£30-00

R. B. Rutherford is Tutor in Greek and Latin
Literature at Christ Church, Oxford, and University
Lecturer in Classical Languages and Literature.

OXFORD CLASSICAL MONOGRAPHS

*Published under the supervision of a Committee of the
Faculty of Literae Humaniores in the University of Oxford*

The aim of the Oxford Classical Monographs series (which replaces the Oxford Classical and Philosophical Monographs) is to publish outstanding theses on Greek and Latin literature, ancient history, and ancient philosophy examined by the faculty board of Literae Humaniores.

THE MEDITATIONS OF

MARCUS AURELIUS

A STUDY

R. B. RUTHERFORD

CLARENDON PRESS · OXFORD
1989

Oxford University Press, Walton Street, Oxford OX2 6DP

Oxford New York Toronto
Delhi Bombay Calcutta Madras Karachi
Petaling Jaya Singapore Hong Kong Tokyo
Nairobi Dar es Salaam Cape Town
Melbourne Auckland

and associated companies in
Berlin Ibadan

Oxford is a trade mark of Oxford University Press

Published in the United States
by Oxford University Press, New York

British Library Cataloguing in Publication Data
Rutherford, R. B.
The Meditations of Marcus Aurelius: a
study).—(Oxford classical monographs).
1. Prose in Greek, to ca 500. Marcus
Aurelius, Emperor of Rome 121–180
I. Title II. Series
878′.0108
ISBN 0-19-814879-8

Library of Congress Cataloging in Publication Data
Rutherford, R. B.
The Meditations of Marcus Aurelius.
(Oxford classical monographs)
Bibliography: p.
Includes index.
1. Marcus Aurelius, Emperor of Rome, 121–180.
Meditations. 2. Ethics. 3. Stoics. 4. Life.
I. Title. II. Series.
B583.R88 1989   188   88–20834
ISBN 0-19-814879-8

Set by the Alden Pess, Oxford

Printed and bound in
Great Britain

TO MY PARENTS

... habetur quod, cum Marcus mortuum educatorem
suum fleret vocareturque ab aulicis ministris ab ostenta-
tione pietatis, ipse dixerit: 'permitte' inquit 'illi, ut homo
sit. neque enim vel philosophia vel imperium tollit affectus.'

(*Historia Augusta*: *Vita Pii* 10. 5)

Preface

SOME of the limitations of this work are deliberate. It is not a biography of Marcus Aurelius or a detailed narrative of his reign, for which the reader may consult the standard life by Anthony Birley. Nor is it a full account or analysis of Marcus' philosophy or of his relation to earlier thinkers. Although I have said a good deal about his Stoicism and its effect upon his writing, I doubt if evidence permits us to determine in detail from what sources an educated Roman of the second century AD derived his knowledge of specific ideas and theories. The principles and vocabulary of Stoicism were well known, if in a somewhat diluted and non-technical form, and the overlap with other schools of philosophy at this date was considerable. The details of academic discussion and philosophic polemic may at an earlier age have been congenial to Marcus, but it is not these concerns which dominate the *Meditations*.

The object of this study is to explain the background, purpose, and character of the *Meditations*, and to suggest the ways in which the work may most fruitfully be read and interpreted. Marcus' book, once an accepted spiritual classic, is not much read nowadays, and literary criticism of his work is almost non-existent. I have attempted to show that this work, although intimate and private, is more varied and richer in texture than is sometimes supposed. The author recognisably draws upon more established literary traditions, his style and thought are enriched by wide reading, and the intensity and severity of his writing are modified by quotation and allusion, satirical wit, rhetorical virtuosity—in general, the skills of a self-conscious literary artist. I have drawn frequent comparisons with more well-known philosophic writers in antiquity, especially Plato, Lucretius, Horace, Seneca, Epictetus, and Plutarch. Sometimes this is because their works were known to or influenced Marcus, but the comparisons are also intended to show that despite the unusual character of his work, Marcus Aurelius is not an isolated or freakish figure lurking in the obscurity of late classical literature: the tasks of moral self-discipline and preparation for death, the purposes which the *Meditations* chiefly serve, have a central and honourable place in the work of artists and thinkers throughout antiquity. I hope that in the process of illustrating Marcus' book I have also kept this wider picture in mind. Some of the material I have collected, particularly in the notes, may be of some use to those interested, like myself, in the interaction of philosophy and rhetoric in the intellectual world of Greece and Rome.

The original focus of my research was on the style and literary aspects of the *Meditations*, but it is an unrealistic and reductive enterprise to separate the things said from the way in which they are said. I have therefore discussed Marcus' view of life, and in particular his religion, at some length, always attempting to relate my conclusions closely to the text of the *Meditations*. The obscurity and ambiguity of some passages have meant that certainty, always hard to obtain in these areas, has been impossible. Here even more than elsewhere it has been my aim to gather and comment on some evidence that others may find relevant in amending or refuting the picture of Marcus Aurelius which the present study offers.

This is in some ways a personal work, and I will not conceal the fact that, with some qualifications, I find the view of life expressed in the *Meditations* both sympathetic and admirable. But this study is not intended as hagiography (Marcus has suffered often enough in the past fron naïve or extravagant praise), and I have often criticised or questioned Marcus' outlook, or offered contrasting quotations from other moralists. My own temperament and preferences must inevitably colour some of my evaluations. But I have tried to make my subjectivity explicit; readers will doubtless apply their own correctives.

I have many debts to recount, but none more lasting and important than those I owe to my parents, whose faith, encouragement, and constant support made it possible for me to come to Oxford and impelled me to make a success of my time here. As an undergraduate and a research student at Worcester College my enthusiasm for classical studies was quickened by the inspiring teaching of Robin Lane Fox, Michael Winter-bottom, and the late Martin Frederiksen, all of whom readily advised and helped me at every stage. Donald Russell of St John's College supervised my research, and it was he who first

turned my attention to the Second Sophistic and the world of
Marcus Aurelius. Those who have also worked under him will
best know how well he combines solid learning with a humane
and sympathetic understanding of the difficulties of research. I
have gladly adopted many of his suggestions, and am grateful
for his patience and kindness. I must also thank the Craven
Committee of the University of Oxford for electing me to a
Craven Fellowship which enabled me to spend the Michaelmas
term of 1980 at the University of Heidelberg; during my time
there, Professor and Mrs A. Dihle and Dr Gerard O'Daly did
much to make my visit both tolerable and profitable. Mr E. L.
Bowie and Professor I. G. Kidd examined this work as a D. Phil.
thesis in 1985, and made many helpful comments and corrections. Since October 1981 I have been able to pursue my work in
ideal surroundings, and in the company of an unrivalled circle of
classical scholars, first as a Research Lecturer and then as a
Tutor at Christ Church. I am very grateful to the Governing
Body for electing me to these posts, and to my colleagues for
their constant kindness and courtesy, which have made the
college a home from the beginning. Friends in Oxford and
elsewhere have helped me in countless ways: for their tolerance
and generosity I thank especially Stephen and Ruth Halliwell,
Victoria Harris, Doreen Innes, Emily Kearns, Barbara
Macleod, Peter Parsons, Nicholas Purcell, Corinne Richards,
Oliver Taplin, and Catherine Whistler. I must also mention
here the meticulous work of those who typed the text of thesis
and book, namely Glenys MacGregor, Alison Menzies, Rachel
Woodrow, and especially Caroline MacNicoll; the notes and
other appurtenances are my own responsibility.

One debt remains to be acknowledged. Of all my teachers,
Colin Macleod most deeply influenced my critical approach; at
the most difficult stage of my research he generously offered
advice and suggested numerous lines of thought which have
invariably proved rewarding; and his integrity, dedication, and
humanity made him an example in life as well as scholarship.
The first draft of this study was completed on the day before his
death. I am deeply conscious how much his close and careful
scrutiny would have enhanced its value. For his teaching and
friendship, I wish to record my belated thanks.

R. B. RUTHERFORD

Contents

Abbreviated Titles for Works of Reference

ANRW	*Aufstieg und Niedergang der römanischen Welt*, ed. H. Temporini and W. Haase (Berlin and New York, 1972–).
Arndt–Gingrich	W. Bauer, *A Greek–English Lexicon of the New Testament and Other Early Christian Literature*, ed. W. F. Arndt and F. W. Gingrich (Chicago 1957).
ERE	*Encyclopaedia of Religion and Ethics*, ed. J. Hastings (Edinburgh 1908–26).
LSJ	H. G. Liddell, R. Scott, H. S. Jones, *A Greek–English Lexicon* (9th edn., Oxford 1940; with Supplement, 1968).
OCD	*The Oxford Classical Dictionary*, 2nd edn., ed. N. G. L. Hammond and H. H. Scullard (Oxford 1970).
ODCC	*Oxford Dictionary of the Christian Church*, ed. F. L. Cross and E. A. Livingstone. (2nd edn. with revisions, Oxford 1983).
OLD	*Oxford Latin Dictionary*, ed. P. Glare (Oxford 1968–82).
PIR[1] and *PIR*[2]	*Prosopographia Imperii Romani* (Berlin, 1st edn., 1897–8, 2nd edn. 1933–).
RE	*Real-Encyclopädie der classischen Altertumswissenschaft* (Stuttgart 1893–).
RLAC	*Reallexicon für Antike und Christentum*, ed. T. Klauser *et al.* (Stuttgart 1950–).
SVF	*Stoicorum Veterum Fragmenta*, ed. H. von Arnim (Leipzig 1903–24).
TDNT	*Theological Dictionary of the New Testament*, ed. G. Kittel, tr. G. W. Bromiley (Grand Rapids and London 1964–76).

Other Conventions

DIFFERENT editions of the *Meditations* use widely varying systems of subdividing chapters. My references follow the divisions in Farquharson's text. Fronto is cited according to volume and page of the Loeb edition by C. R. Haines. Musonius Rufus is cited from the edition by O. Hense (Leipzig 1905); this text is reproduced, with different pagination and without critical apparatus, in the study by C. E. Lutz, *YCS* 10 (1947).

Abbreviations for classical authors follow the conventions laid down in LSJ and the *OLD*. Abbreviations for periodicals normally follow the system of *L'Année Philologique*, though I have occasionally expanded some titles which are less commonly found.

Marcus Aurelius: A Biographical Note[1]

MARCUS AURELIUS, born at Rome in AD 121 as M. Annius Verus, was of Spanish extraction, son of a consular who was also brother-in-law of Antoninus Pius. He lost his father in early childhood (see *Meditations* i. 2), but was soon favoured with the patronage of the emperor Hadrian, who had assumed the throne in 117. Hadrian gave him the nickname Verissimus, and in 136 betrothed him to the daughter of L. Ceionius Commodus, consul of that year, Hadrian's proposed successor. Ceionius died in 138, whereupon Hadrian turned to the sober and trustworthy Antoninus Pius, adopting him and requiring him to adopt both Marcus and Ceionius' son Lucius Verus.[2] Pius' accession was untroubled, and he governed responsibly and well from 138 to 161, a period of prosperity, senatorial freedom, and relative peace on the frontiers.[3] Meanwhile Marcus was educated by the most eminent rhetorical and philosophic teachers of his day, and at an early stage began to serve under Pius (he was quaestor in 139, consul with Pius in 140, consul for the second time in 145, and received the *tribunicia potestas* and proconsular *imperium* in 146). In 145 he married Pius' daughter Faustina, and a daughter was born in the following year. Marcus was clearly senior to Lucius Verus (consul only to 154), but upon his accession insisted that they should reign as colleagues, Verus' titles and powers being immediately augmented. Verus' reputation has suffered from much gossip reported in the unreliable *Historia Augusta*, which paints him as a playboy; yet his ties with Marcus were close, and he seems to have been a reliable administrator and adequate general.[4] Verus died in 169.

[1] This summary makes no pretence of originality: it is simply intended as a brief introduction to Marcus Aurelius' career for those previously unfamiliar with the period.

[2] T. D. Barnes, *JRS* 57 (1967) 65 ff. argues forcefully that Hadrian intended Verus to be Antoninus' successor. *Contra*, see A. R. Birley, *Marcus Aurelius* (rev. ed., London 1987) 240. (References to this work are always to the revised edition.)

[3] On the reign of Pius see A. Garzetti, *From Tiberius to the Antonines* (Eng. tr. London 1974) 441–71, with ample bibliog.; also Birley, ch. 3–5. Despite Marcus' tributes in i. 16 and vi. 30, he remains a rather shadowy figure.

[4] P. Lambrechts, *Antiq. Cl.* 3 (1974) 173–211 = R. Klein (ed.) *Marc Aurel* (Darmstadt 1979) 25 ff., attempted a rehabilitation, but has not been generally followed. See also Barnes (n. 2), P. A. Brunt, *JRS* 64 (1974) 5–6.

Marcus himself reigned from 161 to 180. Frontier problems and indeed invasions occupied his attention for many of those twenty years. Britain, Parthia, and especially the many tribes of the German provinces and the free Germans north of the Danube all caused recurrent problems, and Marcus campaigned himself in north Italy and Germany in 168 and 170–5 (against the Marcomanni, the Quadi, and the Sarmatii), and again in Pannonia and Germany from 177 until his death from illness, on campaign near Vienna, in March 180. In 175 he was also hampered by internal strife, with the revolt of Avidius Cassius, governor of Egypt and Syria. Cassius claimed that news had reached him of the emperor's death, and the full extent of his guilt remains doubtful.[5] Scandal implicated Faustina, Marcus' wife, as Avidius' lover and and fellow-conspirator. The rebellion failed and Avidius was murdered by a centurion; the historian Dio Cassius presents Marcus' reaction to the revolt as one of pity, sorrow, and readiness to forgive.[6] (Modern readers have sometimes attempted to find references to this affair, and to Faustina's supposed infidelities, in the *Meditations*. All such enquiries remain speculative, however intriguing. Of Faustina, as of Verus, he says nothing but good in Book I.[7])

Another disaster of Marcus' reign was the plague of 166–7 and later, apparently brought back from Parthia by Verus' armies.[8] It is not clear how far this affected population. Meanwhile, wars and generous donations of largesse diminished the treasury dangerously. Bureaucracy and busy officialdom flourished, but no strong threads of long term policy can be readily discerned. Nevertheless, Marcus' lifetime was soon idealised as a Golden Age (Dio Cassius 71. 36. 4), partly because of the violent contrast provided by the disastrous reign of his son Commodus (born 161, reigned 180–192), who was eventually assassinated and execrated as a tyrant.

---

[5] See Birley 182–9; R. Syme, *Roman Papers* v (Oxford 1988) 689–701.

[6] Dio, *Epit.* 72. 17–31 is the fullest account.

[7] For speculation of this kind see Brunt (n. 4) 13, 18–19. On Faustina see *Med.* i. 17. 8, in which the author thanks the gods 'that my wife is as she is, so obedient, so affectionate, so simple'; on Verus ibid. § 4: 'that I met with such a good brother, able by his character not only to rouse me to take care of myself but at the same time to cheer me by his respect and affection.' See also viii. 25, 37.

[8] See J. F. Gilliam, *AJP* 82 (1961) 225–51 = Klein (ed.), *Marc Aurel* 144–75.

In retrospect, Marcus' reign also arouses interest in modern readers because of the continuing growth of Christianity (already familiar and persecuted in the time of Nero, and judiciously controlled by Trajan).[9] The emperor must have known about the existence of the cult, but it may still have seemed of little importance at this time. In the *Meditations* he mentions Christians only once, with disapproval (xi. 3, in a phrase which has been doubted as possibly a later gloss); his teacher Fronto denounced them with the ignorant clichés of polemic; and two episodes of persecution occurred under Marcus' authority and presumably with his knowledge: the martyrdom of the apologist Justin (AD 167?), after a trial conducted by Marcus' close friend Rusticus,[10] and the executions at Lyons in response to a public outcry in 177 (though the date has been questioned).[11]

The *Meditations*, unknown to the authors who describe his reign, were presumably written during his final years. They offer exceptional access to the thoughts of a Roman emperor in a period which is, even by ancient standards, very ill-documented. For narrative accounts of Marcus' life and reign we have to turn to an epitomized portion of Dio Cassius' monumental history of Rome, written in Greek between AD 197 and *c.* 225,[12] and to a sketchy biography included in the notoriously unreliable *Historia Augusta* (probably compiled in the late fourth century).[13] There is also a valuable, though fragmentary, collection of letters exchanged by Marcus and his tutor Cornelius Fronto (occasional letters by others such as Verus also appear), but these are badly preserved and many are hard to

---

[9] See Tac. *Ann.* xv. 44. 3–8; Suet. *Cl.* 25. 4; Plin. *Ep.* x. 96–7; Epict. iv. 7. 1–6; Fronto ii. 282 (= Minucius Felix, *Octavia* 9. 8). See further ch. v, nn. 30–2.

[10] *Acta Iustini*, in H. Musurillo, *Acts of the Christian Martyrs* (Oxford 1972) 42 ff.; different and perhaps more authentic version in R. Knopf, G. Krüger, and G. Ruhbach, *Ausgewählte Märtyrerakten* (4th edn., Tübingen 1965) 15 ff.

[11] Eusebius, *Hist. Eccl.* iv. 16. 7–9, v. *praef.* (partly reproduced in Musurillo 62 ff., Knopf–Krüger–Ruhbach 18 ff.). On the date see T. D. Barnes, *JTS* 19 (1968) 517–19, and in *Les Martyres de Lyons* (Paris 1978).

[12] See esp. F. Millar, *A Study of Cassius Dio* (Oxford 1964). G. W. Bowersock, in his review in *Gnomon* 37 (1965) 469–74, criticises Millar's arguments for dating the beginnings of Dio's work as early as 197.

[13] There is a convenient Penguin translation of the earlier Lives, with a detailed introduction, by A. R. Birley, *Lives of the Later Caesars* (Harmondsworth 1976); see also his *Marcus Aurelius* 229–30.

date.[14] The majority of these letters come from the period before Marcus Aurelius became emperor. The social, political, and economic background, though not the personalities of the period, can be further illuminated from public documents and inscriptions, though only in a very few cases is there reason to suppose that the formulation bears much relation to Marcus' own views and words.[15]

[14] The most accessible edn. is that of C. R. Haines (Loeb Classical Library, London and New York 1919–20); the fullest critical edn., that of M. P. J. van den Hout (Leiden 1954). For an outstanding modern study see E. Champlin, *Fronto and Antonine Rome* (Cambridge, Mass., 1980). Champlin discusses the chronology of the correspondence in detail, in *JRS* 64 (1974) 136–59.

[15] See esp. J. H. Oliver and R. E. A. Palmer, *Hesperia* 14 (1955) 320 ff.; J. H. Oliver, *Marcus Aurelius: Aspects of Civil and Cultural Policy in the East, Hesperia* Suppl. 13 (1970); W. Williams, *ZPE* 17 (1975) 37 ff.; id., *JRS* 66 (1976) 78–82. On Marcus and the law see Birley 133–9, 179–83, 199–200.

I

The Form and Function of the *Meditations*

fervet avaritia miseroque cupidine pectus:
sunt verba et voces quibus hunc lenire dolorem
possis et magnam morbi deponere partem.
laudis amore tumes: sunt certa piacula quae te
ter pure lecto poterunt recreare libello.
invidus, iracundus, iners, vinosus, amator,
nemo adeo ferus est ut non mitescere possit,
si modo culturae patientem commodet aurem.

(Horace *Ep.* i. 1. 33–40)

The sentences of Seneca are stimulating to the intellect; the
sentences of Epictetus are fortifying to the character; the
sentences of Marcus Aurelius find their way to the soul.

(Matthew Arnold, 'Marcus Aurelius', in *Essays in
Criticism: First Series*, 367)

1. *Critical Orientation*

Marcus Aurelius Antoninus, emperor and philosopher, has
generally been approached and criticised in terms of one or
other of these roles. In consequence, Marcus the writer, through
whom we have our most intimate knowledge of both, has
suffered from a surprising neglect. From the historians his
campaigns in Germany, his legal rulings as preserved in the
Digest, and his behaviour concerning the Christians have
received due attention, and in some recent work there have been
attempts to reinstate the *Meditations* and their author in the
cultural history of the period.[1] Much, however, still remains to
be done. On the philosophic side, Marcus finds a place in all
accounts of late Stoicism: often he is used as a source for
information or speculation about earlier thinkers, notably

---

[1] Esp. G. W. Bowersock, *Greek Sophists in the Roman Empire* (Oxford 1969); Champlin,
Fronto. In general, see the bibliography in Klein (ed.), *Marc Aurel* 503–29.

Posidonius.[2] Yet these philosophic accounts usually include some apologetic proviso to the effect that, for all his influence, Marcus' thought was in fact disappointingly unoriginal. Thus Professor A. A. Long writes:

The unfortunate fact is that our evidence is best from a period when Stoicism had become an authorized doctrine rather than a developing philosophical system. What matters above all to Epictetus and Marcus Aurelius in the second century AD is moral exhortation within the framework of the Stoic universe. On details of physics, logic or theory of knowledge they have little to say.[3]

Another authority on the Stoics, Professor F. H. Sandbach, finds it possible to reduce Marcus' philosophic content to three basic ideas.[4] It sometimes seems that scholars would gladly exchange all or most of the *Meditations* for a work of the early Stoa, for instance by Chrysippus. Yet originality is not the only quality we look for in a writer, or even a philosopher. Marcus Aurelius' communings with himself have been a spiritual classic for generations, both in the original Greek and through many translations; and if we believe that the task of the literary critic is to illuminate the qualities of a text in such a way as to enhance other readers' appreciation and understanding of it, then the formal aspects and the more purely literary merits of the *Meditations* demand our attention.

This is not to argue that the biography and historical career of Marcus, or the philosophic school to which he belonged, are irrelevant to the study of his writings. To dismiss either of these would be impossible and undesirable. Clearly, when Marcus writes (x. 10) 'A spider is proud when he traps a fly, a man when he snares a leveret, another when he nets a sprat, another boars, another bears, another Sarmatians', the reader misses the full force of the sentence if he does not know that the concluding mention of the Sarmatians is neither random nor inconsequential, but has a precise reference to Marcus' own victories over

---

[2] Esp. R. Neuenschwander, *Marc Aurels Beziehungen zu Seneca und Poseidonios* (Bern 1951). See also M. Pohlenz, *Die Stoa* (3rd edn., Göttingen 1964) i. 341–53, ii. 167–72; Poseidonios *Die Fragmente*, ed. W. Theiler (Berlin and New York 1982) ii. 396–8. For a recent contribution see J. M. Rist, 'Are you a Stoic? The Case of Marcus Aurelius', in B. F. Meyer and E. P. Saunders (eds.), *Jewish and Christian Self-Definition*, iii. *Self-Definition in the Graeco-Roman World* (London 1982) 23–45.

[3] A. A. Long, *Hellenistic Philosophy* (London 1974) 115; similarly 239.

[4] F. H. Sandbach, *The Stoics* (London 1975) 176.

them in the 170s.[5] The dismissal of military pride comes not from an armchair moralist sniping safely from the sidelines (as does the prolonged condemnation of military glory by Juvenal in his tenth satire, 133–87), but from the victor himself, who finds only triviality and disillusionment in his achievement, and yet, we may add, none the less continued to fight and eventually died on campaign.[6] But such allusions to his own actions, to his political or even his personal life, are extremely rare in the *Meditations*, to the frustration of the historian. (See the Appendix to this chapter.) Unlike Seneca—who is himself much more reticent concerning his own life and experiences than at first appears[7]—Marcus almost never refers to an event in his own life in order to point a moral or to place a resolution in its context. This is one of many negative attributes which characterise his work.

Nor is it possible to consider the writings of Marcus without regarding them as above all philosophic. Direct and immediately apprehensible they may often seem, but although it often appears that a man is addressing us simply and solely as a man, it is rare to find a chapter which is not distinctively philosophic, and usually Stoic, in some respect. Marcus himself disclaimed the title of a philosopher (viii. 1), but he was well read in theory and constantly concerned to translate precept into practice. The *Meditations* reflect that preoccupation. They do not themselves constitute a moral treatise, but they assume familiarity with such works, as is natural and inevitable when an author so versed in them writes to and for himself. But that same familiarity with doctrine means that Marcus' references are often allusive, his arguments incomplete or selective, his terminology undefined.

On the other hand, philosophic purpose and content do not exclude a more self-consciously literary form and composition.

[5] Marcus took the title Sarmaticus in 175: Dio 71. 17; SHA *Marcus* 24–5; *CIL* viii. 2276; see also Birley, *Marcus Aurelius* 189.

[6] The evidence on Marcus' death is muddled by gossip and imprecision. It seems most likely that he succumbed to the plague, perhaps reinforced by other weaknesses, while on campaign near Vienna (or preparing for a new campaign at Sirmium; the sources contradict each other): Dio 72. 33–4; SHA *Marcus* 28; Victor, *de Caesaribus* 16. 4; *Epit. de Caes.* 16–17; Tert. *Ap.* 25. See Birley 209–10; H. Bannert, in Klein (ed.), *Marc Aurel* 459–72. The stories of poison administered by doctors in Commodus' sevice are part of the stock paraphernalia of any imperial demise.

[7] See esp. M. T. Griffin, *Seneca: A Philosopher in Politics* (Oxford 1976) ch. 1 and *passim*.

Much of ancient literature, including some of its greatest books, is directed towards moral and didactic ends. The nature and object of Marcus' writings, of which more is said below, required not only, or even primarily, the lucid exposition of philosophic dogma, but persuasive and memorable phraseology, words and ideas that 'bit at the heart' (ix. 3. 2: ἀψικάρδιον), argumentation and elaboration which invite the description 'rhetorical'.[8] Contrary to some modern assumptions, Marcus Aurelius is not an exception to the general expectation in the ancient world that ethical and philosophic writing should aspire to the level of literature (compare, for example, Cicero's complaints about the literary deficiencies of the Latin Epicurean writers[9]). The emphasis of the present study is upon the literary background, techniques, and qualities of the *Meditations*. On the whole, students of Marcus who have discussed this side of the work in the past have confined themselves to brief and rather impressionistic sketches. In his biography of Marcus, Anthony Birley devoted a chapter to the *Meditations*, as before him had A. S. L. Farquharson in his shorter, posthumous volume entitled *Marcus Aurelius: His Life and His World*, a by-product of his years of work on a distinguished commentary on Marcus' book. Both Birley's and Farquharson's books, while very different, are of real value; but both authors seem to feel ill at ease in describing and drawing conclusions about the *Meditations*; both, like others before them, occasionally lapse into vague generalisations, and prefer to let Marcus speak for himself by including a selection of favourite passages. Birley writes:

[8] It seems proper to stress here what is still too often left unsaid: that 'rhetoric' is not necessarily an art (or pseudo-art) of deception, and that 'rhetorical' need not be a merely pejorative term. In this work I try never to use the words in that way. By 'rhetoric' I understand the formal and rational codification of the techniques and styles required for clear and persuasive communication in a wide range of circumstances. Rhetorical discourse may be based on, and used to convey, philosophic argument, and it must also rest, as Plato saw, on a knowledge of human psychology. For ancient attempts to define and delimit rhetoric, especially in relation to philosophy, see R. Volkmann, *Die Rhetorik der Griechen und Römer* (2nd edn., Leipzig 1885) ch. 1, esp. 1–15; H. Lausberg, *Handbuch der literarischen Rhetorik* (Munich 1960) sections 18–22, 32–6. Note esp. Quint. ii. 15 ff. (with M. Winterbottom's comm., diss. Oxford 1964). For modern formulations and discussions see P. Dixon, *Rhetoric* (Critical Idiom series, 19, London 1971); G. A. Kennedy, *Classical Rhetoric and its Christian and Secular Tradition* (Univ. of N. Carolina Press 1980).

[9] Cic. *Tusc.* i. 6, ii. 7–8 (*Fin.* i. 14–15 is disingenuous). Further, see J. S. Reid's introd. to his comm. on Cicero's *Academica* (London 1885) 20–4; A. D. Leeman, *Orationis Ratio* (Amsterdam 1963) 198–206.

Reading the *Meditations* for long periods can be conducive of melancholy. The atmosphere is certainly strongly tinged with darkness, although in many places it is lightened by vivid imagery—figs and olives, the drooping heads of ripe corn, rosebuds and saplings, vines bearing another summer's grapes, scuffling puppies or quarrelsome children [citing iii. 1, iv. 20, v. 6, v. 33]. But he was not trying to achieve 'fine writing'. 'Forget your thirst for books, or you will die muttering' [ii. 3].[10]

Birley here alludes to the variation of tone and mood in some passages, but the scope of his chapter does not allow him to examine the different effects achieved by the diverse metaphors and images which he cites. Nor does he explore further the question of the role that self-conscious stylistic aspirations might play in the composition of Marcus' work.

Farquharson, like Birley, detects no 'fine writing' in the *Meditations*.

This book, like Caesar's, is a soldier's book, a model of directness, a guide to men in like warfare [i.e. of the spirit] ... The purity and simplicity remain, but all else has been stripped away or trebly refined; the rhetoric lessons of that pompous old tutor have been forgotten, the youthful desire for learned attainment has faded ...[11]

This is eloquent but careless description. The passage cited by Birley (ii. 3), referring to Marcus' continuing thirst for books, finds several parallels elsewhere in the *Meditations*. This shows that the desire for learning was one which the author still felt, however difficult he found it to satisfy that longing. The contemptuous dismissal of Fronto as 'that pompous old tutor' finds no confirmation in the sole reference to him in the *Meditations*, which acknowledges a serious and valuable moral lesson (i. 11); and despite Marcus' rejection of rhetoric as an end in itself, the extant correspondence with Fronto amply shows how cordial their relations remained.[12] Finally, the parallel

---

[10] Birley 222.

[11] A. S. L. Farquharson, *Marcus Aurelius: His Life and His World* (Oxford 1951) 122–3. Cf. his comm., vol. i, p. lxvi.

[12] See Champlin, *Fronto* 121–3, with some qualifications which I hope to develop elsewhere. Brief conspectus of important passages (including those in which Marcus seems to dismiss rhetoric as of little value) in Brunt, *JRS* 64 (1974) 4 n. 22; add x. 16 (cf. i. 17. 1). On the same page Brunt remarks: 'It would have been surprising if one who had spent so much time in youth and even after his accession in literary exercise showed no trace of their effect.' This might serve as an epigraph to much that I wish to say here.

drawn between the *Meditations* and Caesar's *Commentarii* is
inexact for several reasons, not least because of the narrative
form of the latter work. Also, it is not necessary to accept the
more extreme statements of the view that Caesar's works offer a
distorted account of historical events to see that they are works of
propaganda, of self-praise and self-exoneration.[13] And it is
worth remembering that Cicero, in a famous characterisation of
Caesar's style, saw his soldierly directness and lack of ornament
as a self-conscious and superbly effective way of writing (Cic. *Br.*
262).[14] In the case of Marcus Aurelius, Farquharson's praise
may be equally misleading.

Comparison with the *Res Gestae Divi Augusti*, an actual public
inscription which recorded supremely public deeds, has also
been made. But the austerity and impersonality of Augustus'
disingenuous account of military and political achievements
only serve as a contrast with the intensity and privacy of
Marcus' inner life. It cannot be assumed that the juxtaposition
of completely diverse works will provide much enlightenment
simply because both authors occupied the throne of the Roman
Empire.

Such comparisons and their critical implications do, however,
illustrate the most immediate problems which face the student
of the *Meditations*. The scholars quoted feel hampered by the
absence of a familiar generic background, by the extraordinary
character and form of the work. The *Meditations* fall into no
obvious literary category: hence the attempt to draw parallels
with the work of comparable men, which is essentially an effort
to localise and to clarify its generic status. This is not a futile
effort, since more illuminating comparisons can be drawn
between Marcus and a number of writers in both Greek and
Latin. The *Meditations*, while they are not themselves to be
classed in any single genre recognised by ancient theory, are in
fact influenced by a number of traditions, mainly of moralistic
texts, and share some of their characteristics. It is important,

---

[13] On Caesar's style in the *Commentarii* see F. E. Adcock, *Caesar as Man of Letters*
(Cambridge 1956); P. T. Eden, *Glotta* 40 (1962) 74 ff. The aims and possible distortions
of his works have been much discussed, notably by P. Rambaud, *L'Art de la déformation
historique dans les commentaires de César* (Paris 1953); for a less sceptical view see J. P. V. D.
Balsdon, *JRS* 45 (1955) 161–4.

[14] See the commentaries of Kroll and Douglas ad loc.; also Suet, *D. Iul*, 56, with
Butler and Carey's note.

however, to emphasise that no single genre will provide the master key. In what follows I demonstrate broad categories into which chapters from throughout the collection may be grouped; but first I offer a number of observations on the character of the work as a whole.

It is immediately striking that Marcus should have written his thoughts down in Greek. Here the influence of the earlier Stoic teacher Epictetus is of paramount importance.[15] Marcus' language and thought are deeply influenced by the teachings of Epictetus as recorded by Arrian, perhaps within Marcus' own lifetime.[16] (To a lesser extent older Stoic authors, and Epictetus' own teacher Musonius Rufus, may have been influential.) He frequently quotes or imitates extant passages of Epictetus, and also undoubtedly had access to material now lost.

Moreover, Greek was the language of philosophy. The technicalities of Stoic theory, which Marcus constantly employs, have no really satisfactory Latin equivalents. Our perspective is marred by the survival of three supremely gifted Latin philosophic writers, Lucretius, Cicero, and Seneca. But even Lucretius complains of the 'patrii sermonis egestas' (see i. 136–9, 830 ff., iii. 218 ff., etc.),[17] and Cicero's achievements in translating and inventing terms were consciously nationalistic (*Ac. Post.* i. 4 ff.; *Fin.* i. 1–5; *ND* i. 8, etc.).[18] Although Cicero goes as far as to claim that Latin is actually more fertile in philosophic terminology than Greek, his interlocutors sometimes express surprise and scepticism, with reason (*Fin.* i. 10, iii. 5; *ND* i. 8; contrast Cato in *Fin.* iii. 51). Roman authors continued to remark on the deficiencies of Latin in comparison with Greek, in numerous fields: the *locus classicus* is the careful discussion of Quintilian (xii. 10. 27–39).[19] Roman youngsters were begun on

[15] On Epictetus see Pohlenz, *Die Stoa* i. 327–41; O. Halbauer, *De Diatribis Epicteti* (diss. Leipzig 1911); M. Billerbeck, *Epiktet vom Kynismus* (Leiden 1978) with full bibliog. Many connections between Epictetus and Marcus are charted by G. Breithaupt, *De M. Aurelii Antonini Commentariis Quaestiones Selectae* (diss. Göttingen 1913) 45–64. For Musonius see esp. C. E. Lutz, *YCS* 10 (1947) 3–147; A. C. van Geytenbeek, *Musonius Rufus and Greek Diatribe* (Assen 1963).

[16] Schenkl's edn. of Epictetus, *Testim.* iii–viii. On Arrian's role see T. Wirth, *MH* 24 (1967) 149–89, 197–216; P. A. Stadter, *Arrian of Nicomedia* (Chapel Hill 1980).

[17] Cf. e.g. E. Marouzeau, '*Patrii sermonis egestas*', *Eranos* 45 (1947) 22 ff.; B. Farrington (ed.) *Primus Graius Homo* (Cambridge 1972), an interesting anthology.

[18] Leeman, *Orationis Ratio* 198–206.

[19] See Austin's comm. ad loc.; also Sen. *Ep.* 58. 1; Plin. *Ep.* iv. 18; Quint. ix. 4. 145.

Greek even before Latin (Quint. i. 1. 12–14), and intellectuals were generally competent in both; *utraque lingua* becomes a cliché.[20] For two or three centuries after Seneca we do not know of even one philosopher who wrote exclusively in Latin.[21]

One argument need not be used to explain Marcus' choice of Greek, namely the assumption that like Hadrian he was a philhellene and an admirer of the Second Sophistic, the period of the supposed Greek revival.[22] The chief representatives of that movement, men like Aristides and Maximus, represented precisely the spirit of vanity and preciosity which Epictetus and Marcus as his disciple condemn in the strongest terms (Epict. iii. 21, 23; M. Aur. i. 7; i. 17 *ad fin.*).[23] There is no reason to suppose that he felt much affinity with these sophists; and in general, as argued further below, his literary and philosophic tastes were somewhat out of harmony with contemporary trends in both Latin and Greek literature. Marcus' Greek is more backward-looking, an attempt to steep himself in the spirit of Epictetus. This is not to deny that his fluency in the language does reflect the prominence of Greek culture at Rome; but this is not something that appears only in the Second Sophistic (see e.g. Sen. *Ep.* 95. 45 on Brutus' περὶ καθήκοντος; 59. 7 on Q. Sextius, 'Graecis verbis, Romanis moribus philosophantem').[24]

2. *Self-Discipline and Self-Address*

The work has often been misleadingly described, and thus over-simplified. It is not, as a brief perusal immediately makes plain, a diary or a journal in any ordinary sense; we have here no Roman precursor of Pepys or Boswell. Indications of date,

[20] M. Crawford, in P. D. A. Garnsey and C. R. Whittaker (eds.), *Imperialism in the Ancient World* (Cambridge 1978), at 335 n. 47. Note also Apul. *Apol.* 4: 'tam Graece quam Latine', and Butler–Owen ad loc. For Roman epigrammatists writing in Greek see A. S. F. Gow and D. L. Page, *The Garland of Philip* (Cambridge 1968) i. xxi–xxiii. Juvenal (6. 187 ff.) inveighs against Roman women who think it clever to converse in Greek.

[21] Further, see R. Kaimio, *The Romans and the Greek Language* (Helsinki 1979) 239 ff.; also 130 ff. (emperors), 262 ff. (Roman verdicts on Greek as a literary language). Fronto chastises Marcus for writing in Greek (i. 28 Haines), but seems to assume that he would use it for philosophic discussion (ii. 78, 82).

[22] So apparently Mayor on Juv. 15. 110; J. Wight Duff, *A Literary History of Rome in the Silver Age* (London 1927) 503; Bowersock (n. 1) 15–16, on the analogy with Hadrian; J. H. W. G. Liebeschuetz, *Continuity and Change in Roman Religion* (Oxford 1979) 203–4; Birley 52.

[23] See further ch. II. 4 below.   [24] See Kaimio (n. 21) ch. 5–6.

circumstances, or place of writing are few and ambiguous. Nor is it a commonplace-book or collection of edifying thoughts, although it does include many quotations and sometimes a string of these occur in succession (esp. vii. 33–52, 63–6, xi. 23–29). Some of the passages Marcus quotes were particularly well known and used in similar contexts by other moralists, such as Cicero and Plutarch. In later times the *Meditations* themselves were valued for the same qualities of edification and 'quotability'. Themistius in the fourth century AD speaks of the value of Marcus' παραγγέλματα (*Or.* vi. 81c), and Tzetzes and Planudes in later antiquity quoted or collected passages from the work.[25] In one of the principal manuscripts, Vaticanus Graecus 1950, the *Meditations* are grouped with other edifying works such as Xenophon's *Memorabilia* and *Cyropaedia*, a collection of Epicurus' aphorisms, and the *Manual* or *Encheiridion* of Epictetus. But this does not identify the *Meditations* themselves as an ordinary moral treatise or handbook of Stoic ethics. The author commonly takes the principles of Stoic philosophy for granted: they receive no formal exposition or defence, but are referred to allusively. Technical terms are introduced without definition, and quotations from the older Stoics are used for confirmation rather than being subjected to detailed comment.[26]

What, then, was the origin and purpose of the work? In the Palatine manuscript used by Xylander in the sixteenth century to produce the *editio princeps*, the title was Μάρκου Ἀντωνίνου αὐτοκράτορος τῶν εἰς ἑαυτὸν βιβλίον αʹ ('The first book of those composed to himself by the emperor Marcus Antoninus'). Naturally we cannot be certain that this has ancient authority. The scholia to Lucian, which are attributed to the tenth-century bishop Arethas, cite *Meditations* viii. 37, saying that Marcus refers to Panthea ἐν τοῖς εἰς ἑαυτὸν Ἠθικοῖς, and elsewhere use a similar phrase, Μάρκος ἐν τοῖς Ἠθικοῖς αὐτοῦ.[27] This late and casual evidence is of no more value than the assertion of an

---

[25] Farquharson i. xiii–xviii; J. Dalfen's Teubner edn. xxv–xxvii. G. Loisel, *BAGB* 15 (1927) 18–27 adds little. See now N. G. Wilson, *Scholars of Byzantium* (London 1983) 146.

[26] Technicalities: see Brunt, *JRS* 64 (1974) 2 n. 6; Haines, Loeb edn. index iii (Glossary). Examples (omitting terms in fairly common use): iv. 1 et al. ὑπεξαίρεσις; iv. 7 and often, ὑπόληψις; v. 14 κατορθώσις; v. 20 ἐνέργεια; vi. 37 et al. ἐπακολούθησις; vi. 38 τονικός; viii. 7 et al. ἔκκλισις; viii. 41 ἀνυπεξαιρέτως; ix. 1 ὑποστασις. For a whole cluster of technical terms see e.g. v. 20.

[27] Schol. Lucian *pro Imag.* 3, p. 207 Rabe; *de Salt.* 63, p. 189 Rabe.

ecclesiastical historian, Nicephorus Callistus Xanthopoulos (1295–1360), that Marcus composed the book for the instruction of his son Commodus (*Hist. Eccl.* iii. 31). More important is the internal evidence of the work itself. The unbiased reader usually concludes that this is indeed a private work of self-analysis and devotion. This view receives confirmation from detail, since there are many admonitions and allusions which seem to have point and significance for Marcus himself, in his role as emperor, but for no one else.[28] The examples and counter-examples of his predecessors fall into this category, as do the oblique and difficult allusions to his early life and to various formative events and experiences which we read in Book I. These would have meaning and continued significance for the author, but are surely not intended for the eyes of the public at large.

In his invaluable paper in *JRS* 64 (1974) P. A. Brunt argued powerfully that the *Meditations* were originally intended for the author's eyes alone; and this helps account for the absence of reference to the work by historians or ancient biographers of Marcus. The books were never 'published', but were privately preserved, presumably by his family or by loyal scribes. Their survival at all is miraculous. The first possible allusion to them is by Themistius (cited above) two centuries later; recent argument that Themistius' contemporary Julian knew the *Meditations* is unconvincing.[29]

Brunt's treatment, though exemplary, raises further questions, of which I single out two which seem essential preliminaries to more detailed study. Firstly, if it is true that the *Meditations* are not aimed at an outside audience, has criticism any validity or scope? In other words, does the work have any real literary status? Secondly, does this kind of self-address have any parallel in ancient literature and philosophy?

Matthew Arnold in a famous essay paid high tribute to the religious sense and spirit of Marcus, but also maintained that even the scholar might prefer to read him in the translation of George Long (1862). 'For not only', wrote Arnold, 'are the contents here incomparably more valuable than the external form, but this form, the Greek of a Roman, is not exactly one of

[28] See Brunt, *JRS* 64 (1974) 2–3.
[29] Argued by P. Lacombrade, *Pallas* 14 (1967) 9 ff.

those styles which has a physiognomy, which are an essential part of their author, which stamp an indelible impression on the reader's mind . . . he [the reader] will find crabbed Greek, without any great charm of distinct physiognomy.'[30] And again, he later describes the entries in the *Meditations* as 'jotted down . . . without the slightest attempt at style, with no care, even, for correct writing, not to be surpassed for naturalness and sincerity.'[31]

Arnold's contention that Marcus' book lacks a distinctive style or 'physiognomy' has not gone unchallenged,[32] but some basic points of principle should be made here. The *Meditations* constitute a body of considerable size, in which themes recur constantly but are treated in different ways and with widely varying degrees of obvious stylistic elaboration (such as the use of figures, similes, and metaphor). There are 490 chapters in the twelve books (473 if we omit Book I as exceptional). These vary in length from a few words to several pages. Thus viii. 12 consists of only three words, paraphrased from another chapter, iii. 5, in which the same thought occurs at the end of a series of loosely connected admonitions; and ix. 20 consists of only six words. The longest chapters outside Book I (16–17) are xi. 18, which amounts practically to a sermon on anger, iii. 4, and iv. 3.

Obviously Marcus sometimes had leisure to develop his thoughts at greater length, and hand in hand with this comes a wider range of stylistic choices and decisions, which the written word preserves for our analysis—decisions ranging from the use

---

[30] Arnold, 'Marcus Aurelius' 279. Similar remarks by Breithaupt (n. 15) 7: 'nullaque arte elaborata'; C. Clayton Dove, *Marcus Aurelius Antoninus: His Life and Times* (London 1930) 254; F. A. Wright, *A History of Later Greek Literature* (London 1932) 251: 'The *Meditations* is too informal to admit of analysis', 253: 'Marcus makes no pretensions to elegance of style . . . if he had, his book would have lost half its reality'; J. Jackson, introduction to *The Thoughts of M. Aurelius Antoninus* (Oxford 1906) xxi: 'the style is, in general, unattractive . . . uncouthness of diction . . .'.

[31] Arnold, op. cit. 364.

[32] E.g. by C. R. Haines in the Loeb edn. of Marcus (1916) p. xix. He does not, however, elaborate his rejection of Arnold's dictum. Cf. his preface, p. ix: 'I have preferred to err . . . on the side of overfaithfulness, because the physiognomy of the work owes so much to the method and style in which it is written. Its homeliness, abruptness, and want of literary finish (though it does not lack rhetoric) are part of the character of the work.' Haines, like others, fails to define his critical terms, and in particular what he means by contrasting 'finish' and 'rhetoric'. In fact the chapters of the *Meditations* differ very greatly in stylistic elaboration, yet a consistent directness and brevity of expression combine with an intensity of analysis in most of the work. See text.

of one word in preference to another, through the use of figures, to larger issues such as the sequence of an argument, or the alteration of pace, mood, and stylistic level. Other considerations also arise: if Marcus sometimes had the leisure to compose at length, we cannot assume that the preponderance of short chapters, often only a sentence or two in length, is solely the consequence of external necessity or exhaustion. Brevity was acclaimed as a virtue of style in Stoic theory,[33] and the aphorism or sequence of aphorisms was a traditional medium of ethical teaching.[34] Many of Marcus' shorter chapters look very much as if they were complete in themselves, not awaiting or requiring development (see e.g. vi. 6, vi. 54, vii. 21, x. 16). It follows that sometimes, though by no means always, the literary artist may be at work alongside the philosopher. The simplicity or naturalness of writing which Arnold and others so much admire is not without its own self-effacing art.[35]

Arnold finds in Marcus Aurelius 'a spirit of gentleness and sweetness; a delicate and tender sentiment'; in his view, 'it is this very admixture of sweetness with his dignity which makes him so beautiful a moralist.'[36] But the content and spirit which he values so highly, the beauty of the moralising, are conveyed to the reader through words, style, language: they cannot be divorced from the 'external form' which Arnold dismisses as 'crabbed Greek'. Modern literary critics would see a more intimate relation between form and content: language is not simply 'the dress of thought', as tended to be the assumption of the ancient rhetorical tradition (e.g. Quint. viii. *praef.*).[37]

---

[33] For Stoic συντομία (*brevitas*) see Diog. Laert. vii. 18, 20, 59; Cic. *Paradoxa* pr. 2; Brink on Hor. *Ars* 25; J. F. D. Alton, *Roman Literary Theory and Criticism* (London 1931) 477–8; F. Striller, 'De Stoicorum Studiis Rhetoricis', *Breslauer philol. Abh.* 1 (1886).

[34] For the early history of gnomic sayings and aphorisms see M. L. West's introd. to his comm. on Hesiod's *Works and Days* (Oxford 1978) 22–5 (cf. 3–22 on Eastern and other parallels). For theory see Arist. *Rh.* ii. 21, 1394a–5b; Caplan on *ad Her.* iv. 24; J. F. Kindstrand, *Eranos* 76 (1978) 71–85; J. Russo, *Journal of Folklore Research* 20 (1983) 121–30. Gnomic letters may also be a possible influence, given that the epistolographic tradition already prescribed brevity (cf. Plut. *Br.* 2 on his Laconising style). See further Sykutris, *RE* Supp. v. 185 ff., e.g. 193, 202 f.

[35] For the art which conceals art in ancient theory, see Calboli on *ad Her.* iv. 10; Colson's commentary on Quint. i. pp. 142, 179; Russell on Long. 17. 1; H. D. Jocelyn, in F. Cairns (ed.), *Papers of the Liverpool Latin Seminar 2* (Liverpool 1979) 122 n. 45–6.

[36] Arnold, op. cit. 368.

[37] Cf. J. Cousin's notes in the Budé edn. of Quintilian, vol. v (Paris 1978) ad loc. For modern formulations see A. C. Bradley, *Oxford Lectures on Poetry* (Oxford 1909) ch. 1; R. Wellek and A. Warren, *Theory of Literature* (New York 1949) ch. 12–15; F. R. Leavis,

Rather, the form itself is an inseparable part of the message, which changes as the language in which it has been couched is modified.

Even if we come to the *Meditations* with presuppositions about the character and career of Marcus derived, for instance, from a modern reference book, the impression which we take away from reading the work is the product of the words on the page, the effect of which depends on the style and manner of the author, and on the peculiar characteristics of the form—brevity, abruptness, and all. The author may have a plain style, but he cannot have *no* style (cf. Cic. *Orator* 75–90). And if we are to apprehend the precise nature of the effect which conveys so strongly the ethos of the writer, and which has moved so many readers through precepts derived from philosophic principles which they did not share,[38] then we pass, as was said above, out of the realms of biography and exegesis. Criticism is not only to the point, but of the essence.

Inasmuch as rhetoric was and is commonly defined as the art of persuasive discourse, whether in speech or in writing, the *Meditations* can be described as rhetorical in this sense. Their traditional title is therefore inadequate in this respect, suggesting as it does a purely introspective and probably non-verbal process; preferable is the Greek heading τὰ εἰς ἑαυτὸν. These are not predominantly reflections, *pensées*, or miniature essays; Marcus tends to be talking to and at himself. The object of this address is moral enlightenment. The aim of the *Meditations* is therapeutic: to revive and bring home to himself, in suitably striking and memorable form, the moral truths that the author has accepted in the past, to revivify them (cf. vii. 2) by rephrasing and reiteration. Marcus' practice illustrates the

The Living Principle (London 1977) 71–154; J. Culler, *Structuralist Poetics* (London 1975). These vary greatly in their applicability to Marcus Aurelius, but I have learned from all of them.

[38] I know of no detailed study of Marcus' *Nachleben*, and have not attempted this myself. For some fragments of the story see Farquharson i, introd., esp. lv–vii; Long (n. 3) 239 f.; R. Jenkyns, *The Victorians and Ancient Greece* (Oxford 1980) 86, 335. For translations and editions see J. W. Legg, *A Bibliography of Marcus Aurelius* (1908), and Klein (n. 1) 503–5, adding *Living Stoically*: selections arranged and translated by R. A. Lawes (Ilfracombe, 1984). Seneca has been better served and generally found more accessible: see G. M. Ross in C. D. N. Costa (ed.), *Seneca* (London 1974); L. Zanta, *La Renaissance du stoicisme au XVIe siècle* (Paris 1914). For a classic statement of Marcus' appeal to a devout Christian reader, see Gataker's *Praeloquium* to his comm.

dictum of Cicero that eloquence is the same whatever the theme
or audience, even if the speaker is addressing only two or three
listeners, or simply himself (*de Or*. iii. 23).[39]

This brings us to the second question raised above, whether
ancient literature offers parallels to the kind of soliloquising and
self-criticism which we find in Marcus Aurelius' work. In fact,
self-analysis in soliloquy appears as an accepted formal device
from earliest times, in a wide variety of genres. Already in
Homeric epic we find formalised monologues by heroes on the
battlefield, facing a choice in a dangerous situation (*Iliad* xi.
404–10, xvii. 91–105, xxi. 553–70, xxii. 99–130).[40] Each passage
is introduced by the same line, ὀχθήσας δ' ἄρα εἶπε πρὸς ὃν
μεγαλήτορα θυμόν ('deeply moved, he spoke to his proud heart');
each soliloquy includes a moment of self-assertion and decision,
signalled by the line ἀλλὰ τίη μοι ταῦτα φίλος διελέξατο θυμός;
('But why has my own heart said such things to me?'). In
envisaging a mental dialogue with his θυμός, the seat of his
passions, the hero articulates a moral dilemma, and recognises
the paradox of the divided self.

This kind of tension appears elsewhere in the *Iliad*, as when
Zeus tells Hera that he will consent to the destruction of Troy
ἑκὼν ἀέκοντι γε θυμῷ ('willing, with a heart unwilling', *Il*. iv.
43), and in the *Odyssey*, where again it is presented to soliloquy,
as Odysseus verbally subdues his first impulse to take revenge:
τέτλαθι δή, κραδίη· καὶ κύντερον ἄλλο ποτ' ἔτλης (*Od*. xx. 18:
'Endure, my heart; you have endured even worse than this in
the past'). As so often, the Homeric conception fuels the more
elaborate style of Greek tragedy, in which we often find such
torment of decision embodied in self-address.[41] The inner

[39] Cf. Sen. *Ep*. 27. 1, bringing the idea closer to Marcus; Themistius, *Or*. 21. 245c–d.
Contrast Quint. i. 2. 9, and context (rhetoric inconceivable without an audience).

[40] On these speeches see E. R. Dodds, *The Greeks and the Irrational* (Berkeley and Los
Angeles 1951) 15–17, 20 n. 31, 25; B. C. Fenik, in id. (ed.), *Homer: Tradition and Invention*
(Leiden 1978).

[41] Besides the passages cited in the text, I note the following (the list is illustrative, not
exhaustive): Solon composed εἰς ἑαυτὸν ὑποθήκας, of which nothing is known (Diog.
Laert. i. 61); further, Theogn. 695–6, 877, 1029; Pind. *Ol*. 9. 35–6; *Py*. 3. 61; Eur. *Alc*.
837 ff.; *HF* 268; *Ion* 859; *IT* 344 ff.; Men. *Sicy*. 397 ff.; *Samia* 111 ff., 134; *Dysc*. 213 ff.
(torment of indecision); *SVF* i. 616; Theocr. 11. 72 ff., 30. 11; Meleager *AP* xii. 117;
Plaut. *Pseud*. 397–400, 453 ff.; Catull. 8, 68. 135 with Fordyce's note; Virg. *Aen*. iv. 596 ff.
For Greek tragedy see further F. Leo, *Der Monolog im Drama* (Göttingen 1908); W.
Schadewaldt, *Monolog und Selbstgespräch* (Berlin 1926); D. Bain, *CQ* 25 (1975) 18 n. 2; id.,
Actors and Audience (Oxford 1977). For Menander see J. Blundell, *Menander and the*

conflict of Euripides' Medea is the most famous instance (*Med.* 1056 ff.); the motif and the particular case are familiar enough to be parodied by Aristophanes (*Ach.* 450, 480 ff., esp. 483–9 which involve address to the soul: θύμ'... ὦ τάλαινα καρδία).[42] Marcus Aurelius too appeals ὦ ψυχή ('O (my) soul': e.g. ii. 6, x. 1), not just ἄνθρωπε ('man', 'mortal': as in xii. 36); and he constantly speaks of his mind or soul in the abstract (e.g. xii. 19). The effort to distance himself from his inner self by metaphor is an attempt to objectify, and so to overcome, the conflict within.[43]

More specifically, we may identify a tradition of *philosophic* self-scrutiny, which goes back to Plato, and indeed to Heraclitus (B 101).[44] The fundamental principle of Greek morality, γνῶθι σεαυτόν,[45] originally an acknowledgement of human limitations and of divine power, gradually acquired a more cognitive and introspective sense. This new significance found more detailed expression and interpretation in the insistence of several philosophic schools on habitual self-examination. Pythagoras is said to have advised his disciples on entering their homes at the end of each day to pose the questions: πῆ παρέβην; τί δ᾿ἔρεξα; τί μοι δέον οὐκ ἐτελέσθη; ('Where have I gone wrong? What have I done? What duty has not been carried out?').[46] The line appears in the *Aureum Carmen* attributed to Pythagoras, and is quoted by Epictetus (iii. 10. 2, iv. 6. 32). Socrates' quest is presented by Plato as having its origins in his own ignorance (*Ap.* 21b); he in turn seeks to awaken others' self-awareness and to teach them to be their own self-critics (*Laches* 187e–188c; cf. *Phaedo* 78a).[47]

Monologue (*Hypomn.* 59, Göttingen 1980). For Latin poetry, G. Williams, *Tradition and Originality in Roman Poetry* (Oxford 1968) 461 ff.; C. W. Macleod, *Collected Essays* (Oxford 1983) 252 ff. For Senecan tragedy, S. F. Bonner, *Roman Declamation* (Liverpool 1949) 164, 166; R. Tarrant on Sen. *Ag.* 108–9.

[42] Cf. Soph. *Tra.* 1260 ὦ ψυχὴ σκληρά.

[43] For the use of the speaker's own name in the second or third person see Eur. *Med.* 401 ff., *Hec.* 736 ff., *Tro.* 99 ff.; Catull. 8 (more jocularly in Catull. 52); M. Aur. vi. 26, 44. For this device of ἔμφασις (*affectus*) see R. Mayer on Lucan viii. 80.

[44] On which see W. K. C. Guthrie, *History of Greek Philosophy* i (Cambridge 1962) 411, 414–16; and Marcovich ad loc. (fr. 15 in his 1978 edition).

[45] Mayor on Juv. 11. 27; P. Courcelle, *Connais-toi toi-même* (Paris 1974–5); G. O'Daly, *Plotinus' Philosophy of the Self* (Shannon 1973) ch. i.

[46] Diog. Laert. viii. 22; 'Pythagoras' *Aur. Carm.* 42 (with Theognis and others, ed. D. Young, Leipzig 1961, 86 ff.). See also the ancient comm. on this work by Hierocles, ed. F. W. Koehler (Stuttgart 1974) xix, p. 80 ff.

[47] See C. W. Macleod, *Collected Essays* (Oxford 1983) 285.

Plato himself, according to an anecdote used several times by Plutarch, used to say to himself after any encounter with bad men 'Could I ever become like that?' (Plut. *Mor.* 40d, 88e, 129d, 463e). Horace too describes such a review of the day:

> neque enim, cum lectulus aut me
> porticus excepit, desum mihi: 'rectius hoc est:
> hoc faciens vivam melius: sic dulcis amicis
> occurram: hoc quidam non belle; numquid ego illi
> imprudens olim faciam simile?' haec ego mecum
> compressis agito labris; ubi quid datur oti
> illudo chartis.

(*Sat.* i. 4. 133–9)[48]

Nor, when my couch or a colonnade has given me refuge, do I neglect myself: 'that is the better course; if I do this I shall be living more virtuously; thus people will meet me with more pleasure; so-and-so did that not at all well—surely I couldn't do anything like him, in a careless moment?' These are the words I voice within my closed lips; and when I have a moment to spare, I toy with my sheets of paper.

Horace's last question here (136–7) is particularly close to the story about Plato. In similar vein, Seneca describes how the neo-Pythagorean Sextius would consult his conscience each evening about the day's activities, rendering account to himself: 'interrogaret animum suum, "quid hodie malum tuum sanasti? cui vitio obstituisti? qua parte melior es?" ' (Sen. *de Ira* iii. 36. 1). Seneca claims to follow the same procedure himself, when he is lying in bed with the light out and his wife has stopped talking 'moris iam mei conscia'. Again he gives a sample, which focuses on particular episodes and draws the moral for future behaviour:

totum diem meum scrutor factaque ac dicta mea remetior; nihil mihi ipse abscondo, nihil transeo. quare enim quicquam ex erroribus meis timeam, cum possim dicere: 'vide ne istud amplius facias, nunc tibi ignosco. in illa disputatione pugnacius locutus es: noli postea congredi cum imperitis; nolunt discere qui numquam didicerunt. illum liberius admonuisti quam debebas, itaque non emendasti sed offendisti . . . (*de Ira* iii. 36. 3–4)

I examine my whole day, I retrace my path through my actions and

---

[48] On this poem see F. Muecke, *Prudentia* 11 (1975) 55 ff., with bibliography. In general on self-address and self-criticism in Horace see Macleod, *Collected Essays* 262–91, and my own remarks in *CQ* 31 (1981) 375–80. On self-exhortation see further Lucr. iii. 1024 'hoc etiam tibi tute interdum dicere possis', with Kenney's comm. p. 232.

words; I hide nothing from myself, nothing do I omit. For why need I fear anything from my own mistakes, when I can tell myself: 'For the moment I pardon you, but see that you do that no further. You spoke rather too aggressively in that discussion; hereafter, do not mingle with the uneducated. Those who have never learned have no desire to learn. You rebuked him more outspokenly than you need have done, and so you did not improve but annoyed him . . .'

Marcus is never so specific, but the parallel with his writing a little at the end of each day in his private notebook is unmistakable.

There are many further parallels throughout Epictetus' lectures. He insists that philosophers should study, write down, and exercise themselves with edifying thoughts or episodes: the examples he gives concern the proper replies to make to a tyrant (i. 1. 25). He says that such meditation ($\mu\epsilon\lambda\epsilon\tau\hat{a}\nu$) should be carried out from dawn to dusk (iv. 1. 111). Like Plato, Horace, and Seneca, he advocates examination of the conscience: 'Am I also guilty of the same faults, and if so how shall I stop?' (iv. 4. 7, cf. 17–18). One should count the days passed without anger (ii. 18. 12 ff., esp. § 14 σήμερον οὐκ ἐλυπήθην κτλ.). Like Marcus, he uses the metaphor of having one's maxims 'close to hand' ($\pi\rho\acute{o}\chi\epsilon\iota\rho o\nu$): 'The only way to real peace—let this rule be at hand in the morning, at the end of the day, and during the night . . .' (iv. 4. 49); 'To what, then, am I to attend? Why, in the first place, to those general truths ($\kappa\alpha\theta o\lambda\iota\kappa o\hat{\iota}\varsigma$) which you must have always at hand, and not sleep, or get up, or eat, or converse without them: that no one is the master of one's own choice, and it is in moral choice alone that good and evil consist.' (iv. 12. 7); 'And so let death come to me thinking on these maxims, writing them down, reading them.' (iii. 5. 11; cf. iii. 26. 39; also *Ench.* 52). These examples from the author most influential on Marcus show that self-address and writing are both accepted aspects of the moral self-discipline of the philosopher: as Epictetus says in another passage, what a philosopher writes should be the embodiment of his self-examination (ii. 1. 32–3).[49]

[49] Pl. *Grg.* 490e, 517c; *Smp.* 221e are important for the Socratic background to the idea that philosophers are habitually repeating themselves (further, Kindstrand on Bion fr. 57 σύνεχες); and the centurion's mockery of the sage in Pers. 3. 78 ff. implies that soliloquy is a regular silly practice of philosophers. Further connections and contrasts: Pl. *Rep.* vii. 532a f., *Tht.* 189e–90a, *Soph.* 263e–4a, on thinking as an inner dialogue; Cleanthes, *SVF* i. 570 (*ap.* Posid. fr. 166 E.–K.), for an imagined exchange between

Communion with oneself leads to clearer realisation of the lasting truths of human nature and human life, and this was recognised and applied by others besides professional philosophers. We see this belief in, for instance, the famous consolatory letter of Servius Sulpicius to Cicero (*Fam.* iv. 5).[50] Servius describes how, as he journeyed past the ruined cities of Greece, 'coepi egomet mecum sic cogitare . . .' (§ 4); this introduces reflections on mortality which are then applied to Cicero's personal loss. At a later date, Cicero himself composed a consolatory work addressed to himself, still concerned with the loss of his daughter; in this he collected all the best arguments of the philosophic authorities (*Att.* xii. 21, cf. xii. 14. 3).[51] Consolation-literature was an accepted genre especially at Rome, and its themes and convictions have in fact influenced many passages in the *Meditations*. Marcus himself had lost children; and death and its inevitability is a central theme of his work, which thus continues what Plato and others saw as the proper task of the philosopher: preparation for death (*Phado* 67d).[52]

This self-scrutiny is an important part of a whole series of self-disciplinary methods which philosophers of the Graeco-Roman period had prescribed as principles of moral health. This undoubtedly had much background in Hellenistic literature and thought; but the major texts surviving today are the philosophic works of Cicero (especially *Tusc.* iii–v), Seneca, and Plutarch (especially *de Tranquillitate Animi* and *de Cohibenda Ira*).

---

reason and passion; K. Thomas, *Religion and the Decline of Magic* (London 1971) 187 f., on diaries as psychologically akin to prayer; P. Brown, *Augustine of Hippo* (London 1967) 165–7, on philosophy as prayer in the *Confessions*; G. Steiner, *On Difficulty* (Oxford 1978) 56, quoting a *mot* of Saint-Simon: only an absolute monarch can soliloquize *out loud*, in his essential apartness (see also much of Steiner's next chapter, esp. 81 ff.).

[50] On which see esp. R. Kassel, *Untersuchungen zur gr.-röm. Konsolationsliteratur* (Munich 1958) 98–103. Many of the topics of the genre are paralleled in Marcus; see further pp. 161–7. Passages which are recognisably related to consolation include iii. 3, iv. 32, 33, 48, 50, vi. 24, 47, vii. 49, viii. 5, 25, 31, x. 27, 34, xii. 27. Cf. also vi. 53, vii. 6, 19, viii. 37, ix. 14 (cf. ii. 4, iv. 32), ix. 36.

[51] See the fragments of Cicero's *Consolatio* collected in the Teubner edn. iv. 3, ed. Mueller (1890) 332–8; R. Philippson, *RE* viiA, 1123 ff.

[52] Further, Epicurus fr. 250 Usener; Cic. *Tusc.* i. 74; Hor. *Ep.* ii. 2. 207, 210 ff.; Sen. *Ep.* 70. 18; Epict. *Ench.* 21; Libanius, *de Silentio Socratis* 22, etc. Much material is assembled in the monograph by B. Wallach, *Lucretius and the Diatribe against the Fear of Death* (*Mnem.* Suppl. 40, Leiden 1976), and in Griffin, *Seneca* ch. 11. For Seneca see also A. L. Motto, *Guide to the Thought of L. Annaeus Seneca* (Amsterdam 1970) 60.

These techniques of psychotherapy or *Seelenleitung* have been studied at length in works by P. Rabbow, I. Hadot, and H. G. Ingenkamp (see Bibliography).[53] Here it will be sufficient to single out a few aspects in which other authors offer particularly close parallels to the methods and the language of Marcus. Cicero is particularly emphatic about the medical parallel to philosophy: philosophy is 'animi . . . medicina' (*Tusc.* iii. 1, cf. 5 ff.). But all the authors speak in these terms.[54] The soul suffers from diseases: φλεγμονή (Cleanthes, *SVF* iii. 467, 474) or *tumor* (Sen. *de Ira* i. 20. 1); the soul possessed of excessive pain, joy, or fear is like a swollen or feverish body (Plut. *Virt. Mor.* 452a). The aim for the Peripatetics is to moderate and control the passions (μετριοπάθεια); for the Stoics, with some exceptions, to eliminate them completely (ἀπάθεια). The medicine for this end is words, λόγοι, δόγματα (e.g. Plut. *Garr.* 502b, *Tranq.* 476c). They need to be repeatedly used and applied in the task of training the reason (Plut. *Tranq.* 465b λόγος εἰθισμένος καὶ μεμελετηκώς). ἐθίζειν, ἀσκεῖν, μελετᾶν (practise, exercise, rehearse) are the key words here as in Epictetus and Marcus. In this task precepts, quotations, and *exempla* are the tools of the healer.

The ultimate object of this training is to infuse in the student/patient's mind a true understanding of the state of man: of the insecurity and transience of his material well-being, and the supreme value of his independent moral purpose. Hence the need to train the emotions, so that the individual will be able to view any change of circumstance without feeling anger, resentment, grief, or envy. This project also explains the numerous treatises composed in antiquity which deal with exile, poverty,

---

[53] See also P. Hadot, *RTP* 22 (1972) 225–39; *BAGB* (1981) 183–91 (these and other papers are now collected in his *Exercices spirituels et philosophie antique* (Paris 1981); H. D. Betz et al., *Plutarch's Ethical Writings and Early Christian Literature* (Leiden 1978) general introduction and *passim*. P. Lain Entralgo, *The Therapy of the Word in Classical Antiquity* (Eng. tr., Yale 1970; originally Madrid 1958) is a thoughtful study of earlier material up to Aristotle.

[54] In the *Meditations* see esp. iii. 13 and v. 9. For medical metaphors applied to philosophy see Pl. *Charm.* 155e–7d; *Grg.* 463 ff., 475d, 479a, etc. (such imagery is frequent throughout Plato; see e.g. H. Ruess, *Gesundheit, Krankheit, Arzt bei Plato* (diss. Tübingen 1957)); Diog. Laert. vi. 6; Cic. *Tusc.* iii. 1–6; Hor. *Odes* ii. 2. 13 with Nisbet–Hubbard; Sen. *Ep.* 50. 9, 72. 6, 94. 24, 117. 33; Musonius p. 22. 9; Epict. iii. 22. 73, 23. 30 (cf. A. Bonhöffer, *Epiktet und die Stoa* (Stuttgart 1890) 4 f.); Tert. *de Anima* 2. 6 with Waszink's n. See also W. Jaeger, 'Aristotle's Use of Medicine as a Model of Method in his *Ethics*', *JHS* 77 (1957) 54–61; L. Edelstein, *BHM* 26 (1952) 299–316; V. Pöschl (ed.) *Bibliographie zur antiken Bildersprache* (Heidelberg 1964) 521.

reputation, slavery, above all with death and loss (e.g. of children). These works were intended to set these supposed hardships in a truer philosophic light.[55]

This whole method of self-discipline and self-preparation is well summed up in a phrase of Cicero's, in his chief discussion of the subject: 'praemeditationem futurorum malorum' (*Tusc.* iii. 34; see the whole discussion, 28–end, esp. 34, 55–8, 60, 77, 79). Cicero's language and tone here strongly resemble those of Marcus' *Meditations*:

For the man who reflects upon nature, upon the diversity of life and the weakness of humanity, is not saddened by reflecting upon these things, but in doing so he fulfils most completely the function of wisdom. For he gains doubly, in that by considering the vicissitudes of human life he has the enjoyment of the peculiar duty of philosophy; and in adversity he finds a threefold relief to aid his restoration: first because he has long since reflected on the possibility of mishap, and this is by far the best method of lessening and weakening all vexation; second, because he understands that the lot of man must be endured in the spirit of a man (*humana humane ferenda*); lastly because he sees that there is no evil but guilt, but there is no guilt when the issue is one against which a man can give no guarantee. (§ 34)

Similar to this method of consolation is that which teaches that all that has happened is natural to human life. For such an argument not only includes a recognition of the facts of man's condition, but indicates that what the rest of men have borne, and are bearing, is bearable. (§ 57)[56]

The spirit of these extracts is close to the more humane and compassionate Stoicism which we find in Marcus' work (especially in the references Cicero makes to nature and to the weakness of human life); and, not surprisingly, we find much in the *Meditations* which can be broadly classed as (*prae*)*meditatio malorum*. Marcus too emphasises the divine perspective, the 'view from above', which teaches the philosopher the triviality of human conflict and discontent.[57] He too insists on the need to

[55] On the typical themes of such literature see A. Oltramare, *Les Origines de la diatribe romaine* (Lausanne 1926) esp. 44–65. See also n. 60 below. A table comparing Epictetus' subject-matter with that of other known 'diatribal' authors is given in Halbauer (n. 15) 12–13.

[56] For 'meditatio mali' and 'praemunitio' see P. Rabbow, *Seelenführung* (Munich 1954) 160 ff. and *passim*; Norden on Virg. *Aen.* vi. 103 ff.; Nisbet–Hubbard on Hor. *Odes* ii. 10. 14.

[57] For the parallel of divine vision and clarity see ix. 34, xii. 2. For the 'view from above' as a philosophic image in Marcus and others see ch. IV. 5 (i) below.

realise the community of man, such that no one is immune to suffering and the other workings of nature's law.[58] Again, he insists that there is a lasting consistency in the way the world works, so that nothing is novel or unexpected: 'how ridiculous and how like a stranger in the world is he who is surprised (θαυμάζων) at any one of the events of life' (xii. 13); 'Only a madman expects a fig in winter; such is he who expects a child when it is no longer permitted.' (xi. 33). The *Meditations* go further than either Cicero or Plutarch in condemnation of the human world and of mortal pursuits (see esp. iv. 32, v. 33, vii. 3, ix. 29); and Marcus is more restrained in his claims for his moral and philosophic progress, as is appropriate in a work which deals with the improvement of the self rather than of others. These factors together bring out more sharply both the dignity and the sternness of the moral ideals involved in Stoic *praemeditatio*.

3. Contributory Influences

Turning to the more strictly generic background of formal philosophic discourse, we may single out four areas in which the *Meditations* owe something to more conventional styles of writing.[59] Firstly, Marcus' style and subject-matter are influenced by the popular philosophic tradition to which modern scholars generally give the title 'diatribe'.[60] Examples of this tradition include the essays of Teles and Musonius, and it seems to have influenced authors as diverse as Lucretius, Horace, Plutarch, Lucian, and St Paul. This is not a genre recognised in ancient theory; it is characterised more by a certain style of writing on practical ethical matters than by

[58] See e.g. vii. 18, and note the importance of συν-compounds in Marcus' vocabulary. See Dalfen's index s.v. συγγενής, συγγινώσκειν (vii. 26), συζῆν, συμβιοῦν, συμβλαστάνειν, συμπνεῖν, συμφρονεῖν, συμφωνία, συνεργεῖν, and many others. Imagery reinforces this: e.g. the metaphor of the closely woven web: see ii. 3, iii. 11, iv. 26, 34, 40, v. 8, vii. 57, x. 5.

[59] On philosophic styles and forms see esp. H. Cherniss, *Selected Papers*, ed. L. Taran (Leiden 1977) 14–35; A. D. Leeman, *Orationis Ratio* (Amsterdam 1963) ch. 8 and 11. On the influence of diatribe and dialogue in particular on Marcus' work, see also J. Dalfen, *Formgeschichtliche Untersuchungen zu den Selbstbetrachtungen Marc Aurels* (diss. Munich 1967) esp. ch. 2–3.

[60] See H. Usener, *Epicurea* (Leipzig 1887) lxix; N. Rudd, *The Satires of Horace* (Cambridge 1966) ch. i; Griffin, *Seneca* 13–16; *RLAC* ii. 990 ff.; Wallach (n. 52); J. F. Kindstrand's comm. on Bion of Borysthenes (Uppsala 1976) 97–9.

stricter formal conventions. The style is often abrupt, sometimes coarse and colloquial, often full of striking and yet usually simple or homely images, drawn from nature and the animal world. The argument is delivered in a sermonising way, involving rhetorical questions, imagined interruptions or protests, enumeration of virtues and vices. Diatribe concerns itself with central moral questions, but with a strong practical slant—how to conduct one's personal relationships, how best to achieve peace of mind, how to face up to exile, enslavement, hardship, illness, and death. The essence of these arguments comes from the Socratic paradoxes;[61] and Socratic also is the use of simple, even vulgar style[62] and homely analogies: the artisan, as in *Meditations* v. 1. 3;[63] the helmsman, physician, and general, as in *Meditations* vi. 55;[64] the ant as a symbol of diligence, as in *Meditations* v. 1.[65] Much of Marcus' vivid range of metaphor and simile may derive from this kind of background; but in general he is more technical, less jocular than the diatribe with its tradition of serio-comic style (σπουδαιογέλοιον);[66] his approach to ethics is more concentrated and his range of subject-matter more restricted.

Another class of chapters may be related not so much to popular philosophic sermons and texts as to the more serious Stoic discussions, fragments of which survive through Plutarch and other sources (collected by von Arnim in *Stoicorum Veterum Fragmenta*; for an extended imitation of their style, see Cic. *Tusc.* iii. 14–22).[67] The two classes are not altogether distinct, but we

---

[61] Pl. *Grg.* 481bc; and e.g. *Rep.* vi. 471a (παράδοξον λόγον), ix. 587b f.; Bond on Eur. *HF* 151; M. J. O'Brien, *The Socratic Paradoxes and the Greek Mind* (Chapel Hill 1967). Important too are the Stoic paradoxes, for which see esp. Cicero's *Paradoxa*, with the introd. to the Budé edn.; also *Fin.* iv. 55. See further E. V. Arnold, *Roman Stoicism* (London 1911) 460 s.v. Paradoxes. In Epict. i. 25. 32 his interlocutor remarks that philosophers say παράδοξα (cf. iii. 24. 111, Cleanthes *ap.* iv. 1. 173).

[62] See Kindstrand, *Bion* 43, 51; esp. Pl. *Grg.* 490c, 491a, 497c. The vulgarity and even obscenity in this procedure was taken further by the Cynics (Kindstrand 51–5; D. R. Dudley, *A History of Cynicism* (London 1937) 44–53). For Stoics, Diog. Laert. vii. 187 (Chrysippus); Cic. *Tusc.* i. 108, *Off.* i. 159 (Posidonius); Clem. Al. *Strom.* v. 9. 58. 2 (= *SVF* i. 43). More examples from Marcus are given below in ch. IV. 3.

[63] See Pöschl, (n. 54) 489.

[64] See Pease on Cic. *ND* iii. 76; 1 Peter 4: 12.

[65] Cic. *ND* i. 79, iii. 21; Hor. *Sat.* i. 1. 33–5; Proverbs 6: 6–8; van der Horst on ps.-Phocyl. 164–70. Town and country mouse: *Med.* xi. 22; cf. Aesop 297 H.; Hor. *Sat.* ii. 6 (Rudd (n. 60) ch. 9).

[66] On which see Kindstrand, *Bion* 47 f.; Rudd (n. 60) 96–8.

[67] See also the very valuable collection by A. A. Long and D. N. Sedley, *The*

can recognise a different note in the more argumentative, occasionally pedantic chapters such as ii. 11 (arguing for divine providence), v. 8, vi. 16, vi. 44 (touching on a controversy prominent in Cicero's *de Natura Deorum*, esp. ii. 164, iii. 86 ff.), vii. 55, ix. 1 (a long and rather ponderous chapter, in the manner of the Stoic handbooks), ix. 9, ix. 40 (on prayer), ix. 42, and xii. 5. Many of the topics and arguments are obviously traditional: formal exposition of reasons to believe in the gods, for example, goes back at least as far as Plato's *Laws*.[68] These chapters are in a very small minority, and the handling of the arguments is often clumsy or casual. Clearly, Marcus' heart was not in such extended demonstration. This alone should have been enough to disprove the theory that the *Meditations* are the draft for a moral treatise.[69]

Thirdly, mention should be made of the literary genre known as protreptic (λόγος προτρεπτικός; in Latin, *exhortatio*), a type of rhetorical exhortation of which the most prominent species encourages the reader to embark upon the contemplative or philosophic life. (Other types are also found: Galen in his *Protreptic* exhorts readers to study medicine.) Traces of this genre are already discernible in Plato (esp. *Euthyd.* 278e–282d[70]), and early examples are to be seen in the Cyprian discourses of Isocrates, especially *ad Nicoclem*. The classic document, however, was Aristotle's *Protrepticus*, largely lost to us but immensely influential in ancient times.[71] The tendency of these works is to stress the supreme importance and value of philosophy as pleasant, honourable, and beneficial. Here as elsewhere, the fundamental difference in the *Meditations* lies in their author's

---

Hellenistic Philosophers (Cambridge 1987) i (translations with philosophical comm.) and ii (texts). Arnold, *Roman Stoicism* quotes extensively from Stoic sources and from Cicero, though his analyses are often superficial. For Plutarch see the very learned work of D. Babut, *Plutarque et le stoïcisme* (Paris 1969).

[68] Pl. *Lg.* x. 884–91, 899–907. Further, Pease on Cic. *ND* ii. 3; M. Dragona-Monachou, *The Stoic Arguments for the Existence and Providence of the Gods* (Athens 1976). For their modern successors see the account by J. L. Mackie, *The Miracle of Theism* (Oxford 1982).

[69] For which view see Farquharson i. lxiv–lxv.

[70] See now R. F. S. Hawtrey's comm. (Ann Arbor 1981). Much of relevance to protreptic literature in S. R. Slings, *A Commentary on the Platonic Clitophon* (Amsterdam 1981). Of older bibliography, note esp. P. Hartlich, *De Exhortationum a Graecis Romanisque Scriptarum Historia et Indole* (Leipzig 1889). On the Roman side Cicero's *Hortensius* was particularly important (fragments ed. A. Grilli, Milan 1962).

[71] See esp. I. Düring, *Aristotle's Protrepticus: A Reconstruction* (Göteburg 1961).

addressing himself, rather than an audience. Although we find praise of philosophy (esp. in ii. 17; see also vi. 12), it is more tentative and modest: both the potential power of the art and the ability of the aspirant are subject to a numbing doubt and questioning. There are points of contact between Marcus and Aristotle[72] on the supreme importance of philosophy, on the superiority and divinity of reason, on the priority of the life intellectual; but the differences of tone and emphasis are more striking than the similarities. The emperor needs no persuasion that philosophy is worth pursuing: what he lacks is not the will but the leisure, and, at least in his own eyes, the intellectual ability.

Fourthly, Marcus seems influenced by collections of anec-dotes about famous men of the past (cf. iii. 14, quoted on p. 28 below), moral tales known as χρεῖαι. These stories often followed a recognisable pattern, laid down by rhetorical theorists.[73] In particular, they had to be short and memorable, and should contain a valuable maxim. Often they were associated with historical characters, such as philosophers, and a frequent convention was for them to end with a witty and exemplary saying by such a figure. Hence these stories are closely related to gnomic sayings and proverbs, which Marcus also includes in his *Meditations*.[74] Anecdotes about great men are not nearly as common in Marcus as moral quotations or γνῶμαι, but they do occur: examples are Socrates' refusal to live at the court of a tyrant (xi. 25), and his behaviour after Xanthippe had taken his coat (xi. 28, rather allusive).

More obscure references also fall into this category: the citation of a saying on Monimus the Cynic (ii. 15: note especially δῆλον δὲ καὶ τὸ χρήσιμον τοῦ λεγομένου), or the dictum of Crates about Xenocrates, where for us the point is lost (vi. 13). Marcus also, like Seneca in his letters, quotes sayings of Epicurus with qualified approval (vii. 64, xi. 26,[75] xii. 34[76]); both authors are

---

[72] For one clear echo cf. *Med.* xi. 7 with Arist. *Protr.* fr. B1 Düring.

[73] Cf. Marcus' frequent use of χρήσιμος (examples follow in the text). On χρεῖαι, their use and definition, se G. Gerhard, *Phoinix von Kolophon* (Leipzig and Berlin 1909) 248 ff.; Kindstrand, *Bion*, 22–3, 99–100. For rhetorical precepts on their use see e.g. Aphthonius 3 (pp. 3–6 Rabe).

[74] Cf. n. 34 above. See Haines's index i, s.v. Proverbs, for some (rather uncertain) examples.

[75] Cf. Sen. *Ep.* 11.8.

[76] Cf. Cic. *Fin.* ii. 96–103(!); *Tusc.* v. 119–20.

eclectic rather than dogmatically anti-Epicurean as is Epictetus (e.g. ii. 20. 10 ff., ii. 23, iii. 7, iii. 24. 38 ff.).[77]

In particular, Marcus quotes Epicurus' brave words in his final illness, as a model to imitate (ix. 41 = Epicurus fr. 191 U). This is the proper use of such sayings and such examples: they inspire emulation, spurring the reader on to action and achievement. This again is plain from Seneca's letters on precept and moral education, or from Plutarch's essays. The association with good men is beneficial to morals: frequent seeing and hearing of them 'descendit in pectora' (Sen. *Ep.* 95. 40), and this is analogous to the function of precepts. The same applies to the mere *descriptio* of a good man such as Cato the Younger, Seneca's particular hero: 'proderit non tantum quales esse solent boni viri dicere formamque eorum et lineamenta deducere, sed quales fuerint narrare et exponere.' (*Ep.* 95. 71, with context.[78])

Marcus was familiar from his youth (i. 14) with the same gallery of virtuous men and philosophic heroes as Seneca, while in the flesh and in his memories he drew lessons for himself from more recent figures, those named in the first book of the *Meditations* and above all his adopted father and predecessor, Antoninus Pius (i. 16; vi. 30). Even the now obscure allusion in the tribute to Pius, 'think how he dealt with the customs official at Tusculum when the latter apologised' (i. 16. 8), has the makings of a χρεία. In the next paragraph he explicitly transfers to Pius qualities famous in the literary tradition concerning Socrates ('what is recorded about Socrates would fit him precisely . . .'). It is easy for the modern reader to be misled by the impersonal schematising of the rhetorical handbooks when they discuss *exempla*.[79] Marcus' statement of his debt to Pius, so

---

[77] Cf. W. Schmid, *RLAC* v. 767 ff. On Epicureanism under the Empire see also C. W. Chilton, *Diogenes of Oenoanda* (Oxford 1971) xxii–xxviii. Abuse of Epicureans and their doctrine is traditional for Stoics: see *SVF* ii. 1115, 1126; D. Babut, *La Religion des philosophes grecs* (Paris 1974) 173.

[78] Cf. 95. 66, and see the discussions of these letters cited in n. 99 below. *Descriptio* in philosophic contexts normally means 'definition' (*OLD* s.v., 3b; e.g. Cic. *de Or.* i. 222), but here we have another case of philosophic persuasion drawing on rhetorical tools (Cic. *de Or.* iii. 205; *ad Her.* iv. 51).

[79] E.g. Arist. *Rh.* ii. 20; *ad Her.* iv. 62; Cic. *Brut.* 145; Quint. v. 11. Cf. H. W. Litchfield, *HSCP* 25 (1941) 1 ff.; F. G. B. Millar, *JRS* 59 (1969) 13; T. P. Wiseman, *Clio's Cosmetics* (Leicester 1979) ch. 3.

intimately related to the pattern he himself seeks to follow, shows how they had real meaning.

4. *What to Read and How to Write*

In many of the passages cited earlier in which Epictetus deals with philosophic self-discipline, he is concerned not only with this philosopher's thoughts but with his reading; and he pronounces on this theme at greater length elsewhere, especially in iv. 4. For him, as for Seneca, reading must not be mere enjoyment or aesthetic appreciation, it must be profitable ethically. This was the traditional Stoic position, as expressed in the opening chapters of Strabo's *Geography*, or in the Stoicizing interpretations of Homer put forward in the second epistle of Horace's first book (i. 2. 1–31).[80] Epictetus also interprets Homer through a moralist's eyes (e.g. iv. 10. 31–6). Mere study for its own sake, even of the works of philosphers, is deplored: what matters is to apply one's reading to one's moral life (iv. 4. 15–18). Both Seneca and Epictetus contrast mere learning with philosophy: Seneca complains 'quae philosophia fuit facta philologia est.' (*Ep.* 108. 24).[81] Similarly, Epictetus treats with contempt anyone who preens himself on being able to interpret Chrysippus' writings:

But when I find the interpreter, what remains is to put his precepts into practice; that is the only thing to be proud about. If, however, I admire the mere act of interpretation, what have I done but turned into a grammarian instead of a philosopher? The only difference, indeed, is that I interpret Chrysippus instead of Homer. (*Ench.* 49)

This fiercely reductive attitude to literature is bound up with Epictetus' condemnation of epideictic or sophistic rhetoric: not only are such practices a waste of time, but they involve much hypocrisy and moral corruption (see esp. iii. 21, e.g. 7; ii. 17. 34–6, 40;[82] ii. 23, esp. 40–7; iii. 10. 10; and above all iii. 23. 7–38[83]).

---

[80] See esp. P. De Lacy, *AJP* 69 (1948) 241–271, an outstanding survey to which I am frequently indebted. Note also F. Buffière, *Les Mythes d'Homère et la pensée grecque* (Paris 1956); R. Pfeiffer, *History of Classical Scholarship* i (Oxford 1968) 140, 166, 237 ff.; much in E. Valgiglio's commentary on Plutarch, *de Audiendis Poetis* (Turin 1973); Kindstrand on Bion fr. 3.

[81] Cf. also Porph. *Vit. Plot.* 14.

[82] Cf. Hor. *Ep.* ii. 2. 87 ff.

38[83]). Here as in their moralistic approach to poetry the Stoics are the true heirs of Plato.[84]

The attitude of Marcus in the *Meditations* is close to that of Epictetus, and also to Stoic-influenced works such as Plutarch's educational treatises.[85] Marcus quotes memorable sayings of poets and philosophers, especially Epictetus himself, Socrates in Plato, Heraclitus, and Democritus; but he makes clear that his reason is that they have salutary moral lessons to teach. *Meditations* xi. 6 on the didactive value of tragedy is particularly illuminating. Tragedy was created, he says with striking simplicity,

to remind you of what comes to pass, and that it is in the course of nature that things should happen so . . . for you see that those events were bound to reach that ending, and that they endure them, even the men who cry out aloud 'Alas! Alas! Cithaeron' [Soph. OT 1389, also quoted by Epict. i. 24. 16] . . . There are also valuable sayings (λέγεται δέ τινα . . . χρησίμως) in the dramatists.

Marcus goes on to quote three favourite lines, all from tragedies and all quoted by him elsewhere. Old Comedy too, with its educational outspokenness (παιδαγωγικὴν παρρησίαν), provided a profitable reminder to avoid pomposity (τῆς ἀτυφίας);[86] and New Comedy also includes τινὰ χρήσιμα (cf. Plut. *Comp. Ar. et Men.*, *Mor.* 853). We see the same tendency to apply poetry to ethics elsewhere in the *Meditations*: for instance, x. 34: 'for one bitten by true doctrines, even the briefest, most familiar saying is reminder enough to dispel sorrow and fear (εἰς ὑπόμνησιν

[83] A detailed study of these portions of Epictetus would be of considerable value. For recitation and its literary and moral resonances, see Mayor on Juv. 3. 9 (a *locus classicus*); for hypocritical and uncritical applause see J. C. Bramble, *Persius and the Programmatic Satire* (Cambridge 1974) 106–8 (add esp. Pl. *Euthyd.* 276cd, 303b; *Prt.* 334b, 339de).

[84] On the continuity of the Platonic critique of rhetoric and its accompanying evils see G. Kennedy, *The Art of Persuasion in Greece* (Princeton 1963) 321 ff.; H. von Armin, *Lebe und Werke des Dio von Prusa* (Berlin 1898) ch. 1; A. Boulanger, *Aelius Aristide et la sophistique* (Paris 1923) 218–70 (on Aristides' attempted reply to Plato).

[85] Or ps.-Plut. *de Liberis Educandis*, a work now equipped with a lavish commentary by N. J. S. Abbot (diss. Oxford 1980). See generally K. W. Weataway, *The Educational Theory of Plutarch* (London 1922); G. Pire, *Stoicisme et pédagogie* (Paris 1958), though both works are somewhat diffuse. Better are Abbot and Valgiglio (n. 80); on *Aud. Poet.* see also Babut (n. 67) 87 ff. On *de Recta Ratione Audiendi* see now the admirable commentary by B. P. Hillyard (New York 1981).

[86] For the moral value of comedy, besides Aristophanic passages such as *Ach.* 500 (on which see O. Taplin, *CQ* 33 (1983) 331–3) or *Ran.* 389 ff., 1009 ff., see Hor. *Sat.* i. 4. 1 ff., with M. Coffey, *Roman Satire* (London 1976) 224 n. 116; Muecke (n. 48) 57.

ἀλυπίας καὶ ἀφοβίας), such as "leaves, some of which the wind scatters to the ground; such are the generations of men" [Iliad vi. 146 ff., slightly abbreviated]'.

Many collections of gnomic sayings by poets and philosophers existed in antiquity for the use of students, both for writing exercises in early education and as an instrument of moral instruction.[87] Most seriously inclined students would doubtless continue this practice in later life. Compilation for oneself is expressly recommended by Seneca to Lucilius, using the traditional bee-imagery: 'nos quoque has apes debemus imitari et quaecumque ex diversa lectione congessimus separare, melius enim distincta servantur.' (*Ep.* 84. 5). He also, however, finds it necessary to insist that some writers must be read in their entirety (*Ep.* 33).[88]

Marcus did not have the leisure of Seneca. In considering his reading-habits, as in other areas, we should contrast the circumstances of his old age, the time at which the *Meditations* were being composed, with his younger days as revealed to us retrospectively in Book I and more directly in the correspondence with Fronto. In *Meditations* i. 7 he thanks Rusticus for teching him how to read books attentively (τὸ ἀκριβῶς ἀναγινώσκειν); but elsewhere he complains of having no time to read (viii. 8). More interesting is iii. 14, in which he specifies what he would be reading if he could: 'you have no time now to read your memoranda, nor the acts of the ancient Greeks and Romans and the extracts from their writings which you have laid up against your old age.'[89] Memoranda (ὑπομνημάτια) is so

[87] See esp. Horna, *RE* Suppl. vi. 74 ff.; J. Barns, *CQ* 44 (1950) 126 ff., esp. 132–7; id., *CQ* (NS) 1 (1951) 1–19; Machon, ed. A. S. F. Gow (Cambridge 1965) 12 ff.; H. Chadwick, *RLAC* vii. 1131–60, esp. 1152–4, on Florilegia. For the bee-imagery referred to in the text see Isoc. i. 51 f., ii. 44; Lucr. iii. 10 ff.; Plut. *Mor.* 32e, 41e, 79c, 467c, 494a, etc.; note also the use of words such as κηρίον and μέλισσα as titles for anthologies (Barns, loc. cit.).

[88] For Seneca's reading-programme for Lucilius see Scarpat on Sen. *Ep.* 2; Hadot, *Seneca und die griechisch-römische Tradition der Seelenleitung* (Berlin 1969) 54–6. For similar methods used by Epicureans see ibid. 48–54; N. W. de Witt, *Epicurus and his Philosophy* (Minnesota 1954) 110 ff. Commonplace-books: *commentarii* in Plin. *Ep.* iii. 5. 17 (on his uncle); Sen. *Ep.* 33. 7 'turpe est enim seni . . . ex commentario sapere'; Gell. pr. 2–3, 11–13, 22. Plutarch kept a commonplace-book for philosophic matter: *Cohib. Ira* 457d; *Tranq.* 464 f. See also ps.-Plut. *Lib. Educ.* 8b; Philostr. *VS* ii. 1, 565 (on Herodes Atticus, one of Marcus' teachers). Meditation on texts: see Rabbow, *Seelenführung* 218 ff., 358 ff. Note esp. Hor. *Ep.* i. 1. 36–7 (discussed on p. 38); Sen. *Ep.* 108. 8 ff., 24 ff.; Epict. i. 1. 25, etc.; *Ench.* 53; Plut. *Aud. Poet.* 34b f., August. *Conf.* ix. 4.7–8.

[89] For the phraseology cf. Pl. *Phdr.* 276d; contrast the lighter or more euphemistic

vague a word as to be almost impossible to pin down: it could mean lecture-notes or *commentarii* (informal draftings for a projected work), but it seems unlikely to refer to the *Meditations* themselves.[90] If Marcus had the leisure to write more, he could presumably look back. The context suggests a more pleasurable pursuit. But the other type of reading-matter, historical extracts, may be suggestive, for in rhetorical theory history is 'philosophy drawn from examples' (ps.-Dion. Hal. *Ars Rh.* II. 2, p. 398 U.-R.), and this kind of exemplary literature, as found in the collection of Valerius Maximus or in Plutarch's *Lives*, would be well suited to Marcus' interests'.[91] There are both connections and contrasts here with Marcus' earlier years: in AD 143 he was already diligently extracting others' works: 'feci tamen mihi per hos dies excerpta ex libris sexaginta in quinque tomis' (!), he writes to Fronto (i. 138 Haines), but there the extracts are from Atellan farces and Scipio's orations. Contrast, again, a letter to Fronto around 161, asking him to send him something light for relaxation, something by Cato, Cicero, Sallust, or Gracchus or some poetry, 'χρῄζω γαρ ἀναπαύλης, et maxime hoc genus quae me lectio extollat et diffundat ἐκ τῶν κατειληφυιῶν φροντίδων.' (i. 301: 'For I have need of recreation, and it is particularly with this kind of writing that I find reading it exhilarates me and releases me from the cares that have me in their grip.'). In the *Meditations* his literary horizons are narrowed, his preoccupations more sombre.

In x. 34 Marcus states that even the briefest quotation can be sufficient reminder of doctrine. This corresponds to his principle regarding the truths embodied in the *Meditations* also. The clearest statement of the purpose of his work occurs in iv. 3, where Marcus speaks of the common wish—which he himself shares—to withdraw into a retreat from the world (ἀναχώρησις),

---

tone of Hor. *Ep.* i. 1. 12 ('condo et compono quae *mox* depromere possim'); see also Plut. *Cohib. Ira.* 454a.

[90] As supposed by e.g. Brunt, *JRS* 64 (1974) 3 n. 12. In general on the word ὑπόμνημα see Kindstrand, *Bion*, pp. 21-2; add Pfeiffer (n. 80) index s.v.; A. Momigliano, *The Development of Greek Biography* (Cambridge, Mass. 1971) 90 n. 24; G. Avenarius, *Lukians Schrift zur Geschichtsschreibung* (Meisenheim am Glan 1956) 85-104; C. B. R. Pelling, *JHS* 99 (1979) 92-5.

[91] On exemplary literature see n. 79 above and further in ch. II. 2. For Valerius Maximus and his genre see C. J. Carter, in *Empire and Aftermath*, ed. T. A. Dorey (London 1975) 35 ff., with bibliog. Note also Nisbet-Hubbard on Hor. *Odes* i. 12 (introductory note).

to find privacy in the country, the sea-shore, the hills. This is an important topic in ancient discussions of the philosophic or contemplative life, conspicuous in the Epicureanism of Lucretius or Horace.[92]

Marcus, however, insists that there is a sufficient retreat within the individual's own mind,

> especially one who has within such things that he need only look into them, and become at once in perfect ease. . . . Continually, then, grant yourself this retreat and renew yourself. But let them be brief and fundamental truths that you find there (βραχέα δὲ ἔστω καὶ στοιχειώδη) which will suffice at once by their presence to cleanse away all sorrow, and to send you back, without repugnance, to the life to which you return. (iv. 3. 1)

'Continually' (συνεχῶς) is a favourite word in Marcus, as are its synonyms. The phrase 'Always remember' often begins a chapter ('some forty times', according to Brunt[93]). The emphasis on brevity in the passage above is also striking. Elsewhere (iii. 5) Marcus bids himself be μήτε πολυρρήμων μήτε πολυπράγμων ('neither a busy talker nor a busybody'). In the *Meditations* he seeks to lay down a set of axioms which will provide comfort and guidance amid life's turbulence. They are 'brief and fundamental' because they are thus more memorable, and because they should take effect 'at once' (iv. 3. 1 εὐθύς). Further, the stylistic simplicity of the *Meditations* is intended to mirror the moral simplicity of Stoic principle. Stoics such as Seneca and Epictetus endorsed the ancient assumption that style and ethics are intimately related (esp. Sen. *Ep.* 114. 1 ff.).[94] So also in the

---

[92] On withdrawal, Epicurean or other, see esp. A. J. Festugière, *Personal Religion among the Greeks* (Berkeley and Los Angeles 1954) ch. 3; E. R. Dodds, *Pagan and Christian in an Age of Anxiety* (Cambridge 1965) ch. i; J. M. André, *L'Otium dans la vie morale et intellectuelle romaine* (Paris 1966). This topic is closely linked with the contrast between the active and contemplative lives, on which see ch. II n. 81. The country as a place of withdrawal associates the philosophic retreat with the primitivist assumptions of idyll and pastoral: the countryside thus becomes a symbol, as in Virgil's *Georgics* or Horace's *Epistles*. See A. E. Lovejoy and G. Boas, *Primitivism and Related Ideas in Antiquity* (Baltimore 1935).

[93] *JRS* 64 (1974) 3.

[94] On the Senecan letter see esp. E. Norden, *Die Antike Kunstprosa* (Leipzig and Berlin 1909) 306 ff.; further, C. N. Smiley, in *Classical Studies in Honour of Charles Foster Smith* (= Univ. of Wisconsin Studies in Language and Literature vol. 3, 1919) 50–61; H. MacL. Currie, *BICS* 13 (1966) 76–87; Leeman (n. 9) 271–8. More broadly on this theme see M. H. Abrams, *The Mirror and the Lamp* (Oxford 1953) ch. 9; Bramble (n. 83) *passim* (esp. ch. 2 and excursus). Cf. nn. 120 ff. below.

Meditations, when the author writes 'throw all else aside, and hold fast only to these few things' (iii. 10), this demand for a return to the essentials of ethics has its stylistic corollary.

The aphoristic style of early Greek poetry and philosophy also has some influence on Marcus' stylistic choices.[95] He frequently quotes Heraclitus, who was generally popular with Stoics,[96] and also cites Hesiod and Democritus. In a famous passage of the *Protagoras* Socrates had referred to the laconic quality of the sayings of the Seven Sages, the wise men of archaic Greece— ῥήματα βραχέα ἀξιομνημόνευτα ἑκάστῳ εἰρημένα ('brief and memorable words uttered by each of them')—sayings such as 'know thyself' and 'nothing in excess'; Socrates declared this brevity to be the ancient style of philosophy (Pl. *Prt.* 343ab and context; cf. *Hipparchus* 228de; Plut. *Garr.* 510e ff.). Aristotle later asserted that proverbs were fragments of the philosophy of earlier ages (fr. 13 Rose).[97] In the *Ars Poetica* Horace states the principle of brevity with his usual economy, the style itself deliberately brief:

> quicquid praecipies esto brevis, ut cito dicta
> percipiant animi dociles teneantque fideles.
> omne supervacuum pleno de pectore manat.

> (*Ars* 335–7)[98]

Whatever your instructions, be brief, so that responsive minds may swiftly grasp your words and guard them faithfully. All that is superfluous overflows a full heart.

Seneca makes a very similar point, more positively, in his discussion of precepts and doctrine in the long and elaborate

---

[95] See Cherniss (n. 59) and West (n. 34). Further, e.g. Demetr. 274; Diog. Laert. ix. 7 on Heraclitus; Sen. *Ep.* 94. 27–8, 94. 43, 108. 8–9. The special effect of such brief and pungent phrases is partly rooted in the fascination of linguistic ambiguities and oracular opacity (proverbs, riddles, and oracles can be regarded as akin: cf. αἶνος, αἰνίσσομαι, αἴνιγμα; see West on Hes. *Op.* 202; Heracl. B92–3; Plut. *Pyth. Or.* 407a ff.). In Cic. *Fin.* ii. 20 Epicurus' *Kuriai Doxai* are described as oracular; cf. ibid. 102, v. 79.

[96] Pease on Cic. *ND* iii. 35; A. A. Long, *Philosophia* 5–6 (1975–6) 123–56.

[97] Further, Kindstrand (n. 34).

[98] On brevity see n. 33 above. For Stoic rhetoric as pure and brief (!) see also Lucan ix. 188–9 '*pauca* Catonis/verba sed a pleno venientia pectore veri . . .' (a speech of 24 lines follows). For Cato's speech as oracular (cf. n. 95) see Lucan ix. 564–5, and the whole scene. In real life, note Cato *ap.* Cic. *Fam.* xv. 5. 3: 'atque haec ego idcirco ad te contra consuetudinem meam pluribus scripsi . . .' (pointed in a reply one-sixth the length of Cicero's own!).

pair of letters on these subjects (*Ep.* 94–5).[99] By 'precept' he means an edifying maxim, remark, or command which is applied independently of logical argument or proof. The opposite is doctrine (δόγμα, *decretum*). Precepts depend upon doctrine, they are particularised advice (95. 12). Precept alone, according to Seneca, would be weak and rootless[100] unless fully integrated within a philosophic system. Yet precepts are of real value: advice even without proofs may be of help in liberating the chained mind from error (94. 27, 31). It is not superfluous to point out things already known: 'interdum enim scimus nec adtendimus . . . admonere genus adhortandi est . . . ingerenda est itaque illi notitia rerum notissimarum.' (94. 25; cf. 21, 23, 37). The moral facts which we accept intellectually should be kept not 'reposita' but 'in promptu' (ibid. 26[101]). The salutary effect of moral quotations is stressed (94. 46–7; cf. 59, where our guiding preceptor[102] whispers 'salubria verba'). Seneca especially emphasises the powerful impact of compressed, proverbial sayings, which instantly affect and convince even the 'imperitissimos':

velut his brevissimus vocibus, sed multum habentibus ponderis: 'nil nimis [cf. Pl. *Prt*, quoted above]; avarus animus nullo satiatur lucro; ab alio exspectes alteri quod feceris.'[103] haec cum ictu quodam audimus, nec ulli licet dubitare aut interrogare 'quare?'; adeo etiam sine ratione ipsa veritas ducit. (94. 43; cf. 108. 8 f.)

In the same way oracular sayings and proverbial wisdom in prose or verse are referred to at 94. 67, and are there associated with the *Dicta* of the elder Cato.[104] In each case simplicity and epigrammatic brevity effect a moral and emotional impact.

[99] On these letters see the comm. by G. Scarpat (Brescia 1979); also A. Dihle, *JHS* 93 (1973) 50–7 (arguing for background in Posidonius); I. G. Kidd, in J. M. Rist (ed.), *The Stoics* (California and London 1978) 251 ff.

[100] See *Ep.* 95. 12; cf. Pl. *Euthphr.* 11bc, 15b; *Meno* 97d f. and Thompson's note.

[101] Cf. Sen. *Ben.* vii. 1. 3, and the use of πρόχειρος in Epictetus and Marcus.

[102] For the teacher and spiritual director in Seneca and others see S. Dill, *Roman Society from Nero to Marcus Aurelius* (London 1904) 289–333; A. M. Guillemin, *REL* 30 (1952) 202–19, 31 (1953) 215–34, 32 (1954) 250–74; Rabbow, *Seelenführung* 260 ff.; Hadot, *Seneca* part i. See further on masters and pupils, and on 'philosophic chaplains', in ch. II. 3 below.

[103] Cf. the so-called 'Golden Rule', 'do as you would be done by' (*Matt.* vii. 12), on which see esp. A. Dihle, *Die Goldene Regel* (Göttingen 1962), with D. A. Russell's review, *Gnomon* 35 (1963) 213–15.

[104] On Cato's dicta cf. Cic. *Off.* i. 104; *de Or.* ii. 271; A. E. Astin, *Cato the Censor* (Oxford 1978) 186 ff. Samples in Plut. *Cat. Mai.* 8–9.

Marcus Aurelius likewise includes older quotations and aphorisms in his *Meditations*, as well as coining many of his own. There are many 'chapters' which consist of single sentences of a terse, memorable, epigrammatic form: e.g. vi. 54 τὸ τῷ σμήνει μὴ συμφέρον οὐδὲ τῇ μελίσσῃ συμφέρει ('What does not benefit the hive does not benefit the bee'); ix. 20 τὸ ἄλλου ἁμάρτημα ἐκεῖ δεῖ καταλιπεῖν ('Another's wrongdoing one should leave where it lies'; cf. ix. 38, the same idea less epigrammatically phrased); vi. 6 ἄριστος τρόπος τοῦ ἀμύνεσθαι τὸ μὴ ἐξομοιοῦσθαι ('The noblest kind of self-defence is not to become like one's enemy'); xii. 17 εἰ μὴ καθήκει, μὴ πράξῃς· εἰ μὴ ἀληθές ἐστι, μὴ εἴπῃς ('If it is not right, don't do it; if it's not true, don't say it'), and many others. Longer chapters can often be seen to be composed of a series of disconnected sayings or admonitions: examples are iv. 26 (note especially the banal τὸ δ' ὅλον, βραχὺς ὁ βίος—'to sum up, life is short'), vii. 29 (consisting of seven injunctions, many of them used or elaborated elsewhere), vii. 31, ix. 7. Closely related are chapters which consist of κεφάλαια, ungrammatical lists of topics to be considered. These often resemble the titles of philosophic essays (such as those prefixed by Arrian or a later editor to the diatribes of Epictetus). Good examples of this class are ii. 9, vii. 26–7, xii. 7–8 (note especially τί πόνος · τί ἡδονή · τί θάνατος · τί δόξα; 'What is the nature of pain? of pleasure? of death? of reputation?'; these questions are not answered here).[105]

These categories certainly do not exhaust the content of the *Meditations*, but they do illustrate an essential aspect of the work's function for the author. It sums up, in pithy and memorable terms, his central preoccupations and principles.

The language in which Marcus refers to his writing serves as helpful confirmation of the conclusions outlined above. His admonitions are referred to as παραστήματα ('aids'?, iii. 11) and as παραπήγματα ('supports, props', ix. 3. 2).[106] The recollection

---

[105] Further on *gnomica* in Marcus see Dalfen, *Formgeschichtliche Untersuchungen* 232–4; for κεφάλαια, ibid. 243 ff. Dalfen sees the construction of these chapters as analogous to that of Book I (τὸ . . . ὅτι . . ., etc.); see his p. 6 f.

[106] Editors and translators generally take Marcus' words at the beginning of iii. 11 (τοῖς δὲ εἰρημένοις παραστήμασιν . . .) to refer to his precepts; for the suggestion of an architectural metaphor ('props, stays, supports') see Farquharson's note. Strictly the word may be presumed to mean 'that which παρέστη', i.e. what has occurred to his thought (cf. Arndt–Gingrich s.v. παρίστημι 2γ); perhaps 'that which comes to help'? For παραπήγματα, Professor Kidd suggests 'pegs', like the markers on a common type of ancient calendar; cf. Shackleton Bailey on Cic. *Att.* v. 14. 1. Marcus also refers to his

of the deaths of great men is an ἰδιωτικὸν μέν, ὅμως δὲ ἀνυστικὸν βοήθημα ('an unprofessional but none the less effective aid', iv. 50); and at x. 34 a quotation from the *Iliad*, one which is in fact a classic tag in moralistic literature,[107] can serve εἰς ὑπόμνησιν ἀλυπίας καὶ ἀφοβίας ('as a reminder to dispel sorrow and fear'; cf. xi. 6). Similarly, in vii. 75, 'to remember this will make you face many things in a calmer frame of mind'. Often the particular vice that is to be counteracted will be specified, as in iv. 49, 'in every event that inclines you to sorrow, remember to use this axiom . . .'; viii. 1, 'this is a good cure for vainglory, that you no longer have it in your power to have lived your whole life from boyhood as a philosopher'; and also ix. 28, ix. 42, and especially xi. 18, a long chapter which lists ten prescriptions against anger, always a central topic in ancient moralistic writing.[108]

The metaphorical language used of the work and its value for the author is powerful and imaginative, though again it stands in a recognisable tradition. We have already mentioned the frequent use of the word πρόχειρος ('ready to hand'), which can be seen as analogous to the title of Epictetus' *Encheiridion* ('The Handbook') and broadly resembles the usage of Seneca and Plutarch.[109] The axioms which he is to ponder will 'renew' Marcus (iv. 3. 1 ἀνανέου); they are living principles (vii. 2 ζῆ τὰ δόγματα); they cannot become lifeless as long as he continually

---

'rules' or 'standards' (κανόνες: v. 22, x. 2). The term is common in Epictetus, and suits the precision-measurement of Stoic ethics (cf. e.g. Pers. 1. 6, 64–5; Bramble, *Persius* 117).

[107] See Gataker ad loc., citing amongst others Pyrrho *ap*. Diog. Laert. ix. 67; ps.-Plut. *Cons. Apoll.* 104e; Plut. *de Sera Num. Vind.* 560c; Clem. Al. *Strom.* vi. 2. 5. Cf. V. Pöschl, *Bibliographie zur antiken Bildersprache* (Heidelberg 1964) 459; see below, ch. iv n. 28. Another stock quotation, used by Marcus in vii. 40 and xi. 6, is Eur. *Hyps.* fr. 757N. (= 60.90 ff Bond); cf. Cic. *Tusc.* iii. 59; ps.-Plut. *Cons. Apoll.* 111a; Kassel, *Untersuchungen* 11–12. Also famous is vii. 50 (Eur. *Chrys.* fr. 836N.). Marcus seems often to quote from memory, as at xi. 25 (where other sources name Archelaus, not Perdiccas), xi. 33 (from Epict. iii. 24. 86, but not verbatim). In xi. 39 the saying attributed to Socrates is not to be found in Plato or Xenophon. In xi. 32 Marcus or his source amends the text of Hes. *Op.* 185 to give it a more philosophic flavour. Arrian/Epictetus also quotes from memory: e.g. ii. 5. 18 ff. (Pl. *Ap.* 26e f. has Meletus, not Anytus). Likewise Plutarch: see D. A. Russell, *Plutarch* (London 1973) 46; W. C. Helmbold and E. N. O'Neill, *Plutarch's Quotations* (Philadelphia 1959).

[108] P. Rabbow, *Die Therapie des Zorns* (Berlin 1914); Nisbet–Hubbard on Hor. *Odes* i. 16; Brunt, *JRS* 64 (1974) 10–12 (including valuable comparisons between Marcus, Seneca, and Plutarch on this theme); van der Horst on Ps.-Phocyl. 57, 63. Language similar to that of the passages cited can be found in Epict. i. 27. 1–6; Plut. *Tronq.* 467e, 470a, 476e.

[109] See Rabbow, *Seelenführung* 334–6.

kindles them anew (ibid. ἀναζωπυρεῖν).[110] He urges himself to continue until he has assimilated these truths into himself (ἐξοικειώσῃς σεαυτῷ), 'as a strong stomach assimilates any food, and a bright fire turns whatever you throw into it to flame and light' (x. 31; cf. 35; iv. 1). The springs of goodness lie within the soul, waiting to be tapped (vii. 59; cf. viii. 51; Plut. Tranq. 467a, 477b). He acknowledges that the soul is 'dyed' to match the character of its inner thoughts; 'so dye her with a continual stream of thoughts like these . . .' (v. 16; here συνέχεια is akin to his regular use of συνεχῶς). Similarly in iii. 4. 3 he longs to be 'deep-dyed with justice' (δικαιοσύνῃ βεβαμμένον εἰς βάβος).

A particularly suggestive image occurs at xi. 19, where Marcus speaks of four unsatisfactory mental states against which he must keep constant guard, wiping them out when they appear by pronouncing a spell (ἐπιλέγοντα), repeating it in every case. This is almost a technical term in the vocabulary of self-discipline: compare, for example, Epict. Ench. 1. 5; 3; 4; 9; 12; also Plut. Cohib. Ira 463e ἐπιφωνεῖν . . . ἐπιφθεγγόμενος and the whole context, or Tranq. 477a ἐπιθρηνοῦμεν.[111] Moreover, the regular use of these words draws attention to a central fact of ancient philosophic literature, that the appeal of philosophy is to the emotions, and the innermost convictions, as well as to the reason. The philosopher is the opposite of the rhetorician, a recurrent contrast, because the former's goal is truth, not probability (e.g. Pl. Phdr. 267a[112]); but throughout antiquity each learns from the other. The rhetorician needs to acquire and use some of the philospher's understanding of human nature;[113] the philosopher, even the Stoic, needs to recognise that his

---

[110] The image may derive from the brilliant passage on spiritual contact and intellectual awakening in Pl. (?) Ep. vii. 341cd.

[111] See esp. P. Lain Entralgo, Hermes 86 (1958) 298–323; also E. R. Dodds, The Ancient Concept of Progress (Oxford 1973) 111; Rabbow, Seelenführung 347 ff.; E. Belfiore, Phoenix 34 (1980) 128–37.

[112] Further, Smp. 198b ff.; Phdr. 272de. For such critics, rhetoric is most potent with the ignorant (Grg. 459) and lacks any true knowedge of its subject-matter (Phdr. 268). See G. E. R. Lloyd, Magic, Reason and Experience (Cambridge 1979) 79–86, 98–102.

[113] See esp. Cic. de Or. i. 29–34, 202, iii. 55–60, 133–42. On what philosophy (and other arts) can and should give to rhetoric see P. A. Brunt, Miscellanea in onore di E. Manni i (Rome 1979) 323–6. On Cicero's views see also D'Alton (n. 33) 149–53; M. L. Clarke, Rhetoric at Rome (London 1953) ch. 5; K. Barwick, Der rednerische Bildungsideal Ciceros (Abh. Sächs. Ak. Wiss., Phil.-Hist. Kl. 54. 3, Leipzig 1963) esp. 35–42. For later views see Tac. Dial. 30–2; Quint. xii. 2 with Austin's notes.

purpose too is not only to instruct, but to move and inspire his hearers, to transform intellectual assent into the motivation for action.[114] Here too we discern the Socratic background, as when Alcibiades in Plato's *Symposium* declares that although he has heard the speeches of Pericles and the other orators, they never affected him or threw his soul into a turmoil as does the conversation of Socrates (*Smp.* 215de);[115] 'In my dealings with this man alone have I experienced what some people might think it wasn't in me to experience—to feel ashamed.' (ibid. 216b).

Shame and self-reproach are effects which many ancient philosophers sought to instil in their audience or interlocutor: like Socrates or Seneca, they aimed to use rhetoric in order to make their pupils look beyond criteria of mere stylistic appreciation. Epictetus praises the lectures of Musonius Rufus in these terms:

Rufus used to say, 'If you are at leisure to praise me, I speak to no purpose.' And indeed he used to speak in such a manner that each of us who heard him supposed that someone had informed on us to him: he so hit on what was done by us, and placed the faults of every one before his own eyes. (Epict. iii. 23. 28)[116]

Very similar is Arrian's description of Epictetus himself, in his preface to the collection:

It was evident even when he uttered them [his discourses] that he aimed at nothing more than to excite his hearers to virtue. If they produce that one effect [sc. in my versions], they have in them what, I think, philosophical discourses ought to have. (Arrian, *praef.*, p. 1 Schenkl)

So too Marcus thanks Rusticus because from him he gained an

---

[114] Note esp. Cicero's *mot* in *de Or.* i. 47: 'legi Gorgiam: quo in libro in hoc maxime admirabar Platonem, quod mihi in oratoribus inridendis ipse esse orator summus videbatur.' Indeed, the jibe (which recurs at Quint. ii. 16. 1) has more truth than the author perhaps realised, for in the *Gorgias* Socrates himself becomes the practitioner of the purified rhetoric that is outlined at 480bd, 503ab, 527c; cf. *Phdr.* 269–72. (Cf. Brunt (n. 113) 323 n. 27.)

[115] See further Muson, fr. 49 *ap.* Gell. vi. 1; Plut. *Recta Rat.* 46 with Hillyard ad loc.

[116] A positive and moral use of the familiar rhetorical concept of vividness (ἐνάργεια), on which see esp. Nisbet-Hubbard on Hor. *Odes* ii. 1. 17, Russell on Long. 15. 1; M. Winterbottom, *Fondation Hardt Entretiens* 28 (1982) 263–5.

impression of the need for reform and treatment of his own character (*Med.* i. 7).[117]

The image of philosophy as a spell or incantation also has Platonic background, in the *Charmides*, in the *Republic* (where the magic of philosophy is needed in order to counter the bewitchment of poetry: x. 608a, answering 607c), and above all in the *Phaedo*, a work which was particularly dear to the Stoics (notably Cato and Seneca) and to which Marcus often alludes. In that dialogue Socrates gently mocks Simmias and Cebes for being children, afraid that after death the wind may literally blow their souls away. Cebes replies:

'Try to reassure us, Socrates, as if we were afraid; or rather, not as if we were afraid ourselves, but maybe there is a child inside us who has fears of that kind. Try to persuade him, then, to stop being afraid of death as if it were a bogy-man.'
'Well, you must sing spells to him every day (ἀλλὰ χρή ... ἐπᾴδειν αὐτῷ ἑκάστης ἡμέρας)', said Socrates, 'until you have charmed the terror away (ἐξαπᾴσητε).'
'And where', he said, 'shall we find so excellent a charmer, now that you, Socrates, are leaving us?' (*Phaedo* 77e–78a)

Socrates' answer is to urge them to scour the earth for this priceless enchanter; but he then adds that they must seek among themselves too: 'for perhaps you may not readily find anyone more capable of achieving this than yourselves.' This subtly points to the importance of friendship in dialectic;[118] it also encourages his followers to become their own critics as well as each other's. Later in the *Phaedo* the myth of the afterlife is described as the kind of thing they should recite to themselves (114d ἐπᾴδειν); like the myth of the *Gorgias*, it seems to be a recognition that there are some things which cannot be proved by argument alone. The child within us needs to be placated also; and Plato's philosophy appeals through his art to the whole man.

Marcus certainly knew this passage; but the imagery of

---

[117] Cf. A. D. Nock, *Conversion* (Oxford 1933) ch. 11; Macleod, *Collected Essays* 285 n. 30; and add Pl. *Tht.* 177b. Further, ch. II n. 33 and ch. III nn. 35 ff. below.

[118] Cf. *Ep.* vii. 340c7. Friendship, with the frankness and readiness to accept criticism that should go with it, are important throughout Plato's work and especially in the more dialectical dialogues: see e.g. *Grg.* 485e, 508a, etc.; Ast. *Lexicon Platonicum* s.v. φιλία, etc. On friendship as a theme of ancient philosophy see below ch. III n. 24; ch. V n. 3; also Kindstrand on Bion fr. 49–53.

philosophy as magic, as of it as medicine, had a continuous history from Plato onwards, for instance among the Epicureans, whose τετραφάρμακος (p. 69 Usener = *Kuriai Doxai* 1–4) neatly combines the two ideas. Horace too speaks of 'certa piacula' which will cure the mind of its unhealthy and irrational states (*Ep.* i. 1. 33–40). Particularly significant here is line 37 of the first epistle, 'ter pure lecto poterunt recreare libello'. The use of 'recreare' resembles Marcus' use of ἀνανέου in iv. 3. 1 (and elsewhere), while 'ter lecto libello' wittily moves between ritual magic using books of charms, and the meditation on philosophic texts which was widely practiced in antiquity, as illustrated above. Further, the *libellus* is from another viewpoint Horace's own, appropriately in a poem of self-address and self-exhortation, a poem which introduces a book explicitly committed to philosophy and self-improvement.[119] These 'verba et voces' (34), these 'piacula' (36), are identifiable with the 'elementis' with which he proposes to rule and soothe his mind (27); 'elementis' corresponds to στοιχειώδη in Marcus Aurelius (iv. 3. 1 again). Horace's whole approach to philosophy is recognisably in the same tradition as regards method, poles apart though the two authors may be in taste and philosophic temperament. Seneca also seems to allude to the same strand of imagery, for instance in *Ep.* 98. 4–5 (esp. § 6 'carmen'). In Epictetus iii. 24. 88–9 we find an extension of the same concept: there the father, lisping to his child, is advised to murmur 'tomorrow you will die'—again, a *meditatio mali*, and again addressed partly to the child *in himself*.[120] Here too we find the Platonic word ἐπαοιδῶν. (This passage is paraphrased by Marcus at xi. 34.[121])

More examples could be given; but this should suffice to show

[119] Cf. M. J. McGann, *Studies in Horace's First Book of Epistles* (Brussels 1969); Macleod, *Collected Essays* 280 ff.

[120] For a striking parallel see J. McManners, *Death and the Enlightenment* (Oxford 1981) 199, citing a manual of piety published in Avignon, 1777; 'As you climb between the sheets reflect, this very linen may one day form your shroud'. Cf. ibid. 229. McManners' whole discussion (pp. 197–233) of books on preparation for death has much of relevance to Marcus' *Meditations*.

[121] In general for Marcus' quotations see the Oxford Classical Text by R. Leopold, index auctorum (adding Antisth. fr. 20b Caizzi = *Med.* vii. 36). Farquharson is very unsatisfactory here, as his index conflates genuine quotations, possible allusions, resemblances, and testimonia. The most frequently quoted authors are Epictetus, Plato, Heraclitus, Euripides, and Homer. For the contrast with Marcus in the Fronto correspondence see Haines' index to the Loeb Fronto, p. 337 (s.v. 'Marcus, reading'); also the index nominum to van den Hout's edn.

the close and numerous connections between the *Meditations* and better-known examples of philosophic therapy and philosophic eloquence. The general observations on Marcus' 'rhetoric' above, however, open up further questions. I therefore conclude this chapter with some preliminary remarks on the style of the *Meditations* against the background of Stoic pronouncements on the appropriate style for philosophy.[122] These comments will be supplemented in later chapters by more detailed discussions of stylistic techniques and individual passages.

5. *Rhetorical Philosophy and Stoic Stylistics*

As with many ancient authors, including Seneca, we need to distinguish between the writer's statements and claims about style—his programmatic declarations, as it were—and what he actually achieves. Marcus makes a number of statements which fall into the programmatic category. He insists on a simple style when addressing the senate and anyone else (viii. 30: λαλεῖν καὶ ἐν συγκλήτῳ καὶ πρὸς πάνθ᾽ ὁντινοῦν κοσμίως, μὴ περιτράνως· ὑγιεῖ λόγῳ χρῆσθαι.).[123] Elsewhere he quotes an Athenian prayer for rain and comments that one ought either not to pray at all, or else to pray like this, οὕτως ἁπλῶς καὶ ἐλευθέρως ('with this kind of simplicity and freedom', v. 7).[124] True speech and just action are regarded as parallel in iii. 16, and elaborate style is explicitly rejected at iii. 5: μήτε κομψεία τὴν διάνοιάν σου καλλωπιζέτω· μήτε πολυρρήμων μήτε πολυπράγμων ἔσο ('Let no affectation ornament your thought. Be neither a busy talker nor a busybody'). Marcus lays heavy stress on the virtues of frankness and openness (e.g. i. 6, iii. 4, xi. 15) and, in the Stoic manner, associates these with simplicity of style.[125]

---

[122] Cf. Striller (n. 33), esp. 1–14, 35.

[123] Cf. Epict. *Ench.* 33. 2; cf. and contrast Quint. viii. 3. 14: 'nam et in suadendo sublimius aliquid senatus, concitatius populus, et in iudiciis publicae capitalesque causae poscunt accuratius dicendi genus': on this, see L. Laurand, *Études sur le style des discours de Cicéron* (Paris 1907) 310.

[124] On prayers of this kind see further W. Burkert, *Homo Necans* (Eng. tr. by P. Bing, Berkeley 1983) 293 n. 89; F. Heiler, *Das Gebet* (Munich 1919) 48 f., 55, 157 f. ἁπλοῦς is a favoured word of Marcus (21 instances including cognates), as also of Plato. See further *RLAC* iv. 821–40 (832 on Marcus); Van der Horst on ps.-Phocyl. 50.

[125] For other evidence relevant to Marcus' style see Farquharson i. xii. f. (esp. Philostr. *Dial.* ii, p. 258 Kayser: πρὸς γὰρ τῷ κεκριμένῳ τοῦ λόγου καὶ τὸ ἑδραῖον τοῦ ἤθους ἐντετύπωτο τοῖς γράμμασιν; and Herodian i. 2. 3: λόγων τε ἀρχαιότηρος ἦν ἐραστής . . .

Above all, the references to rhetoric in the first book illustrate Marcus' attitudes. He praises Pius for being 'no sophist, not . . . a pedant, but a ripe man, a complete man' (i. 16. 4; cf. vi. 30). He thanks the gods that he made no more progress than he did in rhetoric and poetry (i. 17. 4). His tribute to Rusticus in particular carries the stamp of the traditional conflict between literary or rhetorical studies and philosophy:

From Rusticus . . . not to be diverted into sophistic emulation (εἰς ζῆλον σοφιστικόν) . . . to avoid oratory, poetry, and urbanity (ἀστειολογίας); not to parade at home in ceremonial costume or do things of this kind; and to write letters in the simple style (ἀφελῶς), like his own from Sinuessa to my mother . . . to read books accurately, and not to be satisfied with superficial thinking about things, or agree hurriedly with those who talk around a subject (περιλαλοῦσι); to have made the acquaintance of the treatises [?] of Epictetus, of which he let me use his copy. (i. 7)

Striking here is the way in which literary and philosophic overtones are combined. ζῆλος evokes not only literary emulation (*imitatio*)[126] but also the superficial imitation of the wrong qualities, whether literary, as in Hor. *Ars* 24 ff., or moral, as in Epict. iii. 22. 9 ff.[127] It also suggests the rivalry and antagonism characteristic of distinguished littérateurs and in particular of the second-century sophists.[128] ἀφελῶς, while a common term of literary criticism in Demetrius and others, is elsewhere used in a moral sense by Marcus (xii. 27); like another of his favoured words, ἁπλοῦς, it can readily slide between a stylistic and an ethical application. His usage of τραγῳδία, τραγῳδός, in pejorative moral criticism is comparable (iii. 7, v. 28, ix. 29; see also e.g. κομψός, ὑγιής, ὑπόκρισις). It is plain therefore that Marcus subscribed to the general view in ancient literary criticism that

δηλοῖ δὲ ὅσα καὶ εἰς ἡμᾶς ἦλθέν ἢ λεχθέντα πρὸς αὐτοῦ ἢ γραφέντα). See also the excellent study by W. Williams, *JRS* 66 (1976) 67 ff., which discusses possible traces of individual style in the imperial rescripts (pp. 78–82 on Marcus). I have been unable to see G. Ghedini, *La lingua greca di M. Aurelio Antonino* (Milan, n.d.).

[126] On which see D. A. Russell, in D. West and T. Woodman (eds.), *Creative Imitation and Latin Literature* (Cambridge 1979) ch. 1; also Nisbet–Hubbard on Hor. *Odes* i. 26. 10.

[127] For the topos of 'virtutum vitiorumque vicinia' see L. Radermacher, *WS* 38 (1916) 72 f.; cf. Hor. *Ars* 24 ff., with Brink's notes; Russell on Long. 3. For literary and ethical aspects combined see Macleod, *Collected Essays* 269–70.

[128] Cf. Pl. *Prt.* 318de; Hor. *Ep.* ii. 2. 91–103. On professional quarrels among the great men of the Second Sophistic see esp. Bowersock, *Greek Sophists* ch. 7.

'talis hominibus fuit oratio qualis vita' (Sen. *Ep.* 114. 1).
Simplicity of style is bound up with moral sincerity.[129]

Specific parallels can be adduced which are particularly
concerned with philosophic writing. Quintilian writes of Brutus
(one of Marcus' heroes; see *Med.* i. 14): 'scias eum sentire quae
dicit' (x. 1. 123).[130] Seneca says something very similar in
defending the style of Fabianus, which Lucilius thought tame:
'denique illud praestabit, ut liqueat tibi illum sensisse quae
scripsit. intelleges hoc actum ut tu scires quid illi placeret, non ut
ille placeret tibi.' (*Ep.* 100. 11).[131] This is paralleled by what
Seneca says of his own style. He claims to eschew the merely
ornamental or eye-catching:

hoc unum plane tibi adprobare vellem, omnia me illa sentire quae
dicerem, nec tantum sentire sed amare ... haec sit propositi nostri
summa: quod sentimus loquamur, quod loquimur sentiamus; concordet sermo cum vita. ille promissum suum implevit qui et cum videas
illum et cum audias idem est. videbimus qualis sit, quantus sit: unus
est. (*Ep.* 75. 3–4; see the whole context.)

this alone I would like to make thoroughly clear to you, that I believed
everything I said, and not only believed it but was in love with it . . . let
this be our golden rule: let us say what we think, and think what we
say; let life and language agree. A man who is the same when you are
watching him and when you listen to him has accomplished what he
promised. We shall see the kind of man he is, how great a man he is: he
is one.

So too Aulus Gellius calls Epictetus 'verus atque sincerus
Stoicus' (i. 12. 7). In general, Stoics insisted that true rhetoric
was to say 'what is actually necessary' (Diog. Laert. vii. 59;
contrast e.g. Demetr. 103); as one theorist records: οἱ Στωϊκοὶ δὲ
τὸ εὖ λέγειν ἔλεγον τὸ ἀληθῆ λέγειν ('The Stoics maintained that

---

[129] On the letter, see n. 94 above; on the principle itself, Bramble (n. 83) esp. ch. 1–2
(but the theme runs through his whole book); also G. Lieberg, *Poeta Creator* (Amsterdam
1982); Macleod, *Collected Essays*, index s.v. Poet.

[130] Cf. Quint. xii. 10. 11 on his 'gravitation'; Tac. *Dial.* 25. 6 'simpliciter et ingenue';
note also Cic. *Att.* xv. 1a.

[131] Note also Cic. *Sest.* 61 on Cato's speech in the debate of Dec. 63; 'ea quae sensit
prae se tulit'. On Brutus' style see further Malcovati, *ORF*³ 460 ff., and the modern
studies listed by A. E. Douglas in his comm. on Cicero's *Brutus*, xiii–xxi; R. Syme, *The
Roman Revolution* (Oxford 1939) 57–8. On Fabianus and the Senecas see Leeman (n. 9)
261–71; M. Griffin, *JRS* 62 (1972) 16.

to speak well was to speak the truth'; *Rhetores Graeci* vii. 8. 20 Walz).[132]

Cicero found much to criticise in Stoic standards of eloquence, which he thought unrealistically rigorous and unworthy of their high subject-matter. 'Their pathetic little syllogisms are mere pin-pricks: they may convince the intellect, but they cannot convert the heart, and the reader goes away no better than he came. What the Stoics say may be true, it is certainly important: but the way they say it is all wrong, it is much too petty.' (*Fin.* iv. 7.) Elsewhere, with Stoic writings in mind, he associates philosophy firmly with the plain style, with its didactic aims and its limited rhetorical pretensions (*Orator* 62–4).[133]

It will be clear that Cicero is here polemically oversimplifying, and that the literary realities are more complex. The hierarchy of styles set out in the *Orator* does less than justice to the potential of a 'plain' style (though concessions are made, e.g. 76, 78, 90, 98); nor does it seem likely that any author, or any individual work, could be confined within a single such category. As Quintilian saw (xii. 10. 66 ff.), there was no reason to restrict the number of styles to three, for they were not sharply separated from one another. This was merely a convenient academic division, and subtler gradations could be made.[134] Further, Cicero's schematisation allows the 'plain' style only to instruct or prove (*Orator* 69), and makes this the special province of the plain styles and that style only.[135] Such an analysis is restricting rather than illuminating. It is clear that the plainest of styles can in the proper circumstances be supremely moving

[132] See further *Rh. Gr.* ii. 102 Walz (= *Prolegomena*, ed. Rabe, p. 103); *SVF* i. 491–2, ii. 292–3, iii. 267; Leeman (n. 9) 277. In general on the proper style for philosophic exposition, and related issues, see Douglas's comm. on Cic. *Brut.*, xxv–xxxvi; also xliii for moral-stylistic vocabulary (*sanus, simplex, sincerus*, etc.) of a kind comparable with Marcus' use of ἁπλοῦς, ἀφελής, ὑγιής, etc.

[133] See further D'Alton (n. 33) 153 ff.; Leeman (n. 9) 198 ff. The classic exposition of the qualities of the Plain Style is Cic. *Orator* 76–90, but the polemical purpose of the work must be borne in mind; see Douglas's comm. on Cic. *Brut.*, xii–xvii; Winterbottom (n. 116), esp. 258 ff.

[134] Thus Demetrius, as is well known, uses a four-style system (Demetr. 36 ff.), as do others (see D. A. Russell, *Criticism in Antiquity* (London 1981) 137); Aristides Quintilianus uses two (ii. 8–9), and Hermogenes an indefinite number of ἰδέαι. See further Russell, op. cit. ch. 9.

[135] A. E. Douglas, *Eranos* 55 (1957) 18–26 suggests this is Cicero's own contribution.

(as both Homer and Thucydides amply show),[136] and that a momentary rise to grandeur and eloquence can be the more powerful and significant against a background of greater restraint.

The style of Marcus' *Meditations* can be called plain if that term is explained and qualified: it is true, for instance, that the author does not regularly employ periodic structure, that he shows little concern for prose-rhythm or σύνθεσις, that he does not observe the Atticist canons of 'authorised' vocabulary, that upon occasion he descends to simple, consecutive sentences with a single clause in each, omitting even connectives and particles.[137] Nor does he make extensive use of word-play or *sententia* in the manner of Seneca.[138] He favours compression and aphorism rather than amplitude; his use of rhetorical figures (asyndeton, assonance, tricola, formal balance, etc.) is sparing, and such devices are usually employed, like his imagery, to add emphatic force to a moral point. But this does not mean that his style lacks its own selfconscious artistry—even if it is that of the *ars quae celat artem*.[139] The pupil of Fronto uses the rhetorical techniques to frame his thoughts in the most pungent and effective form.

Moreover, as demonstrated earlier in this chapter, while the *Meditations* have their overall unity of purpose and method, the different classes of chapter are not to be judged by the same

[136] On Homer see now J. Griffin, *Homer on Life and Death* (Oxford 1980), esp. ch. 4; N. J. Richardson, *CQ* 30 (1980) 275 ff.; on Thucydides, e.g. S. Hornblower, *Thucydides* (London 1987) 34–5, 115–16. This function of plain style is not, of course, a new discovery; it is interesting to compare instances of the recurrent criticism of the 'low' style of the Scriptures from late antiquity onwards: see Origen, *Cels.* vi. 2 with Chadwick's notes (it is particularly noteworthy that Origen praises Epictetus and criticises Plato on the ground that the former is plain and comprehensible to the common man); Norden, *Kunstprosa* 512 ff.; E. Auerbach, *Literary Language and its Public in Late Latin Antiquity and the Middle Ages* (Eng. tr. London 1965), ch. i. Augustine's *de Doctrina Christiana* (esp. book iv) is the fundamental defence of the style of the Scriptures in terms of classical (Ciceronian) rhetorical theory.

[137] On Marcus' style, syntax, and relation to Atticism, the dissertations by Schekira and Zilliacus (see Bibliography) collect much of interest; the former is by far the more valuable. See also Breithaupt 65 ff. For neglect of hiatus see Schekira 183 f.; neglect of definite article, Breithaupt 66–73; Latinisms, ibid. 93 f. (esp. i. 16. 4 οὐερκλανος; ἐν Τούσκλοις; iv. 48 Ἡρκλᾶνον). Absence of connectives: e.g. iv. 26, vii. 29 (and often).

[138] For ornamental prose at this period see Norden, *Kunstprosa* 344 ff. On Seneca's style see W. C. Summers, *Select Letters of Seneca* (London 1910) introd.; also Currie (n. 94); A. Bourgery, *Sénèque prosateur* (Paris 1922).

[139] Cf. n. 35 above.

standards. Some of the more argumentative and doctrinal passages may adhere to Stoic standards of style, and in his use of aphorism and quotation Marcus is certainly writing in a well-established educational tradition. But there are other places, especially the more reflective or poetic passages, which recall genres such as consolation or protreptic, in which the philosopher, like the preacher, must seek to move the emotions, to convince on a level deeper than reason alone can reach. And the central preoccupation of the *Meditations* is one that ultimately defies and mocks all reason: namely, the death of the individual and the extinction of the conscious moral will. It is Marcus' confrontation with this topic, and with the place of human life and death against the background of change and inconstancy in the world as a whole, which makes the work enduringly compelling and powerful; and it is through his writing and his style that he seeks to make these themes comprehensible and bearable to himself. We need, then, to read the *Meditations* in such a way as to do justice to their author's purpose, as well as to define the ways in which the book itself suggests the difficulties and complexities which are inherent in that purpose, and which make the *Meditations* a profound, rewarding, yet intensely disturbing work.

The difficulty of dating any part of the *Meditations* is another problem which has long irritated both critics and historians. It is aggravated by the obscurity of the chronology of Marcus' campaigns, which means that the mysterious headings to Books II and III, τὰ ἐν Κουάδοις πρὸς τῷ Γρανουά ά ('the part (?) written among the Quadi, on the river Gran: ι') and τὰ ἐν Καρνούντῳ ('the part written at Carnuntum') are not helpful in dating either of those books. In any case, it has often been held that these should be taken as subscriptions to Books I and II respectively. Further, except in the case of Book I, which follows a clear and logical order, we cannot be sure that the books, or even the individual chapters, stand in a sequence which has any genuine authority. The actual division into chapters is not authenticated by any ancient evidence: as Breithaupt wrote, 'in editione principe capita non distinguuntur nisi paucis locis, partim recte, partim inepte.'[140] In fact even in our modern texts there are divisions which are probably wrong.

The importance of specific dating of any part can, however, be exaggerated. The essential data are as follows. Marcus regularly refers to his old age (ii. 2 γέρων εἶ; ii. 6, v. 31, x. 15, xii. 1) and to imminent death. Since he died just before his fifty-ninth birthday, we are presumably entitled to assign these references to his last decade. Much in the references to his station, above all vi. 30. 1 ὅρα μὴ ἀποκαι-σαρωθῇς, presupposes that he himself is emperor. Pius is referred to as dead in iv. 33, and it is natural to suppose that i. 16 and vi. 30 are also tributes to his memory rather than eulogy of a living man. A later *terminus post quem* is supplied by the references to the death of L. Verus in viii. 25 and 37: this occurred in 169. The present infinitive used of Faustina in i. 17 ('that my wife *is* so obedient, so affectionate . . .') suggests that she is still alive, but other uses of the present tense in this chapter forbid any definite conclusion here. Two other passages may be specific references to contemporary events: ix. 2, where Marcus speaks of flight 'from the plague'—probably the disastrous plague brought back by Verus' armies in 168–9; secondly, x. 10 'another man feels proud at capturing Sarmatians' (quoted more fully above, p. 2). It is very tempting to link this with Marcus' own victory after which he took, in 175, the title 'Sarmaticus' (see n. 5 above), but the inference cannot be proved. Further speculation is generally unconvincing or at best unprovable. It is possible, though perhaps unnecessary, to suppose that 'the vivid language surely reflects personal experience'

[140] Breithaupt 14.

(Birley, *Marcus Aurelius* 215) in a passage such as viii. 34 ('If you have ever seen a dismembered hand or foot or severed head . . .'). But even if this is so, it does not place the passage any more precisely within the last twelve or so years of Marcus' reign, during many of which he was himself campaigning. Our ignorance of the detailed background to the *Meditations* is frustrating, but it is only in a few allusive passages, mostly in the first book, that it seems actually to inhibit our understanding of the work.

Another question which should be raised, if not answered, concerns the relation of Book I to Books II–XII. The first book is clearly a planned whole: does the same follow for the rest of the collection? Surely not, since the nature and function of the other books, as described above, is such that Marcus could have gone on writing them as long as he lived, and probably did. Even if they stand in their original order, they do not constitute a coherent treatise, nor does each book have a character of its own.[141] But Book I clearly could be planned and executed once and for all: even if Marcus had added reminiscences about other teachers, he would still have been working within a clear and limited framework.

There are many thematic connections between Book I and the rest of the work (most of these are discussed and illustrated in Chapter III of this study), but one very prominent link is unique: in vi. 30, after some of his habitual aphorisms, Marcus gives a eulogy of Antoninus Pius, similar to that in i. 16 but very much shorter. Which is the earlier? Together with this should be noted the injunction in vi. 48 to reflect upon and take comfort from the qualities of one's fellow men, and keep the images of their virtues close at hand (πρόχειρα again). Obviously this is what Book I does, although it is notable that vi. 48 refers to contemporaries, whereas Book I treats of men who were mostly dead. We might, then, see in vi. 48 the seed of Book I, and in vi. 30 a shorter sketch of Pius prior to the composition of the first book. This seems more probable than the reverse, though it is possible to imagine Marcus wanting to return to the topic of Pius' virtues, especially if he did not have the pages including that portrait with him at the time. What does not follow, however, is that Book I post-dates all of the other books, still less that it was written as some kind of 'preface or misplaced epilogue',[142] a suggestion which betrays a quite misconceived idea of the work's aim and character. Book I could easily have been compiled separately but simultaneously with the other books.

How important is it to know the chronology and order of the work?

[141] Farquharson, in his commentary, pp. 297, 487–9, 540–1, seems to exaggerate the integrity of Books II–III.
[142] R. G. M. Nisbet, *JRS* 69 (1979) 150.

Clearly, if the conclusions of the present chapter are correct, there is no question of an artistic, planned coherence to *Meditations* ii–xii or any portion thereof. Each chapter should be considered independently of its neighbours, and we are entitled to lay down categories which embrace passages throughout the collection, as I have tried to do in this chapter as a whole. We can also document predominating themes in the collection, as Brunt has studied the topics of anger and social relationships.[143] I try to pursue his insights and go further in Chapters iv–vi of this study.

The order of composition would be significant if (and only if) we could trace or suspected a change in Marcus' philosophic convictions. But conversely, since we do not know the chronology of the work in any more detail, it becomes less likely that we can establish any such change even if we think it probable. In fact no such change of view need be postulated. Marcus remains a professed Stoic[144] throughout: his language and his opinions show no development.[145] We may legitimately distinguish positive change of doctrine (of which there is no sign) from natural agnosticism and wavering. On some topics Marcus makes no claim to certainty (see esp. v. 10). The inconsistencies and doubts, the expressions of scepticism frequent in the work, seem not to arise from chronologically identifiable progress or regress; they are, rather, a continuous phenomenon in many aspects of Marcus' thought, and represent not so much inconstancy in his beliefs as his complex and humane response to the austerity and bleakness of Stoicism.[146]

---

[143] *JRS* 64 (1974) 7–14.

[144] This comment perhaps needs some qualification in view of Rist's observation (art. cit., n. 2, 23 f., 27, 43) that Marcus never refers to himself as a Stoic or explicitly avows allegiance to the school. But I would attach little significance to this: it is something he took for granted, too obvious even to mention. That is not to deny that there are elements in Marcus' thought and language which are hard to reconcile with his Stoicism.

[145] See Brunt, *JRS* 64 (1974) 2 n. 7; 14 f.; 16 n. 100; 19.

[146] Questions of dating and order of composition are discussed also by Breithaupt, esp. 27–39; H. Schenkl, *WS* 34 (1912) 82–96; C. R. Haines, *JPh* 33 (1914) 278–95; Brunt, *JRS* 64 (1974) 18–19.

II

The First Book:
Literary and Cultural Background

memoria teneo solitum ipsum narrare se prima in iuventa
studium philosophiae acrius, ultra quam concessum
Romano ac senatori, hausisse, ni prudentia matris incen-
sum ac flagrantem animum coercuisset.

(Tacitus, *Agricola* 4.3)

... that I did not make more progress in rhetoric and
poetry and my other studies, in which I might perhaps
have become engrossed, had I felt myself making good
progress in them.

(Marcus on himself, *Meditations* 1.17)

THE first and shortest book of the *Meditations* differs in character
entirely from the rest of the collection. It consists of seventeen
chapters of roughly increasing length, stating the debts which
the emperor feels that he owes to his relations, his teachers and
friends, and finally to his adoptive father, the emperor Antoninus Pius (ch. 16), and to the gods (ch. 17). Further remarkable
characteristics, such as the extreme selectiveness of these
accounts, and the peculiarity of some of the items singled out,
will become evident later; but this much will suffice to show the
strangeness of Marcus' enterprise. There is quite simply nothing
else like Book I of the *Meditations* in the whole of classical
literature. Even its links with the rest of the work have never
been very satisfactorily established.

When this has been said, however, a number of qualifications
are in order. It is certain that the first book cannot be said to
belong to any of the regular categories of ancient writing. But in
the first chapter, when considering the rest of the collection, we
concluded that although unparalleled as a whole, it had many
affinities with more familiar genres. Thus the hortatory and
castigatory tone recalls the ethical diatribe to which Lucretius,
Seneca, Epictetus, and others are all indebted; the themes of self-

discipline and spiritual fortification are shared with the main-stream tradition of philosophic *Seelenleitung*; and the bitter comments on the futility and selfishness of human activity and experience find close parallels in satire and declamation. It will not, then, be surprising if closer examination of Book I reveals the influence of better-known branches of literature. In Chapter III I hope to establish that such influence is present, and that it extends to details of phraseology and motifs as well as embracing larger areas of subject-matter.

I propose, then, briefly to survey a range of genres and forms in which Marcus might have been expected to write, but did not, or which involve themes which do actually appear in his book. This enquiry is intended to show what kind of works might have given him the idea for his own unique and individual enterprise, and how these partial models might seem inadequate in his eyes: how he diverged from them and why. Next, I offer a general statement of the exemplary nature of Roman literature, emphasising its ethical function. I then briefly summarise some familiar history of those exemplary figures, the Stoic 'martyrs', whom we know to have been among Marcus' ethical models (i. 14). Finally, I attempt to explain the historical and cultural background which can place the education of Marcus Aurelius, and to some extent his own record of it, in a more clearly defined context. In the following chapter I go on to analyse the book itself, its themes and literary character, in more detail.

1. *Biography and Panegyric*

Many of the Roman emperors wrote memoirs of their lives, campaigns, and public achievements; in this they followed both Hellenistic precedent[1] and the practice of generals and states-men under the late republic. Notable examples are C. Gracchus' record of his brother's life, which probably included an account of his own shared aims (Plut. *Ti. Gr.* 8); the autobiographies of

---

[1] See F. Jacoby, *FGrH* nos. 227–38. In general for much of what follows see Momigliano, *The Development of Greek Biography* 89–100, a clear and concise account of the genre's emergence at Rome. I am much indebted to the whole of this excellent book: for later aspects see *ASNP* ser. iii, 16 (1986) 25–44. P. Cox, *Biography in Late Antiquity* (Berkeley and Los Angeles 1983) does something to continue the story, esp. in ch. 1. For a neglected area involving Marcus' own physician, see V. Nutton, *PCPhS* NS 18 (1972) 50–62, reprinted in id., *From Democedes to Harvey* (London 1988).

P. Rutilius Rufus and M. Aemilius Scaurus;[2] Sulla's *Commentarii de Vita Sua*; and Cicero's accounts in prose and verse of his consular achievements (see esp. Cic. *Att.* ii. 1. 1-2).[3] Perhaps consciously emulating Sulla, Julius Caesar wrote self-exonerating narratives of his campaigns (see above, ch. 1. n. 13); and Augustus composed not only the *Res Gestae* but a more lavish autobiography, of which substantial fragments survive (Suet. *Aug.* 85; Malcovati's edition of Augustus' works, 4th edn. 84 ff.).[4] Tiberius' notebooks survived long enough to be consulted assiduously by Domitian (Suet. *Dom.* 20 'praeter commentarios et acta Tiberi Caesaris nihil lectitabat'), and he also wrote an autobiography with strongly self-defensive elements (Suet. *Tib.* 61). Autobiographies or similar works were also composed by Claudius (Suet. *Cl.* 41. 3 'octo volumina, magis inepte quam ineleganter'[5]), Vespasian (*commentarii* on his Jewish war, Josephus, *Vita* 342), Trajan (on his Dacian wars), and Hadrian (SHA *Hadr.* 3,16; Peter, *HRR* i.324 f.). Other figures near the throne also wrote historical accounts more or less tendentious, notably the younger Agrippina (explicitly Tacitus' source at *Ann.* iv. 53, and probably for much else[6]). Generals continued to write up their campaigns: for instance, Suetonius Paullinus on his campaign in Mauretania (Plin. *NH* v. 14) and Domitius Corbulo on the Armenian war (Plin. *NH* ii. 180, al. ; Tac. *Ann.* xv. 16).

By contrast, Marcus, while he may not reveal as much of himself in purely biographical terms as we would wish, is so far from self-glorification that the dominant note of his work is one of self-castigation. And although the work was written, at least in part, during campaigns, there is no account of these, hardly even an allusion. Momigliano[7] observes that Sulla's autobiography (probably like Augustus', and certainly like Caesar's

---

[2] See Ogilvie–Richmond on Tac. *Agr.* 1. 3.

[3] Further, *RE* Suppl. vii. 1245-53, 1267-9.

[4] F. Blumenthal, *WS* 35 (1913) 113-20, 267-88; 36 (1914) 84-103; R. Syme, *The Roman Revolution* (Oxford 1939) index s.v. 'autobiography of Augustus'; Z. Yavetz, in F. Miller and E. Segal (eds), *Caesar Augustus* (Oxford 1984) 1 ff. Also deserving mention are the memoirs of Agrippa: Philarg. Virg. *Geo.* ii. 162; H. Bardon, *La Littérature latine inconnue* ii (Paris 1956) 100.

[5] Cf. A. Momigliano, *Claudius: The Emperor and his Achievement* (Oxford 1934) 6 ff.

[6] See R. Syme, *Tacitus* (Oxford 1958) index s.v. Agrippina. P. J. Parsons, *Omnibus* 7 (Mar. 1984) 21, comments: 'they must have been a sort of *He, Claudius*'.

[7] Op. cit. (above, n. 1) 94.

Commentarii or the *Res Gestae*) 'conformed to Greek patterns in saying little about private life and much about political struggles and warfare'. In Marcus' *Meditations* the case is quite the reverse: private details and apparent trivia abound in Book I (for an explanation of this see below, pp. 96–100), and in the rest of the work his central concern is with the warfare of the spirit.

The first book of the *Meditations* is an account of Marcus' spiritual education, but couched entirely in the form of descriptions of the qualities he admired most in his teachers. It is, therefore, in a sense a piece of autobiography, but of a very oblique and reserved kind. It is also a tribute to those teachers and a list of their virtues, and to this extent reminds the reader of more formal commemorations such as eulogies, funeral speeches, or testimonials (the more so if some or most of those named were then dead: cf. ch. III, p. 123). But again the differences are very great. Family pride, strong and approved at Rome, justified self-elevation through written and oral laudation of one's ancestors,[8] and from very early times the achievements of great men were preserved in *elogia*, career-records, and epitaphs. The inscriptions thus commemorating the Scipiones are well known;[9] the tradition was continuous. Augustus erected a series of *elogia* and statues of the great men of Rome in his new forum (Suet. *Aug.* 31; Dessau, *ILS* 50–60). Such inscriptions were generally erected by relatives, being a more durable kind of funeral eulogy. They recorded above all the public career and offices of the dead man. In Book I of *Meditations* the references to Marcus' natural relatives are among the briefest; and even in the chapter on Pius there is no explicit allusion to his status or magistracies. Although there are some items singled out for praise from his behaviour as emperor, these are of a much more specific, less conventional kind. In most passages of Book I the attributes of his teachers have no clear connection with politics and public life at all—except insofar as social graces and *civilitas* are necessary to any monarch.[10]

---

[8] Ibid.; Syme (n. 4) ch. 2.

[9] See esp. D. C. Earl, *The Political Thought of Sallust* (Cambridge 1961) 26 f. His ch. 1–3 skilfully set such memorials in the wider context of Roman traditions of *virtus* and the family. See also id., *The Moral and Political Tradition of Rome* (London 1967).

[10] Cf. Champlin, *Fronto* 119; A. Wallace-Hadrill, *JRS* 72 (1982) 35, 40; id., *Suetonius: The Scholar and his Caesars* (London 1983) part ii.

Roman funeral ceremonies on the death of illustrious men were impressive enough to be given an enthusiastic description by Polybius (vi. 53–4). He is particularly concerned to emphasise the potential inspiration for the young men present, which derives from the sight of all the *imagines* of their ancestors, worn by men who resemble them closely:

For who would not be inspired by the sight of the images of men renowned for their excellence, all together and as if alive and breathing? What spectacle could be more glorious than this? Besides, he who makes the oration over the man about to be buried, when he has finished speaking of him, recounts the successes and exploits of the rest whose images are present, beginning from the most ancient (vi. 53. 10–54. 2).

Again we may discern remote analogies with Marcus' book, which follows a roughly chronological order beginning from the author's grandfather and father. But although Marcus' book also has an exemplary aim, in that the descriptions of these men are intended to inspire him to follow in their footsteps, the subjects dwelt on are far from those of the conventional funeral speech, in which the 'successes and exploits', as in Augustus' *Res Gestae*, would be above all military. For Marcus the campaigns and physical courage of others are of as little relevance to his primary, ethical concerns as are his own wars.

Precise parallels and contrasts between Marcus' references to his tutors and more public forms of eulogy reinforce this picture. In this area it is interesting to contrast Marcus' brief statement of his debt to Alexander of Cotiaeum (*Med.* i. 10) with the ἐπιτάφιος by another of Alexander's pupils, the sophist Aristides (*Or.* xxxii Keil). The formalised fullness of the Greek rhetor is fully in accord with the prescriptions of the theorists (e.g. Menander Rhetor iii. 418–22 Spengel). Marcus has no thought of recalling the γένος of his teacher, of eulogising his learning, or of listing his benefactions to his city; rather, he concentrates on a single, well-remembered point, precisely described: how Alexander corrected Marcus, not severely but with a touch of scholastic irony. Alexander is said to have capped his pupils' mistakes or excesses by replying himself with the correct phrase: a veiled but effective form of reprimand (ἐμμελοῦς παρυπομνή-σεως), which besides being an appropriate response to the student of a *grammaticus*, also has an element of sharp-wittedness and point (as ἐπιδεξίως implies[11]). Both these elements are implicit in the adjective ἐμμελής. But the stylistic precept is, as often, attached to a moral lesson which is given first place in the chapter: τὸ ἀνεπίπληκτον καὶ τὸ μὴ ὀνειδιστικῶς ἐπιλαμβάνεσθαι ('not to be captious, nor to find fault in carping fashion'); and the passage also touches on larger issues in the insistence that the dialogue between pupil and teacher should concern 'the thing itself, not just its verbal expression' (περὶ αὐτοῦ τοῦ πράγματος, οὐχὶ περὶ τοῦ ῥήματος).[12]

Thus exactness of diction is essential; but Alexander's tuition went beyond that and contributed something to the lasting preoccupations of his pupil: the concern for precision and for a clear grasp of distinctions (διάληψις); the determination to see 'the thing itself'; the consciousness of a need to correct others, but without undue severity or resentment. These topics pass into the other, introspective books of the *Meditations*. There is in general a clear connection between Book I and the rest of the work: Marcus in Books II–XII performs for himself many of the tasks of instruction and criticism which his tutors had performed for him in the past. Indeed, the *Meditations* themselves, even including Book I, may be seen as exemplifying some of the lessons of which Marcus remembers in this book: stylistic simplicity combined with a search for the exact word and phrase (as here); concern for fundamental issues and for moral improvement; choice of important subjects (i. 7. 1–2); modesty, frankness, and tolerance (i. 9. 1; i. 16. 5). Gratitude to and respect for teachers is specified as a moral lesson in i. 13, and this is of course the motivating force behind the whole book; it is also a topic of ethical discussion, as in Sen. *Ep.* 44. 9, 73. 4; *Ben.* vi. 15–17; or, in poetry, the fifth satire of Persius.[13]

Also interesting for its generic affinities is the longest chapter of Book I, that which records Marcus' debt to Antoninus Pius

[11] For ἐπιδεξίως cf. Arist. *NE* 1128ᵃ17; Plut. *Virt. Mor.* 441b (Chrysippean terminology). In literary criticism, cf. Dover on Ar. *Nu.* 148 for δεξίως; Kindstrand on Bion fr. 3 for ἀστείως and similar terms.

[12] For the related principle 'concordet sermo cum vita' (Sen. *Ep.* 75. 4), see Griffin, *Seneca* 8 n. 3; A. D. Leeman, *Orationis Ratio* (Amsterdam 1963) 271 ff.; W. C. Summers, *Select Letters of Seneca* (London 1910) lxx f. (note esp. *Ep.* 100. 2); D. A. Russell, in C. D. N. Costa (ed.), *Seneca* (London 1974) 73–4, 84–5. See also ch. 1. 5, above.

[13] For the earlier history of this theme see F. Préchac's introd. to the Budé edn. of Sen. *Ben.* (Paris 1961) xxvii f.; also Breithaupt 43; van der Horst on ps.-Phocyl. 80.

(i. 16), especially as the proper form and subject-matter of a βασιλικὸς λόγος, or of a panegyric, had been laid down in detail by rhetorical teachers.[14] Praises of the ideal king were commonplace in both Greek and imperial Latin literature: the ultimate roots are, as usual, Homeric (*Od.* xix. 109 ff.; Hes. *Op.* 225 ff.). Such praises are exemplified in works as widely different as Pindar's *Odes*, Isocrates' *Evagoras*, Theocritus' seventeenth idyll, Pliny's *Panegyric of Trajan*, and the speech εἰς βασιλέα attributed to Aristides (*Or.* xxxv Keil), which some have held to be addressed to Antoninus Pius or even to Marcus Aurelius himself.[15]

Equally abundant was theoretical or pseudo-philosophic literature on the subject of kingship. These works discussed the king's duties and responsibilities, usually contrasting him with the sinister figure of the tyrant. Descriptions of the typical tyrant also have a very long history, apparent first in Hesiod's protests against unjust kings (*Op.* 202 ff., 248 ff.) and schematised by the sophists and authors influenced by them (Hdt. iii. 80; Eur. *Suppl.* 429 ff.; Pl. *Grg.* 509–10). This tradition, fully developed by major thinkers like Plato and Aristotle, was still in full flow under the Roman empire. Famous imperial examples are Seneca's *de Clementia*[16] and the first four essays of Dio Chrysostom, which include strongly Stoic ideas. The subject is frequently touched upon in other genres, for instance in hortatory and epideictic rhetoric (as in Cicero's *Caesarianae*; also Philo, *Leg. ad Gaium*, e.g. 49–50), in poetry (Horace's political odes, esp. iii. 4, iv. 5), or in historical works such as Velleius' account of Tiberius, which has recently been set firmly (almost too firmly) in the panegyrical tradition by A. J. Woodman.[17] Nearly all these authors are concerned to relate their discussion to a particular monarch. That such issues were considered important by Marcus is proved by *Med.* i. 14, in which he wishes

[14] T. C. Burgess, *Epideictic Literature* (Studies in Class. Philol. 3, Chicago 1902) 113 ff.; O. Murray, *Peri Basileias* (diss. Oxford 1970); *RLAC* viii. 555 ff.; Wallace-Hadrill, *Suetonius* ch. 7. See e.g. Menander Rhetor, iii. 368 ff. Spengel, with Russell and Wilson's comm. (Oxford 1981).

[15] For recent discussions see C. P. Jones, *JRS* 62 (1972) 134–52; S. A. Stertz, *CQ* 29 (1979) 172–97; R. Klein, *Hist.* 30 (1981) 337–50; C. P. Jones, *CQ* 31 (1981) 224–6.

[16] On which see Griffin, *Seneca* ch. 4; cf. her ch. 3 and 6.

[17] In his comm. on the 'Tiberian Narrative' (Cambridge 1977) and in *CQ* 25 (1975) 272 ff. Cf. and contrast P. A. Brunt in *Miscellanea in onore di E. Manni* i (Rome 1979) 331; R. Syme, *Roman Papers* iii (Oxford 1984) 1090 ff.

for a πολιτείας ἰσονόμου, κατ' ἰσότητα καὶ ἰσηγορίαν διοικουμένης, καὶ βασιλείας τιμώσης πάντων μάλιστα τὴν ἐλευθερίαν τῶν ἀρχομένων ('a constitutional state founded on the principles of equality and freedom of speech, and a monarchy the chief ideal of which is the liberty of its subjects'). This passage echoes the terminology of such discussions, especially by Stoics.[18] Treatises on the proper form of government were as common as those on kingship itself, and works on constitutional theory were written, for instance, by Zeno and Chrysippus (Diog. Laert. vii. 33 f.; *SVF* iii. 743–56). Marcus must have been familiar with this kind of work. In assessing the true virtues of his predecessor he himself took a rather different line, but parallels with the attributes of the ideal monarch can still be discerned.

2. *Exempla and Ideals*

From exemplary kings we turn to exemplary characterisation in general. The patterns of eulogy (ἐγκώμιον) and its opposite, invective (ψόγος), early expounded in rhetorical treatises,[19] were extended to biography and indeed to most ancient character-portrayal. Thus the earliest extant biographies, Xenophon's *Agesilaus* and Isocrates' *Evagoras*, are straight forward laudations with an exemplary purpose; and even a superior artist such as Plutarch was essentially working within a fairly straightforward and restricted scheme. Marcus Aurelius, of course, was in no sense writing a biography even of Pius, the man whom he describes at greatest length; but his picture of his predecessor may be illuminated by comparison with the techniques of characterisation and the stated or evident aims of other ancient writers, for instance Plutarch and Tacitus, both near-contemporaries, both concerned with the study of men's moral character, and above all that of men in high places— kings, emperors, and statesmen. For such writers the idiosyncrasies of behaviour in their principals and incidental anecdotes or experiences are of interest not merely as gossip and colourful details, but because they throw light upon the moral character of the agent (see esp. Plut. *Alex.* 1, quoted below, ch. III p. 110).

[18] See C. Wirszubski, *Libertas as a Political Idea at Rome* (Cambridge 1950) 145 f., 148 f., 155–8. See also n. 14 above.

[19] See esp. the introduction to D. A. Russell and N. G. Wilson's edn. of Menander Rhetor (Oxford 1981).

Part of the explanation for the sometimes over-simplified characterisation in ancient oratory, historiography, and poetry lies in the ancient, and especially Roman, passion for exemplary figures. Except in the hands of a great artist, the personalities of the past were in general portrayed in terms of very clearly defined virtues and vices. This was encouraged by the philosophic (especially Peripatetic) discussion of individual moral and social qualities, as in Aristotle's *Nicomachean Ethics* iii–iv, or Theophrastus' *Characters*. As for later times, it has been observed that the characterisation of heroes in Plutarch's *Lives* is such as almost to make them into moral essays on Peripatetic themes.[20] A Roman who encountered the names of Camillus, Cincinnatus, Fabricius, and the like, whether in oratory, history, or poetry, was expected to respond enthusiastically and predictably, with approval, admiration, and a desire to imitate these great and good men (cf. Plut. *Per.* 2. 4–5). Cicero and Quintilian recommended the deployment of such *exempla* by the orator (Cic. *Brut.* 322; *Cael.* 39; Quint. xii. 2. 29 f., xii. 4). Livy and Tacitus were conscious of the moral value, whether hortatory or deterrent, of their portraits (see esp. Tac. *Ann.* iii. 65), though perhaps they did not always realise just how stereotyped their characters might become.[21]

Similar strategies were followed by the philosophers, whose long-standing feud with the practitioners of rhetoric did not prevent them from profiting from their techniques. Indeed, the Roman idealisation of the past and deep concern with the traditions of both family and state made the study of one's ancestors automatically a source of moral imperatives.[22] The heroic past is a touchstone by which to judge, and usually to condemn, the degenerate present.[23] Another principle that spans the different genres is the primitivist assumption that the

[20] A. Dihle, *Studien zur griechischen Biographie* (Göttingen 1956) 57–76; Russell, *Plutarch* ch. 6–8.
[21] For these tendencies in Roman historiography see Woodman (n. 17) 30–45; T. P. Wiseman, *Clio's Cosmetics* (Leicester 1979) ch. 1–4, a very valuable treatment; C. W. Fornara, *The Nature of History in Ancient Greece and Rome* (Berkeley and Los Angeles 1983) 106–20. See also G. Williams, *Tradition and Originality in Roman Poetry* (Oxford 1968) 619–33. On stereotyping see B. Walker, *The* Annals *of Tacitus* (Manchester 1952) ch. 10–12; Wallace-Hadrill, *Suetonius* ch. 7.
[22] See Wiseman (n. 21), who promises a further study.
[23] See Bramble, *Persius and the Programmatic Satire* (Cambridge 1974) 29 ff.; Nisbet–Hubbard on Hor. *Odes* ii. 15.

simple life of peasant-farmers is more conducive to virtue than sophistication, city-dwelling, and cosmopolitan luxury.[24] Philosophers, like historians, approved the life of poverty, and many, especially the Cynics, imposed it upon themselves as an aid to virtue.[25] Like Seneca (*Ep.* 108), Marcus Aurelius was inspired to a marked asceticism in youth by the preaching of a teacher who in his case had clear Cynic sympathies (*Med.* i. 6; cf. i. 3); and he continued to admire moderation and sobriety throughout his life (cf. i. 16. 4, 8–10; note also SHA *Pius* 2. 1; Jul. *Caes.* 317c).

To the eye of the satirist most moralists are sure to be hypocrites;[26] such criticism was directed particularly at the ostentatious simplicity of the Cynics.[27] But in the case of a true philosopher like Socrates or Zeno, abnegation of worldly possessions and indifference to the standards of the masses reflected his strength of character and single-mindedness. For these qualities such men were remembered and commemorated by their pupils (in Marcus note the χρεῖαι at xi. 25, 28). In particular the Platonic dialogues preserve the memory, the personality, and the example of Socrates for future generations, and that recollection is not merely an expression of gratitude, but is didactic. By extension, Socrates remained an *exemplum* for later philosophic writers who had never known him, including Epictetus.[28]

Other eminent thinkers were also venerated, whether the founders of schools (Epicurus, Pythagoras, and others) or the tutors of individual writers: thus Persius, as already mentioned, records the inspiring teaching of the Stoic Cornutus in a poem dedicated to him (*Satire* 5); Seneca writes of his teachers

---

[24] *Loci classici* are Virg. *Geo.* ii. 493–540; Hor. *Odes* iii. 6; Sen. *Ep.* 90; Apul. *Apol.* 18–20. Further, A. O. Lovejoy and G. Boas, *Primitivism and Related Ideas in Antiquity* (Baltimore 1935); Mayor on Juv. 11. 77 ff., 14. 160 ff.; E. Courtney's comm. on Juvenal, pp. 24 ff.

[25] See R. Vischer, *Das einfache Leben* (Göttingen 1965).

[26] See Epict. iii. 22 with M. Billerbeck's comm. (Leiden 1978). A recurrent theme of satire and also of polemic among philosophers: see esp. Juvenal 2 with Courtney's comm. The theme is ubiquitous in Lucian, e.g. *Menippus* 4 ff.; *Icaromen*, 16, 2, 29–30; see J. Hall, *Lucian's Satire* (New York 1981) 182 ff. For false Stoics see further Gell. i. 2, ix. 2; Favorinus *ap.* Gell. xvii. 19; Epict. iv. 8. 15 (cf. iii. 22. 9, 60, 80); Apul. *Fl.* 7.

[27] See Bramble (n. 23) 154 f.; Nisbet–Hubbard on Hor. *Odes* ii. 2. 18–19.

[28] See works cited by Billerbeck (n. 26) 7 n. 32, adding K. Düring, *Exemplum Socratis* (*Hermes* Einzelschr. 42, 1979); J. L. Moles, *JHS* 98 (1978) 98.

Fabianus, Sextius, Sotion, and Attalus (*Ep.* 108 et al.);[29] Epictetus and a more enigmatic figure named Lucius quote and refer to their teacher Musonius;[30] Arrian records the lectures and in his preface describes the eloquence of Epictetus;[31] and Pliny in his letters describes several of his teachers, including the Stoic Euphrates, a philosopher-rhetor, pupil of Musonius and of Dio Chrysostom (*Ep.* i. 10; also ii. 3 on Isaeus; iii. 11 on Artemidorus).[32] Lucian describes his 'conversion'[33] by the wonderful eloquence of Nigrinus and elsewhere records, more fragmentarily, the wit and wisdom of the Cynic Demonax.

In other genres or fields of study the same awareness of one's models and teachers may be observed, for ancient writers delighted in expounding their literary pedigree and intellectual development. Cicero tells us a good deal about his education in the *Brutus* (304–24). Ovid in his autobiographical poem *Tristia* iv. 10 and in *ex Ponto* iv. 16, Propertius in ii. 34b, and more elliptically Virgil in some of the *Eclogues*, all have something to say about the poets whom they knew personally and by whom they were most influenced. Horace's account of his father in *Sat.* i. 6, and still more in i. 4. 105–39, shows clearly not only that he regards him as a valuable example, but that this example has shown him the way to write satire and lead an aware and self-disciplined moral life. The relevance of all this to the first book of the *Meditations* must be obvious.

Moreover, we may single out a common philosophic idea: that the example of a revered moral preceptor should be kept continually in one's mind. Seneca in *Ep.* 11. 8 ff. endorses the

[29] See Griffin, *Seneca* 36 ff.

[30] See Lutz, *YCS* 10 (1947) 3 ff.; van Geytenbeek, *Musonius Rufus and Greek Diatribe* (Assen 1963) ch. 1. Good surveys of Musonius by K. von Fritz, *RE* xvi. 1. 893–7; Mayor on Plin. *Ep.* iii. 11. 5.

[31] Quoted in ch. 1 above, p. 36. On Arrian's work see further ch. VI below, esp. nn. 1–3; P. A. Brunt, *Athen.* NS 55 (1977) 19–48; T. Wirth, *MH* 24 (1967) 149–89, 197–216.

[32] For further examples of Pliny's character sketches, and of his 'obituaries', see Sherwin-White's comm. (Oxford 1966) 45.

[33] For this conception in ancient philosophy see above all Nock, *Conversion* (Oxford 1933) ch. 11; id., *RLAC* ii. 105–18; and 'Conversion and Adolescence' in id., *Essays on Religion and the Ancient World*, ed. Z. Stewart (Oxford 1972) i. 469–80 (p. 472 briefly discusses the case of Marcus, with important parallels from Epictetus; see also ch. III 3 below). Further, O. Gigon, *MH* 3 (1946) 1–21; Macleod, *Collected Essays* 285. On the *Nigrinus* itself see Hall, *Lucian's Satire* 157–64; it has probably been taken too seriously in the past (see Hall 6 ff., 35 ff., against extravagant claims for Lucian as a philosopher; also C. P. Jones, *Culture and Society in Lucian* (Cambridge, Mass., 1986) 13 f., 25).

view of Epicurus (fr. 210 Us.) that a good man should be
selected and kept ever before our eyes, so that even when alone
we shall be ashamed to do wrong.[34] Such a man will be a
'custodem nobis et paedagogum'.[35] He need not be one of our
friends and contemporaries, for Seneca suggests Cato or Laelius
(cf. *Ep.* 25. 4–7 for very similar ideas; Scipio Aemilianus is there
added).[36] Marcus seems to recall the same principle as Seneca
at *Med.* xi. 26, where he says: 'The writings of the school of
Epicurus lay down the injunction to remind oneself constantly
(συνεχῶς ὑπομιμνῄσκεσθαι) of one of those who practised virtue
in days past.' It is in this spirit that Marcus recalls the memory of
his friends' virtues (vi. 48), and bids himself do all things as a
disciple (μαθητής) of Antoninus (vi. 30). Ancient authors
generally recognised the virtue of this method in education: it is
recommended, for instance, in the (Stoic-influenced) treatise *de
Liberis Educandis* attributed to Plutarch (10e).[37] Marcus in Book
I combines a traditional Roman regard for his elders with
philosophically-inspired contemplation of ethical models.
Though these models are mainly of personal acquaintance, he
does make allusion to figures of an earlier generation, enemies of
tyrants and heroes of the 'Stoic opposition', in i. 14: 'From
Severus, . . . to have got by his help to know Thrasea, Helvidius,
Cato, Dio, and Brutus.' The verb here, γνῶναι, is the same as
that used in i. 17. 5, where Marcus thanks the gods that it was
granted to him 'to have got to know Apollonius, Rusticus,
Maximus'. The parallel is more than verbal: in both passages
the same conceptions of inspiration and learning are present.

3. *The Stoics and the Empire*

The reference to Cato and the others is of more than ethical
significance: it presents Marcus as the paradoxical culmination

[34] On this motif ('behind closed doors') see ch. v n. 67 below.

[35] Cf. *Ep.* 52. 7 'adiuvare nos possunt non tantum qui sunt sed qui fuerunt'. For
further parallels in Seneca see G. Scarpat, *Lettere a Lucilio libro primo (epp. 1–12)* (Brescia
1975) 251–7. For the related principle that 'longum iter est per praecepta, breve et
efficax per exempla' (Sen. *Ep.* 6. 5) see ibid. 114 f., 251 f.; Kindstrand, Bion, 37 f. A
contrast: *exempla* from the Old Testament offered to Christians, e.g. 1 Cor. 10: 6 (our
τύποι). On early 'imitation of Christ', 1 Cor. 11: 1; see A. D. Nock, *Saint Paul* (London
1938) 244.

[36] Cf. further Muson. fr. 11 Hense; Plut. *Prof. Virt.* 85a.

[37] Further, N. J. S. Abbot's comm. on ps.-Plut. *Lib. Educ.*, 318 (on 14a6 f.).

of a continuous tradition which began with the charismatic figure of Cato. Not only was the younger Cato a committed Stoic, but his moral ascendancy and refusal to compromise, while condemned in his own lifetime as political *naïveté* (esp. Cic. *Att.* ii. 1. 8), earned him lasting renown under the empire, when his resolute stand against the faction of Julius Caesar, and his suicide at Utica, were considered glorious and heroic.[38] Cato committed suicide after rereading Plato's *Phaedo* (Plut. *Cat. Min.* 67–8; perhaps twice, cf. 70!); Cicero paired his end with that of Socrates (*Tusc.* i. 71–5); and it seems clear that Cato himself took Socrates' end as a model for his own.[39] Biographies of Cato, largely hagiographic, began to appear soon after his death: noteworthy are those by Cicero himself (*Or.* 35; *Att.* xii. 4, xiii. 28), by Brutus (*Att.* xii. 21), by M. Fadius Gallus (*Fam.* vii. 24–5), and by Munatius Rufus, Cato's close friend (Val. Max. iv. 3. 2; Plut. *Cat. Min.* 25. 1; Peter, *HR* ii, pp. lix, cxxx f.). The idealisation of the first 'Stoic martyr' was surely reinforced by the antagonistic attitude of the victors, first Caesar in his notorious *Anticato*, and later, more temperately, Augustus in his *Rescripta Bruto de Catone*.[40]

Although Cato may have undergone rehabilitation under the early principate—enough to receive Augustus' qualified praise, and the poetic eulogies of Virgil and Horace—his name was still one to conjure with, and could be both potent and dangerous. The same applied, in lesser degree, to the tyrannicides Brutus and Cassius, symbols of liberty. It was tactful to omit the *imagines* of these two from the funeral procession of Junia, although they were among her most distinguished relatives (Tac. *Ann.* iii. 76, pointedly set at the close of a book). The historian Cremutius

[38] See R. MacMullen, *Enemies of the Roman Order* (Cambridge, Mass., 1966) 295 ff.; Griffin, *Seneca* 182–94; P. Pecchiura, *La figura di Catone Uticense nella letteratura latina* (Turin 1965); R. Syme, (n. 4) index s.v. 'Porcius Cato Uticensis, laudations of'; T. Geiger's comm. on Plutarch, *Cato Minor* (diss. Oxford 1971) 1–97.

[39] See J. M. Rist, *Stoic Philosophy* (Cambridge 1969) ch. 13, esp. 244 ff.; Griffin, *Seneca* ch. 11. R. Hirzel, 'Der Selbstmord', *ARW* 11 (1908) 75–104, 243–84, 417–76 (reprinted as a book, Darmstadt 1966) remains a masterly survey. More recently, see Y. Grisé, *Le Suicide dans la Rome antique* (Montreal and Paris 1982), with M. T. Griffin's review in *Gnomon* 57 (1985) 437–40. For a modern study, see A. Alvarez, *The Savage God* (1971).

[40] The evidence for Caesar's *Anticato* has now been collected by H. J. Tschiedel, *Caesar's Anticato* (Impulse der Forschung 37, Darmstadt 1981). For Augustus' work see E. Malcovati's edn. of the emperor's writings, (4th edn. Turin 1962) xxxix f., 80. See further MacMullen (n. 38) 295 n. 4 and works there cited. Note also Macr. ii. 4. 18, with Syme (n. 4) 506 f.; id., *Roman Papers* i (Oxford 1978) 205–17.

Cordus was condemned at least partly on the grounds that he had praised Brutus and Cassius in his writings (Tac. *Ann.* iv. 35–6; Sen. *Marc.* 1. 3–4; Dio 57. 24. 2–4).[41] Similarly, under Nero suspicion attached to Thrasea Paetus because of his laudatory biography of Cato (Tac. *Ann.* xvi. 21 f.; with Plut. *Cat. Min.* 37), and under Domitian two other Stoic men of principle followed his example and met with comparable ends in the purge of AD 93. They were Q. Arulenus Iunius Rusticus, a younger friend and ally, as well as biographer, of Thrasea, and Herennius Senecio, who wrote a life of the elder C. Helvidius Priscus, son-in-law and intimate friend of Thrasea.[42] Biography had become a weapon of resistance; the pamphlet-warfare of the late republic lived again.

By contrast, the *delator* Aquilius Regulus composed an attack upon the younger Helvidius Priscus, executed under Domitian (see Plin. *Ep.* i. 5. 3): the work was presumably in the manner of Caesar's *Anticato*. This provoked in turn Pliny's own 'libros de

[41] The scepticism of R. S. Rogers, *TAPA* 96 (1965) 351–9 seems extreme, and in any case he only aims to refute the view that the history was the formal cause of Cremutius' prosecution. Wider and more stimulating is F. H. Cramer, 'Book-Burning and Censorship in Ancient Rome', *JHI* 6 (1945) 157–96. Brief résumé: Mayor on Juv. 1. 152 and on Plin. *Ep.* iii. 5. 5.

[42] The relationships of this closely knit group are more easily set out diagrammatically: for stemmata see e.g. MacMullen (n. 38) 42–3. Concise summaries of the careers of Iunius Rusticus (*PIR*² I 730), Thrasea Paetus (*PIR*² C 1187), Herennius Senecio (*PIR*² H 128), and Helvidius Priscus (*PIR*² H 59) in Ogilvie–Richmond's notes on Tac. *Agr.* 2. 1. Fuller discussions are abundant: G. Boissier, *L'Opposition sous les Césars* (5th edn., Paris 1905) is a classic account; since then note esp. J. M. C. Toynbee, *G&R* 13 (1944) 43 ff.; Wirszubski, *Libertas* ch. 5, esp. 136–71; Syme, *Tacitus* ch. 41; MacMullen, op. cit. ch. 1–2. P. A. Brunt, *PBSR* 43 (1975) 7–39 reassesses the subject with particular reference to the Stoic principle of the individual's role (τάξις), and is also valuable for his emphasis on the importance of philosophic belief to men like Thrasea (e.g. 23 n. 91), against Syme, Wirszubski, and others. M. T. Griffin, *Nero: The End of a Dynasty* (London 1984) 171–7 is another recent account.

For Thrasea's life of Cato see Plut. *Cat. Min.* 37; Martial i. 8. 1–2. For Herennius' life of Helvidius see Plin. *Ep.* i. 5. 2, iii. 11, vii. 19. 5; Tac. *Agr.* 2. For Rusticus' life of Thrasea see Tac. ibid. Suetonius (*Dom.* 10) attributes to Rusticus 'Paeti Thraseae et Helvidii Prisci laudes', probably conflating him with Herennius (cf. Wallace-Hadrill, *Suetonius* 58).

Primary sources for the Domitianic fortunes of this family are Tac. *Agr.* 45 and several letters of Pliny cited in the text (esp. iii. 11, vii. 19, vii. 30, ix. 30). Sherwin-White's commentary on all of these (esp. on iii. 11) is most helpful, though I do not accept his view that the philosophical views of these men became important for their politics only under the Flavians (expressed on i. 5. 2 and iii. 11 (p. 241)). *Contra*, see Brunt, *PBSR* 43 (1975); Griffin, *Seneca* 363 n. 2; and my text, pp. 68–70. (Sherwin-White's view seems in any case undermined by his admission of the potent influence of Musonius on Rubellius Plautus and Barea Soranus: p. 244, citing Tac. *Ann.* xiv. 59, xv. 71.)

Helvidii ultione' (*Ep.* ix. 13. 1), published in the period after Domitian's death, when this family and its provocative activities had been vindicated and Pliny's friendship with them became respectable. He describes the exploits of some of its members in several letters (iii. 16 on the elder Arria, wife of the Claudian conspirator Caecina Paetus; vii. 19 on the younger Arria, wife of Thrasea, and on Fannia, wife of Helvidius Priscus; vii. 30 and ix. 13 on Pliny's own speeches vindicating Helvidius). Pliny gladly undertook to find a tutor for the orphaned children of Rusticus (ii. 18) and a husband for his daughter (i. 14). He quotes Thrasea's sayings twice with admiration (vi. 29; viii. 22 (misunderstood?)). Most significantly of all, he tries to associate himself with the sufferings and dangers of those executed or exiled by Domitian in 93:

cum septem amicis meis aut occisis aut relegatis, occisis Senecione Rustico Helvidio, relegatis Maurico Grantilla Arria Fannia, tot circa me iactis fulminibus quasi ambustus mihi quoque impendere idem exitium certis quibusdam notis augurarer. non ideo tamen eximiam gloriam meruisse me, ut ille praedicat, credo, sed tantum effugisse flagitium. (iii. 11. 3)[43]

When, with seven of my friends either executed or exiled—Senecio, Rusticus, Helvidius executed, Mauricus, Grantilla, Arria, and Fannia exiled—scorched, so to speak, by all these thunderbolts which were hurled down around me, I foresaw by unmistakable signs that the same doom was hanging over me. But I don't think that I deserved the splendid reputation he gives me; I only consider myself to have avoided disgrace.

In this we discern the changed mood and attitudes of the reigns of Nerva and Trajan (cf. Tac. *Agr.* 1–3; *Hist.* i. 1).

There was, then, a distinctive and polemical tradition of biographical writing, which from its probable similarity to later Christian martyr-acts is usually referred to by modern scholars as 'Stoic martyr-literature'.[44] Biography in general was increas-

[43] Cf. Plin. *Pan.* 90. 5. See Syme, *Tacitus* 76 f., and Sherwin-White ad loc. (also on iv. 24. 4, vii. 27. 14) for doubts about Pliny's actual peril and the degree of his intimacy with those endangered.

[44] MacMullen, *Enemies of the Roman Order* 70–93 stimulatingly outlines the connections: his pp. 310 n. 25, 313 nn. 37 ff. are particularly full. Further, Ogilvie–Richmond, *Tacitus*: Agricola 11 ff.; H. Musurillo, *Acts of the Pagan Martyrs* (Oxford 1954), esp. 236 ff. on the literary fashion for recounting the deaths of famous men. This tradition is particularly important for Tacitus in the Neronian books of the *Annals*, which draw on

ingly in fashion under the empire.[45] Persius wrote verses on
Arria, who was a relation, but they were suppressed on
Cornutus' advice (*Vita Pers.* 30; 46 f. Clausen). A friend of Pliny,
Titinius Capito, contributed a work entitled *Exitus Illustrium
Virorum* (cf. Plin. *Ep.* viii. 12 'funebribus laudationibus seris
quidem sed veris'). Similarly C. Fannius wrote an account 'inter
sermonem historiamque' of those whom Nero had killed or
banished (*Ep.* v. 5). The themes and the author's name surely
imply a family connection with Fannia, daughter of Thrasea
Paetus.[46] (It was common for a writer to have some blood or
marital relationship with the deceased: as Pliny says, memorial
pamphlets were composed 'pio munere' (*Ep.* viii. 12. 5; cf. i. 17.
1 'est adhuc curae hominibus fides et officium'); Tacitus too
makes *pietas* the motive for his life of Agricola, his father-in-law
(*Agr.* 3. 3).)

These works dominated the tradition about such men: they
have left traces in Suetonius (e.g. *Nero* 47 ff.), and influenced
Tacitus' vivid death-scenes in the *Annals*, especially those of
Thrasea and other victims. (Clearly the biographers tended to
focus in most detail on the heroic death, as is explicit in Capito's
title.) Moreover, the *Agricola* itself owes much to this tradition,
against which it is also a reaction. The book commemorated

works such as the Life of Thrasea by Rusticus (cf. K. Marx, *Philol.* NF 46 (1937) 83 ff.;
Syme, *Tacitus* 297–8; O. Murray, *Hist.* 14 (1965) 41 ff.). Later, Socrates could also be
regarded as a precedent for Christian martyrdom: see e.g. Justin, *Ap.* ii. 10, Clem. Al.
Strom. iv. 80. Further, M. Montuori, *Socrates* (Eng. tr., Amsterdam 1981) 6–8.

[45] For examples not connected with Stoics see Plin. *Ep.* iv. 7 (Aquilius Regulus'
memoir (or *laudatio*?) of his son), vii. 31. 5 (Claudius Pollio's Life of Annius Bassus); ix. 9
is only doubtfully a parallel, *pace* Sherwin-White. Pliny himself commemorates the death
of his uncle in two of his most famous letters (vi. 16, 20); see also iii. 5, in which he
describes the old man's way of life in detail. Virginius Rufus, Pliny's former guardian, is
given a similarly affectionate and detailed obituary; for more examples see Sherwin-
White's comm. (Oxford 1966) 45. Suicide, political or private, particularly attracted the
attention of biographers who focused on the final moments: see Griffin, *Seneca* 387; P. A.
Brunt, 'Marcus Aurelius and the Christians', in C. Deroux (ed.), *Studies in Latin Literature
and Roman History* i (Brussels 1979) 484–90. Death in the face of extreme illness was
sometimes the subject of such works: see esp. Nepos, *Vita Attici*; Plin. *Ep.* i. 12, i. 22, iii. 7
(cf. Sen. *Ep.* 30; 48. 32 ff.). Marcus' attitude to suicide is necessarily different from that of
the paradigmatic Stoic escape, in the manner of Cato or Thrasea, from the tyrant
(MacMullen, *Enemies of the Roman Order* 310 n. 25). But he contemplates escaping senile
decay by such means in iii. 1: cf. Lucr. iii. 1039 ff.; Sen. *Ep.* 58. 36, 70. 12; perhaps Plut.
Tranq. 476a; Dio 69. 8. 3 (Euphrates); A. Bonhöffer, *Die Ethik des Stoikers Epictet*
(Stuttgart 1894) 29 ff.; Brunt, loc. cit. See also Epict. i. 2. 25, iii. 10, esp. 12 ff. For an
irrational suicide, ibid. ii. 15. 4–18. A Christian contrast: Phil. 1: 19 ff.

[46] See Sherwin-White ad loc.; Syme, *Tacitus* 92. See *PIR*² F 1818 for Fannia.

Tacitus' father-in-law as a noble and conscientious member of the senatorial class, who was prepared to co-operate with the regime instead of rejecting it, and yet still retained his integrity.[47] On this interpretation the reference to the works of Herennius Senecio and Arulenus Rusticus in the preface (2. 1) may be seen as a subtle challenge to comparison with Tacitus' work and Tacitus' own ideal.[48] He still took advantage, however, of the contrast regularly drawn in this literature between the selfless and honourable aristocrat and the merciless tyrant,[49] and in various ways his work testifies to hs uneasiness with the solution which, as he maintained, Agricola had found and his own generation had accepted (*Agr.* 44–5).

What significance had this pervasive and fruitful tradition for Marcus Aurelius? Two connections are particularly prominent; one is the list of *exempla* quoted from i. 14. As Thrasea idolised and followed Cato (emulating the manner of his death[50]), as his juniors imitated Thrasea himself, so too Marcus looked back with reference at 'Thrasea, Helvidius, Cato, Dio,[51] Brutus'.

[47] See esp. *Agr.* 42. 3–4, with Syme, *Tacitus* 91 ff., 585 ff. For a valuable analysis of Tacitus' ambivalent attitude to the opposition, and of his view of the collective guilt of the senatorial class under the Domitianic terror, see Walker (n. 21) 196 ff.; also MacMullen, *Enemies of the Roman Order*, 45, 80.

[48] For Tacitus' praise of moderates see *Ann.* iv. 20 (cf. iii. 35, 50, vi. 27) on M. Lepidus; vi. 10 on L. Piso; vi. 39. 3 on Poppaeus Sabinus; xiv. 7 on Memmius Lepidus. See also Walker (n. 21) 196 f.

[49] On which see Ogilvie–Richmond's comm. on Tac. *Agr.*, p. 20; Walker (n. 21) 204–25; C. G. Starr, 'Epictetus and the Tyrant' (sc. Domitian), *CPh* 44 (1949) 20–39.

[50] Tac. *Ann.* xvi. 34–5; cf. xv. 60–3 on the death of Seneca. Both emulate not only Cato but, as he himself did, Socrates. Cf. MacMullen, *Enemies of the Roman Order* 4, 21–3; Griffin, *Seneca* 369 f.

[51] It is a long-standing question whether this is the sophist Dio Chrysostom or the Syracusan friend and patron of Plato. The odds seem to me very strongly in favour of the latter (for the contrary view, see most recently P. Desideri, *Dione di Prusa* (Florence 1978) 16–19, part of a chapter discussing ancient judgements of Dio Chrysostom). The most important point is that if Dio of Syracuse is meant, all of these names are those of men who suffered or died for philosophy and in opposition to tyranny. It is true that Dio suffered exile under Domitian, but he was restored to imperial favour before long: he was not a philosophic martyr in the same tradition as the others. A couple of subsidiary points suggest the same conclusion: Epictetus' only reference to Dio Chrysostom (apparently) is hardly flattering (iii. 23. 17–19, cf. Desideri 2–4); and Plutarch's parallel lives group Brutus and the Sicilian Dio as a pair, and these biographies may well have been known to Marcus through Sextus, Plutarch's nephew (*Med.* i. 9). In general on evidence for knowledge of Plutarch's work in this period, see R. Hirzel, *Plutarchos* (Leipzig 1912) ch. 8. (Does *Med.* xi. 13 come from reading Plut. *Phocion* 36?) On the opposite side, note Lucian, *Peregr.* 18, where Peregrinus claims distinction as a philosopher driven into exile, comparing himself with Musonius, Dio, and Epictetus.

Secondly, Q. Arulenus Iunius Rusticus, the biographer of Thrasea and the victim of Domitian, was evidently the grandfather of another Q. Iunius Rusticus,[52] another Stoic, consul in 133 and 162, who was one of Marcus Aurelius' most valued teachers and friends. He is mentioned in i. 17 as one of the three men whom Marcus thanks the gods he was able to know. Rusticus dissuaded him from excessive devotion to poetry, rhetoric and clever writing (ἀστειολογίας i. 7), and introduced him to the works of Epictetus (ibid.). Since Epictetus too was forced into exile under Domitian,[53] the contrast between the philosophic 'monarchy' of the Antonine period and the 'tyrannies' of the first century becomes still more remarkable. The emperor is thus linked with the group of families who were persecuted by Nero and Domitian, and with the philosophic sect which had been most suspect and most frequently attacked not only by these two but also under Vespasian[54] and perhaps Caligula.[55] Marcus' spiritual debts were to the opponents of his predecessors, as well as to Pius.

The paradox is partially explained by remembering that Marcus, like the first-century Stoics, notably Seneca, was opposed not to monarchy as an institution, but to the corrupt form of tyranny.[56] The novelty for Marcus was that he himself, in potentiality, was the tyrant. He was well aware of the danger, warning himself in vi. 30. 1: 'Be not Caesarified,[57] be not dipped in the purple dye; for it can happen.' Writers such as Seneca and Epictetus might achieve brilliant rhetorical heights in imagin-

[52] SHA Marcus 3. 3 'Stoicae disciplinae peritissimus'. See further Med. i. 17. 7; Fronto ii. 36; PIR² I 814.

[53] See Starr (n. 49); PIR² E 74; F. Millar, JRS 55(1965) 141 ff.; Brunt, Athen. 55 (1977) 19 ff.

[54] See Brunt, PBSR 43 (1975) 28–31 with full documentation; also Boissier and Toynbee (both n. 42).

[55] See Brunt (n. 54) 9 n. 9, citing Sen. Tranq. 14 (Julius Kanus); Tac. Agr. 4 and Sen. Ep. 29. 6 (Julius Graecinus).

[56] See Med. i. 11 on ἡ τυραννικὴ βασκανία; i. 14; iv. 28 τυραννικόν; iv. 31, 48; v. 11, vi. 34, perhaps 47; xi. 18 end (a contrast, by ring-composition, with the description of the true ruler at the beginning of the chapter). See further Brunt (n. 54) 7 ff.; Griffin, Seneca 138, 148, 202–7. Seneca's de Clementia is a particularly valuable document for Stoic views of kingship.

[57] The traditional reading ὅρα μὴ ἀποκαισαρωθῇς, retained in Dalfen's recent edition, was questioned by P. Maas, JRS 35 (1945) 145 = Kleine Schriften (Munich 1973) 138, who prefers A's ἀποκαισαριανωθῇς ('do not become one of the Caesariani', i.e. courtiers). Contra, see Birley 271 n. 9; Brunt (n. 54) 24 n. 100. I have no doubt that the latter are correct.

ing the clash of tyrant and philosopher, whether a hypothetical supreme sage or a particular instance drawn from history (as e.g. in Sen. *Const.* 5. 6 f.; Epict. i. 1. 19–32).[58] This kind of vicarious self-consolation and glorification was not available to Marcus. There remained the problem, even more acute for him than for Seneca, of reconciling imperial power with the dictates of philosphy.

The paradoxical triumph of the Stoic school in the person of Marcus has often attracted attention. From the author of the biography in the *Historia Augusta* (esp. 19. 12, 27. 7) onwards, writers have rhapsodically celebrated this realisation of the Platonic dream that kings should become philosophers or philosophers kings.[59] An equal paradox may be seen in an emperor expressing his gratitude to scholars and philosophers alongside, and in the same terms as, his tribute to his royal predecessor. Both these apparent paradoxes may be resolved by a clearer understanding of the place and prominence of philosophers in Roman life, especially under the empire. It may be that the glamour of the tragic victims—of Seneca, Thrasea, and the rest—which beguiled Tacitus, has led in modern times to an overemphasis on the antagonism which existed between philosophers and the principate—the theme which animates even so well-informed and balanced a study as R. MacMullen's *Enemies of the Roman Order* (1966).[60] The conflicts and expulsions distract attention from a more regular and continuous pattern, which is also a part of the larger history of Roman acceptance of, and finally union with, Hellenic culture.

In fact Greek philosophers and their Roman disciples—or patrons—had long been a regular feature of cultivated society. As early as 163 BC Polybius (xxxii. 10) prophesied a great mass of cultured Greeks flocking to Rome, and in the next decade, *c.* 155

---

[58] Further examples: Epict. i. 2. 12–13, 19–24; i. 19; i. 25. 22 (Demetrius to Nero); i. 29. 5 ff.; ii. 13. 22–7; iii. 24. 70 ff.; iii. 26. 35.

[59] Pl. *Rep.* v. 473c ff., vi. 487e, 501e f., etc.; *Ep.* vii. 326b, 328a, 335d. Hence derives Stoic theory, documented by van Geytenbeek (n. 30) 124 ff.; Brunt (n. 54) 18 n. 64 (works by Persaeus, Cleanthes, and Sphaerus; cf. Musonius fr. 8); Griffin, *Seneca* 141–56, 202 ff. For watered-down imperial versions see Plin. *Ep.* i. 10. 9–10; Plut. *Mor.* 776a ff. See further n. 14 above. For modern echoes of the *Historia Augusta*'s idealised portrait see e.g. F. H. Hayward, *Marcus Aurelius: A Saviour of Men* (London 1935) esp. ch. 23.

[60] O. Murray's important review in *JRS* 59 (1969) 261–5 does not really correct this. His remarks on *novi homines* on p. 262 are valuable in another connection; cf. pp. 77–80.

BC, the famous embassy of the three philosophers stunned their Roman audience by arguing in favour of justice on the first day of their visit and next day refuting the arguments they had previously used; for this indifference to orthodox morality they were run out of town by the indignant Cato.[61] Although a much-quoted line of Ennius cheerfully asserted 'philosophari mihi necesse, paucis, nam omnino haud placet',[62] Roman grandees seem to have felt it desirable to have an expert on hand, even resident in the home, to make sure of getting that limited amount of instruction. Hence the custom of maintaining a philosophic 'chaplain',[63] who was often more than just a hireling or tutor for one's sons; he became a respected adviser, a trusted friend. Thus the Stoic Panaetius was an intimate of Scipio Aemilianus,[64] as was the historian Polybius.[65] C. Blossius of Cumae and Diophanes of Mytilene were tutors of the Gracchi, and were thought to have encouraged them in their humanitarian projects.[66] Lucullus had the Academic Antiochus (Cic. *Ac. Pr.* ii. 11), Brutus had Antiochus' brother Aristus (Plut. *Br.* 2. 3), L. Calpurnius Piso had the Epicurean Philodemus,[67] Crassus had the Peripatetic Alexander, who accompanied him abroad (Plut. *Cr.* 3. 3 f.). The Stoic Diodotus was highly esteemed by Cicero, who kept him in his house for many years.[68] The younger Cato had many Stoic guides and advisers, such as Antipater of Tyre and Athenodorus Cordylion, whom he took

[61] Cic. *Rep.* iii. 9 f.; *Acad.* ii. 137; Gell. vi. 14. 18 ff.; Plut. *Cat. Mai.* 22, etc.; A. E. Astin, *Cato the Censor* (Oxford 1978) 174 ff.

[62] Neoptolemus in the *Andromacha, Scaen.* fr. 376 Vahlen³ = 400 W. See H. D. Jocelyn, *The Tragedies of Ennius* (Cambridge 1967) 252. A tirade from the Elder Cato to his son makes much the same point ('quod bonum sit illorum litteras *inspicere*, non perdiscere') though the context is more hostile (Plin. *NH* 29. 13 f.; Astin (n. 61) 170–1).

[63] See e.g. M. L. Clarke, *Higher Education in the Roman World* (London 1971) 71 ff., from whom I derive some of the examples which follow. Further, H. D. Jocelyn, *BRL* 59 (1977) 323–66; J. Glucker, *Antiochus and the Late Academy* (Göttingen 1978) 22 ff.; E. Rawson, *Intellectual Life in the Late Roman Republic* (London 1985) 79–83.

[64] See M. Pohlenz, *RE* xviii. 2. 422; A. E. Astin, *Scipio Aemilianus* (Oxford 1967) appendix vi.

[65] See esp. A. Momigliano, *Alien Wisdom: The Limits of Hellenization* (Cambridge 1975) ch. 2.

[66] Plut. *Ti. Gr.* 8. 4 f.; further, D. R. Dudley, *JRS* 31 (1941) 94 ff.; E. Badian, *ANRW* i. 1 (1972) 679 f.

[67] Cic. *Pis.* 68; Philod. *Epigr.* 23 Gow–Page = *AP* xi. 44; see R. G. M. Nisbet, *Cicero: in Pisonem* (Oxford 1961) 187.

[68] *RE* v. 715; S. F. Bonner, *Education in Ancient Rome* (London 1977) 77, on Cic. *Br.* 309, etc.

back with him to camp after conferring with him at Perga-mum.[69] Apollonides the Stoic and Demetrius the Peripatetic were with him discussing philosophic topics, à la Socrates, on the eve of his suicide at Utica (Plut. *Cat. Min.* 65–7, 69). Of Brutus it was remembered that while in Athens during the crisis of the Republic he combined virtue and learning by making prep-arations for war while also finding time to attend the lectures of Cratippus and Theomnestus (Plut. *Br.* 24. 1). Certainly he managed to attract as a follower a youthful student of philosophy (Hor. *Ep.* ii. 2. 43 ff.; cf. *Serm.* i. 7), who presumably did not believe that *virtus* was an empty word.[70]

It is often said that before the advent of philosophy the Romans were Stoics without knowing it.[71] Certainly the heavy emphasis which the Romans placed on the qualities of resolu-tion, self-sufficiency, endurance of pain, and seriousness of mind made the Stoic ideals thoroughly congenial to many of them, and made it natural to see the heroic actions of Romans past and present in Stoic terms—a process fostered both by Greek chroniclers of Roman history and by Roman orators or historians determined to dignify Rome's past with the flavour of philosophic principle. This influenced works of literature, including the very greatest. Characters in the pages of Livy often approximate to the conventional portrait of the Stoic *sapiens*,[72] and Virgil's Aeneas has long been seen to possess some Stoic characteristics and to use Stoic language upon occasion, however much he may himself fall short of the ideal.[73] When Cato the younger makes his intransigent stand in the Catilinar-

---

[69] Cf. Plut. *Cat. Min.* 4. 1, 10. 1, 16. 1.

[70] Cf. Nisbet–Hubbard on Hor. *Odes* ii. 7. 11; J. L. Moles (diss. Oxford 1979) on Plut. *Br.* 51.

[71] For general accounts of the assimilation of Stoicism at Rome see Arnold, *Roman Stoicism* ch. 5; M. L. Clarke, *The Roman Mind* (London 1960); A. E. Wardman, *Rome's Debt to Greece* (London 1976) (on which see N. M. Horsfall, *JRS* 67 (1967) 179 f.) esp. ch. 2 and 6. An amusing variant: the Epicurean speaker Torquatus, in Cic. *Fin.* i. 34–6, argues that the early Romans were *Epicureans* without knowing it! (Cicero replies in book ii, esp. 70–3.)

[72] See P. G. Walsh, *Livy: His Historical Aims and Methods* (Cambridge 1961) 88 ff., 94; id., *AJP* 79 (1958) 355 ff. N. M. Horsfall, *Prudentia* 8 (1976) 78 f. is more sceptical on Livy's Stoicism.

[73] See commentaries on *Aen.* iv. 331 f., 438–49, v. 709–10, vi. 103 ff.; C. M. Bowra, *G&R* 3 (1933–4) 15 ff.; A. S. Pease's comm. on book iv (Cambridge, Mass. 1935) 36–8; Horsfall (n. 72) 80. Note also Regulus in Hor. *Odes* iii. 5 (illuminated by Cic. *Off.* iii. 99–115; *Fin.* ii. 65).

ian trial, Sallust, probably adapting the original speech,[74] makes him imitate the phraseology and archaic tone of his ancestor the Censor: this was in no way incongruent with the younger man's Stoicism.

The educated class of the Roman republic were conscious of what the Greek schools had to offer, and for many of them philosophy was an important part of their personal and moral lives, a source of inspiration and consolation, and a means of articulating their moral dilemmas (see esp. Cic. *Att.* ix. 4).[75] Of course the interest of many Romans in philosophy may have been superficial and faddish,[76] but the original trend must stem from genuine, and in some cases dedicated, interest in Greek teachings. In 92 BC Rutilius Rufus, a pupil of Panaetius (see Cic. *Br.* 113 f. and Kroll ad loc.), chose exile rather than compromise his Stoic principles (Cic. *de Or.* i. 227 ff.). To men like Cicero, author of many dialogues in which he aimed at expounding Greek doctrines to a wider Roman audience,[77] philosophy did matter. Likewise to Brutus, an Academic strongly influenced by Stoicism through his father-in-law Cato,[78] the assassination of Caesar was an issue of principle, not of personal enmity or jealousy: Plutarch (*Br.* 8. 3) sees him as μισοτύραννος, not μισοκαῖσαρ. The hard-headed realism of a whole school of Roman history, effectively founded by Sir Ronald Syme, finds in the killers of Caesar, not excepting Brutus, the last stand of

[74] R. Syme, *Sallust* (Berkeley and Los Angeles 1964) 111 ff., esp. 116 on Sall. *Cat.* 52; Earl, *Political Thought of Sallust* (n. 9) 100 f.

[75] See also Cic. *Att.* vii. 2. 4, viii. 11. 1, x. 8. 6; *Fam.* iv. 2. 2, v. 19. 1–2 (esp. 'ut, si nos ii sumus, qui esse debemus, id est studio digni ac litteris nostris'); *QF* i. 1. 37; Cassius *ap. Fam.* xv. 19. 2. For further examples, and a valuable general statement along these lines, see Macleod, *Collected Essays* 280 ff. For the ideal of philosophy in action see Cic. *ND* i. 7; *Fam.* xv. 4. 16 (to Cato); n. 81 below.

[76] Vigorously argued by M. Crawford, in P. D. A. Garnsey and C. R. Whittaker (eds.), *Imperialism in the Ancient World* (Cambridge 1978) 193–207, with reference to Pompey's philistine philhellenism. For the empire, note (with caution) Lucian, *de Mercede Conductis* e.g. 36, with detailed material in J. Bompaire, *Lucien écrivain* (Paris 1958) 499–512; Hall, *Lucian's Satire* 241–51.

[77] Cf. the passages cited by J. S. Reid in his edn. of the *Academica* (London 1885) 20–4.

[78] Cf. Syme, (n. 4) ch. 5; J. P. V. D. Balsdon, *Hist.* 7 (1958) 80–94; MacMullen, *Enemies of the Roman Order* ch. i, esp. 2–16. Plutarch's *Brutus* provides the most detailed evidence for Brutus' philosophic education and standpoint, and this has been carefully discussed by Moles in his comm., esp. pp. 29–38. See Plut. *Br.* 2. 1 ff., 29. 2–3, 34. 4, 40. 4–9, 50. 5, and Moles on all of these passages. It is clear that Plutarch was well-informed about Brutus' philosophic allegiances: although he angles the evidence at times to suit his themes and effects, it is not his own invention.

reactionary senatorial privilege. 'It is in no way evident', according to Syme, 'that the nature of Brutus would have been very different had he never opened a book of Stoic or Academic philosophy.'[79] This view cannot stand against the evidence, especially in the works of his contemporary Cicero and in Plutarch's biography, for Brutus' stern and very Stoic commitment. Brutus and his allies may have been wrong, but they were wrong for at least some of the right reasons.[80] Similarly under the empire there were many, including Thrasea Paetus and Helvidius Priscus, whose creed required that their actions be tested and guided by principle. These men were models of Marcus' teacher Severus (i. 14, quoted above) and of Marcus himself. He too was aware that philosophy was ideally not an academic pursuit[81] but a way of life: 'Put an end once and for all to discussion of what a good man ought to be, and be one.' (x. 16); 'How clearly it is borne in upon you that there is no other state of life so suited to the practice of philosophy as this, in which you now find yourself.' (xi. 7).[82]

Under the empire the trend outlined shows no significant change. Greek philosophers and their Roman imitators continued to play a part in the education of the upper classes, and to

[79] Syme (n. 4) 57. (The same line is taken with regard to the opposition under the empire: see Syme, *Tacitus* 552–8, against which see Brunt (n. 54).) Syme's argument in the case of (e.g.) Cato Uticensis appears to rest on the observation that he 'controlled a vast nexus of alliances among the *nobiles*' (*Tacitus* 557, cf. *The Roman Revolution* loc. cit.). The coherence of this argument is perhaps questionable. MacMullen, loc. cit. (n. 78) does more justice to both sides of Brutus and the others.

[80] Cf. esp. A. Momigliano, *Secondo contributo alla storia degli studi classici* (Rome 1960) 407–16, 375–8.

[81] This was not of course an undisputed view even at Rome: see esp. Griffin, *Seneca* ch. 10; A. Grilli, *Il problema della vita contemplativa nel mondo greco-romano* (Milan 1953); R. Joly, 'Le Thème philosophique des genres de vie dans l'antiquité classique', *Acad. Roy. de Belgique Mémoires* 51 (1956) 7 ff. For Greek views see also Dodds on Pl. *Grg.* 484–6; Gauthier–Jolif on Arist. *NE* x. 6 (with very full parallels and bibliography); Festugière, *Personal Religion among the Greeks* 58 ff.; T. B. Eriksen, Bios Theoretikos: *Notes on Aristotle's Ethica Nicomachea x. 6–8* (Norwegian Research Council 1976). For Tacitus see *Dial.* 9 ff.; for Dio Chrysostom, Moles, *JHS* 98 (1978) 95 n. 132. The Stoics in particular, traditionally the opponents of Epicurean quietism, were popularly associated with active public life (e.g. Cic. *Fin.* iii. 68; Hor. *Ep.* i. 1. 16–17 and Kiessling–Heinze ad loc.).

[82] Similar views in Muson. fr. 8. Contrast Agrippina's assumptions in bringing up an emperor, Suet. *Nero* 52. 1: 'sed a philosophia eum mater avertit monens imperaturo contrariam esse', with Bradley's note (for converse, see *Med.* viii. 1). Compare Pl. *Grg.* 484 f.; Sen. Rh. *Contr.* ii. pr. 3–5, vii. pr. 1; Sen. *Ep.* 108. 22, *Helv.* 17. 4; Tac. *Agr.* 4. 3. Further, Brunt, *PBSR* 43 (1975) 8–9, for the reservations of Quintilian and others. Epictetus (i. 26. 5) mentions parents who are angry when their sons study philosophy; cf. Muson. fr. 16; ps.-Quint. *Decl. Min.* 283 with Winterbottom's notes.

support and advise them in later life. That they should attend upon the emperors and offer them, if not corrective, at least protreptic works, is a legacy from both the Hellenistic courts[83] and the Roman Republic,[84] under which, as we have seen, philosophers were part of the cultural entourage of any distinguished patron. Philosophers were among the learned Greeks maintained and employed in various non-philosophic capacities by Augustus.[85] Particularly distinguished in that company were the Stoics Athenodorus of Tarsus[86] and Arius Didymus. The latter compiled a well-known summary of Stoic doctrine and composed an authoritative consolation to Livia after the death of the elder Drusus.[87] Nestor of Tarsus was one of the tutors of Augustus' nephew Marcellus (Strabo xiv. 675 f.), and very probably of Tiberius too, whose virtues, viewed fairly, seem characteristically Stoic.[88] The Peripatetic Athenaeus of Seleucia, another figure probably associated with the imperial household, was also for some time resident in the house of Licinius Murena.[89] Julius Kanus, executed under Caligula, was accompanied to his death by 'his philosopher' (unnamed; see Sen. *Tranq.* 14, an extended account). Tullius Marcellinus, an acquaintance of Seneca's, was persuaded by a friend to starve himself to death rather than submit to an incurable disease (Sen. *Ep.* 77. 5 ff.—the arguments seem Stoic; cf. ibid. 58. 32–6; n. 45 above).

The Romans entrusted their offspring to such men as tutors (as the younger Cicero was entrusted to Diodotus), and the educator of one's youth often remained the companion and

[83] P. M. Fraser, *Ptolemaic Alexandria* (Oxfod 1972) 480–5; Kindstrand's comm. on Bion, 14 f.; Clarke (n. 63) 71.

[84] Cf. n. 14 above. For instance, compare the later treatises on kingship addressed to emperors with Philodemus' work dedicated to Piso and entitled *On the Good King according to Homer* (on which see esp. O. Murray, *JRS* 55 (1965) 161 ff.). Particularly close is Dio Chr. *Or.* ii. For Republican 'kings' see E. Rawson, *JRS* 65 (1975) 148–59.

[85] See G. W. Bowersock, *Augustus and the Greek World* (Oxford 1965) 30–41.

[86] *PIR*[2] A 1288; P. Grimal, *REA* 47 (1945) 261 ff., 48 (1946) 62 ff. For the intellectual prominence of Tarsus see Mayor on Juv. 3. 117, citing esp. Str. xiv. 673 ff. Note the case of Apollonius of Tyana and St Paul.

[87] *PIR*[2] A 1035; Sen. *Marc.* 2 ff.

[88] *PIR*[1] N 54; [Lucian] *Macrobioi* 21; C. Cichorius, *Römische Studien* (Leipzig and Berlin 1922) 278; B. M. Levick, *Tiberius the Politician* (London 1976) 16. Levick 231 nn. 36–7 considers the possibility of Stoic influence on Tiberius; *contra*, see R. Syme, *The Augustan Aristocracy* (Oxford 1986) 365.

[89] Str. xiv. 675; Nisbet–Hubbard's comm. on Hor. *Odes* ii (Oxford 1978) 152. Contrast Syme (n. 88) 387–91.

counsellor of one's maturity. One example is Persius' lasting friendship with Cornutus, under whom he began to study at sixteen (*Vita Pers.* 12 f. Cl.; for a parallel, Plut. *Mor.* 37b–f); another is the Roman philosopher-rhetor Papirius Fabianus, described by the Elder Seneca: his lectures were attended, his books treasured, and his style defended by Seneca the Younger.[90] When we add the case of Seneca himself, writer of hortatory and advisory works to his juniors and relatives, it becomes evident that Roman Stoics are almost professionals themselves, at no disadvantage to Greek thinkers and cultivated as much as them by their contemporaries. Tacitus' account of the killing in AD 62 of Rubellius Plautus, governor of Asia, nicely illustrates this by describing the dual support he had while awaiting his end: 'doctoresque sapientiae, Coeranum *Graeci*, Musonium *Tusci* generis constantiam opperiendae mortis pro incerta et trepida vita suasisse' (*Ann.* xiv. 59), though Tacitus' elegant antithesis masks the fact that Musonius wrote philosophy in Greek. In the same way Romans and Greeks are juxtaposed in the first book of the *Meditations*.

The political persecutions of philosophers have generally been given prominence in the history of philosophy under the empire because both ancient and modern authors tend towards a justified preoccupation with the conflict between ruler and opposition, tyrant and hero. It is, however, worth noting how consistent the functions of a philosopher remain even in extreme cases: consolation, exhortation, exposition of eternal truths.[91] Moreover, Seneca, Musonius, and the family of Thrasea and Helvidius are extreme cases. Many philosophers, not only Epicureans, still advocated the quiet life.[92] The half-Stoic Sextius rejected office and a career (Sen. *Ep.* 98. 13), as did Seneca's brother Mela (Sen. Rh. *Contr.* ii. pr. 3). Tacitus seems to allude to a general tendency for philosophers to use their profession as an excuse for 'segne otium' (*Hist.* iv. 5). So the

[90] Sen. Rh. *Contr.* ii pr.; ii. 1, and the other passages listed in the index to the Loeb edn. See also Sen. *Ep.* 40. 12 ff., 52. 11, 100; *Brev. Vit.* 10, 13; H. MacL. Currie, *BICS* 13 (1966) 76 ff.; A. D. Leeman, *Orationis Ratio* (Amsterdam 1963) 261–71, 282; M. Griffin, *JRS* 62 (1972) 16; H. Bornecque, *Les Déclamations et les déclamateurs d'après Sénèque le père* (Lille 1902) 185–6; J. Fairweather, *Seneca the Elder* (Cambridge 1981), see index.

[91] Cf. Dill, *Roman Society* 289 ff., also ch. 1 n. 102 above.

[92] Brunt, *PBSR* 43 (1975) 9 nn. 12–13; cf. 8 n. 7, 19–21. Also Griffin, *Seneca* ch. 10; Syme, *Tacitus* 553; cf. n. 81 above.

evidence of Seneca (especially in his letters), of Pliny, and of Plutarch on philosophers' activities may be more relevant to our theme than the evidence of Tacitus, who by the very nature of his work does not inform us about the unimportant pursuits of political non-entities.

As Seneca advised and, one hopes, improved Lucilius, Serenus, and the rest, so Epictetus gave specific advice (not simply lectures) to individual Roman clients,[93] and Plutarch offered elegant essays and moral discourses to Roman philhellenes such as Sosius Senecio and Minicius Fundanus.[94] Since both these dignitaries were close friends and colleagues of Pliny, we may fairly see in his letters the other side of the coin, the receiving end of a regular relationship. Other friends in common are the brothers Avidius Quietus and Nigrinus.[95] Pliny may even have known Plutarch himself,[96] but perhaps felt it would be beneath his dignity to include so undistinguished an author among his correspondents (compare the superiority and greater sharpness of letters addressed to social inferiors such as Julius Genitor, esp. *Ep.* ix. 17). No such qualms need be felt about that 'princeps provinciae', the impressive and excellent Euphrates, who receives a positive eulogy (*Ep.* i. 10).[97] The description of Euphrates' style and subject-matter recalls both Dio Chrysostom and Plutarch. Pliny tells how he complains to Euphrates (as he often does to other, less philosophic friends) about the pressures of his work, and describes the great man's counterarguments: 'Ille me consolatur, adfirmat etiam esse hanc philosophiae et quidem pulcherrimam partem, agere negotium publicum, cognoscere iudicare, promere et exercere iustitiam, quaeque ipsi doceant in usu habere.' As usual with Pliny, the relationship and the moral considerations come across as civilised rather than profound. Yet such cases do illuminate the usefulness and general acceptance of philosophers in Roman

---

[93] For a list of those known to have visited him see Brunt, *Athen.* 55 (1977) 20.

[94] On the patrons of Plutarch see above all C. P. Jones, *Plutarch and Rome* (Oxford 1971) ch. 4–5. The *Parallel Lives* are dedicated to Senecio, as are the *Quaestiones Convivales.* Fundanus is the main speaker in the *de Cohibenda Ira* and is also mentioned in the *de Tranquillitate Animi* (464e). For letters of Pliny to these two men see *Ep.* i. 13, iv. 4 (Senecio); i. 9, iv. 15, v. 16, vi. 6 (Fundanus).

[95] Sherwin-White on Plin. *Ep.* vi. 29.

[96] So Jones, *Plutarch* 61.

[97] See also *PIR*[2] E 121; Philos. *VS* i. 25; P. Grimal, *Lat.* 14 (1955) 370 ff. Euphrates is also praised by Epictetus, iii. 15. 8; for a specimen of his oratory see iv. 9. 17–20.

life. Obviously some Romans took them more seriously than others, and some philosophers deserved it more. But although learned Greeks might match their dignity and morality with financial and administrative shrewdness, and were often employed as the emperor's political intermediaries in their own cities,[98] it is over-cynical to see the articulation of the necessity of Roman dominion as their only important function in the eyes of Rome. Romans, even the highest, evidently believed that philosophy had something to tell them.

Philosophers and *grammatici* were with Tiberius on Rhodes (Suet. *Tib.* 11-12), and probably later on Capri.[99] His favoured astrologer, Thrasyllus, was also a distinguished Platonist.[100] They were permitted at the court of Nero, if only for mockery (Tac. *Ann.* xiv. 16; though in view of Tacitus' contempt for Nero's excessive Hellenism this anecdote ought not to be heavily pressed).[101] The younger Agrippina was the patroness of Seneca (though she favoured him as a teacher of rhetoric rather than philosophy). Seneca himself, however hypocritically,[102] addressed philosophic arguments in a consolation to the Claudian freedman Polybius (*Consol. ad Polyb.*). The learned Claudius, it may be conjectured, was interested in Greek thought as well as in history and antiquarianism.[103] Even bad emperors might maintain or patronise philosophic toadies, however unworthy they may seem from the evidence of their enemies. The classic instance is the Stoic P. Egnatius Celer, chief witness against his patron Barea Soranus under Nero, bitterly

[98] Bowersock, *Greek Sophists in the Roman Empire*, inspired above all by the work of Syme, esp. *Tacitus* 504–19 (see also Syme, 'The Greeks under Roman Rule', *Proc. of the Massachusetts Hist. Soc.* 72 (1963) 3–20 = *Roman Papers* ii (Oxford 1978) 566–81); also F. Millar, *The Emperor in the Roman World* (London 1977) 491–506. Bowersock's emphases have been criticised by E. L. Bowie, *YCS* 27 (1982) 28–59): should social status or rhetorical skills be judged the more important factor in explaining the careers of the sophists? No doubt this debate will continue.

[99] For Tiberius' sojourn and pursuits on Capri see esp. Tac. *Ann.* iv. 58; Suet. *Tib.* 40–5, 70; Mayor on Juv. 10. 93; R. Syme, *Hist.* 23 (1974) 490–2 = *Roman Papers* iii (Oxford 1984) 946–8.

[100] *PIR*[1] T 137; *RE* viA. 581 ff.; F. H. Cramer, *Astrology in Roman Law and Politics* (Philadelphia 1954) 92 ff.

[101] For other evidence of Neronian philosophers see *Suda* s.v. 'Alexandros'; Griffin, *Seneca* 64.

[102] See the discussion in Griffin, *Seneca* 415–16.

[103] On his tastes see Suet. *Claud.* 41–2; Momigliano (n. 5) ch. 1. For possible hints of knowledge of moral treatises on kingship see the quotations in Syme, *Tacitus* 706 n. 5.

condemned by Tacitus,[104] and exiled during the subsequent reign. Another of the same, it appears, is the unknown philosopher-informer Seras, who prospered under Domitian and was condemned after his assassination (Dio 68. 1. 2).

Musonius Rufus seems to have been sufficiently in favour under Vespasian to be exempted from the first expulsion of philosophers. He later lost his immunity,[105] but was subsequently recalled by Titus, another philhellene, with whom Dio Chrysostom also seems to have been on good terms.[106] This fits together admirably, since Dio was evidently one of Musonius' pupils (Fronto ii. 50, cf. Dio Chr. *Or.* 31. 122).[107] Flavian emperors indeed granted special privileges to 'grammaticis et oratoribus et medicis et philosophis' (*Dig.* 50. 4. 18. 20 on Vespasian and later confirmation by Hadrian).[108] These edicts were reinforced by the Hellenising Hadrian and by the Antonines. In general we can see a continuity from the Flavian encouragement of education to the activity of Pliny and his friends on behalf of the young, both through the institution of endowed schools and through the careful selection of private tutors.[109] The concern for educational standards is further reflected in the great work of Pliny's teacher Quintilian, in the *Dialogus* of Tacitus, and in the educational treatises of Plutarch. The opening of Juvenal's seventh satire, acclaiming the revival

[104] Tac. *Ann.* xvi. 32; *Hist.* iv. 10, 40; Dio 62. 26. 1; Juv. 3. 116. J. L. Moles, *JHS* 103 (1983) 103–23 discusses the case in detail.

[105] *PIR*[1] M 549; see also Lutz (n. 30); Sherwin-White on Plin. *Ep.* iii. 11. 5.

[106] C. P. Jones, *The Roman World of Dio Chrysostom* (Cambridge, Mass. 1978) 14 f., 44.

[107] Jones, *Dio* ch. 6 and Moles, *JHS* 98 (1978) 78 ff. argue that this is not contradicted by Dio's works attacking philosophy and in particular his (lost) πρὸς Μουσώνιον (Synesius, *Dio* 37b; Moles, op. cit. 82 ff.). This question, and the whole problem of Dio's career and chronology, will shortly be reopened by Oswyn Murray (in a paper a version of which was read to a seminar organised in Oxford by Dr M. T. Griffin, 21 Feb. 1984).

[108] For fragmentary edicts on such *immunitas*, granted by Vespasian and Domitian, see *L'Ann. Épigr.* 1936, no. 128 = M. McCrum and A. G. Woodhead (eds.), *Select Documents of the Principates of the Flavian Emperors* (Cambridge 1961) no. 458; also Sherwin-White on Plin. *Ep.* iv. 13. 5, x. 58. 1 (case of Flavius Archippus). For Nerva see Plin. *Ep.* x. 58. 5 (extract from an edict). *Dig.* 27. 1. 6 contrasts the favour shown by Hadrian to philosophers with the greater strictness of Antoninus; cf. V. Nutton, *JRS* 61 (1971) 56; Williams, *JRS* 66 (1976) 75; Millar, *The Emperor in the Roman World* 494–8; P. J. Parsons, in A. E. Hanson (ed.), *Collectanea Papyrologica; Fest. H. C. Youtie* (Bonn 1976) ii. 409–46, at 441 ff.

[109] See esp. E. de Saint-Denis, 'Pline et la jeunesse', *Révue Universitaire* 1946, 9 ff.; Bonner (n. 68) ch. 9. For the literary milieu of the time of Trajan see esp. Syme, *Tacitus* ch. 8–9.

of letters and learning under the patronage of a new emperor
(Hadrian?), is relevant, though ironically biased.[110] By this
date not only were philosophy and rhetoric intimately inter-
woven (the keynote of the Second Sophistic), but both arts were
in high favour at Rome[111] and promulgated even in the western
provinces.[112]

So the antithesis of emperors versus philosophers is, as it
appears, only a part of the picture. Greek philosophers and their
Roman adherents met with the antagonism of the emperor only
at times of extreme political tension: the conspiracy of Piso, the
dispute over the Flavian succession, the suspicion and alarm of
Domitian in late 93. Two conditions had to be satisfied before
such enmity arose. The opponents had to be of significant rank,
senatorial and therefore potential aspirants to the purple; and
their principles had to be important enough for them to take
active and provocative political steps. The expulsions of
professional philosophers are subsequent to the retaliation
against such dangerous men, and reflect fear of rabble-rousing
(as indicated by Dio 76. 12. 2; Suet. *Vesp.* 15 (accusations against
the elder Helvidius)). In times of conflict with the senate the
emperor might find it advisable to avoid the danger, real or
imagined, of further dissemination of 'treasonable' ideas, for
instance by Cynic popular orators, whose diatribes on the
fundamental liberty of every man could be misinterpreted by
the mob as anarchic and revolutionary doctrine.[113] But
temporary expulsions did not prevent Roman pupils from
gathering around the philosophers in exile. Epictetus sustained
his school at Nicopolis, Demetrius at Athens (*PIR*[2] D 39). Nor

[110] For discussion of this passage see W. S. Anderson, *CPh* 57 (1963) 153 ff.; M.
Coffey, *Roman Satire* (London 1976) 129, 246; Courtney's comm. 348–50. R. Syme, *AJP*
100 (1979) 250–78 = *Roman Papers* iii (Oxford 1984) 1135–57 argues effectively for a
Hadrianic date.

[111] Trajan's wife Plotina (a patroness of Pliny: *Ep.* ix. 28), was of Epicurean
persuasion: see *ILS* 7784, with *SIG*[3] 834; Syme, *Tacitus* 538. (For Epicureanism under
the empire see ch. 1 n. 77 above.)

[112] Cf. Mayor on Juv. 15. 111; Ogilvie–Richmond on Tac. *Agr.* 21; Bonner (n. 68).

[113] On Stoics and Cynics see Juv. 13. 121–2 (on the difficulty of distinguishing
between them); J. M. Rist, *Stoic Philosophy* (Cambridge 1969) ch. 4. For the view that
Cynics, as opposed to Stoics, never fully came to terms with the monarchic regime of the
empire see Toynbee (n. 42). Scholars differ on how naturally or inevitably Stoic and
Cynic philosophy came into conflict with monarchic government, but they were
certainly considered *potentially* subversive at some periods: cf. Sen. *Ep.* 73. 1; Epict. i. 29.
9; Wirszubski (n. 18) 143 ff.; MacMullen (n. 38) 68 ff.

did imperial action in these emergency conditions alter the basic trend which placed Greek intellectuals ever higher in the estimation and the service of Rome.[114] No new era dawns with the assassination of Domitian:[115] it was simply that philosophy in senatorial circles became respectable again, as it was admitted that it should be under all good and popular emperors. That trend culminates in Marcus Aurelius' endowment of chairs in philosophy at Athens.

Again, the tyranny of Domitian overshadows a larger continuity from Flavians to Antonines, which has its roots in the reign and character of Vespasian. In a famous passage, one of the few in which he succeeds in stepping back from his subject and taking a broader view, Tacitus outlines the change from the luxury and indulgence of the Julio-Claudian era, culminating in the decadent irresponsibility of Nero, to the more responsible and restrained government of the Flavians. The old wealthy families of the republican nobility had died out: Nero was the last representative of three patrician *gentes*, the Julii Caesares, the Claudii Nerones, and the Domitii Ahenobarbi.[116]

postquam caedibus saevitum et magnitudo famae exitio erat, ceteri ad sapientiora convertere. simul novi homines e municipiis et coloniis atque etiam provinciis in senatum crebro adsumpti domesticam parsimoniam intulerunt, et quamquam fortuna vel industria plerique pecuniosam ad senectutem pervenirent, mansit tamen prior animus. sed praecipuus adstricti moris auctor Vespasianus fuit, antiquo ipse cultu victuque. obsequium inde in principem et aemulandi amor validior quam poena ex legibus et metus. (Tac. *Ann.* iii. 55)

After the savage massacres in which greatness of renown was fatal, the survivors turned to wiser ways. The new men who were often admitted

---

[114] Bowersock, *Greek Sophists, passim*, esp. ch. 4. For earlier accounts, now somewhat dated, see C. S. Walton, *JRS* 19 (1929) 38 ff.; M. Hammond, *JRS* 47 (1957) 74 ff.; Syme, *Tacitus* ch. 38 (also various reprises such as the paper cited in n. 98, and *Greeks Invading the Roman Government*, S. J. Brademas Lecture, Brookline, Mass. 1982). The authoritative work is now H. Halfmann, *Die Senatoren aus dem östlichen Teil des Imperium Romanum bis zum Ende des 2. Jh. n. Chr.* (*Hypomn.* 58, Göttingen 1979). For Epictetus' school see n. 53 above.

[115] *Contra* Griffin, *Seneca* 364. Earlier, compare the suggestive remark by Murray, *JRS* 59 (1969) 262: 'Talk of Seneca changing sides is out of place in any event: it was Nero, not Seneca, who changed sides—from good emperor to tyrant.'

[116] See T. P. Wiseman, *Titus Flavius and the Indivisible Subject* (Inaugural Lecture, Exeter 1978) 19, to which I am indebted throughout this paragraph; also M. F. Charlesworth, *JHS* 27 (1937) 97–9; Syme, *Tacitus* esp. ch. 3 and 42–5; Brunt, *JRS* 64 (1974) 9, esp. n. 52; Wallace-Hadrill, *Suetonius* 177–89.

into the Senate from the towns, colonies, and even the provinces, introduced their household thrift, and though many of them by good luck or energy attained an old age of wealth, still their former tastes remained. But the chief encourager of strict manners was Vespasian, himself old-fashioned both in his dress and his diet. Henceforth a respectful feeling towards the prince and a love of emulation proved more effective than legal penalties or terrors. (tr. A. J. Church and W. J. Brodribb)

This remarkable passage, so contrary to the usual view of Roman historians that everything is always going from bad to worse,[117] finds confirmation elsewhere in the *Annals*, especially at xvi. 5 (municipal visitors to Rome outraged by Nero), and in Pliny's letters.[118] Thrasea Paetus himself came from Padua, famous for its upright morality and strictness. Pliny exalts the merits of his contemporaries and juniors from the Italian *municipia*, and his attitude to the remnant of the old nobles is ambiguous, like that of both Tacitus and Juvenal. *Epistle* iii. 1 on the *antiquitas* (§ 6), health, propriety, and dignity of Vestricius Spurinna, whose wife too is a model to her sex ('singularis exempli'), is a typical document, and valuable even if biased. Though Tacitus may have overschematised, the change in Roman manners and society is there, and has as its chief ornaments several of the emperors.[119] Domitian passed moral legislation as censor; although his behaviour was condemned by contemporaries as hypocrisy (Plin. *Ep.* iv. 11. 6; Juv. 2. 29–33), it may indicate what was expected of the emperor. Trajan cultivated the image of a stern and responsible literary man, unlearned (Philos. *VS*. i. 7. 2), dignified, but fond of his drink—a true Roman, in fact. With the rise of the provincial emperors a new spirit of severity and a consciousness of public service enters the principate.[120]

[117] See e.g. Ogilvie on Livy i. 19. 4; McGushin on Sall. *Cat.* 6–13; Earl (n. 9) ch. 4. The idea is a *topos* in other genres also: of countless possible examples, see e.g. Hor. *Odes* iii. 6. 45–8; cf. Nisbet–Hubbard on ii. 15; Bramble, *Persius* 29 ff.

[118] See esp. *Ep.* i. 14. 4; Sherwin-White on vii. 24. Note also *Pan.* 46 (banning of pantomimes). For more devotees of the simple life see *Ep.* i. 22. 4, ii. 9, iii. 3. 5 (cf. ix. 17), iii. 5. 10, vi. 8. 2 and 5. For Pliny's prudishness, iv. 14, v. 3, vii. 24. See further Dill (n. 91) 141 ff.

[119] For Vespasian see further Suet. *Vesp.* 2, 4. 5, 8. 3, 9. 2, 12; Tac. *Hist.* ii. 5. He had a reputation for stinginess; Suet. *Vesp.* 16–19, 23, etc. (Pius was abused for the same fault; see *Med.* i. 16. 3 and Farquharson's n.). For Domitian see Suet. *Dom.* 8–9.

[120] See esp. Syme, *Tacitus* 26–9.

This is relevant to the case of Marcus Aurelius, and to the themes of this chapter, because the change described by Tacitus and recognised by his contemporaries involves a reversion to moral values which are constantly endorsed by philosophers. In the area of sumptuary legislation and the vices it seeks to curb, Roman traditionalism and philosophic principle coalesce. Moralists' praises of the *victus simplex*[121] were combined with the belief that Roman greatness was founded on the qualities of frugality and piety which had so distinguished her race in the days before she rose to empire.[122] It is not sufficient to dismiss these as clichés, for 'a cliché need not be a lie'.[123] Rather, the recurrence of these ideas indicates their potency, and they provide the moral background and presuppositions for writers and thinkers of the empire. Whatever the degree of distortion which we as historians may discern in the schematic history of Sallust and others, it was none the less received doctrine in Roman educated circles, reinforced by the literary prestige of the authors in whose works these ideas were enshrined. For some purposes the myth is more important than the facts. The literary conventions of philosophy and diatribe are not easily separable from what Romans actually believed. Ethical assumptions, underlying literary models, influenced the way a man acted, the way he wrote, even the way he looked at life. This is above all the case with a bookish, contemplative writer like Marcus Aurelius, himself a philosopher in aspiration if not in profession (viii. 1).

A ruler should protect morals, and be an example to his citizens,[124] as Nero conspicuously was not (Tac. *Ann.* xv. 67; Mayor on Juv. 8. 211 ff.), but as Vespasian was, and to good effect (Tac. *Ann.* iii. 55, quoted above). This is relevant to Marcus' judgements of his predecessors, and particularly his praise of Pius, whom he is contrasting with Trajan, Hadrian, and others (see ch. III, p. 108 f.). The same ideals of simplicity and self-discipline appear in several places in Book I: 'from my mother . . . to live the simple life, a life far from the habits of the rich' (ch. 3); 'from my tutor . . . not to shirk toil, and to have small needs; to do my own work and not to interfere . . .' (ch. 5).

---

[121] See e.g. *SVF* iii. 705–15; Nisbet–Hubbard on Hor. *Odes* i. 31. 16–17, ii. 16. 13.

[122] See esp. Pease on Cic. *ND* ii. 8 f.; Horsfall (n. 72) 81.

[123] R. M. Ogilvie, *Commentary on Livy i–v* (Oxford 1965) 23.

[124] See Woodman on Vell. ii. 126. 5; Wallace-Hadrill, *Suetonius* 134.

These ideals are especially prominent in the description of Pius' simple life (i. 16. 8) and the rejections of the pomp of a court (i. 17. 3), where the vocabulary (τῦφος, κόμπος) comes straight from the pages of the moralists. Marcus continues, perhaps more self-consciously, the trend begun by Vespasian after the civil wars; as Rostovtzeff saw,[125] though he overstated the directness of the influence, the popular ethics which permeated Roman thinking had an important part to play in the change.

4. *The* Meditations *and the Second Sophistic*[126]

With the friendship of Dio Chrysostom with Nerva and Trajan, the praises Pliny showers on Euphrates, Isaeus, and Artemidorus, and the patronage of Plutarch by eminent consulars, we reach the threshold of the Second Sophistic, a period of political and intellectual resurgence in the Greek world, a period and cultural milieu which Marcus Aurelius inhabited without being entirely typical of it. This revival is represented for us by the voluminous productions of the Greek sophists, men like Dio of Prusa, Aelius Aristides, Maximus of Tyre, the historian Arrian, and others; on the fringes of the movement were more gifted but less successful men, such as the philosopher Plutarch and the satirist Lucian, possibly a sophist *manqué*.[127] The definition of the term 'sophist', for contemporaries and for the modern scholar, is a matter of considerable dispute,[128] as it had been in the fifth century BC, the era of the original sophists. Rhetorical ability, linguistic purity (defined by the canon of classical Greek prose, a verbal cult known as Atticism), and the capacity to speak with expertise on a technical or learned subject were *de*

---

[125] M. Rostovtzeff, *Social and Economic History of the Roman Empire* (2nd edn., Oxford 1957) ch. 4. The criticisms by Jones, *Dio* ch. 13 (esp. 115, 118–20) are too strong.

[126] On the period in general see Boulanger, *Aelius Aristide* esp. part i; Bowersock, *Greek Sophists*; F. Millar, *JRS* 59 (1969) 12–29; E. L. Bowie, in M. I. Finley (ed.), *Studies in Ancient Society* (London 1974) 166–209; and his paper cited in n. 98 above; G. W. Bowersock (ed.), *Approaches to the Second Sophistic* (University Park, Pa., 1974); B. P. Reardon, *Courants littéraires grecs des IIᵉ et IIIᵉ siècles après J.-C.* (Paris 1971) (pp. 268–74 on Marcus).

[127] On Plutarch see Russell, *Plutarch* 6–7; on Lucian, Bowersock, *Greek Sophists* 114–15.

[128] See recently Bowersock, *Greek Sophists* ch. 1; G. R. Stanton, *AJP* 94 (1973) 350–64; C. P. Jones in Bowersock (ed.), *Approaches* 11–16; G. Anderson, *Philostratus* (London, Sydney, and Dover, NH, 1986) 8–13. Such terminology is also discussed by Moles, *JHS* 98 (1978) 88–91.

rigueur. Some of the sophists also laid claim to the title of philosopher, although in general they peddled second-hand ideas and richly wrought trivialities. We know them most fully through the enthusiastic survey of Philostratus, writing in the next century, who compiled a series of miniature biographies,[129] and through the fierce but effective satires of Lucian, who never tired of pillorying them as pompous frauds (the most important of his works for this theme is the *Rhetorum Praeceptor*[130]).

In the early years of the second century AD the Roman C. Caecilius Plinius Secundus and the Bithynian Greek sophist Dio Chrysostom of Prusa both declaimed with equal eloquence (and with many common themes) on the wisdom and virtue of Trajan, the ideal monarch.[131] The confrontation, or rather the concord, of these two literary men is the spirit of the age, and heralds a number of other well-known instances of the merging of the two worlds of Greece and Rome. In AD 143 two tutors of Marcus Aurelius, Cornelius Fronto and Herodes of Athens, both celebrated consulships, the former *suffectus*, the latter *ordinarius*. So too in the chapters describing Marcus' mentors in Book I of the *Meditations*, Romans and Greeks are juxtaposed: here we find distinguished ex-consuls and Greek professional philosophers, eminent littérateurs and rhetoricians. The combination of literary and political prominence is characteristic of the age.[132]

Marcus Aurelius has often been regarded as a typical figure of the Second Sophistic, a patron of philosophic learning and a philhellene, even a worthy heir of Hadrian.[133] He was, after all, taught Greek and Latin rhetoric by the most distinguished authorities in those fields, Herodes Atticus and Fronto himself. External evidence, particularly in Philostratus' *Lives of the Sophists*, shows him attending the public orations of the sophists and participating fully in the literary fervour of the age. In 176

[129] See esp. Anderson, *Philostratus* ch. 1–6, more successful, in my judgement, than his treatment in the subsequent chapters of the *Life of Apollonius*. See also Jones (n. 128); id., *GRBS* 21 (1980) 373–80 (prosopographical notes).

[130] Also *Lexiphanes, Pseudologista, adv. Indoctum*. See Jones, *Culture and Society in Lucian* 101–16; Hall, *Lucian's Satire* 252–73.

[131] For more detail see J. Mesk. *WS* 23 (1911) 72 ff.; Jones, *Dio* ch. 13; M. Durry's edn. of Pliny's *Panegyricus* (Paris 1938) 27 ff.

[132] See n. 98.

[133] See ch. 1 n. 22 above (esp. Bowersock, *Greek Sophists* 15–16).

he endowed chairs in rhetoric and philosophy at Athens, and Herodes Atticus was given the task of selecting the honorands (Philos. *VS* ii. 2, 566). These chairs were to be among the most prestigious cultural appointments in the empire.[134] But despite this public support for the sophists, the evidence for Marcus' attitudes is not uniform. The *Meditations* suggest that his private view of these men and their professions and pretensions may have been less favourable; diplomacy and the obligations of a monarch may sufficiently explain his involvement in the Second Sophistic. Before turning to the relevant passages in the *Meditations*, however, it is necessary to consider some of the external evidence, and to see more of the sophists themselves.

To modern eyes the sophists, lionised in their own time, often appear absurd in their pretensions, extravagant in their histrionic self-importance.[135] Unsympathetic ancients may have felt the same. There is fairly substantial evidence that Antoninus Pius at least had a more jaundiced attitude to these notables. Alexander the Platonist, who late served as Marcus' secretary (*ab epistulis Graecis*) in the 170s, arrived in Rome during Pius' reign on a mission on behalf of his native Seleucia. On this occasion, Alexander, feeling that the emperor was not listening closely enough, said 'Pay attention to me, Caesar' (an impertinently direct mode of address). Pius crossly replied: 'I *am* paying attention, and I know you well. You are the fellow who is always arranging his hair, cleaning his teeth, polishing his nails, and who always smells of perfume.' (Philos. *VS* ii. 5). Another admired teacher mentioned in the first book of the *Meditations* is the Stoic Apollonius of Chalcedon (i. 8; i. 17. 5). Again, this man had no doubts about his own importance. On arrival in Rome he is said to have demanded that Marcus be sent to his residence to be taught there, to which Pius replied: 'So it was easier for Apollonius to come from Chalcis to Rome than from his own house to the palace.' (SHA *Pius* 10. 4.) Jealous satire did not spare the pompous Apollonius: his progress to Rome, surrounded by admiring disciples, to instruct the young prince was

---

[134] Lucian, *Eunuchus* 2; Philos. *VS* ii. 2, 566–7; J. H. Oliver, *AJP* 102 (1981) 213–25 = *The Civic Tradition and Roman Athens* (Baltimore 1983) 85–96.

[135] See Hall, loc cit. (n. 130) for satire on the arrogance and preciosity of the sophists; also ibid. 268 f., on their ostentatious dress; B. Baldwin, *Studies in Lucian* (Toronto 1973) 70–2. See also Galen, *On Prognosis* 1. 2 (p. 68. 12 Nutton, with the editor's note).

compared by one observer with Jason and the Argonauts setting off in search of the Golden Fleece—that is, of extraordinary wealth (Demonax in Lucian, *Demonax* 31).

Arrogant and self-important behaviour of this kind was common among the great and wealthy sophists, and Pius seems regularly to have been unlucky in his encounters with these self-styled sages. In a notorious phrase, the great Polemo was described as conversing 'with cities as his inferiors, with emperors as not his inferiors, and with gods as his equals' (Philos. *VS* i. 25, 535). Philostratus described him in this way just after recounting an episode in which Polemo, returning home, evicted Antoninus Pius from his house, in which the future emperor, then a mere proconsul of Asia, had taken up temporary residence. Polemo would have no truck with such lesser mortals! Another story told how Pius and Herodes Atticus had come to blows over right of way on Mount Ida (Philos. *VS* ii. 1, 554–5).

The behaviour of the sophists in Marcus' reign was not significantly different. The emperor may have tolerated their excesses, but he can hardly have failed to be amused. In one of Philostratus' anecdotes this is explicit. Like Pius with Apollonius, Marcus has to send for Aristides in Smyrna if he is to hear him perform, and the sophist promises him a declamation the next day, with an additional request.

> 'Permit my students also, O Emperor, to be in the audience.'
> 'They have my permission', replied Marcus, 'for that is democratic.'
> And when Aristides added, 'Grant them leave, O Emperor, to shout and applaud as loud as they can', the Emperor smiled and retorted, 'That rests with you.' (Philos. *VS* ii. 9, 583)

On a later occasion, when Aristides delivered in Marcus' presence his Lament for Smyrna (which had been devastated by an earthquake), the emperor was moved to tears—by the rhetorician's eloquence, or by the intrinsic sadness of the subject-matter? Philostratus naturally attributes Marcus' subsequent financing of the city's reconstruction to Aristides' efforts, but admits, with cautious courtesy, that the emperor might well have done the same of his own accord (*VS* ii. 9. 582–3).

Many of the incidents in Philostratus involving Marcus

centre on the colourful figure of Herodes Atticus, wealthiest and most eminent of the sophists and Philostratus' particular favourite.[136] A complex tangle of incomplete evidence—letters between Marcus and Fronto, separate passages and allusive references in Philostratus—suggests that Marcus was at one stage friendly toward the Greek sophist, who had indeed been one of his own teachers, friendly enough to caution Fronto against excessive invective when appearing on the other side in a court case involving Herodes; that subsequently a certain coolness developed; and, most startling of all, that in the course of another hearing, in which Marcus himself as emperor was presiding, Herodes denounced and hurled abuse at his monarch and former pupil. This hysterical outburst, vividly recounted by Philostratus, was due to Herodes' deep distress at the death of his daughters, shockingly struck down by lightning; nevertheless, it says something about the self-assertiveness and emotional instability of the egotistic sophists. Philostratus describes the emperor's response to this display as

among Marcus' conspicuously philosophic actions . . . for he never frowned or changed his expression . . . but turned to the Athenians and said 'Make your defence, Athenians, even though Herodes does not give you leave.' And as he listened to the speeches in defence, he was greatly pained, though without showing it, by many things that he heard [about Herodes' tyrannical behaviour towards the Athenians]. (Philos. *VS* ii. 1, 561)

Although at a later date Herodes seems to have sought a reconciliation with the emperor, and Marcus publicly proclaimed his eagerness to resume their former friendship,[137] it is difficult, despite Philostratus' protestations, to imagine that they were ever again on easy terms.

It is striking that Herodes, like a number of other teachers of Marcus, makes no appearance in the *Meditations*. The biography

---

[136] For Philostratus' facination with Herodes see Anderson (n. 128) 82–3. On Herodes see *PIR*[2] C 802; Bowersock, *Greek Sophists* 92 ff.; Champlin, *Fronto* 63–4, 104–7; P. Graindor, *Un milliardaire antique: Hérode Atticus et sa famille* (Cairo 1930). Sophistic feuding and Herodes' quarrels: Russell and Wilson on Men. Rh. iii. 396. 28; Anderson (n. 128) 57–66. Philos. *VS* ii. 17. 598 thinks it worth mention that Rufus of Perinthus did *not* incur the enmity of any city or individual!

[137] Philos. *VS* ii. 1, 562–3; *Hesperia* Suppl. 13, Plaque E, 87–91. An inscription records Herodes' presence at some stage in Marcus' campaigns against the Sarmatians in the 170s (*IG* ii/iii[2] 3606).

of Marcus in the *Historia Augusta* (2–3) supplies a detailed list of Marcus' tutors, and seems here to be using a good source, since all those mentioned in Book I of the *Meditations* figure in the biographer's independent list. The omissions show the mature emperor's priorities:[138] all six of his mentors in philosophy appear in Book I, but of his four tutors in rhetoric only Fronto is commemorated (and not for his technical instruction, but for a moral lesson). We have seen how others might regard the pomp and ceremony of men like Apollonius and Alexander; it is characteristic of the author of the *Meditations* that his brief reminiscences purge away any hint of avarice and conceit, any eccentricities of dress and mannerism of the kind highlighted in the colourful *Lives of the Sophists*. Only the crucial, exemplary points remain.

Pius' sparring with the sophists, Marcus' amusement at Aristides' precious vanity, the turbulent affair with Herodes, the omissions in the first book of Marcus' work, are merely straws in the wind. Were this all, it would be extravagant to suggest that Marcus in any way disapproved of or disliked the activities of the sophists. More significant is the evidence of the *Meditations* themselves, the repository of Marcus' private reflections. In the tribute to Rusticus he thanks his Roman mentor for turning him away from 'poetry, oratory, and urbane writing', and for diverting him from 'sophistic emulation' (i. 7). He praises Pius twice for being 'no sophist' (i. 16, vi. 30). He thanks heaven that he 'did not fall in with any sophist, or sit down to disentangle literary works or syllogisms, or involve myself with heavenly phenomena' (τὰ μετεωρολογικὰ; i. 17. 9), and that he made no rapid progress with eloquence and poetry (i. 17. 4). In these passages we see more clearly that Marcus' primary concern is for philosophy, not for the ambitious yet ultimately vacuous literary and rhetorical products of the sophists. No mention of Fronto's archaistic crusade, or of his lofty claims for the art of rhetoric,[139] survives in the four-line reference to him in the

---

[138] Champlin, *Fronto* 18–19.

[139] On Fronto's tastes and goals see M. D. Brock, *Studies on Fronto and his Age* (Cambridge 1912); R. Marache, *La Critique littéraire de langue latine et le développement du goût archaïssant* (Rennes 1952). Marache has also provided a survey of recent work on Fronto and Gellius in *Lustrum* 10 (1965) 213–25. See further Norden, *Die Antike Kunstprosa* 344 ff.; Sherwin-White on Plin. *Ep.* i. 16. 3; P. Steinmetz, *Untersuchungen zur röm. Literatur der zweiten Jahrhunderts* (Wiesbaden 1982).

Meditations; nor does the Greek of Marcus' book conform to any of the rigorous stylistic demands of the contemporary Atticists. As a ruler and a recipient of appeals and embassies from throughout the empire he must inevitably have encountered and even requested performances from the aristocratic sophists, who often represented their cities of origin; but he was not himself a practitioner of their arts or (we may suspect) a particularly enthusiastic patron.

The sentence quoted from *Med.* i. 17. 9, dismissing not only literary composition but also syllogisms and the study of heavenly phenomena, suggests a more restricted conception of philosophy, as a purely ethical pursuit, than we find in the older Stoa or even in Seneca and Epictetus. The single-minded rigour which we find in the *Meditations* excludes all that the author sees as irrelevant to moral self-improvement. 'A man should get rid not only of actions that are unnecessary, but of imaginations also, for in this way superfluous actions too will not follow in their train' (iv. 24); 'Make use of these rules, then, and do not be troubled about anything besides' (x. 2); 'Therefore throw all else aside, and hold fast only to these few things' (iii. 10); 'No longer spend time discussing what a good man is, but *be* one' (x. 16).[140] Throughout the work he writes of cutting away superfluities, of rejecting extraneous desires and distractions, of exorcising trivial speculations and unanswerable questions.

The intensity and single-mindedness—one might almost say the obsessiveness—of the *Meditations* may be contrasted with the diversity and polymathy of much contemporary literature, just as the clipped brevity of Marcus' sentences stands at the opposite extreme from the immense length and quantity of writings by Dio and Aristides, Plutarch and Galen. Since at least the age of Pliny the literary and intellectual climate of the Graeco-Roman world had been spectacularly polymath. Pliny's own versatility in many genres is well documented in his letters (especially iv. 14, ix. 10), in which he also describes the practice of others (e.g. i. 16, ix. 22).[141] A still more striking example is the

---

[140] Cf. e.g. Sen. *Ep.* 24. 19, 75. 4, 108. 36, and Stuckelberger on 88. 42; also, closer to Marcus' thought, Epict. *Ench.* 46. For a startling parallel from another king and thinker see J. D. Spence, *Emperor of China: Self-Portrait of K'ang Hsi* (London 1974; Penguin edn. 1977) 40.

[141] On Pliny's recitations see Sherwin-White on *Ep.* i. 13. 3–4. For Pliny's optimsm about the literature of the age see *Ep.* iv. 27, v. 17, vi. 11, 15, 21, ix. 2; also iv. 25 (!). A

self-satisfied Apuleius, who, in a passage from one of his declamations, which can be seen as a classic document of the sophistic age, writes on his own brilliant career as follows:

The first cup [of the Muses], from the schoolmaster, relieves the spirit; the second, from the grammarian, forms learning; the third, from the rhetorician, arms one with eloquence. Up to this point many have drunk. But I have drunk from other goblets at Athens: the inventive cup of poetry, the limpid one of geometry, the sweet one of music, the austere one of dialectic, and above all the cup of universal philosophy—inexhaustible and nectareous. Empedocles composes poems; Plato, dialogues; Socrates, hymns; Epicharmus, mimes; Xenophon, histories; Crates, satires; your Apuleius embraces all these genres and cultivates the nine Muses with equal zeal. (*Florida* 20, tr. J. Tatum)[142]

In the world of the Greek sophistic Dio and Aristides, Maximus and even Plutarch may be less forthright in their claims, less flamboyant in their style, but the background of their studies and their literary presuppositions is the same as that of Apuleius.

The polymathy of the age makes itself apparent also in the blurred borderlines between professions: not only the difficulty of distinguishing between rhetors, sophists, and philosophers (as in the cases of Dio and Favorinus),[143] but also the association of philosophy and magic (Apuleius again provides lively evidence),[144] or of philosophy and medicine, reflected in the portmanteau titles ἰατροσοφιστής (doctor-sophist) and ἰατροφιλόσοφος (doctor-philosopher). Marcus' own physician, Galen, is a conspicuous example, author not only of an essay arguing that 'the best doctor is also a philosopher', but also of commentaries on philosophic writers and studies of verbal expression and philology.[145] Sophists had been a byword for Protean versatility

---

more qualified and defensive view appears in Tacitus' *Dialogus* (cf. *Ann.* iv. 32, xvi. 16; Juv. 7), as also in Quintilian (x. 1. 122; contrast ii. 5. 23 f.; M. Winterbottom, *JRS* 54 (1964) 90–7, at 96). Further, see Champlin, *Fronto* 53; Syme, *Tacitus* 86 ff.

[142] J. Tatum, *Apuleius and the Golden Ass* (Ithaca and London 1979) 125. Cf. *Fl.* 5, 13; *Apol.* 10. Note also, particularly revealing for the literary climate, the preface to Athenaeus' *Deipnosophistae* (e.g. 1d on philosophers πολυμαθείᾳ πάντας ὑπερηκοντικότες). Further, see Champlin, *Fronto* ch. 4; A. Cameron, *HSCP* 84 (1980) 127–75, esp. 164–5; Champlin, *HSCP* 85 (1981) 189–212.

[143] Anderson, *Philostratus* 99–104.

[144] Cf. MacMullen, *Enemies of the Roman Order* 320 n. 16, 322 n. 20; also ch. v. 2 below.

[145] See Bowersock, *Greek Sophists* 66–9; V. Nutton, *Galen on Prognosis* (*CMG* v. 8. 1, Berlin 1979). Nutton remarks on p. 59: 'Aelius Aristides' Hieroi logoi show a sophist's knowledge of medicine: "On prognosis" shows a doctor's knowledge of sophistry.'

in the fifth century BC (Pl. *Hipp. Min.* 368), and the tradition continued.[146] Serapion, one of Plutarch's addresses, combined the professions of Stoic philosopher, orator-sophist, physician, and epic poet! Bibliophilia and learned compilation also flourished, as we see in the erudite pages of Aulus Gellius and Athenaeus. Needless to say, multiple pursuits of this kind need not have led to superficiality in all cases, but it is plain that in some instances profound but pointless learning was combined with a trivial or undemanding attitude to more serious moral, philosophical, and religious questions. Encyclopaedic erudition, scholarly polemic, ostentatious feats of memory, and abstruse system-building—all are equally alien to the thought-world of the *Meditations*.

We might endorse and sympathise with Marcus' determination to focus on the single task of making ethical progress, by and for himself, without necessarily approving his exclusively ethical conception of philosophy. Certainly the early Stoics might have accepted that ethics was primary, but they would also have insisted that ethics was founded in physics, and that the triad ethics–physics–logic was indissoluble. A famous series of images to describe this relationship goes back to the Stoic fathers:

they [Zeno, Chrysippus, and others] compare philosophy to a living being, likening logic to bones and sinews, ethics to the fleshier parts, and physics to the soul. They make a further comparison to an egg: logic is the outside, ethics what comes next, and physics the innermost parts; or to a fertile field: the surrounding wall corresponds to logic, its fruit to ethics, and its land or trees to physics. (Diog. Laert. vii. 40)

Whatever the order, the three are inseparable.[147] Marcus' rejection not only of indiscriminate erudition but also of logic ('syllogisms') means that he is opting for a diluted and unsupported set of axioms, familiar and comforting but deprived of their intellectual roots.

But Marcus, as we have seen, was not trying to produce a textbook or a fresh approach to any major philosophic issues; his purpose is more personal and more limited, his pretensions humbler. We may fittingly end this chapter with one more

---

[146] See also Pl. *Euthyd.* 297c and *Soph.* 240 (hydra); *Euthyd.* 288b (Proteus); 299c (Briareos).

[147] See A. A. Long and D. N. Sedley, *The Hellenistic Philosophers* i (Cambridge 1987) 158–62.

anecdote from Philostratus' compendium of gossip and praise, a
story which presents the ageing emperor as still a student:

> Here is another admirable saying of this Lucius [a philosopher,
> pupil of Musonius and friend of Herodes]. The Emperor Marcus was
> greatly interested in Sextus the Boeotian philosopher [the same man as
> is thanked in *Med.* i. 9]. Lucius had just arrived in Rome and asked the
> emperor, whom he met going out, where he was going and for what
> purpose. Marcus answered: 'It is a good thing even for one who is
> growing old to acquire knowledge. I am going to Sextus the
> philosopher to learn what I do not yet know.' At this Lucius raised his
> hands to heaven and exclaimed: 'O Zeus! The Emperor of the Romans
> is already growing old, but he hangs a tablet round his neck and goes to
> school, while my emperor Alexander died at thirty-two!' What I have
> quoted is enough to show the kind of philosophy cultivated by Lucius,
> for these speeches suffice to reveal the man as a sip reveals the bouquet
> of wine. (*VS* ii. 1, 557)

As usual, Philostratus appreciates the *bon mot*, the snappy put-
down line; in this story Lucius is the star and Marcus Aurelius
the straight man.[148] But the humour is of a fairly crude variety,
and on reflection we may be inclined to value the humility of the
emperor (and the toleration which made such outspokenness
possible) more highly than the impertinent mockery of the
Greek wit.[149] Lucius speaks of the emperor as old; the date of the
anecdote and the spirit of Marcus' response thus suit the period
of his life when the *Meditations*, equally lacking in self-satisfac-
tion or hauteur, were being composed.

---

[148] Anderson, *Philostratus* 47–8.
[149] For toleration of freedom of speech and criticism under Marcus see SHA *Marcus*
8. 1; cf. *Med.* i. 6, i. 16. 1, vi. 21, vi. 30. 1 on παρρησία.

III

The First Book:
An Ethical Self-Portrait

what we must look for here is, 1st, religious and moral
principles; 2ndly, gentlemanly conduct; 3rdly, intellectual
ability.

(Thomas Arnold, 1795–1842)

THE last chapter outlined the background, in literature and in
life, which helps to explain the first book of the *Meditations*. The
present chapter examines the book itself, its form and subject-
matter, the philosophic ideas which give coherence to its
apparent disorder, and the indications it gives of its author's
character and preoccupations. The book is not straightfor-
wardly autobiographical; but it is a commonplace that we may
learn something about a man from the qualities he praises in his
friends. In the last section of this chapter I offer a broader
comparison between Book I and the rest of the collection, and
comment on the selectivity of the subject-matter of the work as a
whole. These limitations are in part deliberate, in part the
consequence of Marcus' position, time of life, and general
outlook. Comparison with the Fronto correspondence, and with
other evidence concerning the emperor's earlier years, provides
many poignant contrasts.

1. *Formal Aspects*

The seventeen chapters of Book I are themselves far from
homogeneous. The seventeenth in particular, although brought
into formal alignment[1] with the rest by the opening παρὰ τῶν
θεῶν, is distinctive in that it does not describe any particular
lessons which the gods have taught Marcus, but rather names
the aspects of his life for which he feels he ought to thank them
most fervently. These are past facts and events, whereas

[1] See in general F. Martinazzoli, *La 'Successio' di Marco Aurelio: Struttura e spirito del
primo libro dei Pensieri* (Bari 1951) esp. ch. 7.

elsewhere in the book the emperor is referring less to his experiences than to the moral lessons inculcated by his tutors. Contrast, for instance, i. 1 παρὰ τοῦ πάππου Οὐήρου τὸ καλόηθες καὶ ἀόργητον ('From my father Verus, honourable character and evenness of temper') with a passage from i. 17 like the following: 'From the gods . . . that my body has held out so well in a life like mine; that I did not touch Benedicta or Theodotus . . .'. Chapter 17 has indeed something in common with philosophic essays on the objects for which we should pray to, or thank, the gods.[2]

In general we can see a change as we read through Book I, as the chapters become more expansive and longer, in a roughly chronological sequence (grandfather, father, mother, mother's grandfather, early tutors, and so forth[3]). This is in part understandable in view of the fragmentary memories which are all most adults retain from their earliest years. But the selection of qualities is too precise to be fully explained thus. As the book progresses, not only do the qualities which are recorded increase in number, but they also become more varied, and more concrete. Experience and recollection of individual occasions creep in, somewhat unnaturally and ungrammatically expressed in the same syntactical form as was used at first with neuter abstracts. Thus καὶ τὸ φερέπονον καὶ ὀλιγοδεὲς (i. 5) is perfectly good Greek, and indeed the expression of mental attributes by neuter nouns rather than the classical feminine abstracts is characteristic of the period. But τὸ μὴ ὀρτυγοκοπεῖν

---

[2] On this topic see *Med.* ix. 40 (discussed in ch. v. 6 below). How, and for what, a man should pray is a topic of ethical discussion: Democr. B 234; Pl. *Lg.* iii. 687c–8b, vii. 801ab; *Alc.* 2; Hor. *Odes* i. 31; *Ep.* i. 18. 106; Pers. 2; Petron. 88; Juv. 10; Arnold, *Roman Stoicism* 233 ff. See also Epict. ii. 16. 42 (cf. M. Aur. iv. 23, viii. 45, x. 14); *Ench.* 8.

[3] In SHA *Marcus* 2. 2 ff. we have an independent and overlapping list which adds some further names (of which one, Caninius Celer, may perhaps be identified with the man named Celer in *Med.* viii. 25; cf. also Philos. *VS* i. 22, p. 524; SHA *Verus* 2. 5). On this passage of the *vita* see E. Birley, *Hist. Augusta Colloquium, Bonn, 1965* (1966) 36–7; A. R. Birley, *HA Colloq. 1966–7* (1968) 39–42. The former doubts the authenticity of some of the names, 'with undue warrant', according to R. Syme, *Ammianus and the* Historia Augusta (Oxford 1968) 170. On the *vita Marci* see above all J. Schwendemann, *Der historische Wert der* vita Marci *bei den SHA* (Heidelberg 1923); also K. B. Pflaum, *HA Colloq. 1968–9* (1970) 199–232 (201 ff. on this passage). Certainly this passage, even if erroneous in points of chronology, does not conflict with the evidence of the *Meditations* and seems to retain substantial truth. Why, then, are certain names not included in Marcus' first book? Were the lessons they taught so trivial, had he failed to learn from them, or had they failed as teachers and examples? The omission of Herodes Atticus (SHA *Marcus* 2. 4; see ch. II p. 85) is particularly intriguing.

μηδὲ περὶ τὰ τοιαῦτα ἐπτοῆσθαι (i. 6) is distinctly odder and more
laboured; while καὶ τὸ ἀεὶ ὅμοιον, ἐν ἀλγηδόσιν ὀξείαις κτλ. (i. 8) is
simply an unnatural and very elliptical way of describing any
kind of debt or lesson. Some other examples are equally bizarre,
and one sometimes has to read for several lines before finding the
infinitive which accompanies the definite article (e.g. i. 7. 3, p. 6.
6–8 Farquharson: τὸ . . . διακεῖσθαι).

This grammatical peculiarity, combined with the fact that
most of the chapters commence with a simple item such as
wholly composed the first few (e.g. i. 6 παρὰ Διογνήτου τὸ
ἀκενόσπουδον; i. 8 παρὰ Ἀπολλωνίου τὸ ἐλεύθερον καὶ ἀναμφι-
βόλως ἀκύβευτον . . .; i. 9 παρὰ Σέξτου τὸ εὐμενές), suggests that
Marcus may have intended to make them all parallel and all
very brief, but found himself drawn to develop his clipped
acknowledgements into more extensive statements. These allow
us to glimpse, albeit partially, certain aspects not only of the
character of his mentors, but also of his own development. By
chapters 14–15 the particular detail is considerable, but the lists
of abstract qualities still form the basis of each chapter. In
chapter 16 this is almost completely transformed, and each
point is elaborated, made more concrete and particular.
Chapter 17 is the fullest and frankest about Marcus himself, and
also the freest of this formal structure. The style has become
more fluent, the sentences more flexible and more consciously
balanced. (This increase of freedom and of stylistic self-
consciousness may well have been paralleled in the original
development of the *Meditations* as a whole.)

Hence the ambiguous status of this book. Various key points
in Marcus' development are isolated but not placed in any
context, and hardly described in any detail (see esp. i. 3–4, 6–7,
11, 14. 1, 17. 3). For instance, although what Marcus describes
as his debt to Rusticus in i. 7 recalls the pattern of 'conversion' to
philosophy,[4] we remain a world away from the lushness of
Lucian's *Nigrinus* or the intimate self-revelation of Augustine's
Confessions, a fascinating contrast with Marcus' work in many
ways.[5] In the *Meditations* there is a sense of reserve and restraint,

[4] See ch. II n. 33 above, and n. 35 below.
[5] For a very brief preliminary σύγκρισις see C. H. Cochrane, *Christianity and Classical Culture* (Oxford 1940) 386. Further, see G. Misch, *History of Autobiography in Antiquity* (Eng. tr. London 1950) 404 ff., 574 ff., 626 ff.

which goes beyond the Stoic principles of brevity and severity of style. Readers often raise their eyebrows at the intimacies of i. 17. 2 and 7 (on his sexual experiences; quoted below, p. 118 f.). But equally striking is the allusiveness of Marcus' references to himself and his life: no continuous narration of any episode, no clear location of events in place or time, no account of experiences we might assume were influential or painful—the loss of his real father, for example, or of children (a topic presented more abstractly in the chapter on Apollonius, whose loss is there in question, i. 8. 1).[6] Perhaps Marcus in fact found it difficult or embarrassing, even in his private writing, to commit his feelings and memories to paper with complete openness or at length. He may even have thought it somehow demeaning or undignified for a professed Stoic to spend long dwelling on the past or on individuals, rather than in contemplating the task before him at that moment, or the larger horizon of the divine order.

Marcus is also understandably reluctant to compare himself with his teachers. He counts himself still a μαθητής of Antoninus also (vi. 30). Educational theory often held that a father is the best teacher (compare Cato the Elder and his son in Plutarch's life; or Plin. *Ep.* viii. 13; 14. 4 ff.). He declines to say what he himself has achieved or has to offer. It is noteworthy too how many of the statements about himself in Book I are negative statements, of faults he has managed to avoid without necessarily doing the positive thing (esp. i. 17. 1–2, 5), or even statements of his continuing inadequacy (i. 17. 6 ἀπολείπεσθαι δέ τι ἔτι τούτου παρὰ τὴν ἐμὴν αἰτίαν: 'that I still fall short of this through my own defects'). The form of expression in Book I generally

---

[6] Stoic teaching on the subject of personal loss was sternly demanding, to modern eyes almost brutal: see above ch. 1 p. 38; Epict. iii. 24. 88–9; *Ench.* 3, 11, 26; M. Aur. xi. 34 (cf. viii. 49, ix. 40, x. 35). SHA *Marcus* 21. 3 f. tells us that Marcus did not mourn his son for more than four days; it is difficult to say whether this has any foundation or is merely part of the 'idealised' Stoic austerity which the author regularly attributes to him (see below, ch. IV n. 130). Stoic influence is probably to be seen in the harsher forms of consolation mentioned and deprecated by the gentle Pliny: *Ep.* v. 16. 10 'memento adhibere solacium non quasi castigatorium et nimis forte, sed molle et humanum'; see Sherwin-White's note, and also Sen. *Polyb.* 18. 5; *Marc.* 4. 1 (C. G. Grollios' edn. (Athens 1956) 73–7). In Lucian, *Demonax* 24, the sage derides the extravagant grief of Herodes Atticus for his son. Finally, note the powerful protest against the false comforts of philosophy by Fronto, on the death of his grandson (ii. 222–8). In later literature see e.g. Shakespeare, *Much Ado* v. 1. 1–37; Johnson, *Rasselas* (1759) ch. xviii.

leaves it ambiguous whether Marcus learned the lesson or not,[7] except where the use of παρά is extended to mean 'under the teaching/influence of' (e.g. i. 6 καὶ τὸ γράψαι διαλόγους). More than self-depreciation, this is an indication of Marcus' honesty, and indeed of his pessimism; it should be related to other evidence throughout the *Meditations* for his negative attitude to life (see section 5 below).

In vi. 48 Marcus recommends the contemplation of the merits of one's συμβιούντες as a source of pleasure (ὅταν εὐφρᾶναι σεαυτὸν θέλῃς . . . οὐδὲν γὰρ οὕτως εὐφραίνει). Yet the aim of Book I is surely, like that of the rest of the work, primarily a didactic one;[8] that is, by the recollection of these men and their virtues Marcus continues to instruct himself in those same virtues. They are *exempla*, models for his moral improvement. But at the same time there is obviously a great deal of affectionate attention lavished on these portraits, which however brief are in the main strongly individualised. This mixture of motives helps explain the way that the more restricted lists of moral qualities tend to expand into longer character sketches with more incidental detail. Thus in i. 5 a sudden rash of proper names accompanies the vivid specifics of a lesson about the triviality of popular enthusiasm for racing and gladiatorial games. Other names besides the main figures of the book make an appearance here and more elliptically in chapter 13. Chapters 10 and 12 seem to capture a scene, an occasion, rather than a gradual lesson derived from a man's general bearing and character. We can sense the strong impression which the reproofs or disapproval of the two Alexanders made upon Marcus. In the chapter concerning Fronto (i. 11) we do not, of course, need to depend upon our intuition for the origin of Marcus' reminiscence, since the passages in which Fronto made his observation about the deficiencies of the Latin language and of Roman patricians in φιλοστοργία are actually extant (Fronto i. 280, ii. 154).

This close correspondence brings home the undeniable fact that some at least of these recollections are real and concrete, referring to specific occasions (cf. i. 16. 8, i. 17. 9). This applies to

---

[7] Martinazzoli (n. 1) 81–9.

[8] Pleasure and instruction are a traditional antithesis in ancient (and modern) analysis of the purpose of a work of art: see e.g. Ar. *Ran.* 1413; Thuc. i. 22. 4 (ἀτερπέστερον . . . ὠφέλιμα); Pl. *Rep.* x. 607d; Hor. *Ars* 334 ff.; G. Avenarius, *Lukians Schrift zu Geschichtschreibung* (Meisenheim-am-Glan 1956) 22 ff.

several points in the chapter on Rusticus. Marcus remembers a letter that Rusticus wrote from Sinuessa to Marcus' mother, and acknowledges the loan of Rusticus' own copy of some works by Epictetus. Similarly, he seems to be recalling lessons from Severus on the role of the Stoic opposition in recent Roman history (i. 14, discussed in the last chapter). Yet these incidents and anecdotes rub shoulders with philosophic technicalities,[9] Peripatetic and Stoic, words which are clearly drawn from regular and serious reading. Often they are rare words, occasionally they seem to have been coined by Marcus himself.[10] The personal and the abstract are constantly alternating, above all in the long chapter on Pius. The abstract truths and qualities are contained in the personal experience.

The process of self-instruction consists for Marcus in distilling these truths from his memories of individual men and specific events. Analogous is the way that Seneca in his letters frequently draws a moral lesson from a recent (perhaps often fictional) event, moving swiftly from the particular to the general.[11] Comparable in a different way is the strongly didactic use which ancient philosophers made of literary works and of individual episodes in epic or tragedy: thus Horace, for example, treats mythical figures as moral paradigms in *Ep.* i. 2. 1 ff., i. 16. 73–9. This is frequent also in Epictetus.[12]

In the first book, then, we find neither a list of abstract virtues to which the *proficiens* should aspire nor a series of life histories or irrelevant descriptions of the people named. Their physical appearance, for example, is almost never alluded to.[13] Much

[9] E.g. i. 12, the contrast between the initial phrases and the more technical τὰ κατὰ τὰς πρὸς τοὺς συμβιοῦντας σχέσεις καθήκοντα.

[10] For ἅπαξ λεγόμενα see Schekira 264–5 (cf. 263–4 for words *first* found in Marcus); Haines, Loeb edn., pp. 411 f.

[11] See e.g. *Ep.* 12. 1 ff.; further, D. A. Russell, in C. D. N. Costa (ed.), *Seneca* (London 1974) 76 ff.; Griffin, *Seneca* (Oxford 1976) 2–5.

[12] Cf. P. de Lacy, *AJP* 69 (1948) 264 n. 140.

[13] Exceptions perhaps in i. 8 (ἰδεῖν ἐναργῶς κτλ.), i. 15. Notice also i. 16. 5 (on Pius) καὶ τὸ τοῦ ἰδίου σώματος ἐπιμελητικὸν ἐμμέτρως οὔτε ... πρὸς καλλωπισμὸν οὔτε μὴν ὀλιγώρως κτλ. (Note that even here it is a negative point that is being made; Pius was *not* fussy or negligent about his appearance.) For Marcus' insistence on moral openness and self-revelation see esp. xi. 15; on this topic see Brunt, *JRS* 64 (1974) 8–10. There are possble analogies between xi. 15 and the scholarly-ethical study of physiognomics, which strongly influenced imperial biography: see esp. E. C. Evans, *HSCP* 46 (1935) 43–84 (citing xi. 15 and also vii. 37, 60); Nisbet–Hubbard on Hor. *Odes* ii. 4. 21 (esp. for other articles by Evans); Wallace-Hadrill, *Suetonius* 67 ff., 176; P. Cox, *Biography in Late Antiquity* (Berkeley and Los Angeles 1983) 14–15.

more important than this is the impression which the man conveys to others, his exemplary influence (e.g. i. 16. 2 καὶ τὸ φαιδρόν, 'and his good humour'; i. 16. 4; i. 16. 5 ἔτι δὲ τὸ εὐόμιλον καὶ εὔχαρι οὐ κατακόρως, 'and furthermore, affability and humorousness, but not taken to excess'). We may contrast the topics of imperial panegyric, in which it is emphasised that the man honoured looks the part of a ruler;[14] often, indeed, he is likened to a god.[15]

This book is an attractive and sympathetic piece of writing to most readers because it does have this quality of honest reflection on people the author loves and admires. This is something which everyone experiences but which few find easy to articulate. The way in which we learn the nature of moral goodness is not by a method of definition; rather, we come to know and understand admirable virtues through admiring the virtuous. Yet there is a danger that the reality of a moral quality may vanish if we abstract it from its context, separating the virtue from both action and actor. This seems to be the difficulty with which Marcus is coping—with considerable originality and success—in this book. There must be due weight given to the ἐμφαινόμενα τοῖς ἤθεσι τῶν συζώντων as well as to the actual ἀρεταί of which they are ὁμοιώματα (vi. 48).

2. Lessons in Virtue

The first book is far from being an autobiography, even of a specialised, spiritual kind. But the reader naturally seeks to know more of the author, and certain parts of the book do provide revealing, although often oblique, insights. Yet there is no narrative; no telling anecdote or significant occasion is actually retold at length. As with the passage on Fronto, we can observe that the original phrase, conversation, or event, stripped of its context, has been made more abstract, generalised as an ethical lesson.

These lessons and examples can often seem incongruous or trivial, as with i. 6: 'not to be a quail-fancier[16] or get excited

[14] See Woodman on Vell. ii. 94. 2, 107. 2.

[15] See Woodman on Vell. ii. 130. 5 (esp. Cic. Marc. 8; Plin. Pan. 1. 3, 7. 5).

[16] 'Cock-fighting' in Farquharson's translation and notes is a slip. For the sport see Pollux ix. 107; D'Arcy W. Thompson, Glossary of Greek Birds (London and Oxford 1936) 124 f.

about such pastimes'. But one thing which is clear about the whole of Book I is that Marcus is throughout viewing experience within the framework of ethical principle. Ancient moralists, in this respect more wide-ranging than most moderns, included in their scrutiny everyday actions and behaviour;[17] their discussions were often concerned with aspects of social tact and courtesy, with the etiquette of commonplace pursuits as well as with loftier issues such as civic duty, conflicts of justice and expediency, or the status of moral absolutes. Thus we find Plutarch writing essays on inoffensive ways of praising oneself, on the proper way to behave at lectures, and on garrulousness. Epictetus too is ready to discuss not only 'wherein consists the essence of Good' (ii. 8 tit.), but also such diverse topics as adultery (ii. 4), fine dress (iii. 1), ascetic exercise (iii. 12), solitude (iii. 13), and cleanliness (iv. 11). Above all his *Encheiridion*, especially ch. 33, a series of injunctions with several parallels in Marcus' book, shows how wide a range of human activities could be considered to fall within the sphere of philosophic prescription, often in terms of τὸ πρέπον (*decorum*).[18]

With this in mind, we can detect many passages in the first book which reflect the topics of ethical textbooks and discussions. These are not, of course, antithetical to 'real life'; Marcus will have been influenced by both his reading and his association with his tutors as friends, as well as by common human experience. But the point is worth stressing that in his own writing he chose to express his debts in recognisably philosophic terms; that he found this a familiar, appropriate, and realistic way of thinking.

Some examples will illustrate this point. In i. 4 Marcus thanks his mother's grandfather for his education at home, with good teachers, rather than at public school; and is grateful 'to have learned that on things like these it is one's duty to spend liberally (ἐκτενῶς)'. This reflects an increased concern for education in

[17] Besides the examples mentioned in the text, see above all Cicero's *de Officiis*, drawing on Panaetius' περὶ καθηκόντων (see H. A. Holden's comm.; P. A. Brunt, *PCPhS* NS 19 (1973) 26-7, etc.). A striking instance is Epict. fr. 15 Schenkl: . . . ἐπεί τοι φιλοσοφία φησίν ὅτι οὐδὲ τὸν δάκτυλον ἐκτείνειν εἰκῇ προσήκει (cf. Epict. ii. 11. 17, iv. 12. 7; contrast Diog. Laert. vii. 104). See also Cic. *Paradoxa* 26.

[18] See Cic. *Off.* i. 93 ff., and esp. 126 ff., 146. Cf. Hor. *Ep.* i. 1. 11, where the poet proposes to enquire 'quid verum atque *decens*'. Cf. M. Pohlenz, *NGG* (1933) 53-92 = *Kleine Schriften* (Hildesheim 1965) i. 100-39; McGann, *Studies in Horace's First Book of Epistles* 10 ff.; Macleod, *Collected Essays* 282 ff.

the Flavian and Antonine period;[19] the preference that Marcus expresses here is also felt by Quintilian (i. 2), and parental reluctance to spend on education is criticised by the satirist Juvenal (7. 187, 217 ff.). Pseudo-Plutarch, in the (Stoic) work *de Liberis Educandis*, ch. 7, insists on the need for trustworthy and upright teachers; Pliny's diligent efforts to obtain a suitable man for Comum may be compared (*Ep.* iv. 13). More broadly, the discussion of liberality (ἐλευθεριότης) is not neglected by the philosophers; examples are Arist. *NE* 1119b 22 f., and Cic. *Off.* ii. 52–87.[20]

Again, when Marcus says how pleased he is 'not to have become a partisan of the Greens or the Blues in the races, or of Thracian or Samnite gladiators' (i. 5), this is a legacy of Pius (see i. 16. 8), and it is also personal preference, as we know from external evidence in Fronto (i. 206);[21] but it is also an approved philosophic attitude. Both topics are barred from sensible men's conversation by Epict. *Ench.* 33. 2: 'We may, however, enter, though sparingly, into discourse when occasion calls for it, but not on any of the common subjects, such as gladiators or horse-races or athletic champions or feasts.'[22] This may seem priggish, but it is one of the recurrent themes of the book, which constantly refers to the purging away of trivial enthusiasms, leaving one free to concentrate on what truly matters. This practice is pursued throughout the pages of the *Meditations*.[23] In the same spirit Marcus repeatedly criticises and rejects the

---

[19] See Colson's notes on Quint. i. 2. For general concern with the moral character of tutors in this period see S. F. Bonner, *Education in Ancient Rome* (London 1977) 104–10; Sherwin-White on Plin. *Ep.* iii. 3. 3; Mayor on Juv. 7. 187, 217 ff., 239, 10. 244. Herodian (i. 2. 1) mentions considerable outlay by Marcus on official tutors for his son Commodus.

[20] Further, ps.-Plato, *Def.* 412d; *SVF* iii. 273; Kindstrand on Bion fr. 38.

[21] In general on the games see esp. Mayor on Juv. 10. 80–1, 11. 193–202; L. Friedlaender, *Sittengeschichte Roms* ii (2nd edn., Leipzig 1919) 151–468; also A. Cameron, *Circus Factions* (Oxford 1976). For the importance of the emperor's attendance at the games (and his displaying enthusiasm!), see Wallace-Hadrill, *Suetonius* 124 ff., 164. Marcus was said to read his correspondence during the games (SHA *Marcus* 5. 1)—the error of Caesar: cf. Suet. *Aug.* 45. 1–2. Fronto i. 206, cited in text, rebukes Marcus for his stand-offishness: 'vel quom in theatro tu libros vel in convivio lectitabas . . . tum igitur ego te durum et intempestivom hominem, odiosum etiam nonnumquam ira percitus appellabam'. Further, n. 84 below.

[22] Cf. and contrast Hor. *Sat.* ii. 6. 44; also Apul. *Ap.* 98. Further on the races, Wallace-Hadrill, *Suetonius* 180. Marcus' co-emperor Verus, by contrast, was a devotee of the 'Greens': SHA *Verus* 6; Cameron (n. 21) 54.

[23] See above, ch. II pp. 86–8.

luxury and high living to which his lofty rank gave him access; and what external evidence we have suggests that he carried this principle into practice.

Another recurrent topic in Book I is friendship, again a theme much treated by ancient philosophers. Cicero, himself the author of a *de Amicitia*, refers to the abundant literature on the subject (*Fam.* iii. 7. 5, 8. 5); Seneca has a thought-provoking and in parts paradoxical discussion of whether the *sapiens* would need or desire friends (*Ep.* 9).[24] Book I of Marcus' work has many references to matters of tact, restraint, generosity, gratitude, and other social virtues;—*humanitas*, in a word. Sextus exemplified for him 'solicitous consideration for friends' (i. 9); he possessed τὸ πρὸς πάντας εὐάρμοστον ('the capacity for harmony towards all men', an attribute of the *sapiens* according to Chrysippus, *SVF* iii. 630), 'so that not only was his conversation more agreeable than any flattery, but he excited the highest reverence in those with him'. From Catulus one lesson was 'not to neglect a friend's remonstrance, even if he may be unreasonable' (i. 13). From Severus, 'to believe in the affection of friends and to use no concealment . . . his friends had no need to guess at his wishes or the reverse, but he was open with them' (i. 14). The references to flattery naturally recall moralistic discussions such as Plutarch's *How to Tell a Flatterer from a Friend*;[25] but there is also obvious personal relevance to Marcus. These passages illuminate the stress he lays elsewhere in the work on openness and honesty as opposed to secrecy and hypocrisy: for the latter are qualities often associated with the tyrant (cf. i. 11: Fronto taught him the worthlessness of ἡ τυραννικὴ βασκανία καὶ ποικιλία καὶ ὑπόκρισις, 'tyrannical envy and subtlety and two-facedness').[26] The openness he admired in Severus may thus be contrasted with the *dissimulatio* of Tiberius or Domitian. Pius too is praised for checking all kinds of flattery, including organised

[24] See further Pl. *Lysis*; Arist. *NE* viii–ix; F. A. Steinmetz, *Die Freundschaftslehre des Panaitios* (Wiesbaden 1967); *RLAC* viii. 418 ff.; P. A. Brunt, *PCPhS* NS 1 (1965) 1–8 = R. Seager (ed.), *The Crisis of the Roman Republic* (Cambridge 1969) 199–206.
[25] See also Theophr. *Char.* 2; Hor. *Ars* 419–52 with Brink's notes; Max. Tyr. *Or.* xiv; Kindstrand on Bion fr. 51; van der Horst on ps.-Phocyl. 91.
[26] See above, ch. II n. 56 for the use of τύραννος in Marcus' work. For the association of secrecy and lies with the tyrant or monarch, see Brunt, *JRS* 64 (1974) 8–10, esp. 9 n. 51 (Tiberius' *dissimulatio*, Domitian, etc.). Marcus declares that he has learned truthfulness from Fronto (*ap.* Front. i. 16). Note also the stress on openness with friends in *Med.* i. 14–15.

applause (ἐπιβόησεις),²⁷ and for having few secrets (i. 16. 3 and 7).

The reference in i. 8 to receiving favours from friends, 'neither lowering oneself on their account, nor returning them insensitively', also has ample background in ethics, notably in Seneca's *de Beneficiis* (e.g. ii. 24–5).²⁸ The reciprocal process of giving favours was of still more concern to a monarch and patron: Marcus praises Pius for desiring to award to every man impartially, according to his desert (i. 16. 1), a conventionally unexceptionable aim. But he strikes a more original note when thanking the gods 'that I made haste to advance my masters to the honours they appeared to desire, and did not put them off with hopes that, as they were still young, I would do it later on' (i. 17. 5). There is a tarter note here as the author implicitly criticises the value placed on these promotions by the recipients; but one also detects an awareness that the power to bestow honours and rewards can be used capriciously, and that it was possible that he might do so. It is again noteworthy that he thanks the gods for these and other experiences: he does not claim credit for them.

These examples sufficiently show that although the subject-matter of Book I includes many traditional topics,²⁹ this is very far from excluding a personal application; rather, the philosophic concepts provide a natural framework for Marcus' thought. They also enable him to view his own experience from a more detached and reflective viewpoint. When we take account of Marcus' obvious reticence even in his private journal,

²⁷ On which see R. MacMullen, *Art Bulletin* 46 (1964) 437 f.; S. Weinstock, *Divus Julius* (Oxford 1971) 107 ff.; for later developments, S. MacCormack, *Art and Ceremony in Late Antiquity* (Berkeley and Los Angeles 1981).

²⁸ See ch. II n. 13 above.

²⁹ A few further examples may be confined to a note. (1) i. 5 (τὸ αὐτουργικόν) may be compared with the Roman idealisation of ruler-farmers (Cincinnatus, etc.), and also with philosophic endorsement of that way of life (Hor. *Sat.* ii. 2; Nisbet–Hubbard on *Odes* ii. 16. 13; Musonius fr. 11 with van Geytenbeek, *Musonius Rufus* 129–34). (2) i. 5 τὸ δυσπρόσδεκτον διαβολῆς may be compared with vi. 30. 3 (on Pius) and with Lucian, *de Calumnia*. (3) i. 6 τὸ ἀνέχεσθαι παρρησίας can be illustrated from the theory of friendship by Cic. *de Amic.* 88 f. or Hor. *Ars* 438 ff. (further, Macleod, *Collected Essays* 278; Kindstrand on Bion fr. 53), and in political terms by i. 14, vi. 30. 4; cf. MacMullen, *Enemies of the Roman Order* 309; Wirszubski, *Libertas* 124 ff.; G. Scarpat, *Parrhesia* (Brescia 1964). (4) For i. 13 τὸ περὶ τὰ τέκνα ἀληθινῶς ἀγαπητικόν (and i. 11, Fronto's remark about Roman patricians) cf. Plutarch's essays περὶ φιλοστοργίας and περὶ φιλαδελφίας (on the latter see H. D. Betz in *Plutarch's Ethical Writings* Betz 231–63, esp. 231–4). There are many such correspondences.

we can plausibly see significance in brief and apparently casual references.

It is significant, for instance, that Marcus says in the chapter on Rusticus: '[I learned] to be easily recalled to myself and easily reconciled with those who provoke or offend,[30] as soon as they are willing to meet me' (i. 7), since he also says elsewhere: '. . . that although I was often angry with Rusticus I never went to extremes for which I should have been sorry' (i. 17. 7). These passages suggest that Marcus refers often to lessons which he found especially hard to learn; and indeed we frequently respect others for the abilities which we doubt that we possess ourselves. The example of anger is a particularly clear one: we may also note the remark that, had he made swifter progress with rhetoric and poetry, he might easily have become absorbed in such pursuits. It is indeed apparent that in the *Meditations* these interests are properly subordinated, not exorcised.

In general, Marcus regularly praises his elders for qualities of consistency and balanced character: Apollonius for being 'always the same, in sharp attacks of pain, in the loss of a child, in long illness' (i. 8); Severus for his 'consistency and uniformity with regard to philosophy' (i. 14); Maximus for 'self-mastery and vacillation in nothing; cheerfulness in all circumstances and especially in illness; a happy blend of character, mildness with dignity' (i. 15).[31] The references to illness may also have seemed relevant to his own condition at the time of writing (see below, pp. 118, 120).

More striking is the delicate balance which Marcus describes these men as having maintained between severity and indulgence, between philosophic rigour and humanity. In Apollonius he saw 'clearly in a living example (παραδείγματος ζῶντος) that a man can at once be very much in earnest and yet at the same time able to relax' (i. 8. 1). Sextus, he asserts, as a true Stoic was able 'never to give the impression of anger or of any other

---

[30] Cf. Cic. *Att.* i. 17. 2; Hor. *Ep.* i. 20. 25 (with E. Fraenkel, *Horace* (Oxford 1957) Plut. *Cat. Min.* i. 5.

[31] Cf. xi. 18. 3, xi. 21 ἀεὶ ὁ αὐτός ἔσται. For the Stoic claims for the consistency of their system see Diog. Laert. vii. 40; S. Emp. *adv. Math.* vii. 17–19; Cic. *Fin.* iii. 74, iv. 53, v. 83; M. Pohlenz, *Hermes* 74 (1939) 7 = *Kleine Schriften* i. 454; I. G. Kidd, *CQ* 5 (1955) 187. That consistency must show itself in the actual life of a true Stoic: Epict. i. 4. 14–16, ii. 19. 13–28; *Ench.* 49; Plut. *Sto. Rep.* 1. 1033ab, with Cherniss's note in the Loeb edn. On consistency as a moral ideal see also, in lighter vein, Hor. *Sat.* i. 3. 1 ff., esp. 9 and 11 (glossed by Sen. *Ep.* 120. 18 ff.). Note also M. Aur. viii. 53.

passion, but to be at once entirely passionless (ἀπαθέστατον) and yet full of affection (φιλοστοργότατον)' (i. 9).[32] Similar, even fuller praise is accorded to Pius: he knew ποῦ μὲν χρεία ἐντάσεως, ποῦ δὲ ἀνέσεως ('where there was need to draw the reins tight, where to relax them', i. 16. 1). And again, 'What is recorded of Socrates would exactly fit him: he could equally be abstinent from or enjoy what many are too weak to abstain from and too self-indulgent in enjoying. To be strong, to endure, and in either case to be sober—this belongs to the man of perfect and invincible soul.' (i. 16. 9.) Elsewhere Marcus sums up this ideal more epigrammatically, telling himself: 'Be sober in your leisure' (νῆφε ἀνειμένος, iv. 6).[33] Or again, as a generality, in x. 12: 'The man who in everything follows the rule of Reason is . . . at once cheerful in expression and composed (φαιδρὸν ἅμα καὶ συνεστηκὸς).'

These reconciliations of apparent contraries well illustrate a tension which appears constantly in Marcus' work. Clearly the references to affection and relaxation are the author's attempts to soften the severity of traditional Stoic principles, modifying the old insistence on detachment and self-sufficiency.[34] These passages offer a goal considerably more sympathetic, but fully as hard to attain. Integrity, consistency, detachment combined with generosity, sympathy, insight into others' characters, even humour: the portraits in this book, once combined and compared, show us the kind of man Marcus admired and sought to be. It is a rigorous yet humane ideal. But it is one thing to admire, and perhaps unconsciously idealise, such qualities in

[32] For Stoic ἀπαθεία see Mayor on Juv. 10. 150; Bonhöffer, *Die Ethik des Stoikers Epiktet* 46–9; *RLAC* i. 484 ff.
[33] For Socrates see esp. Pl. *Smp.* 176c, 220a. In i. 16 there may be a contrast with Trajan, in view of the other glances at predecessors in this chapter; Fronto ii. 8 tells us that Trajan 'potavit satis strenue' (cf. Syme, *Tacitus* 41). But more broadly, these passages recall discussions of the ethics of symposia (prefigured by e.g. Xenoph. B1, and properly initiated by Pl. *Prt.* 347 and *Smp.* 176) and of moderate indulgence: should the wise man get drunk? (see Macleod, *Collected Essays* 264, 282). See further Russell on Long. 16. 4; H. Lewy, *Sobria Ebrietas* (*ZNW* 9, Giessen 1929); for parallels from Philo see H. Chadwick, in A. H. Armstrong (ed.), *The Cambridge History of Late Greek and Early Medieval Philosophy* (Cambridge 1967), 150.
[34] See e.g. Farquharson on i. 15. 3 (his p. 10. 21) συγγνωμικὸν, for Marcus' softening of the Stoic sage. Note also the references to pity (vii. 22, 26; cf. ii. 13 ἐλεεινὰ)—not approved by the Old Stoa; see *SVF* iv s.v. ἔλεος; Diog. Laert. vii. 123 (parodic version: Cic. *Mur.* 61–6). The humanity of Musonius perhaps goes still further: cf. Lutz, *YCS* 10 (1947) 28–30. See also Epict. *Ench.* 16; van der Horst on ps.-Phocyl. 23.

others: it is another thing to seek to acquire them for oneself. Hence the differences in tone between Book I, focused on others, and Books II–XII, the author's self-examination. He sees himself as their pupil, not their equal. Praise of their revered memory leads on to discontent and impatience with his own lack of progress. It is an admirable, but also a saddening attribute of Marcus' character as expressed in his work that, while severe and vehement in his moral demands upon himself, he is also devoid of illusions about his success.

3. Meditations i. 7 and Marcus' 'Conversion'[35]

A unifying theme of Book I is the author's awakening to philosophic self-awareness, to which each of those named has made some contribution. Hence the damning omission from the book of some of his rhetorical teachers, names known to us from the late biographer of Marcus (SHA Marcus ch. 2—again, one must say, if credible). The restrained and concise style disguises but does not wholly mask some of the formative experiences of his earlier years. We have already noted that a rebuke or cautioning must lie behind i. 10 (Alexander's correction of grammatical errors) and i. 12 (Alexander the Platonist's criticism of an attempt to evade responsibilities by pleading ἀσχολία); such cautionings have the flavour of popular ethics. Plutarch's essay de Recta Ratione Audiendi, although concerned specifically with the impact of philosophic lectures, is suggestive for more private, 'tutorial' occasions as well.[36] He describes the proper reaction to a philosopher's reprimand as follows:

... on the other hand, to hear a reproof or admonition to reform character, delivered in words that penetrate like a biting drug, and not to be humbled on hearing it, not to run into a sweating and dizziness, not to burn with shame in the soul, but on the contrary to listen

[35] On conversion to philosophy see above, ch. II n. 33, esp. the works by Nock cited there. Nock's conceptions and method have been criticised as regards Dio Chrysostom by J. L. Moles in a penetrating paper in *JHS* 98 (1978) 79 ff. For Marcus' conversion to philosophy see Nock, *Essays* 472; Theiler's edn. of the *Meditations*, pp. 9–11; Birley ch. 4. It is guardedly accepted by Brunt, *JRS* 64 (1974) 4, and 'Marcus Aurelius and the Christians' 503 n. 57, but attacked by Champlin, *Fronto* ch. 8 (cf. his paper in *JRS* 64 (1974) 144). For an attempted reply to Champlin see what follows in my text, and n. 41 below. See also Misch, *Hist. of Autobiography* index s.v. 'conversion, stories of'.

[36] On this work see now the extensive comm. by Hillyard. On philosophic criticism of epideictic lecturing methods and inadequate audiences see above, ch. I n. 83.

unmoved, grinning, dissembling in the face of it all, is a notable sign of
an illiberal nature in the young, dead to all modesty . . . For not only is
the wound of Telephus, as Euripides says, 'soothed by fine-rasped
filings from the spear', but the smart (δηγμὸν) from philosophy, sinking
deep in men of noble nature, is healed by the very words which inflict
the hurt. So one must endure and feel the bite; the one being
questioned should not be shattered or despondent, but as in the
mystery initiations, as philosophy takes effect on him, he should
endure the first purifications and hubbub in the hope of something
sweet and bright coming out of the present trouble and disturbance.
(Plut. *Recta Rat.* 46d, 46f–47a)

More playfully, but with a full awareness of the issues involved,
Horace describes the education that his father gave him as they
walked together daily: this too involves explicit criticism of what
is wrong and shameful (Hor. *Sat.* i. 4. 105–26).[37]

It is the chapter on Rusticus, i. 7, which most clearly
emphasises Marcus' philosophic self-discovery. It has indeed
been employed to show that he underwent a 'conversion' to
philosophy, although the precise pattern of this process has
never been completely agreed upon. This chapter contains a
tantalisingly brief reference to his becoming aware of the need
for reform and treatment of his own character: τοῦ χρῄζειν
διορθώσεως καὶ θεραπείας τοῦ ἤθους. This clearly marks a key
point in his life, and once again autobiography is cast in a
literary and philosophic mould. The conception of θεραπεία
ψυχῆς ('tendance of the soul') is Platonic; and the idea of a
mentor who arouses feelings of guilt and consciousness of error in
his pupil also recalls the power of Socrates' conversation (e.g. Pl.
Smp. 172c–3e, 215 ff.),[38] or of the ideal philosophic lecturers
portrayed by Seneca and Epictetus. Polemo's experience in the
lecture-hall of Xenocrates may also be compared (Diog. Laert.
iv. 16). Such occasions are characterised by the pupil's conceiv-
ing of a fresh and worthier goal, or of a mission. Nothing so
dramatic or explicit appears in Marcus' words, but we may still
reasonably speak of conversion, or better perhaps of commit-

---

[37] See F. Muecke, *Prudentia* 11 (1979) at 63 ff.
[38] On shame and self-reproach in such contexts see further Hillyard on Plut. op. cit.
46e7–48a6 (cf. *Aud. Poet.* 36c τῶν φιλοσόφων ἀκούοντας αὐτοὺς τὸ πρῶτον ἔκπληξις ἴσχει
καὶ ταραχὴ καὶ θάμβος); I. Hadot, *Seneca* 65–7; W. Schmid, *RhM* 100 (1957) 14 (on
contritio).

ment, to philosophy, though perhaps over a longer period of time than in the conventional model.[39]

One may also be strongly influenced, in literature or in life, by reading or hearing a great literary work which has close relevance to one's own life, and so impresses in a special, personal way. In this respect Marcus' experience with the works of Epictetus, lent to him by Rusticus, also has parallels in conversion-stories: we can compare particularly the powerful effect of Cicero's *Hortensius* on the young Augustine (*Conf.* iii. 7 f.), or of the scriptures on Augustine's friend Simplicianus (*Conf.* viii. 4).[40] In earlier times Aristotle depicted in one of his dialogues a Corinthian farmer who read the *Gorgias* and promptly abandoned farming in order to study under Plato (Arist. fr. 64 Rose). But the aptest parallel to *Med.* i. 7 comes in a letter from Marcus to Fronto, in which he speaks of the profound impression made on him by the writings of the Stoic Ariston:

Ariston's books just now treat me well and at the same time make me ill. When they teach me a better way, then, I need not say, they treat me well. But when they show me how far my character falls short of this better way, how all too often your pupil blushes and grows angry with himself, that twenty-five years old as I am, my soul has still drunk nothing of good doctrine and purer principles. Therefore I do penance, I am angry, I am sad, I compare myself with others, I go without food. (Fronto i. 216)

Champlin, in his valuable book on Fronto, has argued strongly that excessive emphasis has been put on this passage,

[39] Conversions, like miracles and exorcisms, seem conventionally to be sudden: cf. Sen. *Ep.* 6. 2 'tam subitam mutationem mei'; Plut. *Prof. Virt.* 75d; H. D. Betz, *Lukian von Samosata und das Neue Testament* (Berlin 1961) 157; Moles, *JHS* 98 (1978) 100 n. 172. That is, the converted man, looking back, isolates a key moment and focuses or contracts his experience around it. See further J. J. O'Meara, *The Young Augustine* (London 1954) 182, for discussion of the specific case of Augustine's narrative in *Conf.* viii. 25 ff. What biographical data we have in Marcus' case suggests a slower (more realistic?) process, in which reading of both Epictetus (*Med.* i. 7) and Ariston (Fronto i. 216; see n. 41 below) plays a part. as does a more gradual dissatisfaction with rhetorical exercises for their own sake.

[40] Cf. earlier, Justin, *Dial. praef.*; Theophilus, *ad Autol.* i. 14. Gregory Thaumatourgos was converted to Christianity by hearing Origen lecture (*Paneg. i Orig.* ch. 6–7 and 11, in *Patrol. Gr.* x. 1068 ff.; Eus. *Hist. Eccl.* vi. 30). For modern literary instances of 'significant books' see G. Eliot, *The Mill on the Floss* (1860) book iv, ch. iii (Thomas à Kempis); W. Pater, *Marius the Epicurean* (1885) ch. iv (Apuleius, *Cupid and Psyche*). The corrupting book read by Dorian in Oscar Wilde's *The Picture of Dorian Gray* (1890–1) is a reversal of Pater's motif.

and that it is wrong to see Marcus as ever abandoning rhetoric
for philosophy.[41] It is certainly true that Marcus did not give up
rhetorical studies in his subsequent career,[42] but this does not
exclude giving priority to philosophy, and Marcus in i. 7 and i.
17 is explicit on this. Indeed, even if Champlin rightly maintains
that the Fronto passage has been taken too seriously, he himself
understresses the evidence of the *Meditations*. Fronto's vision of
rhetoric and its rightful status can be shown to be anachronistic,
with distant ancestry in the self-styled 'philosophy' of Isocrates.[43] Marcus' choice, and its justice, shoud not be questioned, though this is not to say that Champlin is wrong in
asserting that the antithesis of philosophy and rhetoric in
Marcus' education has often been outlined too crudely or
naïvely.

The religious dimension of philosophy is another aspect
which unquestionably made it more important to Marcus than
rhetoric and stylistics. (I treat this subject further in Chapters V
and VI.) Here we need only note that the final, climactic
chapter of the book thanks the gods for their generosity to him,
and indeed refers to their communications and guidance in
dreams (here too, their commands are couched in Stoic
terminology: i. 17. 6 κατὰ φύσιν ζῆν με). Very speculatively (for
the passage is unclear and probably corrupt), it may be
suggested that another section in i. 17, referring to an oracular

---

[41] Champlin, *Fronto* 76–8, 121–30, and *JRS* 64 (1974) 144, on the passage quoted in
the text. In the latter he argues that 'Ariston' is not the Stoic writer and that Marcus is in
fact referring to his studies in jurisprudence, not philosophy (Ariston being identified as
the jurisconsult T. Ariston). It is argued that this establishes a connection between
sections 1 and 2–3 of the letter. But to my eyes § 1, and that whole topic, are firmly closed
by the words 'sed tamen negotium belle se dedit. Bene est: gaudeo': and the passage
quoted in the text would be very curious and over-emotional if applied to legal studies.
Decision here is difficult, as the tone of Marcus' words is not without humour; but I do
not feel that Champlin has made his case. (For an unsatisfactory compromise position,
see Birley 226–7, 275 n. 13.) Against Champlin's further point, that Panaetius and
Sosicrates rejected all but the letters of Ariston as the work of the homonymous
Peripatetic, see *SVF* i, p. 76 adn. But the point is in any case a weak one, for (a) Marcus
need not have accepted their judgement; and (b) what is to prevent him from reading,
and being moved or disturbed by, non-Stoic philosophy? After all, he quotes Plato often
enough! Compare again the case of Augustine, who ultimately becomes a Christian but
still acknowledges the impact that Cicero's work made on him.
[42] See Brunt, *JRS* 64 (1974) 4 n. 22; Champlin, *Fronto* 121–2.
[43] See H. M. Hubbell, *The Influence of Isocrates on Cicero, Dionysius and Aristides* (Yale
1913) esp. 1–40. Cf. Fronto, *de Eloquentia* i–iv (ii. 52 ff. Haines).

answer given at Caieta, may also be relevant to Marcus' 'philosopher's progress', since oracles often figure in accounts of such men (Socrates, Diogenes, Zeno, Dio Chrysostom, Galen); classic literary examples must in turn have influenced and even shaped or stylised life.[44]

This passage, like the others discussed above, conveys Marcus' recognition of his own deficiencies: 'though I had the kind of disposition which might have led me to behave thus. . .'; 'though I still come somewhat short by my own fault, and by not observing the reminders and almost the instructions of the gods . . .'; 'all these things require the gods to help, and the aid of fortune' (i. 17. 1, 6, 9). Marcus' quest is far from completion. Thus Book I does not simply show us the young prince being trained to assume a position of power,[45] but traces the path of a Stoic *proficiens*, a disciple studying with his mentors and venerating them and the gods. To concentrate on the political and administrative concerns of his teachers to the exclusion of the ethical concerns of their pupil is to ignore the essence of the book, and to miss some of the most important clues to the personality of the author.

4. *The Emperor and his Predecessor*

In general, then, the themes of Book I are not such as to shed much light on Marcus' own policies or on his attitude to the imperial role. The chief exception[46] is of course the admiring portrait of Pius in i. 16, the longest chapter, to which we now turn. But even this is couched very much in terms of social tact, *simplicitas*, attention to people's feelings. Diligence and accuracy are highlighted, but these are not exclusively imperial virtues: they are insisted on by Marcus in whatever he is called upon to do (ii. 5, etc.), including reading (i. 7. 3 τὸ ἀκριβῶς ἀναγινώσκειν) and performing the duties incumbent on us in all our relation-

---

[44] See Moles, *JHS* 98 (1978) 96 ff., on Dio's use of *personae* or 'role-models'; similar argument for Augustan literature by J. Griffin, *JRS* 67 (1977) 17–26. But for the detail of an oracle (?) in Marcus' case we depend on a few cryptic words in *Med.* i. 17. 9, where it is safest to obelise; cf. below, ch. v. 5.

[45] So Champlin, *Fronto* 119 and elsewhere. Contrast the intimate complexities of *Med.* i with the predictable expansiveness of the 'speculum principis' literature (cf. above, ch. II n. 14).

[46] For another exception see above, ch. II, pp. 55, 59 on i. 14.

ships (i. 12; cf. viii. 27; Epict. *Ench.* 30, etc.).[47] Those who
expect, or try, to find a clear statement of Marcus' political
beliefs and theoretical views about the empire in Book I or
elsewhere will be disappointed. Although Brunt has recently
castigated as inadequate a description of the *Meditations* as 'the
reflections of the emperor as a private man',[48] that error is
perhaps less blatant than its opposite.

It is true, however, that there seem to be allusions in i. 16 to
Marcus' predecessors. Pius is praised for qualities which other
recent emperors lacked. Traditional criticisms of these predecessors are implicitly endorsed by Marcus himself, above all where
Trajan and Hadrian are concerned. Certainly, comparisons
between himself and earlier emperors or dynasties must have
been frequently on his mind. They are often mentioned by
name: an obvious and unsurprising example is iii. 16. 1,
condemning Nero as a monster, a creature of bestial impulses.[49]
But under the Roman empire the personal character and habits
of the ruler were as important to his subordinates as his
policies.[50] In Marcus' chapter on Pius the implicit comparison
seems to condemn the taste of Trajan, and still more notoriously
Hadrian, for young boys (i. 16. 2).[51] Other allusions and
reminiscences may be suspected. Marcus praises Pius for being
'no sophist' (i. 16. 4, vi. 30. 3); perhaps a contrast is intended
with the philhellene and dilettante Hadrian, patron of sophists
such as Favorinus and Heliodorus. This was the man whom

---

[47] Cf. *Ench.* 17 and often; Muson. fr. 7, 13–16, and often. The word τάξις itself is more
frequent in Epictetus than in Marcus, but the concept is identical. See further Brunt,
PBSR 43 (1975) 33 f.

[48] P. A. Brunt, *JRS* 69 (1979) 169, on J. R. Fears, *Princeps a diis electus* (Rome 1977)
190.

[49] On Marcus and his predecessors see further ch. IV n. 102 below. On the swift
formation of a damning judgement on Nero in Roman historiography, see K. Heinz, *Das
Bild Kaiser Neros bei Seneca, Tacitus, Sueton und Cassius Dio* (diss. Bern 1948). Philostratus
paints Nero as a ravening monster (*V. Ap.* iv. 38: 'I know not how many heads he has, nor
whether he has crooked talons and jagged teeth . . .' etc.). For some complexities in the
tradition see O. Murray, *Hist.* 14 (1965) 41 ff.; Griffin, *Seneca* 423–7; Dio Chr. *Or.* xxi. 9–
10; and esp. Plut. *de Sera Num. Vind.* 567 f. (on which see Jones, *Plutarch* 16–19).

[50] Tac. *Ann.* i. 33, 54, 76, iii. 37, xv. 67 (cf. Mayor on Juv. 8. 211 ff.) supply classic
examples. On the whole subject see Z. Yavetz, *Plebs and Princeps* (Oxford 1969), and
now the important studies of A. Wallace-Hadrill, esp. *JRS* 72 (1982) 32–48.

[51] On paedophilia see SHA *Hadr.* 4. 5 (on both Hadrian and Trajan); ibid. 14. 5 f.
(Hadrian and Antinous). On this whole subject see J. Griffin, *JRS* 66 (1976) 100 ff. On
Hadrian see further n. 83 below.

Julian was later to describe as the 'sophist' (*Caes.* 311d).[52] Pius is also praised for acting 'according to ancestral custom' in all things (i. 16. 6), ostensible conservatism being a virtue in the emperor from the beginning.[53] That virtue was conspicuously absent in some of the worst emperors, notably Caligula and Nero. Hadrian too defied Roman tradition.[54] Pius had the ability to keep and place a proper value on his friends (i. 16. 2); not so Hadrian (SHA *Hadr.* 15. 1 ff., 16. 8 ff). Marcus' attitude can be confirmed from the frankness of Fronto, writing to his pupil and referring to his unease with, even his disapproval of, Hadrian: 'I wished to appease and propitiate Hadrian, as I might Mars Gradivus or Father Dis, rather than loved him' (i. 110). Here the contrast with Pius is explicit: 'Antoninus, however, I love, I cherish like the light, like day, like life, etc.'[55]

Developing this topic, I suggest that there are further implicit comparisons in *Med.* i. 16 between Pius and other predecessors; or at the very least, that typical criticisms of these men may have influenced Marcus' choice of points to emphasise. If σοφιστής in i. 16. 4 could carry an allusion to Hadrian, σχολαστικός in the same sentence is no less apt for Claudius. More convincingly applicable is § 8, which also supplies a good example of the moral criticism of apparent trivia. 'He was not one who bathed at odd hours' is likely to be an allusion to the eccentric habits of Caligula (known to us from Philo, *Leg. ad Gaium* 14) and Nero (Suet. *Nero* 27).[56] The continuation of the sentence, 'nor fond of building' is also probably a hit at Nero;[57] 'no connoisseur of the table' perhaps a reference to the notorious gluttony of Vitellius, doubtless enhanced by slander and satire (Suet. *Vit.* 13, 16 (his

---

[52] On the usage of the word 'sophist' in this period see above, ch. II n. 128. Marcus has only four instances, all pejorative (though vii. 66 is perhaps neutral).

[53] E.g. Aug. *Res. Gestae* 6. 1, 8. 5, and *ap.* Suet. *Aug.* 31.

[54] On Hadrian see n. 51, 55, 83; also Dio 69. 5–6, 23 (with Millar, *A Study of Cassius Dio* 60 ff.). The contrast between Hadrian and Marcus Aurelius is well brought out by Marguerite Yourcenar in her *Mémories d'Hadrien* (1951), esp. ch. 1.

[55] On this passage see Champlin, *Fronto* 94–5. On the contrasts between Hadrian and Pius, ibid. 96–7; C. P. Jones, *JRS* 62 (1972) 145–6.

[56] In general on baths, and hours normal or abnormal therefor, see Mayor on Juv. 1. 143, 11. 204; note also Dover on Ar. *Nu.* 837.

[57] For Nero's building-programme see Suet. *Nero* 31; A. Boethius, *The Golden House of Nero* (Ann Arbor, Mich. 1950); Griffin, *Nero: The End of a Dynasty* 125–142. In general on φιλοικοδομία as a vice cf. Nep. *v. Att.* 13. 1 'cum esset pecuniosus, nemo illo minus fuit emax, minus aedificator'; Hor. *Odes* iii. 1. 33 ff.; Mayor on Juv. 14. 86–95.

pastry-cook and chief were with him in his final hours), 17 (paunch)).[58]

Ancient biographical method may be suggestive in considering such passages as these. Suetonius in his life of Julius Caesar writes: 'talia agentem atque meditantem mors praevenit. De qua prius quam dicam, ea quae ad *formam* et *habitum* et *cultum* et *mores*, nec minus quae ad civilia et bellica eius studia pertineant, non alienum erit summatim exponere.' (44. 4).[59] The more thoughtful Plutarch makes the point of such gossipy details explicit and dignifies them when he says, in the methodological preface to his life of Alexander:

I am writing biography, not history, and the truth is that the most brilliant exploits often tell us nothing of the virtues or vices of the men who performed them, while on the other hand a chance remark or a joke may reveal far more of a man's character than the mere feat of winning battles in which thousands fall, or of marshalling great armies, or of laying siege to cities. When a portrait painter sets out to create a likeness, he relies above all on the face and the expression of the eyes, and pays less attention to the other parts of the body: in the same way, it is my task to dwell upon those actions which illuminate the workings of the soul, and by this means to create a portrait of each man's life. (*Alex.* 1, tr. I. Scott-Kilvert (adapted)).[60]

This was not a mere throwaway remark by Plutarch, but his regular practice and belief. The statement here is closely paralleled elsewhere (e.g. *Phocion* 5. 4), and detailed examples have been assembled of the way he uses anecdotes, witticisms, famous sayings, accounts of men's hobbies, entertainments, habits, and literary style.[61] All these elements contribute to a general portrait of character (εἰδοποιία).

Thus it is not strange that the Stoic emperor, himself a pupil of Plutarch's nephew and perhaps familiar with the famous

[58] For moralists on gluttony (γαστρομαργία, etc., Muson. fr. 18) see below, n. 89. See Syme, *Tacitus* 189–90 for Vitellius in Tacitus and Suetonius.

[59] Cf. *Aug.* 61; F. Leo, *Die griechisch-römische Biographie nach ihrer literarischen Form* (Leipzig 1901) 3 ff.

[60] See J. H. Hamilton's comm. ad loc.; Momigliano, *The Development of Greek Biography* 1–7.

[61] See Hamilton's comm. on Plut. *Alex.* (Oxford 1969) xxxvii–xxxix, and esp. A. J. Gossage, in T. A. Dorey (ed.), *Latin Biography* (London 1967) 58 ff., with nn. 34–42. Also C. B. R. Pelling, *JHS* 100 (1980) 135–6 on the *Cato Minor*; C. W. Fornara, *The Nature of History in Ancient Greece and Rome* (Berkeley and Los Angeles 1983) 184–9.

Lives,[62] should dwell upon such characteristics and attach significance to what we might regard as minor issues of etiquette or *mores*. The ancients recognised that there is no private life which is not continuous with a wider public life, and the idiosyncrasies or caprices of an empreror were under constant, often fearful scrutiny by members of his court. The work of Suetonius shows well the importance attached to such things, for precisely the reason that the emperor's whims or excesses—the secrecy and suspicion of a Tiberius, the short temper of a Caligula—might if indulged prove disastrous to his counsellors and subjects. Hence there is no clear dividing line between day-to-day morality and a more elevated realm of important moral decisions: as Cicero put it in his discussion of *decorum*, 'omnis autem actio vacare debet temeritate et neglegentia nec vero agere quicquam cuius non possit causam probabilem reddere; haec est enim fere descriptio offici' (*Off.* i. 101).[63] Politics emerges from ethics, as in the sequence of Aristotle's two great works. Greek sophists and Roman philosophers could see the government of a state as directly analogous to the organisation of a household, a point which may be alluded to in i. 9. 1 πατρονομουμένου, and which certainly is in the title of *pater patriae*, which Marcus assumed in 166.[64]

Of the tributes in Book I of the *Meditations* the chapter on Pius contains the most frequent references to political duties, as is natural when Marcus is writing of the man who shared the same obligations and status (τάξις) as himself.[65] Brunt has observed that there was a consistent expectation of certain virtues in a monarch and especially in a Roman emperor;[66] that eulogy generally attributed the same virtues to successive emperors;

[62] See above, ch. II n. 51.

[63] Cf. above, nn. 17–18.

[64] For the analogy see Pl. *Rep.* v. 463; *Meno* 71–3; *Polit.* 259. Sen. *Clem.* i. 14. 1–3, i. 15. 11–17 compares the good king's duty with the good father's (so already Hom. *Od.* ii. 234, etc.). On the title *pater patriae* see Lucan ix. 601, Dio 53. 18, Mayor on Juv. 8. 244; J. Béranger, *Recherches sur l'aspect idéologique du principat* (Basle 1953) 276 f.; S. Weinstock, *Divus Julius* (Oxford 1971) 200–5. The opposite is, of course, the national parricide: see e.g. Cic. *Cat.* i. 17; *Off.* iii. 83.

[65] On τάξις, a concept regularly applied to emperors, see E. Koestermann, *Phil.* 87 (1932) 358 ff., 430 ff. (reprinted in H. Kloft (ed.), *Ideologie und Herrschaft in der Antike*, (Wege der Forschung Bd. 528, Darmstadt 1979)); Brunt, *PBSR* 43 (1975) 7–39.

[66] Art. cit. (n. 65) 21 ff.; cf. id., *JRS* 64 (1974) 9; *Gnom.* 51 (1979) 443–8; also F. A. Lepper, *JRS* 47 (1957) 95–103; and now Wallace-Hadrill's studies, esp. *JRS* 72 (1982) 32–48 and *Suetonius* ch. 7.

and that the description of Pius has much in common with this standard 'model' of the good emperor.[67] This is true and indeed natural, as the hopes that subjects entertain of a ruler are unlikely to change much. Brunt himself observes that 'the greatest stress is of course laid, for reasons not hard to discern, on *clementia*'.[68]

It is, however, the individual emphases in the account, and the very different form of presentation, which deserve fuller consideration. It is tempting to speculate on the difference between *Med.* i. 16 and the funeral laudation which Marcus, together with L. Verus, is said to have delivered after Pius' death (SHA *Marcus* 7. 11).[69] It is hard to believe that either the presentation or the points most dwelt on were comparable. Schemata for the composition of encomia, particularly of rulers, have come down to us, in a very standardised form, in Quintilian, Menander, and others;[70] they are wholly unlike Marcus' static, non-chronological, unelaborated portrait. Nor are the intellectual attributes which Marcus singles out simply the standard material of the panegyrist, such as Pius himself had mentioned in a letter to Fronto, politely complimenting him on the freshness he had managed to impart to such well-worn themes (i. 126 'in tam trita et assidua tibi materia invenire et posse').[71] Not only is the choice of qualities for inclusion selective and the vocabulary carefully chosen; Marcus' references are also deepened by the philosophic overtones of his wording.

His portrait of Pius, then, may be distinguished on the one hand from vague and facile statements of an ideal, such as the

---

[67] On imperial 'virtues' see M. F. Charlesworth, *PBA* 23 (1937) 105 ff., a seminal paper; also Syme, *Tacitus*, appendix 66; A. Wallace-Hadrill, *Hist.* 30 (1981) 298–323, with full bibliog.

[68] *PBSR* 43 (1975) 22. (But at a seminar organised by Mrs M. T. Griffin in Oxford in February 1984 Professor Brunt retracted this comment; he tells me he would now lay much more stress on the desire for imperial justice.) On the background to *clementia* see Weinstock (n. 64) 233–43.

[69] For such works see S. MacCormack in T. A. Dorey (ed.), *Empire and Aftermath* (London 1975) 147. They were not necessarily rhetorical in the sense of being highly wrought or grand in style; see Cic. *de Or.* ii. 341; MacCormack, op. cit. 194 n. 30.

[70] Men. Rh. iii. 368–76 with Russell and Wilson ad loc.; also e.g. Philo, *Leg. ad Gaium* 143 ff.

[71] For parallel comments see Plin. *Ep.* iii. 13. 2 (apology for his own *Panegyricus*!) 'in hac nota vulgata dicta sunt omnia'; August, *Conf.* vi. 9 (on panegyrics).

Stoics' descriptions of their beloved *sapiens*,[72] who some held had
never even existed,[73] and on the other hand from descriptions
by orators, historians, and others of idealised individuals
(Xenophon's Cyrus, Isocrates' Euagoras, Pliny's Trajan) who
simply have every possible virtue attributed to them.[74] Despite
the severance of Marcus' work from everyday experience, his
portraits in Book I remain effectively distinct and concrete, as
the examples given above of anecdotes and specific references
show. Furthermore, their brevity and unusual vocabulary
prevent them from falling into cliché; and the way that the
description is often related to Marcus' own autobiographical
experience, however veiled, still reminds us of the importance of
all these people to his own spiritual upbringing and environ-
ment.

Panegyric, according to the theorists, required comparison
between the *laudandus* and heroes of history and myth, a
convention twisted by Marcus in i. 16. 9, where he compares
Pius with Socrates; and also between the ruler being praised and
his predecessor.[75] In the latter case the wicked predecessor is
vilified (as Pliny attacks Domitian), while the predecessor who is
generally admired may be praised, but is shown to be slightly
inferior to the panegyrist's own hero: this is how Pliny treats
Titus at *Pan.* 35. 4, and even Nerva at 51. 2, 61. 7, 89. 1. It is in
accordance with this rule that Fronto damns Trajan and

[72] *SVF* iii. 544–656 *passim*, e.g. 567, 603–4, 608; Cic. *Fin.* iii. 75 f. (Cato speaking);
Mur. 58–66; *Paradoxa* throughout. Wise men vs. fools: Pease on Cic. *ND* i. 23. See also
Cic. *Tusc.* ii. 51 (cf. *Orator* 18, 100 f.; Persius 1. 28; Mayor on Juv. 7. 56).

[73] Pease on Cic. *ND* iii. 70, 79; Sen. *Tranq.* 7.4; Plut. *Sto. Rep.* 1048e with Cherniss ad
loc.; *Comm. Not.* 1076b; Mayor on Juv. 13. 26. For a shortlist of possible candidates see
the passages collected in Arnold, *Roman Stoicism* 295 ff.; they included Heracles,
Odysseus, Cyrus, Heraclitus, and especially Socrates, Diogenes, the Stoic fathers, and
Cato. But Posidonius held that Socrates, Diogenes, and Antisthenes could be praised
only as having 'made progress' (Diog. Laert. vii. 91 = fr. 29 Edelstein–Kidd; cf. e.g.
Quint. xii. 1. 18), and Seneca compared the rarity of the *sapiens* with that of the phoenix
(*Ep.* 42. 1; so also *SVF* iii. 658). Nevertheless, the ideal continues: for a startling
development see Clem. Al. *Strom.* ii. 21: Christ is the Stoic *sapiens*! (cf. H. Chadwick, *Early
Christian Thought and the Classical Tradition* (Oxford 1966) 140 n. 39). See also P. A. Brunt,
PCPhS NS 19 (1973) 23 f.; G. B. Kerferd, in J. M. Rist (ed.), *The Stoics* (Berkeley and Los
Angeles 1978) 125 ff.

[74] Again, cf. and contrast Augustine's *Confessions*; see P. Brown, *Augustine of Hippo*
(London 1967) 173, pointing out that Augustine too gives richer and more complex
character-studies than the ideal pictures presented in lives of saints.

[75] See e.g. Plin. *Pan.* 26, 49–50, etc.; Men. Rh. iii. 376; Woodman on Vell. ii. 126. 2;
W. S. Maguinness, *Hermathena* 47 (1932) 46–8.

Hadrian when he sings the praises of Lucius Verus (*Principia Historiae* ii. 206). This offers another example of how such encomiastic themes are transformed in the tribute to Pius; for there, although a contrast with earlier and less worthy emperors is present, as argued above, the real force of the whole chapter lies in the measuring of the writer himself against Pius: no vacuous exultation at the good fortune of the age can be permitted to dissipate the uncompromising severity of this self-scrutiny and self-admiration.

Thus Marcus' presentation of his mentors is sharply distinguished from the lifeless idealisation of encomium, even when the same themes are being treated. His pointed brevity contrasts equally with the expansive manner of epideictic rhetoric.[76] Almost every quality that Pius is said to possess could be given a whole paragraph of elegant *variatio* in Pliny's *Panegyricus*, and specific parallels are not hard to find.[77] Thus when Marcus praises Pius' indifference to flattery and adulation of all kinds (i. 16. 1 καὶ τὸ ἀκενόδοξον περὶ τὰς δοκούσας τιμάς; ibid. § 3 and § 4 ἀκολάκευτος), this corresponds to Plin. *Pan.* 54. The simplicity of Pius' life and the frugality of his dinners (i. 16. 8) correspond to the topic in *Pan.* 49 (esp. sections 4 ff.). The topic of respect for advisors (i. 16. 1–2 *et al.*) can be compared with *Pan.* 85 and other passages such as Plin. *Ep.* vi. 31; Dio Chr. i. 39–40, iii. 86–122. Marcus refers to Pius' concern to keep his friends (i. 16. 2); this corresponds to Pliny's assertion 'praecipuum est principis opus amicos parare' (*Pan.* 85.6; cf. Xen. *Cyr.* viii. 12. 13, Sall. *Jug.* 10. 4). We should contrast the loneliness of the tyrant who can trust no one (e.g. Pl. *Grg.* 510bc), starkly exemplified by Tiberius in Tacitus' *Annals* (especially vi. 6, where Tacitus refers to Plato), and generalised in the abstract sketch of Dio Chrysostom (ii. 75; cf. iii. 86–118). The ideal ruler should protect morals,[78] a topic remotely echoed in *Med.* i. 16. 2

---

[76] See *ad Her.* iv. 54, with Calboli's note; Lausberg, *Handbuch* (ch. 1 n. 8), §§ 413–19; M. Winterbottom, *Anglo-Saxon England* 6 (1977) 62 ff.

[77] On Pliny's *Panegyric* see M. Durry's comm. (Paris 1938), with R. Syme's review, *JRS* 28 (1938) 217–24 = *Roman Papers* i (Oxford 1978) 76–87 (cf. Syme, *Tacitus* 93–5); also F. Gamberini, *Stylistic Theory and Practice in the Younger Pliny* (Hildesheim 1983) ch. 1 and 9.

[78] See 'Antigonus' *ap.* Diog. Laert. vii. 7; Woodman on Vell. ii. 126. 5; Nisbet-Hubbard's comm. on Hor. *Odes* i (Oxford 1970) xv; Wallace-Hadrill, *Suetonius* 172–3, 180. On Marcus' reign, Herodian i. 2. 4 *ad fin.*, with C. R. Whittaker's note in the Loeb edn.

init. His own family life will of course be unexceptionable; there are hints of this topic in the general account of Pius' moderation and simplicity of life (i. 16. 8–9), and Pliny drearily rings the changes on it (*Pan.* 81 ff.).

But what above all comes across in such comparisons is how little Marcus' portrayal has in common with the more leisured and extravagant treatments by Pliny and the others. He barely does more than state the facts about Pius' *victus simplex*, the details being so compressed as to be almost unclear (§ 8). Instead he goes on to emphasise the impression of strength of mind, of power of organisation, which Pius' whole way of life conveyed. The different virtues are here related and intermingled, as is realistic: contrast the rhetoricians' *schemata* with their complex subdivisions.[79] Likewise, the preoccupations of the ruler merge with those of the man.

5. *The World of the* Meditations

Having surveyed both the historical background and the auto-biographical and philosophic content of the first book, we are now in a position to combine these conclusions with the account of the rest of the collection which was given in the first chapter, and to draw some broader comparisons between Book I and Books II–XII. So far we have been for the most part concerned with the traditions and principles which Marcus inherited and modified; the final section of this chapter offers a more critical account of the thought-world of the *Meditations* as a whole. In this survey I lay considerable stress on what is excluded from the *Meditations*, for it is illuminating to appreciate how wide a range of subjects Marcus does *not* discuss.

It has already been noted that datable events or allusions are absent from Books II–XII.[80] Indeed, throughout the work there is no statement of day-to-day experiences, no description, for instance, of his travels or campaigns. Warfare is a topic used only as a metaphor (ii. 17 ὁ δὲ βίος πόλεμος), or very rarely as an example, or to make a separate point, with no personal reference evident from the text (esp. viii. 34 'If you have ever seen a dismembered hand or foot, or a head cut off, lying somewhere

---

[79] Quint. iii. 7. 10 ff. gives the basic framework; others were less restrained.
[80] See appendix to ch. i.

apart from the rest of the trunk, then you have an image of what a man makes of himself . . .'). Even the traditional supposition that x. 10 (victory over Sarmatians) refers to Marcus' own triumph, celebrated in AD 175, can be doubted.

That same chapter alludes with contempt to the recreation of hunting: here we may contrast the cheerful description of a boar-hunt which we find in a youthful letter to Fronto (i. 178, especially the mock-Ennian phrase, 'fortia facinora fecimus' ('doughty deeds we did'); the letter probably dates from the 140s). This is typical of the difference betwen the young man and the emperor, and surely goes beyond considerations of genre, an argument weak in any case with a work as original in form as the *Meditations*. The selectivity of Marcus' subject-matter is the consequence of deliberate choice and taste.[81]

Similarly, the *Meditations* include no reference to scenery, or notable monuments and places, with the sole exception of iv. 48, a list of cities which have perished: Helice, Pompeii, Hercula-neum. This was a *locus communis* of consolation;[82] it stresses the transience of ambition and achievement. Elsewhere, to Marcus as moralist and self-critic, all places are the same (iv. 3), again a traditional motif given unusual poignancy in the work of one who rules and exercises his authority over those places. Here we may contrast the versatile hedonism of Hadrian, 'omnium curiositatum explorator' (Tert. *Ap*. 5. 7), a great traveller, fond of music, a gourmand;[83] we should also note the difference between Marcus' reticence and Seneca's comments on his visits to Baiae, Puteoli, or the villas of Vatia and Scipio (*Ep*. 51, 77, 55, 86). Again Marcus' earlier years offer the aptest contrast, with the lively exchange about holiday resorts written in the earliest part of his reign (Fronto ii. 1 ff.).

---

[81] For hunting as an innocent recreation cf. Cic. *Off*. i. 104, with Holden's note; Hor. *Ep*. i. 18. 48. Similarly there are references to wrestling-exercises in his earlier years at Fronto i. 150, a very zestful epistle; riding: ibid. and i. 180. Note also SHA *Marcus* 4. 9-10.

[82] See esp. Serv. Sulpicius *ap*. Cic. *Fam*. iv. 5. 4; Sen. *Ep*. 91, esp. 9 ff., on the destruction of Lyons. Kassel, *Untersuchungen* 101 n. 1 cites also Sen. *Marc*. 21. 1; *Polyb*. 1. 2; *NQ* vi. 1. 14, 32. 8; Favorinus fr. 109 Barigazzi; R. Helm, *Lucian und Menipp* (Leipzig and Berlin 1906) 168. Further, ch. vi n. 83 below.

[83] For Hadrian as a gourmand see Fronto ii. 8, SHA *Hadr*. 21. 4; see further R. Syme, 'Hadrian the Intellectual', in *Les Empereurs romains d'Espagne* (Paris 1965) 243-9, and H. W. Benario's comm. on SHA *Hadr*. (California 1980). For moralists on food see n. 89 below.

The games at the amphitheatre are referred to in vi. 46 (see also, for different points, x. 8, xii. 9). This passage has often surprised readers who expect the compassionate Marcus to share the revulsion of Seneca and Augustine.[84] Instead he merely expresses weariness at their monotony: 'the similarity makes the spectacle nauseating. So you feel about life as a whole ... how long will it last?'[85] The bitter pessimism here comes close to despair. Again, a contrast with earlier life, though here a less obvious one: in *Med.* i. 5 Marcus thanks an unnamed tutor for teaching him not to be a partisan of one side or another in races or gladiatorial games. Fronto, himself a great fan of the games (i. 308), went so far as to rebuke Marcus' stand-offishness (i. 206). This earlier indifference, reflected in an anecdote in the *Historia Augusta* (SHA *Marcus* 15.1), deepens and becomes part of a general attitude of sombre distaste towards τὰ ἀνθρώπινα.

Food, drink, rich dress, and the pleasures of love are alluded to by Marcus only dismissively, in a spirit of asceticism, although he pays affectionate tribute to his wife Faustina in i. 17. 8.[86] He learned from his mother to live a simple life, far removed from the pleasures of the rich (i. 3); and Diognetus, the tutor who introduced him to philosophy and encouraged him to write dialogues, seems also to have inculcated Cynic practices of ascetic dress (i. 6).[87] Dio Cassius endorses this for his later years: Marcus did not wear attire befitting his rank, but frequently dressed as a private citizen. We may compare the contempt he expresses for purple robes in vi. 13 and ix. 36 (perhaps also vi. 30. 1 μὴ βαφῇς). Again a conventional object of the moralist's wrath has deeper meaning for the imperial ruler.[88]

[84] See esp. Sen. *Ep.* 7 with Summers' notes, adding Philos. *V. Ap.* iv. 22; Dio Chr. *Or.* xxxi. 22 (Musonius?); Aug. *Conf.* vi. 13. See also Cic. *Tusc.* ii. 41; A. W. Lintott, *Violence in Republican Rome* (Oxford 1968) ch. 4. Different again is Juv. 2. 143. See now J. M. Rist, *Human Value* (Leiden 1982) 3, 79–83.

[85] For parallel expressions of ennui or disillusionment see ix. 14; Sen. *Ep.* 24. 26; *Tranq.* 2. 15; August. *Conf.* viii. 28. Also Eccles. 1, esp. 9 ff.

[86] On Faustina, whom Marcus had married in 145, see Farquharson i. 263–4, 266–7, with whom I agree; also Birley 182. Contrast esp. Gibbon, *The Decline and Fall of the Roman Empire* ch. iv, i. 83–4 Bury. There is nothing novel.

[87] Esp. τὸ σκίμποδος καὶ δορᾶς ἐπιθυμῆσαι. For such attire see Kindstrand on Bion T 19. Diognetus also taught Marcus to tolerate freedom of speech, τὸ ἀνέχεσθαι παρρησίας, a very Cynic-sounding lesson: cf. esp. xi. 6 (the Cynic Diogenes took over the παιδαγωγικὴν παρρησίαν of the Old Comedy). See also n. 29 above.

[88] For simple dress as imperial *civilitas* see Brunt, *PBSR* 43 (1975) 22–5; Wallace-Hadrill, *JRS* 72 (1982) 33-4; further, Wirszubski, *Libertas* ch. 5. The moralists regularly

The contempt for foodstuffs (e.g. vi. 13) is also a rich source of material for satirists and philosophers,[89] but again has close relevance to Marcus' own upbringing (i. 3, i. 6) and health. Dio tells us that Marcus took very little food, his stomach and chest being in bad condition, and that he had to take the drug theriac (Dio 72. 6. 3).[90] In sexual matters we can discern more than a touch of prudery: he approves Pius' traditionalism in restricting homosexuality (i. 16. 2 τὸ παῦσαι τὰ περὶ τοὺς ἔρωτας τῶν μειρακίων); here again there is probably an implicit contrast with Hadrian and Trajan.[91] Marcus recurs to the topic at the end of the same chapter: 'he was not one who was obsessed with beauty of body' (in a sentence which contains other allusions to predecessors).

There are also striking confessional passages, though still elliptical, in the final chapter of Book I. Marcus thanks the gods 'that I was not brought up longer than I was with my

condemn luxurious and ostentatious dress: see van Geytenbeek, *Musonius Rufus* 111 ff.; Bramble, *Persius* 102; Nisbet-Hubbard on Hor. *Odes* ii. 16. 33 ff., ii. 18. 8.

[89] For Stoic–Cynic homilies on the subject of food see O. Hense, *RhM* 61 (1906) 1–18; van Geytenbeek, *Musonius Rufus* 96 ff.; also N. Rudd, *The Satires of Horace* (Cambridge 1966) ch. 7; A. L. Motto, *Guide to the Thought of L. Annaeus Seneca* (Amsterdam 1970) s.v. Gluttony. For abstinence earlier in Marcus' lifetime see his remarks *ap.* Front i. 180–2, ii. 18 'tenui cibo contentus' (cf. *Med.* i. 3 παρὰ τῆς μητρὸς . . . τὸ λιτὸν κατὰ τὴν δίαιταν)—a very different tone, however, from the references to foodstuffs in the *Meditations*, esp. vi. 13 (quoted in text).

[90] T. W. Africa, *JHI* 22 (1961) 97–102 (reprinted in German in Klein (ed.), *Marc Aurel* 133–43) seems to me to exceed the evidence in assuming that Dio 72. 6. 3 and Galen xiv. 3 f. Kühn (on Marcus' use of theriac), combined with various passages such as the complaints in *Med.* v. 1 about lack of sleep, can be taken as proving that Marcus was an opium addict. Would a man so alarmed at the prospect of intellectual senility (iii. 1) be likely to accelerate the process in this manner? Africa makes much of the vivid and powerful dream imagery in the *Meditations* ('dreams and reality were indistinguishable', Klein p. 136); but such figurative language finds close parallels in Plotinus and others (see Dodds, *Pagan and Christian in an Age of Anxiety* 9), who can hardly all have been addicts. See further my comments in *EHR* 97 (1982) 395 f. Africa's curious article has met with undeserved acceptance (e.g. from E. Witke, *CPh* 60 (1965) 23–4, whose arguments from various passages of Lucian also seem to me vulnerable). P. Hadot, in E. Lucchesi and H. D. Sattrey (eds.), *Mémorial Festugière* (Geneva 1984) 33–50, has now administered the *coup de grâce*. On dream imagery see further ch. vi n. 37 below.

[91] Cf. n. 51 above. For moralistic works on sexual folly see Rudd (n. 89) 9–12, 24–6. Among the Stoics, Musonius presents a humane but strict set of prescriptions: esp. fr. 12–14, with van Geytenbeek, *Musonius Rufus* 51–77. See further Mayor on Plin. *Ep.* iii. 1. 5; G. E. M. de Ste. Croix, *The Class Struggle in the Ancient Greek World* (London 1981) 98–111. On the wise man and marriage see Diog. Laert, vii. 121; Sen. fr. 58; Epict. iii. 22. 67–76 with Billerbeck's notes; Muson. loc. cit.; van der Horst on ps.-Phocyl. 175–6. Compare 1 Cor. 7: 32–3. For a fascinating comparison of pagan and Christian views see R. Lane Fox, *Pagans and Christians* (Harmondsworth 1986) 340–74.

grandfather's concubine [not 'second wife', as Farquharson renders this!], that I preserved my virginity (ὥραν) and did not play the man before my time, but even delayed longer . . .' (i. 17. 2); '. . . that I did not touch Benedicta or Theodotus, but that even in later years, when I experienced the passions of love, I was cured' (ibid. 7).[92]

In vi. 13 extravagant asceticism is mingled with a still more reductive approach intended to produce a spurious objectivity. 'Surely it is an excellent plan, when you are seated before delicacies and choice foods, to impress upon your imagination that this is the dead body of a fish . . . and in matters of sexual intercourse, that it is friction of an entrail and a convulsive expulsion of mere mucus' (ἐντερίου παράτριψις καὶ μετά τινος σπασμοῦ μυξαρίου ἔκκρισις). The extremity of Marcus' position may be seen if we compare the more relaxed ethic of Epictetus: 'as far as possible one should remain pure before marriage, and if you do indulge in amatory exploits, then let it be done within the law [i.e. with prostitutes, the advice of the Elder Cato and Horace]. But do not therefore be troublesome and full of reproaches to those who use these liberties, nor frequently boast that you do not.' (*Ench.* 33. 8). Marcus does not blame or boast; nevertheless, the comparison with the earlier Stoic shows that it is not only the permissiveness of our age that makes Marcus' pronouncements seem disturbingly austere.[93]

Marcus displays no interest or intellectual pleasure in the sciences, such as mathematics, astronomy, and so forth, nor in music (all approved by Plato, for example), nor in poetry except in so far as it is morally useful. Again, this is in contrast with his earlier life, for we find him improvising a quotation in one of the letters to Fronto (i. 118); elsewhere he lightly refers to his hexameters, mentioning a passage with which he is especially delighted (i. 138 'ut enim verum magistro meo confitear, amo illos'). Nor does he concern himself with art or sculpture. Similarly his approach to philosophy is narrow not only compared with classical and Hellenistic thinkers, but even

---

[92] A striking parallel to this claim to sexual purity is to be found in the remarkable book compiled by J. D. Spence, *Emperor of China* (London 1974) 129. On concubines, ps.-Plut. *Lib. Educ.* 1a with the note in Abbot's comm.; van der Horst on Ps.-Phocyl. 181.

[93] For earlier Stoic views see *SVF* iv s.v. ἔρως. According to them the sage was permitted to feel love but not lust (*SVF* iii. 650–3; cf. Sen. *Ep.* 116. 5: Panaetius prescribed greater restraint for lesser men).

compared with Cicero, whose chief interests were also ethical but who displays a wide knowledge of logic, physics, and metaphysics as well. Marcus' dogged pessimism makes a striking contrast to the hymn to man's intellectual curiosity and endeavour in Cicero's *de Finibus* (v. 48–60). It is frequently asserted that the scope and ambitions of philosophy dwindled in the imperial period,[94] but comparison with the range of titles in Plutarch's *Moralia* or the essays of Dio Chrysostom illustrates the deliberate self-restriction practised by Marcus.

The emperor was often ill, though there are few indications of this in his work. This is a marked contrast with the Fronto correspondence, in which the health of the writers and their respective families is a constant theme.[95] But Dio Cassius tells us that 'as a result of his close application and study, he was extremely frail of body, although at the beginning he has been so vigorous that he used to fight in armour . . .' (72. 36. 2). He also puts a speech in Marcus' mouth including the admission that he was 'already an old man and weak, unable to take food without pain or sleep without anxiety' (72. 24. 4, a speech set in AD 175). Galen too mentions Marcus' insomnia (xiv. 3 Kühn). In the *Meditations* Marcus thanks the gods for allowing his body to hold out so long in such a life (i. 17. 7). Yet he refuses to indulge himself with the sleep he needs (ii. 1, v. 1, viii. 12; perhaps vi. 2; Dio, quoted above), and expresses scepticism about physicians (iii. 3, iv. 48). This is characteristic of his refusal to pamper himself: his clear-sighted awareness of his own weaknesses leads, at least in the pages of his private journal, to an almost vicious extirpation of them. This rigorous asceticism, which amounts practically to cutting out whole areas of experience, helps

[94] The extreme statement by Dodds in *The Greeks and the Irrational* ch. 8 needs considerable modification.
[95] Brunt, *JRS* 64 (1974) 3 n. 13 lists references to pain, etc. in the *Meditations*. For these topics in the Fronto correspondence see Haines, Loeb edn. ii index s.v. 'health'. This is a natural feature of any exchange between friends, and Bowersock, *Greek Sophists* 71 ff. goes much too far in diagnosing Marcus' weakness as a symptom of an age of hypochondria! Bowersock's particular show-piece (Marcus *ap.* Fronto *ad M. Caes.* v. 8 = i. 196 Haines) in fact proves the opposite of what he says, being a record of a series of accidents, not of imagined illnesses. Was it hypochondria that made Marcus tell Fronto about finding a scorpion in his bed? See further on Fronto's health Champlin, *Fronto* appendix 3. The best account of all this (though still a little over-serious as regards the absurd debate over the incidence of hypochondria) is by J. E. G. Whitehorne, *Latomus* 36 (1977) 413–21.

explain the intensity, the claustrophobic concentration, of his writing. Once again, the form reinforces this effect: bitter epigram and morose reflection exist in a vacuum, lacking a context to define and qualify them, and through generalisation and iteration acquire the status of absolute truths.

Not all of the omissions in the *Meditations* need be the result of conscious choice. But it certainly does seem likely that Marcus deliberately excluded the wearisome daily tasks in order to cultivate and exercise his inner self, to turn his mind to higher things. This is the object of the philosopher's withdrawal into himself, that he may be 'renewed' and face the world again (iv. 3).[96] However, the retreat within and the private monologue may imply that no trusted confidant or kindred spirit was available to commune with the emperor. One of the strongest impressions that one derives from the *Meditations* is of their author's loneliness and isolation. Outside Book I hardly a chapter suggests that he derived any pleasure or advantage from the company of his fellow men. Companions and helpers are to be tolerated, endured (ii. 1)—'love them truly' (vi. 39) is a duty, expressed in terms which imply how hard the ideal is to achieve. Again, the evidence of the correspondence with Fronto provides a contrast, in the exuberant affection of the youthful Marcus for his tutor and friend, answered by the teacher's admiration and love, untainted by any trace of flattery or acquisitiveness (of many possible examples see e.g. Fronto i. 14 f., 58 ff., 112 ff.).[97] The whole collection of letters gives a vivid sense of the affection and frankness which existed between the two: they do not hesitate to criticise or advise each other, and there is much about their households, close friends, and so forth. Fronto, after all, was the advocate of φιλοστοργία (i. 280, ii. 154; M. Aur. i. 11; also Marcus to Fronto, ii. 18 Haines, 'vale mi magister optime, φιλόστοργε ἄνθρωπε'). Many passages exchange news about their children and families (e.g. i. 182, 192, 244, 250, ii. 118 ff.). Contrast the sombre thanks which Marcus offers in the

---

[96] See Festugière, *Personal Religion among the Greeks* 58 ff.; cf. e.g. Sen. *Ep.* 25. 6 = Epicurus fr. 209 U. See further Brunt, *JRS* 64 (1974) 4 n. 19; Griffin, *Seneca* ch. 10; A. Meredith, *JTS* NS 27 (1976) 316 f. Also G. Steiner, *On Difficulty* (Oxford 1978) 87.

[97] For many more instances see the biographies, esp. H. D. Sedgwick, *Marcus Aurelius: A Biography* (Oxford 1921) ch. 5–7; also Champlin, *Fronto* ch. 7–8, a shrewd and balanced study of their relationship which does justice to the question of possible difficulties and tensions, without succumbing to the lure of excessive cynicism.

Meditations 'that my children were not deficient in mind nor deformed in body' (i. 17. 4).[98]

Already in the period before his accession Marcus was the object of flattery (see his remarks *ap.* Fronto i. 136–8). Dio remarks that after his accession many pretended philosophic beliefs in order to curry favour (71. 35. 2; cf. *Med.* i. 16. 5, ix. 29).[99] With the passing of years of power he must have grown more and more remote from the members of his court, who praised him but who, as he suspected, in fact disliked him or were uneasy in his presence. Here x. 36 is suggestive: 'will there not be somebody at the end who will be saying in his heart "We can breathe again, at last, free of this schoolmaster . . . I felt all along that he was tacitly condemning us."' Marcus is thinking here of the discontent engendered by the rule of a true *sapiens*, and *a fortiori* by his own rule. Many passages in the *Meditations* suggest that he was conscious of his position as one apart from those he ruled. Particularly striking is xi. 8, in which the separation of a man from his neighbour is compared with a branch which is severed from the united whole of the tree. As often, the analogy from nature implies a moral imperative.[100] Marcus asserts that mankind is favoured by the generosity of Zeus, who makes it possible for a man to be reintegrated (in the simile, regrafted); 'we are enabled to join again with the man we belong to, and again to become complements of the whole'. But there is a qualification: 'yet, if it is often repeated, the effect of such separation is to make it difficult for the separated part to be reunited and restored.' Moreover, the analogy is not complete: for the branch does not feel itself to be alien to the tree, nor does it suffer from the union and proximity as a man may be uneasy or unhappy amid his associates. Marcus sums up the dilemma with an antithesis, the balance of which would indeed be hard to maintain: ὁμοθαμνεῖν μέν, μὴ ὁμοδογματεῖν δέ ('grow with them, but do not share their doctrines').

[98] For Marcus' own children, some of whom died young, see the material gathered in *PIR²* A 697, at pp. 122–4, supplemented by Birley, *Marcus Aurelius* (revised edn., 1987) 241, 247–8. For the ideal of indifference to such loss see e.g. i. 8, xi. 33–4; further, n. 6 above.

[99] On false or unworthy philosophers see ch. II above, esp. n. 26; Jones, *Culture and Society in Lucian* 29.

[100] For equivalent analogies see iv. 29, viii. 34, ix. 9, 23; see also v. 8. 5. For Marcus' use of such analogies see further ch. IV 4 below. They are traditional in ancient moralistic writing, which constantly argues from what is true in nature to what is natural for man.

It has often been pointed out that most of those mentioned in Book I must have been dead by any date when it is likely that the book was composed. Marcus' wife Faustina died in the winter of 175. Pius obviously was dead (see iv. 33), as were Maximus (viii. 25) and almost certainly Fronto.[101] In other cases deaths cannot be either assumed or denied: we lack the evidence. It can, however, be taken for granted that the number of Marcus' old circle of friends had diminished. They seem not to have been replaced. 'After that, pass on to the characters of those who live with you, even the best of whom is hard to endure . . .' (v. 10. 1). Other than vi. 48 (the chapter which seems to state the programme for Book I) there seem to be no references to friends or the pleasures of friendship in Books II–XII. On a purely lexical check, φιλία, φίλος, and φιλεῖν when used by the author in relation to himself will be found always to refer either to the duty of loving one's neighbours (or even the human race as a whole, vii. 31; cf. vi. 39, vii. 13) or else, in more metaphorical vein, to the need to accept and embrace whatever nature sends (e.g. x. 11). Moral obligation has replaced personal contact and private warmth. The communication with others which he does envisage is a relationship of correction and admonition (e.g. ix. 11, x. 4, xi. 18. 4 (the ninth point)). In his most pessimistic state he despairs even of this: 'for who can change men's opinions? And without such a change what else is there but slavery of men who groan and sham obedience?' (ix. 29).[102] Advancing years[103] and the loneliness of supreme power combine to create

---

[101] The arguments for Fronto's survival until AD 175 or 176, most recently advanced by Bowersock, *Greek Sophists* 124–6, are effectively countered by Champlin, *Fronto* 124–6 and in *JRS* 64 (1974) 136 ff.; see also J. E. G. Whitehorne, in C. Deroux (ed.), *Studies in Latin Literature and Roman History* i (Brussels 1979) 475–82.

[102] Again contrast the clichés of panegyric, in which the subjects are said to rejoice in the rule of their king or conqueror: see Virg. *Geo.* iv. 560 'victorque volentis/per populos dat iura'; Nisbet–Hubbard on Hor. *Odes* i. 12. 57; Men. Rh. iii. 377. 19 ff. By contrast, Marcus elsewhere goes so far beyond the pessimism of ix. 29 as to say: 'if they cannot bear him [*a good man*], then let them kill him' (x. 15; viii. 51 may also contemplate assassination). Other emperors were less squeamish: Suet. *Tib.* 59 'oderint dum probent'; *Calig.* 30 'oderint dum metuant'. Cf. and contrast also Macchiavelli, *Il Principe* ch. xvii.

[103] Marcus was a little over 50. 'Age came early in the ancient world' comment Nisbet and Hubbard on Hor. *Odes* i. 31. 18–20 (cf. *Odes* ii. 4. 22–4; Philod. 17 = *AP* xi. 41. 1–2. But, as Professor Russell remarks to me, '*viridis senectus* was common enough!'). Another Horatian passage, from a late poem, is apposite: *Ep.* ii. 2. 55–6 'singula de nobis anni praedantur euntes,/eripuere iocos, Venerem, convivia, ludum'. See also *Ars* 60–3 (perhaps recalled by Marcus as he wrote *Med.* iv. 33, which uses the same analogy

the unique note of unhappiness and disillusionment that permeates the *Meditations*.

Both in Book I and in the rest of the collection we see the characteristic humility and frankness of the author: as we have seen, he does not claim to have acquired the virtues he saw in his benefactors, and in the first book as elsewhere he admits his own inadequacy in philosophic progress (i. 17. 4; cf. viii. 1). The first book, as we have seen, is rather more personal, and often alludes, albeit obscurely, to aspects of Marcus' experience and career. This is a natural consequence of the book's concern with individuals, with whom particular circumstances and events are associated. But at the same time the lessons are moral (though they embrace, as ancient ethics commonly does, *mores* as well as pure morality); and they are social, being concerned more with behaviour and conduct towards others than with the inner advancement of the *proficiens* towards perfection. In Books II–XII the author's concern with social duties is far from being displaced, but there is much more attention given to the mind as a retreat, which must be made into a fortress (viii. 48), purified and immune to external impressions. Again, the lesson Marcus attributes to Severus, concerning the ideal commonwealth (i. 14. 1), seems to show a more optimistic attitude to political government, and a more idealistic image of his own role, than is admitted elsewhere in the work (contrast especially ix. 29 μὴ τὴν Πλάτωνος πολιτείαν ἔλπιζε, 'do not hope for Plato's ideal state'). This does not necessarily imply the priority of Book I, for early inspiration and ideals might well be revived by the memory of an old and beloved teacher. But these differences of emphasis are consistent with the argument of this section. When Marcus looks back to his past, the atmosphere is lighter and more varied; elsewhere, in the present, we find the characteristic notes of brooding melancholy and recurrent pessimism.

Yet the similarity of Book I and Books II–XII is great, for both represent the author's efforts to convince himself of absolute moral truths. Whether through recollection of the virtues of beloved friends and teachers, or through contempla-

---

between the changing of language and the passing of human lives). In general for ancient views on the horrors of old age see Mayor on Juv. 10. 188–288; Mimnermus fr. 1–6 West. Contrast the optimism of Cicero's *de Senectute* (for ancient works in praise of old age see Pease on Cic. *Div.* ii. 3). But although Marcus lacks Cicero's cheerful outlook, he is equally remote from the self-pitying sentimentality of the Greek elegist.

tion of the divine cosmos and the natural laws which must govern human society, the *Meditations* represent a striving towards an ideal. The despondency and dissatisfaction of their author were in part the consequence of the harshness of that ideal; the tensions involved in his repeated efforts to reach it are embodied in a work which, as doctrine and as art, deservedly continues to move and to enlighten readers today.

IV

Aspects of Style and Thought

rem tene; verba sequentur.

(Cato the Elder, *ad Marcum Filium*, fr. 15 Jordan)

THE guiding thread in this chapter is the intimate relation in Marcus' writing between style and thought, between the rhetoric of his prose (vocabulary, metaphor, figures of speech, and so forth) and his philosophic argument. Sections 1–3 discuss various aspects of Marcus' methods of composition; but consideration of his literary techniques can never be wholly separated from the ethical themes which they serve to express, and from Section 4 onwards these assume greater prominence. By examination of his imagery (§ 4) and through the study of his individual use of a number of traditional themes (§ 5), I attempt to define further his outlook and the nature of his pessimism, and so to pave the way for the fuller discussion of his religious attitudes in Chapters V and VI. Some of the limitations of his sympathy, and some negative aspects of his Stoicism, are considered in Section 6.

1. *Theme and Variation*

Many ancient writers develop their ideas by a process conveniently described as 'theme and variation'—the self-conscious literary reshaping of subject-matter and sentiments previously employed by one's models and predecessors, or even by oneself. Ovid and Seneca provide conspicuous examples of this mode of composition, which is not, however, beneath even the greatest poets.[1] It becomes still more marked in the first two centuries AD, and perhaps especially in the period of the Second Sophistic.

[1] For recent essays on this subject see D. West and T. Woodman (eds.), *Creative Imitation and Latin Literaure* (Cambridge 1979), a volume which unfortunately more or less ignores prose; see also G. Anderson, *Lucian: Theme and Variation in the Second Sophistic* (*Mnem.* Suppl. 41, Leiden 1976). This sense of 'theme and variation' is to be distinguished from the smaller-scale device frequent in Latin poetry which was given this title by J. Henry, *Aeneidea* i (London 1873) 206–7, 745–51.

This technique can be shown to be basic to the *Meditations*. Literary topoi and Stoic precepts, often capable of formulation in a very simple, gnomic phrase, are elaborated and argued over by Marcus, developed with different emphasis and at different lengths, throughout the collection.

This kind of variation or remoulding of one's own work, often starting from a maxim and developing it in different ways, was recognised as a compositional technique by rhetorical theorists, including Marcus' own tutor Cornelius Fronto (*ad M. Caes*. iii. 12 = i. 14 Haines).[2] It was essential training for declaimers, whose novelty lay in turning a hackneyed theme to new and striking effect, modifying it with an original *color*, a novel twist.[3] On a larger scale one could write dual speeches arguing opposite sides of the case, in the tradition of the original sophistic age,[4] or several speeches on the same theme, such as Aristides' five 'Leuctrians' (*Or.* xxxiii–xxxvii Dindorf). Not only did these developments influence literature, but some declamations were themselves classed as literature, including Aristides'.[5] Earlier, Latin love-elegy is a good example of a genre in which the conventional situations and attitudes of the poet and his characters are formalised to such a degree that any originality must involve a slightly altered approach, but within an established framework. Philosopher-essayists too were not above reusing or contradicting their own work. Plutarch gives us a pair of set-piece declamations on the good fortune and the bravery of Alexander (*Mor.* 326–45),[6] Maximus of Tyre is equally happy to argue in favour of the theoretic or the practical life (*Dialexeis* xv–xvi), and two of Seneca's longest letters (94, 95) argue, not altogether consistently, about the relative merits of precept and doctrine in moral instruction.[7]

---

[2] Cf. Aphthonius ii. 26 f., 28–32 Spengel; Hermog. 3 f. Spengel; Theon 62 Spengel; Quint. x. 5. 9–11; D. A. Russell, *G&R* 14 (1967) 140–1.

[3] See S. F. Bonner, *Roman Declamation* (Liverpool 1949) 55 f.; M. Winterbottom, in the Loeb edn. of the Elder Seneca (Heinemann 1974) i, p. xviii and index s.v. *color*.

[4] Prt. A. 21 (Diels–Kranz); Arist. *Rh.* iii. 24. 1402ª; Diog. Laert. ix. 55; the *Dissoi Logoi* (D.-K. no. 90); Antiphon's *Tetralogies*; and antilogies in Thucydides, and in Greek tragedy (C. Collard. *G&R* 22 (1975) 58–71). The Thucydidean strand is continued in rhetorical historiography: see e.g. F. W. Walbank, *Historical Comm. on Polybius* i (Oxford 1957) 13 f.

[5] See D. A. Russell, *Greek Declamation* (Cambridge 1983).

[6] On which see J. Hamilton, *Plutarch: Alexander* (Oxford 1969) xxiii–xxxiii.

[7] See above, ch. 1 n. 99. For further examples of 'in utramque disputari posse' (Prt. A 20 = Sen. *Ep.* 88. 43) see Hall, *Lucian's Satire* 384.

In between the pointed, small-scale variation and the remoulding involved in a long rhetorical work should perhaps be put the achievement of the Greek epigrammatists from the Hellenistic period onwards.[8] These authors wrote in a highly stylised genre which had a number of fixed categories: for instance, love-poems of various kinds, dedications, short prayers, epitaphs, symposiastic poems, versified riddles. They regularly imitated one another and revised their own efforts, not necessarily wishing to replace their earlier attempts. Thus Callimachus composed an epitaph for himself (*AP* vii. 415 = 35 Pf.), Meleager composed three (ibid. vii. 417–19 = 2–4 G.-P.). Most epigrammatists also tried their hands at epitaphs on famous men, often dead many generations before them: eminent literary men or mythological figures were favourites. The seventh book of the Greek Anthology preserves such exercises from many periods, arranged roughly in groups according to the chronological order of the subjects of the epitaphs: thus *AP* vii. 1–7 are epitaphs on Homer, 8–10 on Orpheus, 11–13 on Erinna, 14–17 on Sappho, and so on.

These epigrams are not wholly unlike the chapters of Marcus' *Meditations* which deal with the deaths of great men (e.g. iii. 3, vi. 47). To take only one point of contact, Marcus like many of the epigrammatists likes to dwell on the triviality of a man's lifelong efforts when seen in retrospect.[9] For instance, in iii. 3 Marcus waxes satirical on the ignominious ends of Heraclitus and Democritus, after all their elevated speculation on cosmic subjects (cf. viii. 25 on 'those clever people'; similar passages: vi. 47, vii. 19). The anonymous epitaph of Democritus in the Anthology, *AP* vii. 56. 3–4, makes much the same point:

> καὶ γὰρ ἐγὼ σοφίην μετ' ἀπείρονα καὶ στίχα βίβλων
> τοσσατίων, κεῖμαι νέρθε τάφοιο γέλως.

For even I, after all my limitless wisdom and the long series of my written works, lie here beneath the tomb, a laughing-stock.

So too an epitaph on Heraclitus (vii. 127) dwells, like Marcus, on his watery end, though without making the further point which Marcus includes, contrasting this death with his doctrines on fire (*Med.* iii. 3).

---

[8] See F. Cairns, in West and Woodman (n. 1) 124 f., and in *Mnem.* 4/26 (1973) 15–22; S. L. Taran, *The Art of Variation in the Hellenistic Epigram* (Leiden 1979).

[9] For the theme see further Nisbet–Hubbard on Hor. *Odes* i. 28. 1–5.

Reflections on the pettiness and folly of human life in the face of death are also commonplace in the Anthology, and often provide close verbal or metaphorical parallels to some of Marcus' sayings. One example is an epigram by Glycon, *AP* x. 124:

πάντα γέλως καὶ πάντα κόνις καὶ πάντα τὸ μηδέν,
πάντα γὰρ ἐξ ἀλόγων ἐστὶ τὰ γινόμενα

All is laughter, all is dust, all is nothingness; for all things that exist come from the unreasoning.

For parallel expressions in the *Meditations* we may turn to x. 31, 'for in this way you will continually see that the world of man is smoke and nothingness', or xii. 27, 'Where now are they all? Smoke and ashes and a name or not even a name'. Or again, an epigram of Lucian, *AP* x. 31:

θνητὰ τὰ τῶν θνητῶν, καὶ πάντα παρέρχεται ἡμᾶς·
ἢν δὲ μή, ἀλλ' ἡμεῖς αὐτὰ παρερχόμεθα.

All things that belong to mortals are mortal, and all things pass us by; or, if not, we pass them by.

This is paralleled by the river imagery frequent in the *Meditations*, for example in iv. 43: . . . ἅμα τε γὰρ ὤφθη ἕκαστον, καὶ παρενήνεκται καὶ ἄλλο παραφέρεται, τὸ δὲ ἐνεχθήσεται. (' . . . For no sooner is each thing seen that it has been carried away, and another is being carried by, and that too will be carried away.')[10]

Some of the epigrammatists, like Lucian, may have been contemporaries of Marcus Aurelius, and others with whom he shares much, such as the late pagan poet Palladas,[11] drew on themes which go back much earlier than Marcus' time. Palladas too plays on the idea of life and death being interchanged, each really the other, a paradox which goes back to Euripides;[12] and his question in *AP* x. 82, 'Is life really a dream?', while it may have a contemporary reference, recalls a number of Marcus' expressions, especially in vi. 31 (see below, p. 143). Life as a play, another traditional image, also links the two authors (Palladas

[10] See also the passages discussed in section 5 (ii) below.
[11] See C. M. Bowra, *PBA* 45 (1959) 91–5 = *On Greek Margins* (Oxford 1970) 253–66.
[12] Eur. fr. 638 N.; cf. fr. 361, 688, 833; Pl. *Grg.* 492e with Dodds ad loc. See also Kindstrand on Bion fr. 72; Luke 15: 24; Rom. 6: 11; 11: 15.

AP x. 45; M. Aur. xii. 36, etc.).[13] But there are also important differences, above all in the hedonistic moral drawn by Palladas and by many others from their pessimistic observations. This goes beyond choice of genre to choice of ethic, choice of lives.[14] Death is near, so let us make love, 'eat, drink, and be merry . . .'—these are the themes of the sympotic poet, the elegist, the love-poet of the Anthology.[15] Death is near, so we must prepare ourselves for it in spirit, learn to contemplate and face it, be true philosophers—these are the themes of the serious writer, the moral essayist, the philosophic poet.[16] Yet the different genres share many common ideas and images, such as 'only the present moment is ours', a recognition which gives rise both to Horace's 'carpe diem' and to the determination of Marcus Aurelius to 'complete the present work, following the rule of right, earnestly, with all your might, with kindness; and admit no side-issue, but preserve your inner divinity pure and erect, as if you had this instant to restore it' (*Med.* iii. 12). Our sense of the austerity of this philosophic conception is reinforced when we perceive its kinship with the baser morality of self-indulgence: the Stoic emperor weighs the pleasures of the immediate moment against the principles of all time.

[13] For this theme in the *Meditations* see also iii. 8, xi. 1. See further vi. 42, vii. 3, ix. 29, x. 27, xi. 6; Aristo Chius *SVF* i. 351; Bion fr. 16a with Kindstrand's note; Cic. *de Sen.* 5, 48, 64, 70, 86; Aug. *ap.* Suet. *Aug.* 99. 1; Sen. *Ep.* 77. 20; Epict. i. 29. 41, iv. 1. 165; *Ench.* 17; M. Kolokakis, *The Dramatic Simile of Life* (Athens 1960); J. W. H. Walden, *HSCP* 5 (1894) 1 ff.
[14] For the literary topic of the choice of life, see e.g. Hor. *Odes* i. 1, with Nisbet–Hubbard, pp. 1–3; Eur. *Antiope*, ed. J. Kambitsis (Athens 1972) esp. pp. xxii–xxx; Lucian, *Somnium* and *Vitarum Auctio*; Joly, op. cit. (above, ch. II n. 81). In the *Meditations* note v. 1, vi. 51, viii. 43, xi. 21.
[15] Memorable instances include Catull. 5; Prop. ii. 15. 51–4; App. Verg. *de Rosis Nascentibus*; Palladas, *AP* v. 72. See also Nisbet–Hubbard on Hor. *Odes* ii. 14, esp. p. 224.
[16] For meditation on death see ch. I n. 52. See e.g. Lucr. iii. 830 ff.; Cic. *Tusc.* i; Hor. *Ep.* ii. 2; Sen. *Ep.* 12. How closely the philosopher's *contemptus mundi* may come to the hedonist's jaded disgust with life may be seen if we compare Marcus' words in iv. 32 ('call to mind by way of example the time of Vespasian: you will see everything the same: men marrying, bringing up children, falling ill, dying, fighting, feasting, trading, farming, flattering, asserting themselves, suspecting, plotting, praying for another's death, murmuring at the present, lusting, heaping up riches, setting their hearts on offices and thrones...') with a passage from Byron's journal for 7 Dec. 1813: 'went to bed, and slept dreamlessly, but not refreshingly. Awoke, and up an hour before being called; but dawdled three hours in dressing. When one subtracts from life infancy (which is vegetation),—sleep, eating and swilling—buttoning and unbuttoning—how much remains of downright existence? The summer of a dormouse.' (*Letters and Journals*, ed. L. A. Marchand, iii (London 1974) 235).

Of course Greek epigrams of the kind quoted above are far from being the only place outside the *Meditations* in which such motifs occur. But they do provide an interesting parallel to the short, isolated, self-sufficient chapters of the *Meditations*, and to some extent to their subject-matter and techniques. Marcus Aurelius, then, was writing prose epigrams in more than one sense, and there is no reason for him not to have been conscious of the similarity. This suggests that an aesthetic criterion is available to us in comparing versions in which the same message appears in different forms: it makes sense, that is, to ask which version is the best and why. Just as the original compilers of the Greek Anthology thought it sensible to collect together epigrams on comparable subjects, so too some guide-lines through the subject-matter of the *Meditations* may assist the criticism of that work.

There are many topics which appear with sufficient frequency in the work to be considered major preoccupations. Such a topic is built up and elaborated, combined with and related to other topics. The string of κεφάλαια ('headings') in xii. 26, unadorned and undeveloped, give the best examples. Here we have eight topics for reflection which could each provide the starting-point or central idea for a chapter. For example, the aphorism 'every man lives only the present life and it is this which he is losing' is developed at length, in rather Senecan manner, in ii. 14. As in, for instance, Seneca's *Epistle* 93, not much is added to the basic idea, but it is restated in different ways, and a few consequences and precepts deduced. Similarly, the second point made in xii. 26, ὅτι τὸ ἁμαρτανόμενον ἀλλότριον ('the wrong done is not your own, but another's'), is paralleled in ix. 4, where it is put more epigrammatically:

ὁ ἁμαρτάνων ἑαυτῷ ἁμαρτάνει· ὁ ἀδικῶν ἑαυτὸν ἀδικεῖ, ἑαυτὸν κακὸν ποιῶν.

('Whoever does wrong, wrongs himself; whoever does injustice, does it to himself, making himself evil.').

Elsewhere in the collection we can find at least three other variations:

(ix. 20) τὸ ἄλλου ἁμάρτημα ἐκεῖ δεῖ καταλιπεῖν.

('Another's wrongdoing you should leave where it lies.');

(vii. 29, the last of a string of precepts) τὸ ἐκείνῳ ἁμαρτηθὲν ἐκεῖ κατάλιπε ὅπου ἡ ἁμαρτία ὑπέστη.

('Leave the wrong done by another where the wrong arose.');

(ix. 38) εἰ μὲν ἥμαρτεν, ἐκεῖ τὸ κακόν. τάχα δ᾽ οὐχ ἥμαρτεν.

('If he did wrong, then the harm lies with him. But perhaps he did not do wrong.').

All of these are very brief, very similar expressions of the same thought. But the last instance is more interesting as it allows a further thought to cloud the epigrammatic point, so introducing a characteristic note of doubt and questioning. The second phrase picks up the hypothetical εἰ ('if') of the first. Here in miniature we have an important quality of Marcus' morality and thought, his recognition of his own fallibility. The same point, that our view of others' actions is partial, that we cannot judge what may have been right for another in his circumstances, is made more argumentatively and explicitly in the long chapter on anger, xi. 18.[17]

There are many other examples of these recurring themes. Besides those in xii. 26 we may note, for instance (one of Marcus' most famous sayings): 'nothing happens to a man that he is not fitted by nature to bear' (v. 18; cf. viii. 46),[18] or 'only the present moment belongs to us'.[19] Although not technically γνῶμαι, many sentences dependent on imperative verbs are also treated as such. From 'life is short' (e.g. iv. 26; cf. ii. 6) it is a short step to 'you should think like a man who is already on the point of death' (ii. 2, with many parallels, e.g. ii. 11. 1, iv. 17); or from that to iv. 37: ἤδη τεθνήξῃ καὶ οὔπω ἁπλοῦς οὔτε ἀτάραχος οὔτε ἀνύποπτος . . . ('you will presently be dead, and still you are not yet simple, or undisturbed, or unsuspicious . . .'). In the last passage we see a very obvious technique of amplification, the extended list,[20] used to good effect. The curt simplicity of the

[17] This long chapter is excellently analysed by Brunt, *JRS* 64 (1974) 11–12. See also P. Rabbow, *Antike Schriften über Seelenheilung und Seelenleitung* i. *Die Therapie des Zorns* (Leipzig and Berlin 1914) ch. 1.

[18] See also x. 3. Cf. and contrast the thought and spirit of 1 Cor. 10: 13. Note the stress there on temptation, and on God (not the more impersonal Nature) as giving strength and protection at time of need, not once and for all at birth (Marcus comes closer to this concept of divine aid in ix. 40—unorthodox, however).

[19] Parallels are listed by Brunt, *JRS* 64 (1974) 17 n. 115.

[20] For such lists of virtues and vices see ii. 5, 13, 17. 2, iii. 16. 2, v. 33, vi. 16. 4, vi. 30 (τήρησον οὖν σεαυτὸν ἁπλοῦν, ἀγαθόν, ἀκέραιον, σεμνόν, ἄκομψον, τοῦ δικαίου φίλον,

truism 'you will soon be dead' is juxtaposed with the long list of deficiencies still to be remedied, and this emphasises the disproportionate number of unfinished tasks in relation to the small span of life remaining. Sometimes a common image, as well as the topic itself, may link chapters of the same thematic group. In ix. 17 we read: τῷ ἀναρριφθέντι λίθῳ οὐδὲν κακὸν τὸ κατενεχθῆναι οὐδὲ ἀγαθὸν τὸ ἀνενεχθῆναι ('For the stone that is tossed up in the air it is no ill to be carried down again, any more than it was good to be raised up'). Here we have an epigrammatic (and alliterative) formulation of an analogy for life and death. In viii. 20 exactly the same point is being made, but more explicitly: first the general statement, 'Nature has designed the ending of each thing . . .', and the analogy, the only difference being that here it is a ball, not a stone, which is thrown into the air. Then come two more analogies supporting the same point (a bubble forming or bursting; a candle being lit or going out). Or again, the same message with a different image is found in vii. 23: Nature models and breaks down her figures as if modelling wax, each for just a short time; 'Yet it is no hardship for a box to be broken up, as it was none for it to be nailed together'—exactly the same kind of antithesis as in the two previous quotations. In each chapter the homely imagery recalls the moralising style of diatribe,[21] or indeed the noble simplicity of the Gospel parables.

Similarly, there is a clear relation between vii. 15 and iv. 20. In the former Marcus writes that he has his duty to be good, 'just as if gold or emerald or purple were to say continually to itself, "whatever anyone else may do or say, I am bound to be an emerald and to keep my colour." ' In iv. 20 the general principle of intrinsic beauty and virtue is much more fully treated; only at the end does Marcus ask 'Does an emerald become worse than it was, if it is not praised?' (compare 'praised' with 'whatever anyone may do or say' in vii. 15). Then he supplements the

θεοσεβῆ, εὐμενῆ, φιλόστοργον, ἐρρωμένον πρὸς τὰ πρέποντα ἔργα), xii. 3. 1, and many other cases. See further Cleanthes' definition of the Good, *SVF* i. 557; *RLAC* iii. 999 ff.; H. D. Betz *et al.*, *Plutarch's Theological Writings* (Leiden 1975) and *Plutarch's Ethical Writings*, indexes s.v. 'Lists'; S. Wibbing, *Die Tugend- und Lasterkataloge im NT* (Berlin 1959); Arnold, *Roman Stoicism* 423. Such lists are common in Epictetus too (e.g. ii. 23. 42). In the New Testament see e.g. Rom. 1: 28–32; Gal. 5: 19–21.

[21] For the lamp see Sen. *Ep.* 54. 5; for the bubble, Lucian, *Charon* 19 (with R. Helm, *Lukian und Menipp* (Berlin and Leipzig 1906) 167); for wax, ps.-Plut. *Cons. Apoll.* 106a (with Kassel, *Untersuchungen* 74); for the falling stone, Epict. iii. 6. 10, citing Musonius.

thought with further comparisons, again a form of amplification: 'Or does gold, ivory, purple, a lute, a sword-blade, a flower-bud, a little plant?'

Nature and growing things are especially common as moral analogies in the *Meditations* (see below, pp. 148–55); Aristotelian and Stoic theory puts plants, animals, men, and higher powers in a teleological hierarchy, each with its own task and excellence (vi. 16).[22] Several chapters use natural imagery to make the simple point that everything has its role to play in the universal scheme, and is most happy when it is performing that role; so, very briefly, viii. 19: 'Everything has come into being for a purpose: a horse, a vine . . . [and so also with yourself].' Similar is a passage in v. 6, where Marcus further expands the point: 'A horse runs, a hound follows the trail, a bee makes honey, and a man does a good deed, but he doesn't make a to-do about doing it, but simply passes on to the next task, just as a vine goes on to bear once more its grapes in due season.' Alternatively, the teleological point can be stressed still more by reference to the gardener, the vinedresser, or the trainer (vi. 16).

These same images may also be used to illustrate a related but different point, as in viii. 46, where the precept involved is, as often, formally stated at the end of the chapters: οὐ γὰρ ἀφορητόν σοι ἔφερεν ἡ κοινὴ φύσις (there is etymological word-play here: 'universal nature did not *bear* [i.e. bring forth] for you anything you could not *bear*'). Before this come the familiar analogies: nothing can happen to a man which is not an event appropriate to a man, nor to an ox which is not appropriate to an ox, nor to a vine which is not appropriate to a vine, nor to a stone, etc. This kind of naïve repetitiousness is perhaps another trace of popular, or at any rate less literary, writing.

Even what may seem spontaneous and irritable outbursts begin to assume a rather different face when we consider their frequency and regularity of structure. At iv. 38 ('Look at the governing selves of those men, even the wise—what things they flee from, what things they pursue') the exclamation mark comes readily to the translator's pen; yet the οἷος/οἷον ('what' exclamatory) construction is almost a regular formula in a whole set of parallel chapters, some of them much more

[22] See e.g. Arist. fr. 16 Rose; *SVF* i. 529; Cic. *ND* ii. 33–4 with Pease's notes; also M. Aur. v. 16 *ad fin.* with Theiler's note, xi. 18. 1.

THEME AND VARIATION 135

elaborate.²³ In ix. 34 there is a certain artistry in the triple variation:

τίνα τὰ ἡγεμονικὰ τούτων καὶ περὶ οἷα ἐσπουδάκασι καὶ δι' οἷα φιλοῦσι καὶ τιμῶσι.

What governing selves are theirs, what mean ends they have pursued, for what reasons they bestow their love and esteem!'²⁴

In the same chapter there is a formal balance in ὅτε δοκοῦσι βλάπτειν ψέγοντες ἢ ὠφελεῖν ἐξυμνοῦντες ('when they think they do harm by their critiques or do good by their praise').

Such outright condemnation passes easily into melancholy reflection, so that the themes 'what creatures they are!' and 'how soon death will put an end to their petty pursuits—and to mine!' can be combined, as in vi. 59:

οἷοί εἰσιν οἷς θέλουσιν ἀρέσκειν, καὶ δι' οἷα περιγινόμενα καὶ δι' οἵων ἐνεργειῶν. ὡς ταχέως ὁ αἰὼν πάντα καλύψει καὶ ὅσα ἐκάλυψεν ἤδη.

What creatures they are whom they wish to please, and by what kind of results, through what kind of actions! How swiftly eternity will cover all things, and how many it has covered already!

This is not, therefore, a random juxtaposition of two sentences; the chapter is a unity. The second sentence, without passing further judgement on the men referred to in the first, nevertheless sets them and their contemptible ambitions in proper perspective. In vii. 34 Marcus makes the same point with the same verb, καλύπτειν, but clarifies it with a simile:

... ὡς αἱ θῖνες ἄλλαι ἐπ' ἄλλαις ἐπιφορούμεναι κρύπτουσι τὰς προτέρας, οὕτως ἐν τῷ βίῳ τὰ πρότερα ὑπὸ τῶν ἐπενεχθέντων τάχιστα ἐκαλύφθη.

... as fresh sands are constantly carried over one another, hiding the sand that was there before, so in our life what was before is swiftly hidden by what comes after.

So the striving of men for individual fame and glory is futile in the face of natural forces such as the tides, the sand, time itself.²⁵

²³ ii. 12; iii. 4. 4; iv. 3. 2 (πόσοι) and 3 (πόσοι καὶ οἷοι), iv. 38; vi. 18, 34, 59, vii. 6, 34, viii. 3, 31 (πόσα ἐσπάθησαν), ix. 18, 27, 34, x. 13, 19, xi. 18. 1.
²⁴ Cf. vi. 59; for a similar triad see ix. 8: ὥσπερ καὶ μία γῆ ἐστιν ἁπάντων τῶν γεωδῶν, καὶ ἕνι φωτὶ ὁρῶμεν, καὶ ἕνα ἀέρα ἀναπνέομεν.
²⁵ All things are buried in time (vii. 10 ἐγκαταχώννυται τῷ αἰῶνι); time drinks us down (vii. 19 καταπέπωκεν); see also ix. 28 ἐπὶ κυματώσεις τῶν μεταβολῶν. In vii. 23 man is transformed as in the remoulding of wax. In iv. 19 successive generations are like a chain of torches kindled and extinguished in turn. αἰών, ἀχανής, ἄπειρος, ἄιδιος are favourite

Marcus often comes close to poetry in writing about death: his image here recalls Horace, *Epistles* ii. 2. 175 f.:

> sic quia perpetuus nulli datur usus et heres
> heredem alterius velut unda supervenit undam.

Both authors stress the hopelessness of any attempt to stand out as an individual for any length of time. Horace's heirs are not even named, and Marcus does not even personalise the men who vanish—they are merely τὰ πρότερα, 'that which was before'.

The larger structures of long chapters can also (though more rarely) fall into repeated patterns. There is something of this in the arguments about the gods and whether they exist, arguments which are indeed often traditional, with parallels in Cicero's *de Natura Deorum* and elsewhere (*Med.* ii. 11, vi. 44, ix. 40, xii. 5). But the best and fullest examples of this tendency are the chapters on the deaths of great men: these regularly begin 'Think constantly of how many great generals [etc.] have died . . .', then pass to specific *exempla*, and finally draw a conclusion regarding the vanity of human aspiration and the value that subsists in virtuous action alone (further, see pp. 161–7).

From these examples we can begin to see how each topic can be reworked and given fresh treatment each time. On the other hand, the regularity with which Marcus returns to certain themes and images (a repetitiveness which also embraces vocabulary[26]) also enables us to build up a picture of his chief preoccupations and attitudes. In other words, the procedure he followed should not be viewed as a dull, mechanical process, as this kind of tabulation might seem to imply. These themes recur and are elaborated because they matter to the author, and if themes are combined and juxtaposed, this is because they are logically or emotionally associated in his mind. The way that he

---

words of Marcus' in such contexts; for details see Dalfen's index verborum in the Teubner edn. Marcus often contrasts the swiftness of human life and the nearness of its end with the vast span of time past and future (cf. n. 83 below). For Stoic and other ancient notions of time see Rist, *Stoic Philosophy* ch. 15; V. Goldschmidt, *Le Système stoïcien et l'idée de temps* (3rd edn., Paris 1977); G. O'Daly, in H. Blumenthal and R. A. Markus (eds.), *Neoplatonism and Early Christian Thought (Fest. A. H. Armstrong)* (London 1981) 171 ff.

[26] 'Favoured words' can to some extent be observed by study of Dalfen's index, but words are often repeated in juxtaposition, e.g. in lists of good and bad qualities (see above, n. 20). Comparable reflections call forth the same vocabulary and thought-patterns: compare e.g. viii. 34 with xi. 8. See further n. 25 above; nn. 61, 74, 120 below.

approaches a topic traditional to moralists enables us to isolate his individuality.[27]

2. Formal Artistry: Some Examples

The following quotations are intended to provide further evidence of Marcus' self-conscious artistry, in large part the legacy of his rhetorical training. In partcular, they illustrate his fondness for symmetry and formal balance in his epigrams (sustained more intermittently in his longer efforts); they show how he makes use of isocolon, jingling rhymes, and the like.

(iv. 7) ἆρον τὴν ὑπόληψιν, ἦρται τὸ βέβλαμμαι· ἆρον τὸ βέβλαμμαι, ἦρται ἡ βλάβη.

Get rid of the judgement, and you are rid of the 'I am hurt'; get rid of the 'I am hurt', and you are rid of the hurt itself.

(iv. 35) πᾶν ἐφήμερον, καὶ τὸ μνημονεῦον καὶ τὸ μνημονευόμενον.

Everything is ephemeral, both what remembers and what is remembered.

(vi. 6) ἄριστος τρόπος τοῦ ἀμύνεσθαι τὸ μὴ ἐξομοιοῦσθαι.

The best manner of revenge is not to become like your enemy.

(vi. 54) τὸ τῷ σμήνει μὴ συμφέρον οὐδὲ τῇ μελίσσῃ συμφέρει.

What does not benefit the hive does not benefit the bee.

(vii. 21) ἐγγὺς μὲν ἡ σὴ περὶ πάντων λήθη, ἐγγὺς δὲ ἡ πάντων περὶ σοῦ λήθη.

The time is near when you will forget all things, and near also the time when all things will forget about you.

(vii. 65) ὅρα μήποτε τοιοῦτον πάθῃς πρὸς τοὺς ἀπανθρώπους οἷον οἱ ἀπάνθρωποι πρὸς τοὺς ἀνθρώπους.

See that you do not feel to the inhuman what they feel to mankind. [This is a surprise ending, since we expect 'to yourself': this counters any tendency to an egocentric viewpoint.]

---

[27] This important point is still widely ignored by those who find it difficult to recognise the importance of tradition and convention in ancient (and all) literature. Moreover, we should not speak too glibly of 'commonplaces' when we mean (as we often do) universal truths. Both points are well made, and illustrated on the grand scale, by E. R. Curtius, *European Literature and the Latin Middle Ages* (Eng. tr. London 1953) esp. ch. 1 and 5.

(viii. 33) ἀτύφως μὲν λαβεῖν, εὐλύτως δὲ ἀφεῖναι.

Accept modestly, surrender freely.

(ix. 4) ὁ ἁμαρτάνων ἑαυτῷ ἁμαρτάνει· ὁ ἀδικῶν ἑαυτὸν ἀδικεῖ, ἑαυτὸν κακὸν ποιῶν.

Whoever does wrong, wrongs himself; whoever does injustice, does it to himself, making himself evil.

(ix. 5) ἀδικεῖ πολλάκις ὁ μὴ ποιῶν τι, οὐ μόνον ὁ ποιῶν τι.

Often the man who does not act is unjust, not just the man who acts.

(xii. 17) εἰ μὴ καθήκει, μὴ πράξῃς· εἰ μὴ ἀληθές ἐστι, μὴ εἴπῃς.

If it is not right, don't do it; if it is not true, don't say it.

Interesting though these may be for the student of the aphoristic style, they are probably not what one remembers or values most in the *Meditations*. But there are many chapters equally short and simple, which strike the reader differently and carry a more individual stamp. Three examples:

(iv. 15) πολλὰ λιβανωτοῦ βωλάρια ἐπὶ τοῦ αὐτοῦ βωμοῦ· τὸ μὲν προκατέπεσεν, τὸ δ' ὕστερον, διαφέρει δ' οὐδέν.

Many grains of incense [fall] upon the same altar; one falls first, another later, there is no difference.

(iv. 17) μὴ ὡς μύρια μέλλων ἔτη ζῆν· τὸ χρεὼν ἐπήρτηται· ἕως ζῇς, ἕως ἔξεστιν, ἀγαθὸς γενοῦ.

Do not live as if you were going to live on for a thousand years. Fate is hanging over your head. Now, while you are living, while you can, become good.

(xi. 35) ὄμφαξ, σταφυλή, σταφίς, πάντα μεταβολαί, οὐκ εἰς τὸ μὴ ὄν, ἀλλὰ εἰς τὸ νῦν μὴ ὄν

The unripe grape, the ripe bunch, the dried raisin, all are changes, not to what is not, but to what at this moment is not.

The first of these has the brief simplicity of a Japanese haiku. Above all it shows how the strength of the epigrammatic form lies in its lack of elaboration. The comparison which the author is making is undoubtedly between the falling grains and the death of men, some soon, some late (compare the leaf simile in *Iliad* vi. 145 ff., quoted at *Med.* x. 34).[28] But in iv. 15 there is no

---

[28] See further V. Pöschl, *Bibliographie zur antiken Bildersprache* (Heidelberg 1964) 459; Austin on Virg. Aen. vi. 309 ff.; K. F. Smith on Tib. i. 4. 29–30.

explicit reference to humanity, and the writer therefore retains the objective, remote outlook without seeming callous. In the image itself, however, a sacral metaphor is perhaps suggested for mankind's experience: we too fall, like incense or sacrifices on an altar (another common metaphor for death[29]), and perhaps we also fall for a purpose, to please or serve God. This counters the suggestion of futility and randomness which the image at first sight conveys.

Marcus says nothing in iv. 17 that has not been said by moralists since time began: 'tomorrow is too late' is part of all folk-wisdom. Yet the phrase τὸ χρεὼν ἐπήρτηται is unusual, again owing part of its impact to its compression. The perfect tense suggests that necessity has already taken effect, that the moment of truth is already upon us.[30] Could the metaphor recall the sword of Damocles hanging above the uneasy ruler?[31] Finally, the repetition ἕως ζῇς, ἕως ἔξεστιν ('while . . . while') adds a note of urgency, as in ii. 4 οἰχήσεται καὶ οἰχήσῃ καὶ αὖθις οὐκ ἐξέσται ('the time will be gone and you will be gone and there will be no chance again'), or in Epicurus, fr. 204. The last words, ἀγαθὸς γενοῦ, make the demand sound simple, easy to comply with.

In xi. 35 the imagery again provides an analogy with the human life-span (for a development of the thought without the image, see ix. 21, or Sen. Marc. 21. 6). Here again brevity allows detachment; indeed, there seems even to be a touch of playfulness in the antithesis 'not into what is not, but to what at this moment is not'. Such phrasing recalls semi-philosophic disputes on how one can become, or even talk about, what is not (compare the theme of Gorgias' On Not-Being, or Parmenides B6, B8).

Marcus' chapters, then, are seldom careless jottings: instances of real incoherence or discontinuity are in a minority. They frequently show careful structure and offer examples of devices

---

[29] See Nisbet–Hubbard on Hor. Odes ii. 3. 24 f.; Palladas, AP x. 85; James Shirley (1596–1666), 'The Contention of Ajax and Ulysses': 'Upon Death's purple altar now,/ See where the victor-victim bleeds' (quoted in D. J. Enright (ed.), The Oxford Book of Death (Oxford 1983) 12).

[30] On such use of tenses, Macleod, Collected Essays 340. In Marcus see also iii. 6. 3 κατεκράτησεν ἄφνω καὶ παρήνεγκεν; xi. 18. 3 (the sixth point) ὅτι ὅταν λίαν ἀγανακτῇς ἢ καὶ δυσπαθῇς, ἀκαριαῖος ὁ ἀνθρώπινος βίος καὶ μετ᾽ ὀλίγον πάντες ἐξετάθημεν.

[31] Cf. Cic. Tusc. v. 61; Hor. Odes iii. 1. 17 ff.

drawn from formal rhetoric and applied to his moral purpose. Catalogues of this kind of technique are generally tedious, and only a few examples will be given here. Marcus is familiar with the technique known as ring-composition,[32] which is clearly present in iv. 3 (the recurrent theme being that the only true retreat or refuge is within oneself), iv. 45 (οἰκείως . . . οἰκειότητα), v. 5, x. 27 (πάντα τοιαῦτα), xi. 21 (ὁ αὐτός ἐστιν . . . ὁ αὐτὸς ἔσται). At viii. 35 there is an example of the figure known in rhetoric as the *klimax* (*ad Her.* iv. 34; Quint. ix. 3. 55), an argumentative structure which one is unlikely to use accidentally. Although Marcus occasionally runs wild in his enumeration of examples, he also shows awareness of the theorists' preference for a trio of these (Plin. *Ep.* ii. 20. 9 'scholastica lege'; Lucian *Hist. Conscr.* 53). His use of tricola is conspicuous, often deliberate and artistic, as in ix. 14: πάντα ταὐτά· συνήθη μὲν τῇ πείρᾳ, ἐφήμερα δὲ τῷ χρόνῳ, ῥυπαρὰ δὲ τῇ ὕλῃ ('All things are the same: familiar in experience, transient in time, sordid in their substance'). We find a double tricolon in x. 25: ἅμα καὶ ὁ λυπούμενος ἢ ὀργιζόμενος ἢ φοβούμενος οὐ βούλεταί τι γεγονέναι ἢ γένεσθαι ἢ γενήσεσθαι ('He who gives way to sorrow or anger or fear wishes that something had not been or were not now or should not be hereafter'; note the logical order and the polyptoton). We find triple *exempla* in viii. 3: 'Alexander and Caesar and Pompeius, what are they compared with Diogenes and Heraclitus and Socrates?' When Marcus exceeds the rule of three it is often for deliberate effect, as in viii. 25, where the monotonous repetition and the prolonged examples of death and burial emphasise the message (τοιαῦτα πάντα, all things come to the same end), just as the clipped syntax, omitting a main verb in each case, stresses the other message, that of life's brevity (πάντα ἐφήμερα, all things are transitory). Rhyming triple parallelism, though not carried to the extent of Isocratean isocolon, is exemplified in ix. 6 ἀρκεῖ ἡ παροῦσα ὑπόληψις καταληπτικὴ καὶ ἡ παροῦσα πρᾶξις κοινωνικὴ καὶ ἡ παροῦσα διάθεσις εὐαρεστικὴ . . . ('Sufficient are the present judgement that grasps its object, the present action that shares with fellow beings, the present disposition that is well pleased with life . . .').

[32] See Fraenkel on Aesch. *Ag.* 20, 205; F. Cairns, *Tibullus* (Cambridge 1979) 194–5 n. 4.

But this bare enumeration of tropes needs to be subjected to more critical analysis.

As might be expected from what we already know of Marcus' practice, there is little frivolous or merely witty use of words in the *Meditations*. In iv. 50 there is word-play in the phrase ἐν δὴ τούτῳ τί διαφέρει ὁ τριήμερος τοῦ τριγερηνίου; ('In this, what difference is there between a three-day infant and a three-generation Nestor?'). This echoes both Γερηνίος ἱππότα Νέστωρ ('the Gerenian charioteer Nestor', *Iliad* ii. 336, *et al.*) and Νέστωρ τριγέρων ('thrice-old Nestor', e.g. *AP* vii. 144).[33] But such gratuitous paronomasia is not typical. Word-play in the *Meditations* is less frequent and more integrated than in the flamboyant style of Seneca, and this difference is discernible in all the important areas of rhetorical ornamentation. In general, 'point', puns, and repetition, like the reuse of a word in a different sense, all serve to underline the moral point being made.

To take a very simple example, in ix. 13 Marcus writes: σήμερον ἐξῆλθον πάσης περιστάσεως, μᾶλλον δὲ ἐξέβαλον πᾶσαν περίστασιν ('Today I escaped all circumstance, or rather I cast out all circumstance'). Grammatically and conceptually this could hardly be more straightforward, but it still emphasises a basic Stoic dogma (the first item in chapter 1 of Epictetus' *Manual*[34]), that our preoccupations should be solely with what is within us and in our power, but that potentially our control of this is absolute. In Marcus' sentence this crucial distinction is represented by the movement from a purely intransitive verb to an active and emphatic one (ἐξέβαλον, 'I cast out'), by the change from a genitive to an accusative, and by the shift of emphasis, which makes it no longer a question of Marcus escaping or yielding: *he* is the agent and master of his surroundings. At the same time there is point in the simplicity of the amendment: this suggests how easy and conclusive this change of attitude can be.[35] It comes with the realisation of the basic truth which follows: 'for the circumstance was not outside

---

[33] See Nisbet–Hubbard on Hor. *Odes* ii. 9. 13.
[34] In Epictetus cf. e.g. i. 22. 10; *RLAC* v. 607 f. In Marcus, e.g. ii. 11. 4, vi. 41, ix. 15, xi. 11, 16, xii. 22, and constantly elsewhere. See also Theiler on xii. 33.
[35] Compare the Stoic account of the instantaneous transition from folly to wisdom: *SVF* iii. 524–43; Plut. *Prof. Virt.* 75e; *Stoic. Absurd. Poet.* 1058b with Cherniss's note.

me, but within, in my judgements.' There is a paradox also, in that Marcus speaks of casting *out* what is *around* him (ἐξ-, περι-). Paradox is quite often apparent in the *Meditations*, and usually it too underlines a moral lesson, imposing a new way—the true way—of looking at reality.[36] This is an important aspect of Stoic doctrine in general (compare Cicero's essay, *Paradoxa Stoicorum*). The Stoics held that they were reapplying the true names of objects, qualities, and so on. Chrysippus wrote a work entitled *On the Correct Use of Names by Zeno* (*SVF* iii. 617). Closely related is the persuasive definition, which is often itself paradoxical, defying everyday assumptions (e.g. ix. 21 'every change of this kind [i.e. the stages of life] is a death. Is there anything terrible in that?'). Both of these devices are inherited by Cynics and Stoics from Socrates and his followers.[37]

Two final instances will show how these formal devices are fruitfully used by Marcus to express his thoughts in suitably striking and pungent form. In vii. 74 a persuasive definition equates benefit to self with benefiting others:

οὐδεὶς κάμνει ὠφελούμενος, ὠφέλεια δὲ πρᾶξις κατὰ φύσιν· μὴ οὖν κάμνε ὠφελούμενος, ἐν ᾧ ὠφελεῖς.

No one wearies of receiving benefits; and to benefit another is to act according to nature. Do not grow weary, then, of the benefits you receive in doing them.

We may contrast the same point, made more flatly and less neatly, in ix. 4 or in Epict. i. 19. 13.

A similar pointed antithesis is vii. 71:

γελοῖόν ἐστι τὴν μὲν ἰδίαν κακίαν μὴ φεύγειν, ὃ καὶ δυνατόν ἐστι, τὴν δὲ τῶν ἄλλων φεύγειν, ὅπερ ἀδύνατον.

It is ridiculous not to flee from one's own wickedness, which is possible, but from that of others, which is impossible.

---

[36] Cf. vi. 31 (imagery of (re)awakening); n. 41 below. On paradox as a mode of argument, especially in poetry, see M. H. Abrams, *Glossary of Literary Terms* (4th edn., New York 1981) s.v. 'Paradox'. It is particularly at home in religious language; see the interesting critique by R. W. Hepburn, *Christianity and Paradox* (New York 1958) ch. 2 and *passim*. On the specifically Stoic paradoxes see above, ch. 1 n. 61.

[37] See further Nisbet–Hubbard on Hor. *Odes* ii. 2. 19–21; N. Rudd, *The Satires of Horace* (Cambridge 1966) 25 f. On 'correct naming' see esp. *Med.* x. 7 (where φθείρεσθαι is redefined σημαντικῶς), x. 8 (opening) with Farquharson ad loc.

There is a paradox here, since one naturally thinks that it *is* possible to flee from others, but not from oneself. Indeed, the latter point is a moralistic commonplace (e.g. Lucr. iii. 1058-70; Hor. *Ep.* i. 11. 27; Sen. *Ep.* 28). But Marcus' point is rather that the wickedness within oneself can be checked and controlled by one's own effort, whereas that of others is not our concern. Morality begins at home.[38]

3. *Philosophic Outspokenness (παρρησία)*

We have already seen something of the fervour with which Marcus Aurelius excludes 'superfluities' from the pages of the *Meditations*.[39] This has further consequences for his approach to his actual subject-matter. Marcus strives to rise above the petty distractions of individual circumstances and events, in order to discern amid apparent chaos the absolute truths which govern our lives. Hence the rarity of contemporary allusions, and even of personal names.

This process of penetration to reality is described in many passages and in powerful language. Marcus must accustom himself, like God (xii. 2), to see the souls of men in their nakedness (ix. 34; cf. iii. 11, x. 1, xii. 8[40]). The most important thing is to acquire clear vision (x. 35) and see things as they truly are. 'Be sober once more, recall yourself, and when you have awakened anew and realised that those were dreams that troubled you, look again, in your waking senses . . .' (vi. 31).[41] He often urges himself to 'look within' (vi. 3; cf. vii. 30; viii. 11, 13, 22); 'Enter into the governing self of each man, and permit every other man to enter into your own.' (viii. 61). Elsewhere the tone is more superior: 'Penetrate their governing selves, and

---

[38] Even on the theme 'caelum non animum mutant' Marcus shows some lapses from philosophic indifference to place: see esp. iv. 3 (cf. Lucr. ii. 29 ff.), x. 1; Brunt, *JRS* 64 (1974) 8 n. 37.

[39] See ch. iii. 5 above.

[40] Also Pl. *Grg.* 523; Sen. *Ep.* 92. 13; Marcus' speech in Julian, *Caes.* 335b; see also Rabbow, *Seelenführung* 328.

[41] Sleep and waking are traditional images for moral insensibility and awareness (cf. sight and blindness: Soph. *OT* 412 ff.; M. Aur. iv. 29). See *CQ* 31 (1981) 377, and add 1 Thess. 5: 4 ff.; Rom. 13: 11; *Corp. Herm.* i. 27 f. For parallel or related images see M. Aur. x. 35 (cf. v. 9), ophthalmia that affects the mind, not the eyes; ix. 2, corruption of the mind to be feared like a plague (λοιμός); iii. 8, gangrenous sores; viii. 34, mutilation of the body analogous to severance from one's fellow men or abandonment of one's communal duties.

you will see what manner of critics you are afraid of, and just how capable they are of criticising themselves.' (ix. 18; cf. 27). The resolve to go beyond external appearances also has a religious dimension: the man who has a feeling for and a deeper insight into the processes of the universe will find all things beautiful and pleasurable because they are natural (iii. 2; cf. vi. 36, x. 11).

Closely linked with this idea, but very different in tone and effect, is Marcus' insistence on a deliberately dispassionate, diaeretic analysis of objects and actions. Here the philosopher resembles a ruthless surgeon, cutting away illusion and hypocrisy, deriding folly and attacking unsound opinions. The method is outlined in iii. 11:

> To the above aids let one more be added. Always make a figure or outline of the imagined object as it occurs to you, in order to see distinctly what is its essence, naked, as a whole and in its parts, and say to yourself its individual name and the names of the things of which it was compounded and into which it will be broken up. For nothing is so able to create greatness of mind . . .

This description of the method is frequently echoed elsewhere, for instance in xi. 2, 16, xii. 28, 29 ('the salvation of life lies in seeing each thing thoroughly, as it is').

Although this method ostensibly aims at intellectual objectivity, it often passes into a grimly satirical attitude, antagonistic to life and its grossness. In such passages Marcus deliberately employs crude, unpleasant language or examples, occasionally verging on the obscene. This outspokenness ($\pi\alpha\rho\rho\eta\sigma\acute{\iota}\alpha$) is another legacy from Socrates, imitated above all by the Cynics.[42] Thus in Plato's *Gorgias* Socrates annoys and upsets Callicles with his calculatedly coarse examples, so deflating the high-flown pretensions of the Calliclean superman (494b–c, e: Callicles here accuses Socrates of behaving like a mob-orator).[43] Bion the Borysthenite was also accused of using vulgar terms in his writings; and in general this shock technique became

[42] Cf. esp. Diog. Laert. iv. 52 = Bion T 11 (with Kindstrand's notes); Plut. *Amat.* 770b = Bion fr. 56. See Bramble, *Persius* 135; ch. 1 n. 62 above.

[43] Also Xen. *Mem.* i. 2. 29–30. The 'lowness' and vulgarity of Socrates' conversation, and especially his examples, regularly outrage his more sophisticated interlocutors: see above all Pl. *Smp.* 221e. I intend to discuss Socratic style and dialectical tactics further elsewhere. At present see esp. Kindstrand, *Bion* 43, 51.

common in diatribe and satire. In *Meditations* xi. 6 Marcus expresses approval of the practice of 'instructive freedom of speech' employed by Old Comedy and by the Cynics.

One common way for Marcus to use this technique is to describe life in terms which anticipate its end: thus in ii. 2 τῶν μὲν σαρκίων καταφρόνησον· λύθρος καὶ ὀστάρια καὶ κροκύφαντος, ἐκ νεύρων, φλεβίων, ἀρτηριῶν πλεγμάτιον. ('Despise the flesh—blood and bones and a web constructed of nerves, veins, arteries.'); or viii. 37 γράσος πᾶν τοῦτο καὶ λύθρον ἐν θυλάκῳ ('all this just a bagful of stink and filthy gore'); or ix. 36 τὸ σαπρὸν τῆς ἑκάστῳ ὑποκειμένης ὕλης ('the rottenness of the matter which underlies all things'). Other passages express particular distaste for life as manifested in the bodily processes. These include v. 12 (where Marcus sourly quotes the proverbial 'no room left to ease oneself'), v. 28 on bad breath and foul armpits (cf. xi. 15),[44] viii. 24 ὁποῖόν σοι φαίνεται τὸ λούεσθαι—ἔλαιον, ἱδρώς, ῥύπος, ὕδωρ γλοιῶδες, πάντα σικχαντά—τοιοῦτον πᾶν μέρος τοῦ βίου καὶ πᾶν ὑποκείμενον. ('As the process of bathing appears to you—oil, sweat, muck, greasy water, all that is disgusting—such is every part of life and all material things in it.').[45] We find the same distaste in x. 19: οἷοί εἰσιν ἐσθίοντες, καθεύδοντες, ὀχεύοντες, ἀποπατοῦντες, τὰ ἄλλα . . . ('What kind of men they are—eating, sleeping, copulating, excreting, and so on . . .'). In vii. 47 contemplation of the stars is said to purify 'the filth (ῥύπον) of life on the ground' (for the expression cf. v. 10. 2). In a rather different category, we may note the unpleasant use of technical terms for cauterising, suppuration, and mortification in iv. 39.[46]

This approach is exemplified in a particularly gruesome form at vi. 13, in which Marcus argues that it is best always to impress upon one's mind that

this delicacy is the dead body of a fish, and that this is the dead body of a bird or a pig; and again, that the Falernian wine is juice taken from a

[44] Cf. Catull. 69 and 71 with Kroll's notes; Hor. *Epod.* 12. 5. Note how a conventional coarseness of invective is put to more metaphorical, ethical, and paradoxical use by Marcus.

[45] See further ch. VI. 2 below. On hatred of the physical, Dodds, *Pagan and Christian* ch. 1 (p. 8 on Marcus) is a classic account.

[46] τέμνηται, καίηται, διαπυΐσκηται, σήπτηται. The appalling conditions of ancient surgical treatment should be borne in mind here: see e.g. J. Scarborough, *Roman Medicine* (London 1969), esp. ch. 5 on the army. For medical imagery and vocabulary see also iii. 8, v. 9, vii. 64; ch. VI n. 33.

grape, and that robe of purple is just a lamb's fleece dipped in the blood of a shellfish; and as for sex, it is friction of an entrail and a convulsive expulsion of mere mucus (ἐντερίου παρατριψις καὶ μετά τινος σπασμοῦ μυξαρίου ἔκκρισις).[47]

Surely this, he comments, is going to the heart of reality, seeing thing as they really are. The merely plausible must be stripped away: 'bare these objects and inspect their cheapness'. For similar morbid definitions we may compare, in addition to the passages already quoted, vi. 28, 36, ix. 36, xi. 2, and especially iv. 48. 2: κατιδεῖν ἀεὶ τὰ ἀνθρώπινα ὡς ἐφήμερα καὶ εὐτελῆ καὶ ἐχθὲς μὲν μυξάριον, αὔριον δὲ τάριχος ἢ τέφρα. ('always observe how transient and trivial is all human life: yesterday, a drop of fluid, tomorrow, embalmed meat or ash.'). Here verbal parallels with vi. 13 (μυξάριον and εὐτελῆς) reinforce the similarity of thought. This may be realism, but it is of a singularly acid and even cynical kind.

The mockery of satire seems especially close in the rather unusual chapter of exempla (iii. 3)[48] in which Marcus makes the most of the ironic end of Heraclitus, who speculated so long about fire but in the end died of water (dropsy) and attempted to poultice himself with cow-dung (a further reference to the element of earth?). This is followed by an equally atypical play on words: 'Democritus was destroyed by vermin [i.e. devoured by lice],[49] Socrates by vermin of another kind.' This kind of jesting morality (σπουδαιογέλοιον)[50] would not surprise us in Bion, Seneca, or Epictetus, but its appearance in Marcus reminds us how distant any kind of humour generally is from his work. Of the two paradigmatic early philosophers approved by

---

[47] παράτριψις (only here in Marcus) is scientific/technical vocabulary (ps.-Aristotle, Theophrastus, Galen: Schekira 257). σπασμός (again here only) likewise (note that it seems normally to be used of fits of sickness, cramp, etc.); see Schekira 225. For μυξάριον (also in iv. 48; cf. ix. 29 for μύξα) see Schekira 255 f.; n. 125 below.

[48] For an interesting parallel in satirical polemic see Tatian, Or. ad Graec. 2–3 (mentioning the ignominious lives or deaths of Diogenes, Heraclitus, and Empedocles, with much else); also ibid. 25–6; Lucr. iii. 1024–44.

[49] Marcus appears to be in error here; this end is elsewhere attributed to Pherecydes (Diog. Lart. i. 118). But such humiliating deaths were regularly invented for the great and famous by their ungrateful biographers: cf. Sotadea 15 Powell; M. R. Lefkowitz, The Lives of the Greek Poets (London 1981) esp. 96–7.

[50] See Kindstrand, Bion 47 ff.; Curtius (n. 27) 417 ff.; M. A. Grant, Ancient Rhetorical Theories of the Laughable (Univ. of Wisconsin Studies in Lang. and Lit. 21, Madison 1924) 57 ff.

Juvenal (10. 28–53)[51] and mentioned here by Marcus himself, he resembles more the weeping Heraclitus (who strongly influenced Stoicism), rather than Democritus the scoffer, whom the satirist naturally takes as his model. Seneca argued that we should find the vices of the mob ridiculous, not harmful: 'elevanda ergo omnia et facili animo ferenda: humanius est deridere vitam quam deplorare' (*Tranq.* 15. 2). From his writings it appears that Marcus seldom found it possible to smile at others' errors. His combinaton of austere stylistic restraint with an intense and bitter despondency of thought suggests an inherent dilemma: in the effort to achieve the superhuman (xii. 2) Marcus sometimes hovers on the brink of the inhumane.

4. *Imagery*

Marcus' imagery, like the other techniques already discussed, and like his *exempla* and quotations, is rarely developed as ornamentation: rather, it is integral to the structure and effect of the passage in question. In this his comparisons and similes are markedly different from those which crowd the pages of Plutarch's *Moralia*.[52] Plutarch's imagery not only comes from a much wider range of sources, but seems to be developed in much more detail and often for its own sake.

Marcus' comparisons have been helpfully classified, though without any detailed analysis or criticism, in a short paper by C. C. Bushnell.[53] Many of his examples can be seen at once to be traditional: the comparisons of life to a play, a banquet, a voyage at sea; of birth to an arrival and death to a departure— these are familiar from diatribe and its poetic heirs Lucretius and Horace.[54] Life as a river, a torrent, or a confused turmoil

[51] Cf. Mayor's note; Sen. *Tranq.* 15. 2–3; *de Ira* ii. 10. 5.

[52] On Plutarch's imagery see A. I. Dronkers, *De Comparationibus et Metaphoris apud Plutarchum* (diss. Utrecht 1892); F. Fuhrmann, *Les Images de Plutarque* (Paris 1964); Russell, *Plutarch* 28.

[53] *TAPA* 39 (1908) xix–xxi; the author also offers some brief comments in *TAPA* 36 (1905) xxix–xxx. Bushnell's collection is useful but not invariably accurate. For example, though it would suit my arguments well enough if it were so (see ch. III. 5, esp. p. 121), I do not agree with him that Marcus' metaphors of child life are 'always on its unattractive side' (*TAPA* 36, xxx).

[54] For life as a play see n. 13 above; as a banquet, Kindstrand on Bion fr. 68, Brink on Hor. *Ep.* ii. 2. 213 ff. with his appendix 20; voyage and harbour, M. Aur. iii. 3, xii. 22; C. Bonner, *HTR* 34 (1941) 49 ff. (cf. the moralistic interpretation of the *Odyssey* as a tale of man's voyage through life: Sen. *Ep.* 88. 7; August. *Conf.* i. 13. 20; Kindstrand on Bion fr. 5).

described in terms reminiscent of water are regular Stoic metaphors drawn from Heraclitus (esp. fr. B12, which is quoted by the Stoic Arius Didymus).[55] Such imagery naturally appealed to the poets, notably Horace (*Odes* ii. 14. 1 ff.; iii. 29. 33 ff.). Seneca, like Marcus, sustains the delicate balance between poetic and doctrinal use of the image (*Ep.* 23. 8).[56]

Other comparisons are no less traditional, but more philosophic in ancestry: for instance, the battlefield of life (ii. 17 ὁ δὲ βίος πόλεμος, vii. 7).[57] A related image is the 'post' or 'station' (τάξις) in which we have been placed by God, a post which we must not desert (iii. 5, iii. 6. 1, v. 27, xi. 20; xi. 9 speaks of λιποτάκται, deserters). These metaphors go back to Plato, as is shown by vii. 45, in which Marcus quotes the *Apology* (28d; cf. *Phaedo* 61-2).[58]

But the imagery most frequently and extensively employed by Marcus is drawn from the world of nature, usually plant and animal life, but also landscape: seeds, fruit, figs, reaping, branches; stones, rivers, waves; clear weather, calm at sea,[59] a storm dashing against a headland;[60] sand and floods. Animal imagery seems to be more often uncomplimentary than the images taken from inanimate nature: 'men are like puppies snapping at one another, children loving to quarrel, laughing and then at once crying instead' (v. 33). The same note of condemnation can be found in single words: in ix. 37 πιθηκισμοῦ (the 'monkey antics' of human discontent); in ix. 39 τεθηρίωσαι ('have you sunk to the level of a beast?'); in xi. 15 'there is nothing viler than the false friendship of the wolf (λυκοφιλίας)'. But we find also more extended passages, notably vii. 3:

πομπῆς κενοσπουδία, ἐπὶ σκηνῆς δράματα, ποίμνια, ἀγέλαι, διαδορατισ-μοί, κυνιδίοις ὀστάριον ἐρριμμένον, ψωμίον εἰς τὰς τῶν ἰχθύων δεξαμενάς,

[55] See also A6, A15, B49a, B91; W. K. C. Guthrie, *History of Greek Philosophy* i (Cambridge 1962) 450, 488 ff.

[56] See further Pohlenz, *Die Stoa* ii. 170; D. Steyns, *Étude sur les métaphores et les comparaisons dans Sénèque* (Ghent 1907) 73-8; Pöschl (n. 28) 478.

[57] See below, ch. vi nn. 16, 18, 42.

[58] On τάξις see Brunt, *PBSR* 43 (1975) 21, 32-5, and throughout; also Cic. *Somn.* 15.

[59] Compare the metaphor of εὔροια at ii. 5, v. 9, 34, x. 6; note that Zeno, Cleanthes, and Chrysippus defined εὐδαιμονία as εὔροια βίου (*SVF* i. 184, 554, iii. 16, 73; see also Cic. *Off.* i. 90; Epict. ii. 18. 28).

[60] For the image of the virtuous man as the headland that stands firm against the waves compare the similes at Hom. *Il.* xv. 618 ff.; Soph. *OC* 1239 ff.; Virg. *Aen.* vii. 586 ff. (note that the last two examples are both used of aged kings). See also C. J. Herington, in N. Rudd (ed.), *Essays on Classical Literature from Arion* (Cambridge 1972) 219.

μυρμήκων ταλαιπωρίαι καὶ ἀχθοφορίαι, μυιδίων ἐπτοημένων διαδρομαί, σιγιλλάρια νευροσπαστούμενα.

An empty pageant, a stage play; flocks of sheep, herds of cattle; a tussle of spearsmen; a bone flung among a pack of curs; a crumb tossed into a pond of fish; ants, laden and labouring; mice, scared and scampering away; little marionettes, dancing and jerking on their strings[61]—such is life.

Such passages are indictments of the defects of human society, to which Marcus attributes the unthinking acquisitiveness, the random confusion, the absence of moral sanctions, which some moralists saw as typical of the animal kingdom.[62] These comparisons can, however, be used both ways. Animal metaphors can serve to express an idea, as in xi. 18. 1, which alludes to the traditional imagery of kingship: the ram protecting his flock, the bull his herd.[63] Other references are concerned with the animals' place in the natural order, analogous with that of plants below them or with mankind above them (see viii. 19).[64] Marcus is conscious of the paradox (strictly speaking incompatible with the idea mentioned in the last paragraph) that man, who surpasses the animals through the possession of reason (iii. 16. 1, vi. 16. 1, viii. 12), is nevertheless the only creature to ignore what both reason and Nature dictate. This idea is seen in its most developed form in ix. 9, with special reference to social duties:

ὅρα οὖν τὸ νῦν γινόμενον· μόνα γὰρ τὰ νοερὰ νῦν ἐπιλέλησται τῆς πρὸς ἄλληλα σπουδῆς καὶ συννεύσεως καὶ τὸ σύρρουν ὧδε μόνον οὐ βλέπεται.

But see now what happens. It is the intelligent beings, and they alone, who have now forgotten the mutual urge to unite and work together; only among them is the converging force not to be seen.

The observation recalls satirical or declamatory denunciation of

---

[61] For this image compare above all Pl. *Lg.* i. 644de, x. 903d, which were connected with Marcus' words here (and in ii. 2, vi. 28, vii. 29, xii. 19) by Dodds, *The Greeks and the Irrational* 214-15, and *Pagan and Christian* 7-12, 27-30.

[62] Among early writers see above all Hes. *Op.* 276 ff.; for moralistic development see e.g. Plut. *Terrestriane* 963 f-4c; Clem. Al. *Strom.* i. 29. For a substantial collection of rhetorical material on this theme see Winterbottom on ps.-Quint. *Decl. Min.* 260. 15. See also the absorbing work of K. Thomas, *Man and the Natural World* (London 1983).

[63] See e.g. Hom. *Il.* ii. 480 ff., iii. 196 ff., xiii. 492; Cic. *Fin.* iii. 66; Epict. i. 2. 30, iii. 22. 99 (with Billerbeck's note); Dio Chr. *Or.* ii. 68.

[64] See n. 22 above.

human perversity in contrast with the more 'natural' behaviour of the animal kingdom.[65]

Nature imagery is usually employed, like some other comparisons in the *Meditations* (the candle, the falling ball, the soap-bubble),[66] to recommend acceptance of whatever is in store. Marcus writes, for example, in v. 1: 'Do you not see the plants, the sparrows, the ants, the spiders, the bees, all busy with their own particular tasks, each sharing in the formation of the world order? And then are you not prepared to do what is the proper work of man?' This example makes the analogical argument particularly clear (cf. viii. 19 'Each thing is born for a purpose, a horse, a vine . . .', quoted above, p. 134, with parallels).

In other cases the analogy of something beautiful or pleasant in nature is used to show that something else, though it happens to be unattractive or disagreeable to the author himself, serves an equally worthy purpose in the ultimate order, and must be loved and accepted, even found beautiful (iii. 2; also, rather less optimistically, vi. 36). The argument is used of evil men as well: in iv. 6 Marcus comments: 'these are natural and necessary results from creatures of this kind, and he who wants it to be otherwise is wanting the fig-tree not to yield its acrid juice' (paralleled in viii. 15, xii. 16; cf. ix. 12).[67] This is a notion which we find also in the New Testament (Matt. 7: 16; Luke 6: 44; Jas. 3: 12).[68] Similarly in iv. 44 everything is said to be 'familiar and commonplace, as is the rose in spring and the fruit in summer. So too with disease and death and blasphemy and conspiracy and all that gives pleasure or pain to the foolish.' The conclusion implicit here is that illness and the rest are 'indifferent', and that one way of grasping this is to see that they are natural events, and so to accept them without surprise or resentment.

The analogy drawn between the human body and the body politic or the cosmos also figures in Marcus, as it had in earlier

[65] See e.g. Juv. 15. 131 ff., with Mayor's notes; M. Coffey, *Roman Satire* (London 1976) 251 n. 148; also A. O. Lovejoy and G. Boas, *Primitivism and Related Ideas in Antiquity* (Baltimore 1935) ch. 13 'The Superiority of the Animals' (citing from 2nd-c. literature, e.g. Dio Chr. *Or.* vi. 21–8 and Plutarch's treatises *de Sollertia Animalium* and *de Amore Prolis*); in lighter vein, Lucian's *Gallus*. For Marcus on animal virtues see further xi. 18. 4 (p. 226. 18–19 Farquharson).
[66] See n. 21 above.
[67] This is a topos; cf. Plut. *Tranq.* 472ef. See also Epict. i. 15 (end); iii. 24. 86–7, 91 f. is close to Marcus' nature imagery.
[68] See H. Almquist, *Plutarch und das Neue Testament* (Uppsala 1946) 36.

Stoics.[69] Here again metaphor is used as a moral imperative: 'for we have come into the world to work together (γεγόναμεν γὰρ πρὸς συνεργίαν[70]), like feet, like hands, like eyelids, like the rows of upper and lower teeth' (ii. 1; cf. vii. 13, 19; differently, xi. 8).

The homely image recalls fable and folk-tale; indeed, the most famous version of the comparison is surely the tale of the belly and the other parts of the body, the fable told to the rebellious *plebs* by Menenius Agrippa (Livy ii. 32–3 and elsewhere).[71] Already before Marcus' time the comparison had been given a deeper religious sense in St Paul's extended sermon on the Body of the Christian Church (1 Cor. 12: 14–27).[72]

The descriptive resources of simile and metaphor are used to reinforce the emotional weight and message of a chapter: they may provide uplift and add sublimity to good Stoic doctrine, or they may diminish desire and infuse a proper attitude of contempt towards the goods of this world. (We may compare the opposite rhetorical techniques of praise and blame, ἐγκώμιον and ψόγος, which would be familiar to Marcus from his studies under Fronto.[73]) These two objectives cover much of the purpose of the *Meditations*, and comparisons are frequently used as emotional intensifiers. To this end they are often placed, for the fullest effect, at the end of chapters. Perhaps the most remarkable example is the comparison between fruit and man which concludes iv. 48:

τὸ ἀκαριαῖον οὖν τοῦτο τοῦ χρόνου κατὰ φύσιν διελθεῖν καὶ ἴλεων[74] καταλῦσαι, ὡς ἂν εἰ ἐλαία πέπειρος γενομένη ἔπιπτεν, εὐφημοῦσα τὴν ἐνεγκοῦσαν καὶ χάριν εἰδυῖα τῷ φύσαντι δένδρῳ.

Therefore you should spend this fleeting moment of time as nature

[69] See Pöschl (n. 28) 532; Neuenschwander (ch. 1 n. 2) 41 ff.
[70] On συνεργία cf. vi. 42.
[71] See Ogilvie's comm.; W. Nestle, *Klio* 21 (1927) 350 ff. = *Griechische Studien* (Stuttgart 1948) 502–16. For a fierce critique see G. E. M. de St Croix, *The Class Struggle in the Ancient Greek World* (London 1981) 444–5.
[72] Further, Eph. 5: 22–33; Pascal, *Pensées* (ed. Lafuma) 372; A. J. Krailsheimer, *Pascal* (Oxford 1980) 65–6.
[73] See *ad Her.* iii. 10 ff., with Calboli's notes; Quint. iii. 7; J. Cousin in the Budé edn. of Quintilian, vol. iii (Paris 1976) 131 n. 1. The antithesis is perhaps alluded to at *Med.* ix. 34, x. 13.
[74] For Marcus' use of ἴλεως see e.g. xii. 36 (end); further, see Dalfen's index s.v. (11 instances, including the adverb). All but three occurrences refer to a patient and obedient acceptance of death. Contrast the one instance of the word in Epictetus, iv. 1. 43, where the philosopher mocks one who thinks himself unfortunate because Caesar is not ἴλεως!

wills and then go to your rest with a good grace, just as an olive will fall
when it has come to a state of ripeness, blessing the one who bore it, and
giving thanks to the tree that nurtured it.[75]

In this passage, by a procedure sometimes called 'transfusion',[76]
Marcus associates the man and the fruit by combining their
attributes (this is also done in viii. 51, discussed below). Thus the
fruit is personified, it is made to utter the words of thanks and
blessing to the tree from which it falls which man should render
to Nature (cf. Epict. i. 16. 15). The two are further associated
through the echo κατὰ φύσιν . . . τῷ φύσαντι δένδρῳ ('as nature
wills . . . the tree that nurtured it'). The adjective πέπειρος,
'ripe', can also be applied to humans: it is so used of Marcus'
adoptive father Pius in i. 16. 4.[77]

Elsewhere several comparisons may occur in succession. An
example of this is x. 38, or ii. 17. 1, which is noteworthy for the
compression and accumulation of its metaphors (see further ch.
VI, p. 236 below). The effect is one of mutual reinforcement:
each successive simile makes its own independent point, but
because they are so conclusive and unqualified, with the finality
of an equation, we do not have the time, nor does it seem
possible, to question them.[78] This is in general an attribute of
the aphoristic style,[79] whereas a more discursive approach, even
using the same comparisons, creates a very different effect,
inviting more intellectual scrutiny and criticism.

It is not surprising, then, that Marcus' comparisons are for the
most part fully integrated in his argument, and often employ his
favourite emotive words of praise or blame (see n. 20 above). For

[75] For the image of ripe fruit dropping see esp. Cic. de Sen. 71; also Philod. de Morte col.
9. 12 ff.; CIL xii. 533, 1490, 1542-3 (see R. Lattimore, Themes in Greek and Latin Epitaphs
(Illinois 1942) 255). I owe a number of these references to Dr J. Powell.
[76] D. A. West, The Imagery and Poetry of Lucretius (Edinburgh 1969) 43 ff. and index
s.v.
[77] Besides LSJ see Ussher on Ar. Eccl. 896.
[78] As also in the passages in which Marcus presents an equation, often a highly
questionable one, as a kind of definition: e.g. ii. 17 ἡ δὲ ὑστεροφημία λήθη; ix. 21 καὶ γὰρ
τούτων πᾶσα μεταβολή θάνατος; ix. 35 ἡ ἀποβολὴ οὐδὲν ἄλλο ἐστὶν ἢ μεταβολή. Cf.
Heraclitus, e.g. B 119 ἦθος ἀνθρώπῳ δαίμων. For mystery and ambiguity as a
characateristic of at least one strand of ancient philosophic style see M. Schofield, An
Essay on Anaxagoras (Cambridge 1980) 23-4 (with n. 46), 31-3.
[79] See e.g. G. Neumann (ed.), Der Aphorismus (Wege der Forschung Bd. 356,
Darmstadt 1976), with bibliog. Note also Formes brèves de la gnώμη à la pointe:
Métamorphoses de la sententia (Poitiers 1979), which according to L'Année Philologique 1979
contains a piece on M. Aurelius by M. Alexandre. I have been unable to obtain this.

instance, in viii. 51 he recalls the lesson that other men cannot hurt or damage one's intellect, which remains immune—'pure, sane, modest, just'—a characteristic list of praise-words. This thought is now developed in one of Marcus' most beautiful similes:

οἷον εἴ τις παραστὰς πηγῇ διαυγεῖ καὶ γλυκείᾳ βλασφημοίη αὐτήν, ἡ δὲ οὐ παύεται πότιμον ἀναβλύουσα· κἂν πηλὸν ἐμβάλῃ, κἂν κοπρίαν, τάχιστα διασκεδάσει αὐτὰ καὶ ἐκκλύσει καὶ οὐδαμῶς βαφήσεται. πῶς οὖν πηγὴν ἀέναον ἕξεις καὶ μὴ φρέαρ;

Just as if a man were to stand by a clear, transparent spring of sweet water and heap abuse upon it; yet the spring does not cease welling up with fresh and wholesome water; he may cast in mud, he may hurl in dung, but it will quickly dissolve them and wash them away and it will show no stain at all. How then are you to gain a perpetual spring like this, and no mere well?[80]

It seems plain that besides the felicity of word choice here, and the economy with which Marcus makes each word count, there is an additional strength to the imagery: it echoes in detail the Stoic ideas and language to which Marcus constantly gives voice. The metaphor of the spring remotely recalls the river imagery of Heraclitus and still more the definition of happiness as 'a smooth flow of life', found in several of the founders of Stoicism.[81] The comparison also has a model in Epictetus (fr. C2 Schenkl): 'the soul when it associates with virtue resembles a perpetual spring: for it too is pure and undisrupted and wholesome, and such that you return to it and share with it, and wealthy and devoid of harm and indestructible'. But here there is no scene visualised as in Marcus' simile, and Epictetus' string of adjectives is unselective and monotonous. Closest of all is a more abbreviated version of the same idea in *Med.* vii. 59:

ἔνδον σκάπτε, ἔνδον ἡ πηγὴ τοῦ ἀγαθοῦ καὶ ἀεὶ ἀναβλύειν δυναμένη, ἐὰν ἀεὶ σκάπτῃς.

Delve within, within is the spring of goodness, always ready to gush forth, if you will always delve for it.

[80] For the same thought with a very different image see vii. 68. Note also the use of βλασφημία in viii. 41 ('this [your inner, thinking self] not fire, not steel, not a tyrant, not abuse, not anything can touch'). On βλασφημία see further *TDNT* i. 621 ff. (the sense 'blasphemy' is not exclusively Christian: see e.g. Pl. *Rep.* ii. 381e).

[81] See n. 55 above; also e.g. Plut. *Tranq.* 467a, with Betz, *Plutarch's Ethical Writings* on the passage; H. Broeker, *Animadversiones ad Plut. Libellum περὶ εὐθυμίας* (Bonn 1954) 70 ff.

Here too the concept is one of inner purity; and the idea that virtue is within oneself, dependent not on grace but on one's own efforts, is characteristically Stoic.[82] Furthermore, the comparison in viii. 51 is the only passage in the *Meditations* in which the word 'spring' is used literally; this is another indication how close the metaphorical message is to the surface.

The piling of mud and dung into the water recalls Marcus' imagery elsewhere to describe the human world and the moral body. In ii. 17. 1 man's power of perception is 'murky' ($\dot{a}\mu\nu\delta\rho\dot{a}$); in iii. 3 his body is 'earth and gore'; in vii. 47 contemplation of the pure and ordered patterns of the stars serves to wash away 'the vile filth of life on the ground'. In still more pessimistic vein Marcus declares: 'In such a fog and filth, in so great a torrent of being and time and movement and moving things, what can be respected or be at all the object of serious pursuit, I do not see' (v. 10). Marcus loathed the thought of contamination, hypocrisy, impurity: in harmony with this loathing is the stress on the unchanging translucency of the water in the simile. He himself longed for such immunity, but was aware that habitual association with other men dyed the mind (v. 16; cf. iii. 4. 3, vi. 30. 1). Contrast the ideal state of the water: 'it will quickly dissolve them and wash them away and it will show no stain ($o\dot{v}\delta a\mu\dot{\omega}s$ $\beta a\phi\dot{\eta}\sigma\epsilon\tau a\iota$)'. The verb 'wash them away' recalls Marcus' description of the function performed by the *Meditations* themselves: '. . . this will suffice to cleanse away all vexation' (iv. 3. 1, quoted more fully on p. 30). The spring which Marcus hopes to preserve within his own mind will be eternal ($\dot{a}\acute{e}\nu ao\nu$: compare the literal spring, which 'does not cease', and the parallel in vii. 59, '*always* ready to gush forth'). Contrast not only the daily need to renew the moral struggle (e.g. ii. 1, v. 1), to refire the beliefs in his mind (vii. 2), but also the constant brooding throughout the *Meditations* on the constricting brevity of human life, the impermanence of all achievements, and the short span of time which remains for the author himself.[83]

In vi. 43, writing of the provinces allotted to sun, stars, rain,

[82] Cf. Cic. *ND* iii. 86–8; Hor. *Ep.* i. 18. 111–12; Mayor on Juv. 10. 363 'quod ipse tibi possis dare'. For the Stoics see Sen. *Ep.* 41. 1 (contradicted by 73. 16?); Epict. ii. 5. 4; Plut. *Comm. Not.* 1075 e–f.

[83] On the claustrophobic sense of time—human life a dot between two eternities—see Dodds, *Pagan and Christian* 7–8; Brunt, *JRS* 64 (1974) 18. Notice also J. O. Thomson, *JRS* 43 (1953) 47–8.

and so on, Marcus moves from traditional myth (the personifying of the elements) to an implicit statement of doctrine, namely the Stoic principle that every being and every element of the universe has its particular role which it is best suited to perform. But in passages such as the image of the spring he goes further, transforming doctrine itself. Argument and feeling merge perfectly to create something close to poetry. Marcus' imagery and especially his metaphors (the mark of poetic genius for Aristotle) play perhaps the most important part in this synthesis.

4. Selected Themes and their Treatment

(i) The View from Above (*Med.* vii. 48, ix. 30, 32, x. 15 (cf. 23), xi. 1, xii. 24)

This is a perennial motif in ancient philosophic writing, used for many purposes but above all to illustrate the isolation and superior vision of the philosopher, who has the detachment, and also the moral strength and worth, to ascend to the hills or even the heavenly heights, from which he can look down upon mankind. Virtue dwells on the heights already in Hesiod (*Op.* 286 ff., a passage much imitated). We also find in the early poet the idea of divinities abandoning the world in disgust: Aidos and Nemesis return to heaven in *Op.* 197 ff., quoted by Marcus in iv. 33. When this ascent is transferred to the philosopher, it may take place in a dream (as in Cicero's influential *Somnium Scipionis*) or merely in a fantasy (as in Lucian's *Charon* and *Icaromenippus*) or a metaphor. Platonic example, in the myth of the heavens in the *Phaedrus* and the account of the earth in the *Phaedo*, inspired many highly wrought treatments, notably in Plutarch.[84] Philosophers from Plato onwards associate moral and intellectual achievement. The life of contemplation enables the philosopher to scorn the everyday life of mankind (Pl. *Rep.* vi. 486a, quoted by Marcus in vii. 35); it can even be seen as the supreme end of man (Arist. *NE* x. 7). The ascent of the philosopher to heaven is a symbol of the power and vigour of the

---

[84] *Phaedo* 109–11; cf. Plut. *de Facie* esp. 940f f. Note also Nechepso's nocturnal ascent (in Vettius Valens, p. 241 Kroll); Eratosthenes, *Hermes* (J. U. Powell, *Collectanea Alexandrina* 58 ff.).

human mind, as well as the moral superiority of one who is ready
to abandon earthly life with disdain.[85]

One of the most influential passages on this theme, and one
which we can be sure that Marcus knew, occurs in a famous
section of Plato's *Theaetetus* (172 ff.). Here Plato characteristically draws a contrast between those who spend their lives on
trivial cases in the lawcourts and those who engage in philosophic pursuits. Absorbed in their petty concerns, the men of
affairs grow unhealthy and crooked of mind.[86] The philosophers, on the other hand, are helpless in lawcourts which are run
on such immoral principles, and for the most part oblivious to
the snobbery and competition of civic life.[87] It is in fact only the
philosopher's body that is really present in the city, as if there on
a visit (173e3 ἐπιδημεῖ).[88] With his mind the case is very
different:

. . . ἡ δὲ διάνοια, ταῦτα πάντα ἡγησαμένη σμικρὰ καὶ οὐδέν, ἀτιμάσασα
πανταχῇ πέτεται κατὰ Πίνδαρον "τᾶς τε γᾶς ὑπένερθε" καὶ τὰ ἐπίπεδα
γεωμετροῦσα, "οὐρανοῦ θ᾽ ὕπερ" ἀστρονομοῦσα, καὶ πᾶσαν πάντη φύσιν
ἐρευνωμένη τῶν ὄντων ἑκάστου ὅλου, εἰς τῶν ἐγγὺς οὐδὲν αὐτὴν
συγκαθιεῖσα.

. . . while his thought, disdaining all such things as worthless, takes
wings, as Pindar says, 'beyond the sky, beneath the earth', searching
the heavens and measuring the plains, everywhere seeking the true
nature of everything as a whole, and never lowering itself to what lies
near at hand. (*Theaetetus* 173e–174a)

Plato goes on to develop the point that the philosopher is
preoccupied with *real* questions (174b5). In one of our passages,

---

[85] Cic. *ND* ii. 153 with Pease's note; *Tusc.* v. 114; Manil. iv. 905 ff.; Plut. *de Facie*
926d. For the departure of Aidos and Nemesis, or similarly outraged figures, see Hes. loc.
cit.; Theogn. 1135 ff.; Aratus 133 f.; Virg. *Geo.* ii. 473 f.; Nisbet–Hubbard on Hor. *Odes*
ii. 20. 3. In general on the flight of the mind see R. M. Jones, *CPh* 21 (1926) 97 ff.;
Nisbet–Hubbard on Hor. *Odes* i. 28. 5. For intellectual delight see esp. Ptol. *AP* ix. 577
(*Further Greek Epigrams*, ed. D. L. Page *et al.* (Cambridge 1981) p. 112 f.).

[86] The philosophic path of virtue is typically straight; see n. 138 below. This and
similar images express the strength, firmness, and directness of the good man's moral
choices; cf. εὐσταθεῖν, εὔκαιρος, ὀρθός, etc. (and Eng. 'crooked'). He should spurn
distractions that may pull or drag him out of this proper path; cf. Dalfen's index
verborum in his edn. of Marcus, s.v. ἀποσπᾶσθαι, ἀποστρέφειν, διασπᾶν, etc. Cf. ch. vi
n. 30 below.

[87] On the philosopher or artist's incapacity to deal with practical business see Dodds
on Pl. *Grg.* 485d7; Brink on Hor. *Ars* 457 ff.; and the modern stereotype of the absent-
minded professor.

[88] Further, see below, ch. vi. 2, p. 240.

x. 23, Marcus alludes to a phrase in the *Theaetetus* which immediately follows the passage quoted (174d); and in ii. 13 he refers to the same quotation from Pindar (fr. 292 Snell), although not altogether endorsing it. We can be certain, then, that he was familiar with this passage of Plato's works, and with the general theme of the flight of the mind.

The topic has further philosophic and literary associations. Plato refers here to the liberation of the philosopher's mind from his body. This theme, central above all to the *Phaedo* (64–9), had enormous literary influence, quite apart from any independent religious tradition descended from the Pythagorean and other schools.[89] But many passages which exploit this theme are not really concerned with the soul's freedom to philosophise, but with its escape from the body after death, when it will be transformed and purified (e.g. *Phaedo* loc. cit.; Cic. *Tusc.* i. 44 f.; Sen. *Marc.* 25). This is nowhere explicit in Marcus' references to the soul's flight, but we can hardly doubt that it remains as an undercurrent to his thought, charging it with further emotional power. For he regularly refers, in very Platonic terms, to the flesh as a burden and an obstacle,[90] and thinks of the stellar world as a purer region.[91] A traditional definition described the philosopher's task as one of preparing for death, and it seems that Marcus' scepticism about human perfectibility sometimes leads him to see death as the only philosophic fulfilment (xii. 7, 22).

What, then, does Marcus make of this persistent theme of the soul's philosophic ascent? The answer is not, perhaps, surprising in view of the ways we have seen his mind work in other areas. We notice above all that he is not asserting any hope of permanent liberation in the afterlife, as Seneca or Plato might do. Nor does he even describe the vistas which are opened up to the mind as it rises to the heights. The celestial geography and the music of the spheres, which are highlighted in Cicero's *Somnium Scipionis* and seized on by his imitators, find no echoes in these chapters of the *Meditations*. Indeed, we might feel that Scipio Africanus' reproof to his son in Cicero's myth might have

[89] See below ch. VI n. 45.   [90] E.g. x. 38, xii. 1–2, iv. 41 (quoting Epictetus).
[91] vii. 47, xi. 27 (note also ix. 9. 2). See further Sen. *Ep.* 90. 13; Mayor on Juv. 11. 27, 15. 147. For Stoic, Pythagorean, and other views on the stars see Pease on Cic. *ND* ii. 39, 42–3; Woodman on Vell. ii. 123. The heavenly bodies may be considered as gods by Marcus in xii. 28 (quoted below in ch. v. 8).

been still more fittingly addressed to Marcus Aurelius: 'quousque humi defixa tua mens erit? nonne aspicis quae in templa veneris?' (Cic. *Somn.* 17).

In these hypothetical heavenly flights, as on the earth, his attention is still focused on the endless and futile pursuits of the masses. We may note how closely the lists of men's actions in two of these chapters (vii. 48, ix. 30) resemble those in chapters which do not employ the topos of the mind's flight (e.g. iv. 32. 1, vii. 3). Furthermore, his mind is still preoccupied with the question of their approval or disapproval (ix. 30), however much he may dismiss their attitudes as worthless. In none of these passages does he find consolation in something permanent or superhuman.[92] The objects of his thought (especially in ix. 32) remain those which were in his mind on the surface of the earth, in his more everyday entries. There is no escape.

A few other contrasts reinforce this picture. Cicero freely provides us with a detailed account of earthly and cosmic geography, embroidered with pseudo-science (especially *Somn.* 20 on the 'zones'); there is nothing of this in the *Meditations*, nor any interest in the movements of the heavenly bodies. More striking is the absence of any reference to their rationality or divinity, which Stoic theology commonly deduced from the order and beauty of the stellar movements, a traditional form of the argument from design.[93]

Nor do we find any guarantees of the soul's immortality: for Marcus, this imagined flight remains strictly hypothetical, rather than a foreshadowing of the soul's future fate. In Cicero's account all those who have preserved, aided, or enlarged their country are assured of a special place in heaven (*Somn.* 26). He writes of 'true glory' which is specifically the reward of virtue, and Scipio responds with proper enthusiasm (13 'tanto praemio exposito enitar multo vigilantius'). The absence of such an optimistic vision from the *Meditations* is in keeping with the harsher Stoic doctrine that virtue itself is sufficient for happiness,[94] and with Marcus' own reluctant agnosticism about

---

[92] Despite the possible daemon-creatures of xii. 24, on which see ch. v. 7 below.

[93] See ch. v. 8 below; Pease on Cic. *ND* ii. 15, 17, 39–44. On the *Somnium Scipionis* see the notes in the useful translation by G. H. Sabine and S. B. Smith: Cicero, *On the Commonwealth* (Ohio 1929, often reprinted); A. J. Festugière, *Eranos* 44 (1946) 376 ff.

[94] For the sufficiency of virtue see *SVF* iii. 49–67; Cic. *Paradoxa* ii; also Hor. *Ep.* i. 6. 30 f; cf. n. 82 above.

posthumous survival (xii. 5, etc.; see below, ch. v, pp. 206–8, 212–15).

A final point remains, perhaps the most striking and saddest. We have already seen that the theme of the soul's flight is usually associated with mental and intellectual achievement, metaphorically presented as a heroic adventure.[95] A famous example, which could well have been in Marcus' mind when he wrote, occurs in the proem to Lucretius' poem, where the achievement of his master Epicurus in rejecting traditional religious fears is described as a successful conquest, a military campaign that took him beyond the boundaries of the universe itself:

> ergo vivida vis animi pervicit, et extra
> processit longe flammantia moenia mundi
> atque omne immensum peragravit mente animoque
> unde refert nobis victor quid possit oriri,
> quid nequeat . . .
> [. . .]
> quare religio pedibus subiecta vicissim
> obteritur, nos exaequat victoria caelo.

And so the brilliant force of his mind prevailed, and he made his advance far beyond the blazing walls of the cosmos, and traversed the whole vast expanse through his intellect and his thought; from that voyage, victorious, he brought us back the truth, what can come into being and what cannot do so . . . so it was that gradually superstition was subdued and trampled beneath the feet; that triumph sets us on a level with high heaven. (Lucr. i. 72–6, 78–9)[96]

There are a number of similarities between Lucretius' lines and two chapters of the *Meditations*, both employing the same topos of the view from above. Those similarities need not be explained as imitation, but the juxtaposition of the two authors' treatments is suggestive. In *Med.* ix. 32 Marcus writes:

> . . . καὶ πολλὴν εὐρυχωρίαν περιποιήσεις ἤδη σεαυτῷ τῷ τὸν ὅλον κόσμον περιειληφέναι τῇ γνώμῃ καὶ τὸν ἀΐδιον αἰῶνα περινοεῖν . . .

. . . and give yourself an ampler space by taking in the entire universe [cf. Lucretius' 'omne immensum'] through your power of thought [cf. 'mente animoque'] and contemplating the limitless span of time . . .

---

[95] See Jones (n. 85), citing e.g. Cic. *ND* i. 54; Sen. *de Otio* 5. 6.
[96] Besides the commentaries, see E. J. Kenney in D. West and T. Woodman (eds.), *Quality and Pleasure in Latin Poetry* (Cambridge 1974) 18–30.

Similar is xi. 1, where the rational soul has the power to encompass the universe:

... περίερχεται τὸν ὅλον κόσμον καὶ τὸ περὶ αὐτὸν κενὸν καὶ τὸ σχῆμα αὐτοῦ καὶ εἰς τὴν ἀπειρίαν τοῦ αἰῶνος ἐκτείνεται καὶ τὴν περιοδικὴν παλιγγενεσίαν τῶν ὅλων ἐμπεριλαμβάνει καὶ περινοεῖ ...

... it goes on a journey around the whole universe and the vacant space that surrounds it and its form, and reaches out into the infinity of time and embraces and understands the cyclical renewal of the whole structure ...

Here the idea expressed in τὸ περὶ αὐτὸν κενὸν, of some mysterious region lying beyond the boundaries of the universe, is analogous to Epicurus' journey 'extra . . . moenia mundi'.

As in Epicurus, the soul is depicted as grasping the full truths of nature, the way the universe works. In the latter passage, xi. 1, the vastness of the cosmos is stressed (ὅλον, κενὸν, ἀπειρίαν, ἐκτείνεται all contribute), and there is also emphasis on the soul's mastery of this vast universe (note the repeated περι- verbs). But when we ask *what* the soul is extending itself and seeking to apprehend, we are brought back to the gloomy conclusion of eternal uniformity. For the passage continues: '. . . and it understands that those after us will see nothing new, nor did those before us see anything greater, but in a way the man who is forty years old, if he has any understanding at all, has seen all that has been and all that is to be.' (Marcus was a man in his fifties. The same point about the forty-year-old is made in vii. 49, though it may be a commonplace: it occurs also in Lucian, *Bis Acc.* 32; *Hermot.* 13.) Here we have a startlingly reductive interpretation of humanity's state, a grim picture indeed of the only wisdom accessible to mankind.

If the formula 'all that has been and all that is to be' in this chapter recalls the epic formula τά τ᾽ ἐόντα τά τ᾽ ἐσόμενα πρό τ᾽ ἐόντα ('what is, what will be, and what was before', in Homer, *Iliad* i. 80 and elsewhere), as a close parallel in Epicurean writings (see below) suggests, then there is a further point and contrast. In Homer and Hesiod this knowledge is the prerogative of divinities (such as the Muses), poets, and prophets; and it is a source of insight and spellbinding imaginative utterance.[97]

---

[97] See West on Hes. *Th.* 32; further, W. Marg, *Homer über die Dichtung* (2nd edn., Munster 1971); J. Griffin, *Homer on Life and Death* (Oxford 1980) 96–8.

This also seems to be the implication of a fragmentary admonition attributed to Epicurus or his disciple Metrodorus, a passage close to Marcus in its epigrammatic form, yet subtly different in its message:

μέμνησο ὅτι θνητὸς ὢν τῇ φύσει καὶ λαβὼν χρόνον ὡρισμένον ἀνέβης τοῖς περὶ φύσεως διαλογισμοῖς ἐπὶ τὴν ἀπειρίαν καὶ τὸν αἰῶνα καὶ κατεῖδες "τά τ' ἐόντα τά τ' ἐσόμενα πρὸ τ' ἐόντα".

Remember that, though you are mortal in nature and have received a limited span of time, through your discourses upon nature you have ascended to infinity and [eternal?] time and have looked upon 'what is, what will be, and what was before'. (Epicurus, *Gnom. Vat.* 10)

For the Epicurean author man is indeed inevitably mortal, having only a limited time to live, but nevertheless he has also an eternal task, the study of nature and the universe (cf. Epicurus *ap.* Diog. Laert. x. 135). Through this pursuit he can gain knowledge and understanding beyond his own lifespan, and achieve a kind of immortality. But for Marcus the knowledge gained is commonplace, and the expression of bitter disillusionment. All the flight of the intellect or the soul, the struggle for understanding, comes back in the end to these simple and inescapable truths.

(ii) Death and Oblivion (iii. 3, iv. 32–3, 48, 50, vi. 47, viii. 5, 25, 31, ix. 33, x. 27, xii. 27)

πάντα ὅσα ὁρᾷς τάχιστα φθαρήσεται καὶ οἱ φθειρόμενα αὐτὰ ἐπιδόντες τάχιστα καὶ αὐτοὶ φθαρήσονται καὶ ὁ ἐσχατόγηρως ἀποθανὼν εἰς ἴσον καταστήσεται τῷ προώρῳ.

All that you see will speedily perish, and those who saw those things perish will also themselves speedily perish, and the most ancient of men will be at one in death with the boy who came to a premature grave. (*Med.* ix. 33)

The simple but effective artistry of this passage is easily seen. The correlation of 'you see . . . who saw', 'speedily . . . speedily', 'will perish . . . perish . . . will themselves perish' makes plain the progression—one death followed by the death of those who witnessed it, a theme which fascinates Marcus. The same notion recurs in most of the chapters listed above, and elsewhere, elaborated in various ways (the fullest is iv. 19). We find it in iv. 48. 2 expressed thus:

ὁ μὲν τοῦτον κηδεύσας εἶτα ἐξετάθη, ὁ δὲ ἐκεῖνον, πάντα δὲ ἐν βραχεῖ.

The man who performed the burial for him was laid out next, and then the one [who did it for] him, all in a brief span of time.

Here the rapidity of the description itself brings home the rapidity of what is described, a sequence of deaths. So too in viii. 25 ('Lucilla [buried] Verus, then Lucilla [was herself buried]'), in which the Greek sentence omits even a verb. There the long, repetitive series of names also gives a sense of the monotony of this endless chain.

There is artifice again in iv. 50: 'Cadicianus, Fabius, Julianus, Lepidus, and the rest—who carried many to their graves, then were carried themselves (ἐξήνεγκαν, εἶτα ἐξηνέχθησαν)'. Here the use of the same verb makes the relationship between the bearer and the one borne out still more intimate. It is almost as if there were a causal relationship between the act of bearing the corpse and the experience of being carried out yourself. The verbal echoes unite the subjects of each clause, expressing their common share in mortality. The same device is used in the following examples:

(iv. 35) πᾶν ἐφήμερον, καὶ τὸ μνημονεῦον καὶ τὸ μνημονευόμενον.

All is transient, the rememberer and the remembered alike.

(vii. 21) ἐγγὺς μὲν ἡ σὴ περὶ πάντων λήθη, ἐγγὺς δὲ ἡ πάντων περὶ σοῦ λήθη.

Near at hand is your forgetting all things, near at hand is all things forgetting you.

(viii. 21) βραχύβιον καὶ ὁ ἐπαινῶν καὶ ὁ ἐπαινούμενος καὶ ὁ μνημονεύων καὶ ὁ μνημονευόμενος.

A short-lived thing is both the praiser and the man praised, the rememberer and the remembered.

Apparent opposites are grouped together in a wider scheme.

The factual, restrained tone of the first passage quoted, ix. 33, also deserves comment. Even the personal viewpoint ('all that *you* see') disappears from the following clauses: the authorial voice seems unshaken and unemotional, yet his pronouncement carries all the more authority for its lack of regret or overt sentimentality. This becomes clearer when we remember that the premature death of a child in infancy (ἄωρος, πρόωρος), then as now, was considered particularly tragic.[98] That loss had in fact been experienced by Marcus himself. But in the grave the old and the young, the rich and the poor (vi. 24 'Alexander and his stable-boy'), the praiser and the praised (viii. 21 above) meet on equal terms.

Meditations ix. 33 is one of the most concise versions in the work of a theme on which countless authors, not least Marcus himself, have lavished their literary talents. Statements of the equality imposed by universal death begin with Homer (e.g. Il. xxi. 106 ff.), and can be pursued through Greek and Latin, lyric and tragedy, epigram and elegy.[99] The universality of death is often used as a kind of consolation, or more accurately as a quasi-philosophic argument for facing and accepting an inevitable destiny.[100] From early times this was put in terms of specific examples. 'Patroclus also died', Achilles reminds Lycaon (Il. xxi. 107). 'Even Sisyphus could not find a way out', Alcaeus warns Melanippus (fr. 38a. 5). The greatest of men have been forced in the end to submit to death, even Heracles the all-conquering (Hom. Il. xviii. 117 f.).[101] This sequence of thought appears in most of Marcus' longer treatments of death (iii. 3, iv. 33, 48, 50, vi. 47): think constantly, he tells himself, how many physicians, astrologers, philosophers, warriors, tyrants, cities have perished despite all their efforts and their brief moments of glory. Elsewhere he often speaks of specific individuals; philosophers and kings make frequent appearances (another case of conventional topics in a tradition having added point for Marcus himself). Thus in iv. 33 the list of names ranges from early republican heroes (Camillus, Dentatus, Scipio) down

---

[98] See F. Cumont, *After-Life in Roman Paganism* (Yale 1922) ch. 4; Kassel, *Untersuchungen* 80–1, 88–9; Nisbet–Hubbard on Hor. *Odes* ii. 9. 15.

[99] Illustration is almost superfluous, but see e.g. Simonides *PMG* 520–4; Kindstrand on Bion fr. 62–72; Nisbet–Hubbard on Hor. *Odes* i. 28. 16, ii. 14 throughout; Lattimore (n. 75) 250 ff.

[100] See Kassel, *Untersuchungen* 54 f.; Macleod on Hom. *Il.* xxiv. 518–51; Rutherford, *JHS* 102 (1982) 158–60.

[101] For the theme, see again Hor. *Odes* i. 28. 7, ii. 9 (with Nisbet–Hubbard), iv. 7. 25 f.; also e.g. Lucr. iii. 1024 ff.; Kassel, *Untersuchungen* 70 ff.; B. P. Wallach, *Lucretius and the Diatribe against the Fear of Death* (*Mnem.* Suppl. 40, Leiden 1977) 91 ff.; Men. Rh. iii. 414. 4.

to Roman emperors. He names Augustus, Hadrian, Antoninus Pius: the next term in this series is unspoken but obvious.[102]

In the same way we can find additional point in other passages on this theme. For instance, in viii. 31 he refers to the death of 'the whole court' of Augustus: 'his wife, daughter, grandsons, ... sister, Agrippa, ... Arius, Maecenas, doctors, priests, an entire court, all vanished.' The obvious lesson is the usual one of life's transience. But Marcus no doubt also thinks of Augustus' increasing isolation in the final decade of his long reign.[103] Is it irrelevant that Marcus himself was probably the survivor of most of those he cared for?

Again, the preoccupation with leaving an heir to one's house, preferably of one's own blood, is mentioned later in the chapter. Here again Augustus' struggles to ensure that the succession passed to an offspring of the Julii must be in the author's mind. But this does not exclude the likelihood of a secondary reference to his own parallel concern. Commodus, his own successor, was his last surviving son, and Marcus himself was the first emperor in five reigns to be succeeded by his own offspring.[104]

Thirdly, the many references to posthumous fame and reputation should not be considered only in a philosophic context, but also compared with the aspirations of Roman magistrates and earlier emperors to ensure their own undying glory. In the case of Augustus we have the self-glorification of his *Res Gestae*, and also the declaration quoted by Suetonius (*Aug.* 28. 2, especially 'ut optimi status auctor *dicar* et moriens ut feram mecum spem, mansura in vestigio suo fundamenta rei publicae quae iecero'). The same aims may be observed in the great mausoleums of Augustus and Hadrian, modelled on the tombs of Hellenistic kings,[105] and in the emulation of Alexander which

---

[102] For other references to his predecessors see the indexes to Haines' and Dalfen's edns.; e.g. iii. 16 on Nero; xii. 27 on Tiberius; and esp. vi. 30, 'be not Caesarified' (see above ch. II n. 57); x. 31, 'and so, when you look at yourself, visualise one of the Caesars'. Cf. n. 110 below.

[103] See R. Syme, *The Roman Revolution* (Oxford 1939) 431 ff.; id., *History in Ovid* (Oxford 1978) 205 ff.

[104] On the deaths of his own children see above, ch. III n. 98. On the dynastic need, Brunt, *PBSR* 43 (1975) 30. Useful qualification of Rostovtzeff's exaggerated contrast with earlier dynasties is provided by R. M. Geer, *TAPA* 67 (1936) 47–54.

[105] For mockery of a tyrant's pretensions to fame through a mausoleum see Lucian, *Cataplus* 9, *Menippus* 17 (close to *Charon* 24 or Juv. 10. 168–73).

flattery and eulogy fostered.[106] It was not only emperors who hoped for posthumous fame. Literary men also, including philosophers (though not Socrates and Epictetus, Marcus' real heroes), claim lasting significance for their works, often to the extent of asserting their immortality. Alternatively, if they are not fully appreciated now, it will be different after their deaths (e.g. Sen. *Ep.* 79, 13 ff.).[107] By contrast, Marcus knows all too well that emperors are likely to be slandered and criticised much more after their deaths than in their lifetimes (see esp. x. 36).[108] It is in this light that we should read the references to posthumous fame in these chapters (e.g. iv. 33 'what then is everlasting memory, all told? All empty.'), and to the worthlessness of other men's judgements (iii. 4. 4, viii. 53, ix. 12, 18, 27, 34, etc.).

Alexander the Great, mentioned in a number of these chapters, is a charismatic figure for any student of the past, above all for a ruler and a conqueror.[109] Marcus Aurelius, however, in the manner of ancient moralists,[110] mentions

[106] See n. 109 below; Suet. *Aug.* 18, 50, 94; P. A. Brunt, *JRS* 53 (1963) 176; E. Norden, *RhM* 54 (1899) 466 ff. = *Kleine Schriften* (Berlin 1966) 422 ff.

[107] On philosophers' aspirations to fame see P. Wendland, *Hermes* 51 (1916) 481–5, based on a discussion of Tac. *Hist.* iv. 6. 1 ('erant quibus adpetentior famae videretur, quando etiam sapientibus cupido gloriae novissima exuitur'). See also Cic. *Tusc.* i. 34; Plut. *Lat. Viv.* 1128b–c; Mayor on Juv. 7. 39; Brunt, *JRS* 64 (1974) 14, 20.

[108] Cf. Tac. *Ann.* i. 9–10, an account of the criticisms which followed the death of Augustus. After death the tyrant may suffer *damnatio memoriae*, as Marcus knew well: cf. e.g. Suet. *Calig.* 60 (though contrast Dio 73. 17); *Dom.* 23; B. M. Levick, *Tiberius the Politician* (London 1976) 282 n. 50; F. Vittinghoff, *Der Staatsfeind in der röm. Kaiserzeit* (Berlin 1936) 64 ff. Nero was actually condemned to death by the senate in his own lifetime: Suet. *Nero* 49. Commodus: SHA *Comm.* 20. This adds an additional flavour to Marcus' obsession with posthumous reputation, and especially to passages such as ix. 30 ὅσοι δ' ἐπαινοῦντες ἴσως νῦν σε τάχιστα ψέξουσι. Cf. also Tiberius' speech in Tac. *Ann.* iv. 38, with the historian's own comments; Suet. *Tib.* 75.

[109] For details of his continuing fame and popularity as a subject of historiography and rhetoric see Mayor on Juv. 10. 168 ff.; S. F. Bonner, *AJP* 87 (1966) 273–4. For Alexander-imitation in the late Republic and later, Syme, *Rom. Rev.* 30; O. Wippert, *Alexander-Imitatio und Römische Politik* (diss. Wurzburg 1972); P. A. Brunt in P. D. A. Garnsey and C. R. Whittaker (eds.), *Imperialism in the Ancient World* (Cambridge 1978) 178 f. On Stoic views of Alexander, and on Marcus' references, see Brunt, *Athen.* 55 (1977) 37 ff., 39 n. 72.

[110] The dismissal of Alexander's achievements in iii. 3, vi. 24, viii. 3, ix. 29, x. 27 corresponds to the more sustained treatments in Sen. Rh. *Suas.* i; Lucan x. 20 ff.; Juv. 10. 168–73. The contrast of Alexander and Diogenes (viii. 3) recalls their legendary exchange, which tradition embroidered (Mayor on Juv. 14. 303 ff.). Compare also the treatment of Pompey (iii. 3, viii. 3, 31; cf. Juv. 10. 283 ff.) or Caesar (iii. 3, viii. 3; cf. Sen. *Ep.* 14. 12 ff. (see M. T. Griffin, *CQ* 18 (1968) 373 ff.), 104. 30 ff.). Seneca also reflects on the self-destructiveness of Caesar, in terms that recall Marcus' terser references, at *Ep.*

Alexander's ambitions and achievements only to deride them: 'Alexander, Julius Caesar, Pompeius—what were they compared with Diogenes, Heraclitus, Socrates? For these men saw reality and its causal and material aspects; their ruling selves were self-determined. But as for the former, how much they had to worry about, and of how many things they were the slaves.' (viii. 3). The kings and tyrants, then, were themselves the slaves, whereas the minds of the philosophers retained their freedom (αὐτάρκη).[111] Thus a Stoic sermon is compressed into an epigram, even briefer in Greek than in English. There may also be a slight undercurrent of sympathy with the worries of the despots (πρόνοια), the distractions and the duties of power, which Marcus too had to endure. But this is not prominent enough to disturb the broad, powerful antithesis: power versus wisdom, active versus contemplative lives, the false masters and the true.

Alexander also figures in a passage (x. 27) in which Marcus looks back upon past generations and kingdoms, reflecting that they are all alike, πάντα τοιαῦτα (a very common theme and phrase):

... καὶ ὅλα δράματα καὶ σκηνὰς ὁμοειδεῖς, ὅσα ἐκ πείρας τῆς σῆς ἢ τῆς πρεσβυτέρας ἱστορίας ἔγνως, πρὸ ὀμμάτων τίθεσθαι, οἷον αὐλὴν ὅλην Ἀδριανοῦ καὶ αὐλὴν ὅλην Ἀντωνίνου καὶ αὐλὴν ὅλην Φιλίππου, Ἀλεξάνδρου, Κροίσου· πάντα γὰρ ἐκεῖνα τοιαῦτα ἦν, μόνον δι' ἑτέρων.

... and set before your eyes all the plays and sets, all alike, that you know from your own experience or from the history of older times: for instance, the whole court of Hadrian and the whole court of Antoninus and the whole court of Philip, Alexander, Croesus—for all of those were just the same, only different actors played the parts.

Here again we can see how repetition and enumeration contribute to the monotony of the catalogue, and so simulate the eternal sameness described. The names, the individuals, seem not to matter: even chronological order is abandoned. There is a

---

94. 65. Further, Griffin, *Seneca* 182–94. Examples of vice and indulgence are equally traditional: Phalaris (iii. 16. 1; cf. Mayor on Juv. 8. 81) and Nero (iii. 16. 1; cf. Mayor on Juv. 8. 211–30), or Tiberius on Capri (xii. 27; cf. Suet. *Tib.* 42–5; see above, ch. II n. 99). On Marcus and his predecessors see also n. 102 above; here again the traditional *exempla* of power and vice carry unique weight for one who is their successor (cf. vi. 30. 1).

[111] Cf. esp. *SVF* iii. 349–66; Cic. *Paradoxa* v. For 'slaves of passion' see Eur. *Hec.* 864 ff.; Kindstrand on Bion fr. 11; Mayor on Juv. 5. 161. Similar play on senses of *libertas* in Boethius, *Consol. Philos.* e.g. i m ii. 24 ff.

limit to the number of things which human beings, or human societies, can do. Each generation, in Marcus' eyes, seems simply to repeat the actions—more particularly the vices—of its predecessors, to act the same parts. The image of life as a play[112] reinforces the impression of repetition and unreality. The same scenes are endlessly reperformed: everyone knows them by heart. Marcus uses the same image elsewhere to describe the shadowy nature of life (vii. 3). A striking instance is the string of images in x. 9: 'Every day, play-acting, conflict, timidity, sloth, slavishness.' The metaphor is also used to decry pomp and pretension, as in ix. 29 (of Alexander, Philip, and Demetrius): εἰ δὲ ἐτραγῴδησαν ('if they played their grandiose roles'). I discuss this chapter more fully in Section 6 (ii) below.

Yet the antithesis of Alexander and Socrates, of despot and sage, is not the only light in which Marcus considers them. Whereas in viii. 3 (quoted above, p. 166) Epictetus and the others emerge triumphant, as masters of their fate, Marcus elsewhere admits that they too are as helpless as any mortals before the onslaught of time:

πόσους ἤδη ὁ αἰὼν Χρυσίππους, πόσους Σωκράτεις, πόσους Ἐπικτήτους καταπέπωκεν.

How many Chrysippuses, how many Socrateses, how many Epictetuses time has swallowed up. (vii. 19)

The generic plurals even deny these thinkers their uniqueness. And in the longer chapters on death philosophers have their place along with tyrants and military leaders (iv. 48, cf. 33; vi. 47; viii. 25; similarly, x. 31). They enjoy no privileged status. The greatest power in the hierarchy of Marcus' thought is not Zeus, or the cosmos, or virtue, but the all-encompassing force of death. No subject in the *Meditations* is treated with such fascination, such endless variation.[113]

6. Stoicism in Practice: A Reading of Two Longer Chapters

I conclude this chapter with a broad analysis of two longer chapters of the *Meditations*, iii. 4 and ix. 29, both of which provide examples of Marcus' style at its more ambitious, more

---

[112] See n. 13 above.
[113] Cf. n. 25 above and ch. VI 3 below.

self-consciously 'literary' level, and both of which illustrate at some length the hortatory method of the work, as applied to the author's own conduct and social duties.[114] Of these two chapters, the longer (iii. 4) seems also the less successful: its argument and tone involve serious difficulties. The general argument of my account of the *Meditations* has been to emphasise, and to illustrate in detail, the intimate relationship in Marcus' work between style and thought. This is not to say that stylistic unevenness automatically corresponds with an uneasy ethical position: naturally, such unevenness could as well be attributed to inattention, overtiredness, or simple literary incompetence (though I hope that what has been said so far will make the reader slow to have recourse the last explanation). I suggest, however, that the analysis of discrepancies or disharmonies in structure, tone, and style is a valid, though hazardous, tool in the critic's armoury, even when applied to so eccentric a work as Marcus'.

Meditations iii. 4 is a lengthy chapter which might well be criticised as a paratactic composition, a mosaic of familiar themes stitched together without any proper unity being imposed. There is, perhaps, some truth in such criticism, not only of this chapter but of many of the longer discourses of the *Meditations*. They tend (as for instance in x. 8) to fall easily into sections, and we sometimes feel that a passage would run more smoothly with some sentences reordered or cut out. But this impression can easily be exaggerated, and we should in any case attempt to follow the author's line of thought and see whether the separate themes are not more intimately related than by simple juxtaposition. Again, we should consider whether structural difficulties or incoherence may reflect problems implicit in the Stoic system itself, or conflicts in Marcus' own attitudes. In my view iii. 4 does indicate such a problem; and although it ends on a high note, it leaves a dilemma half-exposed and unsolved.

In ix. 29, by contrast, the structure is tighter and more economical; the language is forceful, polemical, memorable; the tone is disillusioned yet resolute. The author defines his position firmly and unambiguously. Yet the starkness of the message is not over-simplifying or cynical: this is, we feel, the writer's

---

[114] See also Brunt, *JRS* 64 (1974) 10–14 on Marcus and his associates. For the Stoic's social duties see e.g. Diog. Laert. vii. 121; Cic. *Off.* i. 12.

considered view, expressed pungently and without distracting qualifications or digressions. The vitality and coherence of the chapter in artistic and rhetorical terms encourage us to feel that, even if it is not Marcus' final word, ix. 29 presents a positive and consistently held point of view. It does not, of course, follow that the position is true or wholly admirable. But the passage well illustrates both the positive qualities of Stoicism as a doctrine and the positive function of therapeutic writing (the *Meditations* themselves) in formulating such doctrine persuasively and coherently. The following pages are intended as detailed corroboration of these judgements.

(i) iii. 4

The theme is, as often, that the author is wasting time, and not much of it is left.[115] But the time-wasting is of a quite specific kind: worrying about what someone else is doing or saying or thinking or planning. This kind of obsession is rejected: rather, look to yourself, make sure that if anyone were to ask you what is on your mind, you could answer openly and freely, without guilt or shame. Curiosity and speculation about other people's schemes is, except in special cases, malicious and self-indulgent, the product of envy and suspicion (§ 2).

The thought here is true to the best strain in Marcus' ethics, self-criticism and frankness. It also gives a new and striking twist to a motif familiar since early Greek poetry. In ancient literature we often find the utopian wish expressed: if only we could look into men's hearts and see what they are plotting, if only God had put a window in their breasts for that purpose.[116] But here Marcus deprecates such a desire, and envisages facing this challenge himself. The ethical point is both more realistic and closer to home than in the conventional conceit.

Section 3 of the chapter refers back to the opening of § 1 (οὐκ ἔτι ὑπερτιθέμενος recalls the earlier μὴ κατατρίψῃς τὸ ὑπολειπόμε-

---

[115] For the theme of procrastination in the *Meditations* see ii. 4–6, iii. 10, 14, iv. 17, 19, 37, viii. 22. For parallels see e.g. Epicurus fr. 204 U.; Hor. *Odes* i. 11. 8, iii. 29. 41 ff.; *Ep.* i. 4. 13.

[116] Theogn. 117 ff.; Eur. *Med.* 516 ff. with Page's note; *PMG* 889. Later, e.g. Tert. *Ap.* 35. 7, and the examples quoted by P. Brown, *The Making of Late Antiquity* (Princeton, NJ, 1978) 128 nn. 60–3.

νον), and goes on to expound, in a long and lyrical period, the positive side of the prohibitions in § 2. A man who can speak out all his thoughts at any time is 'no longer putting off being one of the elect'; he becomes, indeed, a kind of priest or minister of the gods. Both of these conceptions, the 'elect' or 'best of men' (ἀρίστοις) and the virtuous man as priest, are rare and remarkable in the *Meditations*.[117] In this passage the author projects a picture of an ideal man, completely fulfilling his own nature and the divine will, immune to pain and wickedness outside himself. The string of alliterative negatives is a prominent rhetorical device: ἄχραντον . . . ἄτρωτον . . . ἀνέπαφον . . . ἀναίσθητον ('unstained . . . unwounded . . . untouched . . . impervious'). The picture drawn here is very much like that of the traditional Stoic *sapiens*,[118] but Marcus avoids any claim to being such a man himself by putting the whole description in the third person, as a mere account of the potential powers and dignity of a true man (esp. § 3 *init*., ὁ γάρ τοι ἀνὴρ ὁ τοιοῦτος, 'for truly such a man as this'). The personal relevance, however, becomes apparent again at the end of this sentence, where the ideal man is said 'seldom and only under some great necessity or for the common good [an echo of § 1] to imagine what another is saying or doing or thinking'. He will concentrate solely on his own work and Nature's will, which are as one. Other men are irrelevant, even unnecessary.

This too is an authentic and logical Stoic position, since only the reform and improvement of oneself lies fully within one's power.[119] Yet it sits oddly with the demand that man should be a social being (§ 2 ζῴου κοινωνικοῦ; § 3 κοινωφελοῦς, cf. § 1 ἐπί τι κοινωφελές),[120] a condition which recurs in § 4, where the contrast of ideals is made explicit: 'he does not forget the

---

[117] ἄριστος in this sense only here in Marcus. For the priest image see also below, ch. v n. 103.

[118] On the *sapiens* see above, ch. III nn. 72–3.

[119] See also x. 4, x. 30, x. 37, and Farquharson's notes. Ancient moralists regularly concentrate on the reform of oneself, by oneself (cf. ch. I above generally, on self-examination). This should not be regarded as selfishness, but as a response to the most immediate challenge.

[120] κοινός (and cognates) is extremely common in Marcus, as in Epictetus. It is of course constantly linked with the idea of the brotherhood of man, as children of the same God (cf. e.g. Epict. i. 13. 2 ff.). The *sapiens* will be κοινωνικός (*SVF* iii. 628). See further *SVF* iv, s.v.; *TDNT* iii. 791 ff.; A. Bonhöffer, *Epictet und das Neue Testament* (RVV 10, Giesen 1911) 51 ff. Cf. Stoic 'cosmopolitanism' (see below, ch. VI n. 40).

brotherhood of all rational beings, nor that an affection
(κήδεσθαι μὲν) for every man is proper to humanity; but he
knows that it is not the opinions (δοξῆς δὲ) of the world that he
must consider . . .'.[121] In what follows, the note of superiority
and contempt for the inferior race of ignorant men seems harsh
and arrogant, unusually so for Marcus. Like the eulogy of the
sapiens, this scorn and indifference (the reverse side of authority
and self-respect) is made possible because he is not speaking of
himself or his own personal role. But this makes the passage all
the more revealing.

The point about caring for *all* rational beings is in fact rather
out of place in a passage of this kind: it seems to be an attempt on
Marcus' part to qualify or soften the note of arrogance and
superiority. But in fact it points still more to a contradiction,
since it is hard to separate love for other men from concern with
what makes them human and individual, their opinions and
their judgements. Moreover, the final sentences of this chapter
bring us back, from another direction, to a topic close to what
was dismissed at the beginning; for Marcus now declares that
the wise man will think continually of what other men, men
unlike himself, are doing, and of how they live, οἷοι μεθ᾽ οἵων
φύρονται ('the kind of men they are, and in what company they
spend their muddled lives')—and therefore he will hold their
opinions in contempt.

The argument, then, once fully articulated becomes self-
defeating, for to contemplate the misdeeds and the secret vices of
the masses ('the characters they display at home and abroad, by
day or by night') *is* to think of their deeds and thoughts and
desires, and not without some degree of malice and contempt.
The chapter ends by attributing to this idealised figure the kind
of practices Marcus had been reproving in himself. Perhaps the
supreme sage here described would be able to contemplate these
things in a purely public-spirited way; but elsewhere we find
Marcus giving very similar advice to himself; to scrutinise other
men's thoughts and schemes, to observe their deficiencies.[122]
The emperor, for all his justly acclaimed compassion, cannot

[121] Compare my remarks on xi. 8 (esp. the final sentences) in ch. III 5, p. 122 above.
See also vii. 13, vii. 43, ix. 3, and the use of καταφρονεῖν in e.g. xii. 24.

[122] See esp. vi. 53, vii. 30, ix. 27 (cold or two-edged); by contrast, viii. 61, ix. 22, and
x. 37 are more generous or self-critical.

remain 'unconscious of any wickedness' (§ 3), but needs his awareness of others' unworthiness to support his independence from them; which is to say, again, what emerges here and often in the *Meditations*, that the Stoic *sapiens* is an ideal model, and as such must always be undermined by human weakness.[123]

(ii) ix. 29[124]

The second of our examples, which offers one of the most effective expressions of the world-view embodied in the *Meditations*, is short enough to be quoted and translated in full. It provides a more homogeneous and perhaps more memorable model of the author's style: rapid, urgent, full of imperatives, epigrammatic, conveying a sense of strong emotions, controlled but finding outlet through the very process of composition, as in the biting forcefulness of a phrase such as μυξῶν μεστά ('full of drivel').[125]

χειμάρρους ἡ τῶν ὅλων αἰτία· πάντα φέρει. ὡς εὐτελῆ δὲ καὶ τὰ πολιτικὰ ταῦτα καί, ὡς οἴεται, φιλοσόφως πρακτικὰ ἀνθρώπια· μυξῶν μεστά. ἄνθρωπε, τί ποτε; ποίησον, ὃ νῦν ἡ φύσις ἀπαιτεῖ. ὅρμησον, ἐὰν διδῶται, καὶ μὴ περιβλέπου, εἴ τις εἴσεται. μὴ μὴν Πλάτωνος πολιτείαν ἔλπιξε, ἀλλα ἀρκοῦ, εἰ τὸ βραχύτατον πρόεισι, καὶ τούτου αὐτοῦ τὴν ἔκβασιν, ὡς οὐ μικρόν τί ἐστι, διανοοῦ. δόγμα γὰρ αὐτῶν τίς μεταβαλεῖ; χωρὶς δὲ δογμάτων μεταβολῆς τί ἄλλο ἢ δουλεία στενόντων καὶ πείθεσθαι προσποιουμένων; ὕπαγε νῦν καὶ Ἀλέξανδρον καὶ Φίλιππον καὶ Δημήτριον τὸν Φαληρέα μοι λέγε. ὄψονται, εἰ εἶδον τί ἡ φύσις ἤθελε, καὶ ἑαυτοὺς ἐπαιδαγώγησαν· εἰ δὲ ἐτραγώδησαν, οὐδείς με κατακέκρικε μιμεῖσθαι. ἁπλοῦν ἐστι καὶ αἰδῆμον τὸ φιλοσοφίας ἔργον· μή με ἄπαγε ἐπὶ σεμνοτυφίαν.

The working of the whole is like a torrent; it carries all in its stream. How cheap and petty are those little men busy with politics and their philosophic practice, as they suppose it; they are full of drivel. What,

---

[123] For ancient criticism of the *sapiens* see e.g. Cic. *Mur.* 61 ff.; *Fin.* iv. 20 ff.; Hor. *Sat.* i. 3. 121 ff.

[124] I follow Dalfen's Teubner text (and earlier editors and translators) against Farquharson's transposition of ὡς εὐτελῆ... μυξῶν μεστά (p. 89 l. 8–10 Dalfen) to follow διανοοῦ (line 13 D.). Both versions involve some obscurity of thought, but no more than is tolerable and usual in this author.

[125] For μύξα cf. Epict. i. 6. 30 f., ii. 16. 13, iv. 11. 9, iii. 22. 90 (with Billerbeck's note), iv. 11. 32. For μυξάριον cf. M. Aur. iv. 48, vi. 13 (not in Epictetus). Farquharson on ix. 29 aptly compares Pl. *Rep.* i. 343a (Thrasymachus to Socrates: You ought to have a nurse to wipe your face when you are drivelling).

then, man, is your part? Act as Nature asks you to now; set about it, if it is granted you, and don't look around you to see if anyone will know. Do not hope for Plato's state, but be content if the smallest thing goes forward well, and count the outcome of the matter in hand no small thing. For who can change a man's convictions? And without change of convictions what will there be but slavery of groaning men, who pretend to be persuaded. Go now and tell me of Alexander, Philip, Demetrius of Phaleron. If they saw what was the will of Universal Nature and schooled themselves to follow it, they will see to that. But if they played the tragic part, no one has condemned me to imitate them. The work of philosophy is simple and modest; do not lead me astray into pompous pride.

The opening is swift, almost shorthand: Marcus seems to be formulating the briefest possible reminders of thoughts more fully developed elsewhere (for the technique see pp. 131–7 above). Thus the first sentence, with its river imagery, recalls chapters on flux and change, particularly iv. 43 and vi. 15. In this context πάντα φέρει ('carries all things away') perhaps plays on the Heraclitean phrase πάντα ῥεῖ[126] ('all things are in motion'). 'All things' in Marcus' phrase are the object, not the subject: the material world does not just pass away but is forced out, propelled. εὐτελῆ ('cheap') is a typical blame-word, often applied by Marcus to the transient mortal world (ii. 2, iv. 48, v. 10, xii. 27). Marcus here uses it to dismiss self-styled theorists on the philosophic art of practising politics: 'how cheap and petty are those little men . . . they are full of drivel.' We cannot tell precisely what kind of men (or writers) he had in mind— possibly advisers or flatterers who glorified the moral authority of a ruler over his citizens (deploying ideas and doctrines such as we find in Dio Chrysostom's orations or Plutarch's essays on government).[127] Alternatively, he may be condemning actual statesmen who sought to curry favour with their emperor by espousing philosophy without truly understanding its teaching.[128]

In contrast with these men, Marcus sees himself as a realist:

---

[126] Or χωρεῖ? (Pl. *Crat.* 402a = Heracl. A6 D.–K.)

[127] See above, ch. II n. 14.

[128] On flatterers and pseudo-philosophers see ch. III. 5, p. 122 above. Alternatively, Professor Brunt suggested to me (at a seminar in Oxford, Feb. 1984) that Marcus may possibly be referring to himself, yet another variant of his constant self-criticism: Marcus the realist rebukes the idealistic dreamings of his more optimistic (or younger?) self.

'do not hope for Plato's state . . .'. Dismissal of utopian politics, and especially of Plato's detailed yet fantastic schemes, was almost a cliché. We find Cicero saying much the same thing in two passages, both of which, significantly, criticise the unrealistic posturing of Stoic idealists, Cato the Younger and Rutilius Rufus (Cic. *Att.* ii. 1. 8; *de Or.* i. 230).[129] For Marcus the experience of imperial power has led not to wide-ranging social and political reforms, but to a disillusioned appreciation of how little any individual, even an emperor, can influence what really matters, the state of men's minds and souls. (Ironically enough, this is a theme which is itself present in Plato's work, notably in the *Gorgias*: see 511a–18e.) Here again we can contrast the sober pessimism of Marcus Aurelius with the facile enthusiasm of his biographer in the *Historia Augusta*, who maintains that Plato's saying that states would flourish if philosophers became kings or kings philosophers was 'constantly on Marcus' lips' (SHA *Marcus* 27. 1).[130]

'Who can change men's opinions?' reaches a despairing depth uncommon elsewhere in the work.[131] But in the absence of

[129] Marcus may even have had these passages in mind: Seneca and many others (Quintilian, Pliny the Younger, Suetonius, and Gellius) are familiar with the *Letters to Atticus* (cf. D. R. Shackleton Bailey's comm. vol. i, 59 ff. on the 'fata epistularum'). Note also that Plutarch (*Phocion* 3. 2) knows the *ad Atticum* passage, though seemingly at second hand (T. Geiger, 'Commentary on Plutarch, *Cato Minor*' (diss. Oxford 1971) 19).

[130] In general on SHA *Marcus* see J. Schwendemann, *Der historische Wert der Vita Marci bei SHA* (Heidelberg 1923). Much is suspect or fantastic (cf. Brunt, *JRS* 64 (1974) 1 n. 1), but the author has at least one good source, and occasionally the biographer's judgements or characterisations provide a foil to the complexities of the *Meditations* (for one such instance see Brunt, art. cit. 14 para. 2). In particular, Marcus is presented as a model philosophic ruler and indeed as almost a Stoic sage. See e.g. 2. 1 'fuit a prima infantia gravis'; 4. 10 on the perfect balance of his character; 12. 2 on his moral influence upon his subjects, expressed in the banal phrase 'fecitque ex malis bonos, ex bonis optimos' (contrast *Med.* ix. 29); 21. 3 f.; 28. 4 (death-bed scene) 'ridens res humanas, mortem etiam contemnens'; and esp. 16. 5 on his Stoic serenity: 'erat enim ipse tantae tranquillitatis ut vultum numquam mutaverit maerore vel gaudio' (whence *Epit. de Caes.* 16. 7, adding 'a principio vitae'!). Whether or not the dictum is authentic, the remark of Pius in the adjacent life, quoted as an epigraph to the present study, gives a picture of Marcus' character that is truer to the evidence of the *Meditations*.

This idealisation intensifies in the later tradition, in which Marcus becomes an ideal monarch (the philosophic side tends to be understressed): thus already Herodian (i. 2. 3 ff.; see C. R. Whittaker's comments in the Loeb edn., introd. pp. lxxii–lxxiii); S. Aurelius Victor, 16 (esp. §§ 4, 9, 14); *Epit. de Caes.* 16. See further S. A. Stertz, *CW* 70 (1977) 433–9.

[131] Cf. Epict. iv. 6. 5 ff.: not even Zeus has the power to persuade all men of what is good and evil: the only thing possible is to convince yourself. As often in Epictetus (see ch. vi below), we meet a more positive doctrine and a lighter tone. Another contrast: Plut. *Tranq.* 476c–d (difficult, but not impossible).

conviction men will pretend to believe and obey merely because of the emperor's authority: δουλεία στενόντων ('slavery of groaning men'). The word 'slavery' here plays a dual role, denoting both the subjection of those who must obey the ruling power and the condition of a man whom philosophy has not succeeded in 'setting free' (a metaphor prominent in the Stoic paradoxes: Cic. *Paradoxa* 33–41; Sen. *Ep.* 17. 6 'perpetua libertas').

Marcus' difficulty in imposing his principles upon his subjects is a spiritual counterpart to Pliny's paradoxical declaration of allegiance to Trajan: 'You command us to be free; we will be so!' (*Pan.* 66. 4).[132]

Finally, Marcus rejects the models of Alexander, Philip, and Demetrius as examples of true kingship. These can hardly have been seriously proposed to him: we find a severe judgement on Philip in the near-contemporary Plutarch (*Pelop.* 26). But Alexander at least was a common figure in declamation and eulogy of rulers;[133] and it may be that the three monarchs are named in descending order of quality. These rulers are characterised by ancient moralists as, above all, wilful men, defying all laws of man and god for their own glory and power. They knew no masters, and saw no call to discipline themselves; hence the fierce criticism in Marcus' words: 'If they saw what was the will of Universal Nature and schooled themselves to follow it . . .'.[134]

The description of these conquerors as 'playing tragedies on a stage' uses the metaphor of the drama of life[135] to emphasise the illusory status of human ambition. These men knew nothing of the larger drama of nature, but were content to play their bombastic, yet ultimately trivial roles. 'No one condemned me to imitate them', responds Marcus: he has his own models, his own role to play.[136] Moreover, to imitate them would be a positive punishment, as is brought out by the verb he uses: κατακέκρικε ('condemned') is commonly used of the passing of a severe sentence (again a bizarre notion for the supreme master

---

[132] Cf. Wirszubski, *Libertas* 167–71; R. Syme, *Roman Papers* i (Oxford 1978) 76–87.

[133] See nn. 109–10 above.

[134] The text of what follows is far from certain. ὄψονται may be defended as a rather casual extension of a regular idiom in Marcus, illustrated best by v. 25 ἄλλος ἁμαρτάνει τι εἰς ἐμέ; ὄψεται. ('Another does me wrong? He shall see to it.'—i.e. that is his concern, not mine). So also viii. 41, xi. 13, xii. 1. If emendation is needed, Wilamowitz's ἕψομαι seems best.

[135] See n. 13 above.

[136] See Brunt, *PBSR* 43 (1975) 13–16, 34–5. Wallace-Hadrill, *JRS* 72 (1982) 32 ff.

of the Roman world).[137] The verb μιμεῖσθαι ('imitate') in this context carries Platonic overtones: Plato thought that an actor playing the part of an evil man on stage would be corrupted by the emotions which he sought to reproduce (*Rep.* x. 605–6). Marcus, by contrast, would be playing the part on the real stage of the world, and would actually be the tyrant, not just be infected by the associations of the role.

The duplicity of tyranny and of dramatic acting forms a foil in this passage to the singleness and simplicity of philosophy, which (as in viii. 3) is presented in opposition to the conventional ideal of power. The path of philosophy, as of virtue, is straight and direct;[138] and to be led away from it (ἄπαγε) is to betray one's proper task, to be lost in σεμνοτυφία, 'pompous illusion'. As is well known, σεμνός ('pompous, majestic') and its cognates are regularly associated with tragedy.[139] Hence the word σεμνοτυφία, apparently Marcus' own coinage, looks back to ἐτραγῴδησαν ('they played their grandiose roles') and passes final, dismissive judgement on earthly vainglory.

In ix. 29 Marcus rejects cant (even in philosophic guise) and dismisses easy answers, showing a clear awareness of the limited prospects of human progress. The bitterness of his words might be regarded as cynical and uncharitable, but the chapter does not advocate either passive indifference or admission of defeat. Although Marcus' negative verdict on human activities seems un-Stoic, his sense of duty and consciousness of the need for action are Stoic in the most positive sense: 'be content if the smallest thing goes forward well, and count the outcome of the matter in hand no small thing.'[140] To summon up courage in this way, for limited and uninspiring ends, is often harder than flamboyant heroism. Elsewhere we find the same message put more epigrammatically: 'even supposing the gods take counsel

---

[137] See LSJ, and add Epict. ii. 16. 38, iii. 18. 9, and esp. iii. 8. 2, where it is the emperor ('Caesar') who has condemned.

[138] See ii. 7 (final word ἀπευθύνουσιν), iv. 51, v. 3 εὐθεῖαν, v. 14 κατορθώσεις, vi. 17, 22, vii. 55, viii. 7, x. 11; further, West on Hes. *Op.* 9; Th. 85 f.; Pl. *Lg.* iv. 716a1; Nisbet–Hubbard on Hor. *Odes* ii. 10. 1. See also n. 86 above.

[139] E.g. Pl. *Grg.* 502b; Crates fr. 24 Kock; Arist. *Poet.* 22, 1458a21.

[140] I have translated οὐ μικρὸν, the reading of the *editio princeps* and of most editors. The oldest MS reads μικρὸν, which produces a very different thought, bleaker, and more dissatisfied: 'and count the result a small thing'. This seems less likely in view of the more positive injunction in the first part of the sentence; ὡς οὐ μικρόν τί ἐστι διανοοῦ should balance ἀρκοῦ.

about none of our concerns, I am still able to take counsel about myself' (vi. 44; see further ix. 28, x. 31, xii. 14, 15.). Even amid apparent chaos, we cannot afford to abandon some conception of a meaning to our actions and to our very existence; otherwise those actions will grind to a halt in apathy and despair.

V

Marcus Aurelius and the Supernatural

> Man does not know the place he should occupy. He has
> obviously gone astray; he has fallen from his true place and
> cannot find it again. He searches everywhere, anxiously but
> in vain, in the midst of impenetrable darkness.
>
> (Pascal, *Pensées* 400)

1. *The Philosopher's Quest*[1]

Philosophy in the first and second centuries AD looks within, to
the soul and spiritual well-being of the inner man. It also looks
outwards, far beyond the individual and his particular needs
and longings, to embrace the relationship between man and
God, between human life and universal mind. It is, then, at once
a highly personal pursuit and a quest for universal truths: it seeks
to apprehend the divine forces and to understand their relation
to the world; but this enterprise is not a purely intellectual
enquiry, for it is directed toward practical ends, namely to
determine how a man should live, and how he may best serve
God, act as Nature requires of him, and thus fulfil his highest
potential. The answers given by the different philosophic
schools were of course many and varied, but there was much
common ground, not least in their practical assumptions: that
philosophy constitutes a sustained enquiry into the nature of the
good life, and that its function is to enable the practitioner to
become good.

Both of these aims of ancient philosophy—to pursue absolute
truth and to achieve thereby some form of personal fulfilment or
salvation—bring it closer to religion than most modern schools
of thought. The wisdom that the philosopher seeks generally

---

[1] In this section I draw particularly on A. M. Malingrey's interesting study
'*Philosophia': Étude d'un groupe de mots dans la littérature grecque* (Paris 1961). See further
TDNT ix. 172 ff., s.v. φιλοσοφία; van Geytenbeek, *Musonius Rufus* 33–5; Stuckelberger
on Sen. *Ep.* 88; on the origin of the word see W. Burkert, *Hermes* 88 (1960) 159–77.

involves some knowledge of a transcendent reality: thus the pseudo-Platonic *Definitions* speak of philosophy as 'the aspiration to knowledge of what exists for all time' (414b). Plato already saw philosophic religion as a sublime form of love and desire.[2] A number of ancient definitions also speak of philosophy's concern with the divine, often employing the imagery of seeking, longing for, and desiring a beloved object. The emphasis on this aspect of philosophy, as a search for God, seems to increase in this period.[3] Plutarch in a striking passage declares that while we are here below, encumbered by our bodies and by physical desires, we can have no intercourse with God save when, in philosophic thought, we may faintly touch him, as in a dream (*Is. Os.* 78. 382f.). For Dio Chrysostom the philosophic life is one which 'strives for truth and insight and care for the gods and tendance of one's own soul' (70. 7); Justin Martyr's interlocutor remarks that 'philosophers turn every discourse upon God . . . do not questions continually arise among them as to his unity and his providence? Is not this truly the task of philosophy, to investigate deity?'; and Justin agrees that philosophy is an honourable and valuable possession, which leads us and commends us to God (*Dial.* 1–2). For Clement of Alexandria the true philosophy is that which seeks God (*Strom.* ii. 10–11); for the writers of the *Corpus Hermeticum* 'philosophy consists solely in learning to know the deity by habitual contemplation and pious devotion' (*Asclep.* 12); and in some Christian writers, such as Tatian, φιλοσοφεῖν can even mean 'to be a Christian'.[4]

Many ancient writers speak of philosophy as having the

[2] Love and desire of philosophy: esp. *Grg.* 481d (in Stoicism cf. Sen. *Ep.* 89. 4–6; M. Aur. i. 17. 9 ἐπεθύμησα). For the philosopher as lover see e.g. *Smp.* 200–212b; *Rep.* vi. 485b–d); L. Robin, *La Théorie platonicienne de l'amour* (Paris 1933); F. M. Cornford, *The Unwritten Philosophy* (Cambridge 1950) 68–80. Later, e.g. Plot. vi. 9. 1 f.

[3] Contrast the stress in earlier Stoic definitions on the practice and attainment of virtue and wisdom (*SVF* ii. 36, etc.; iv. p. 155; Muson. p. 9. 14 and 87. 7–8 Hense). Another contrast is offered by Epicurean teaching, which stresses the verbal and moral link between φιλοσοφία and φιλία. Philosophy for Epicurus means the art of living happily (e.g. Diog. Laert. x. 122), and for this friendship is an essential ingredient (Gnom. Vat. 13, 52, 78; *KD* 27–8); note Epicurus' use of συμφιλοσοφέω (Diog. Laert. x. 18, Epicurus' will). Further, see A. J. Festugière, *Épicure et ses dieux* (Paris 1946; Eng. tr. Oxford 1955) ch. 3; Macleod, *Collected Essays* 283 f., 288–91. The contrast with Stoicism's relative neglect of friendship is striking: cf. Brink on Hor. *Ep.* ii. 2. 210 (though note Steinmetz on Panaetius, cited above, ch. III n. 24).

[4] See Malingrey, '*Philosophia*', 120 ff.; e.g. Tatian, *Or. ad Gr.* 32, 33; *Cohort.* 12. 12c. Related is the description, often polemical, of Christianity as a 'philosophy': see *Envoi* n. 6.

power to bring us close to God, setting us on his level, even bringing man and God face to face or into some mysterious or mystical union. In some authors, such as Seneca, this appears to be only high-flown metaphor or a moral ideal symbolically expressed. In others the concept is taken more seriously and given a more solid theoretical foundation: the duty and aim of the philosopher is to emulate, and ultimately become like, a god (ὁμοίωσις θεῷ).[5] Various metaphors are used to define this unimaginable union: imitation, participation, assimilation. This concept again has its roots in Plato (*Tht.* 176a ff.; also *Rep.* vi. 500c; *Tim.* 90d; *Lg.* iv. 716ad). It is influential in Stoicism. Cleanthes speaks of man as possessing a μίμημα of God; Balbus, the Stoic in Cicero's *de Natura Deorum*, describes the soul's potential, through contemplation, to become 'equal and like unto the gods, yielding to them in nothing but their immortality' (*SVF* i. 537. 4;[6] Cic. *ND* ii. 153). Seneca too echoes this belief: 'hoc enim est quod mihi philosophia promittit, ut parem deo faciat' (*Ep.* 48. 11). Stoicism, never a popular or an easy doctrine, was easily vulnerable to this and other ways of ameliorating its stern ideals. We can see the reflection of other philosophic and religious paths in the *Meditations*. A tiny but suggestive instance is *Med.* vii. 2 ἀναβιῶναί σοι ἔξεστιν ('it is open to you to live again')—in Marcus, a metaphor for the true life of philosophy, analogous to the imagery of awakening and sight; in other writers, and, it appears, in the mystery religions, a literal promise of rebirth, a guarantee, as in Christian belief, of safety and preservation in the afterlife.[7]

[5] See esp. H. Merki, Ὁμοίωσις θεῷ (Fribourg 1952) esp. 7–17 on the Stoics. Clem. Al. *Strom.* ii. 22 and v. 13–14 discusses the idea and quotes (rather indiscriminately) numerous pagan and Christian parallels. In Marcus note esp. x. 8. 4 with Theiler ad loc. For the related concept of γνῶσις θεοῦ see E. Norden, *Agnostos Theos* (Berlin 1913) 87–109.

[6] Imitated by Muson. fr. 17, p. 90 H.

[7] Of older studies see above all E. Rohde, *Psyche* (Eng. tr. London and New York 1925); F. Cumont, *After-Life in Roman Paganism* (Yale 1922); note also Richardson on 'Hom.' *Hy. Dem.* 480–2. For the Christian promise of immortality see 1 Cor. 15; *ODCC* s.v. 'Immortality'. It has recently been suggested that the importance of the promise of personal survival in the mystery cults has been much exaggerated by modern scholarship; see MacMullen, *Paganism in the Roman Empire* 53–7; W. Burkert, *Ancient Mystery Cults* (Cambridge, Mass., and London 1987) 21–8, 105. Yet it is difficult to deny the force of ancient testimony on this point: see e.g. *Hy. Dem.* already cited; Pind. frr. 129, 133 Snell; Cic. *de Leg.* ii. 36 'neque solum cum laetitia vivendi rationem accepimus sed etiam cum spe meliore moriendi'; Plut. *Cons. ad Uxorem* 611d; Apul. *Met.* xi. 6, cf. 25 (and J. Gwyn Griffiths' comm. on xi. 23, p. 285. 11 f. Helm). Further, Nock, *Essays* 100 ff.,

In the next two chapters an attempt is made to isolate various strands of Marcus' thought which can be fruitfully seen against the richer, if more chaotic, background of religious beliefs and philosophic speculation for which we have evidence among his contemporaries. The present chapter discusses a series of particularly interesting, puzzling, or revealing passages in the *Meditations* which refer to the supernatural or to some form of religious experience. This kind of material is notoriously difficult to handle. To relate the world-view of any individual to the mood of an age presents almost insuperable difficulties, and there is room for justified scepticism about generalisations based on the evidence of a number of scattered individuals, many of them highly literate and articulate intellectual figures. Nor is the interpreter's task made easier by the obscurity and allusiveness of Marcus' words in some of the most significant passages. It may be, however, that enough emerges from examining them together and in the light of parallels from authors more forthcoming on these subjects for the enquiry to be worthwhile, even if conclusions must sometimes be negative or at least tentative, with various possibilities left open. In the final chapter I offer a broader comparison between Marcus' religious beliefs and attitudes and those of Epictetus. The discussion there is based less on the analysis of individual phrases, more on the general implications of Marcus' style, imagery, and treatment of his subject-matter: there I have been rather more positive and perhaps less prudent in drawing conclusions on the basis of both these approaches.

2. Magic[8]

... τὸ ἀπιστητικὸν τοῖς ὑπὸ τῶν τερατευομένων καὶ γοήτων περὶ ἐπῳδῶν καὶ δαιμόνων ἀποπομπῆς καὶ τῶν τοιούτων λεγομένοις.

... scepticism about the statements made by sorcerers and impostors about incantations, exorcism of spirits, and such like. (Med. i. 6)

---

624 ff. (I am grateful to Dr E. G. D. Kearns for advice on this matter, and for a number of these references.) See now Lane Fox, *Pagans and Christians* 95–6.

[8] See *OCD* (2nd edn.) s.v. Magic; and add P. Brown, *Religion and Society in the Age of St Augustine* (London 1972) 119 ff.; Dodds, *The Ancient Concept of Progress* ch. 10; A. M. Tupet, *La Magie dans la poésie latine* i (Paris 1976); A. B. Kolenkow, *ANRW* ii. 23. 2 (1980) 1471–82. For more 'tall stories' about magic, see Plut. *Def. Orac.* 420f f., with Betz (ed.), *Plutarch's Theological Writings* ad loc.

It has been widely held that during the second century AD credulity amongst the upper classes concerning 'signs and wonders' was on the increase, and that this was reflected in the popularity of certain kinds of philosophic or pseudo-philosophic systems and Eastern religious cults (this view is associated particularly with the name of Franz Cumont, and was adopted by Dodds in his masterly *Pagan and Christian in an Age of Anxiety*[9]). Such increase is hard to quantify or prove, and most recent scholars have tended to play down the broad historical changes, and instead to emphasise the continuity of conflicting elements in ancient thought and attitudes. One example will illustrate the difference of approach. We know that under Hadrian the freedman Phlegon was the author of a work *On Marvels*, full of stories of portents, monstrous births, and so forth (*FGrH* 257 F 35 ff.). This has sometimes been rather naïvely regarded as a disturbing sign of declining rationalism. But in this area at least literary history provides a corrective to this kind of diagnosis, for it is clear that the tradition of catalogues such as Phlegon's has its roots much earlier, in Hellenistic paradoxography or indeed in the work of Herodotus himself.[10] Nevertheless, we may still benefit from considering and comparing parallel or opposed attitudes in the works of Marcus' contemporaries, without necessarily giving any of them privileged status as the voice of his age. On the subject of religious belief—not to say gullibility— the most vociferous witness, however mischievous and preju- diced, is the satirist Lucian.[11]

[9] See n. 62 below; also MacMullen, *Paganism in the Roman Empire* 64, 123-4, and elsewhere, against 'periodisation' of history; 200 n. 11 against Cumont; 122-3, 177, 202 against Dodds; 179 n. 35 against Brown. (See also S. R. F. Price's review, *JRS* 72 (1982) 194-5.) Lane Fox, *Pagans and Christians* is a sustained and sympathetic critique of Dodds's already classic book. In part i he attempts to reinstate the lonely men of Dodds's picture in the civic society to which they belonged and in which they worshipped—with much success.

[10] See K. Ziegler, *RE* 28. 2. 1137-66; also edns. of the *Paradoxographi* by A. Westermann (1839), O. Keller (1877), and now A. Giannini (1966). The tradition is already prominent in Callimachus; see P. M. Fraser, *Ptolemaic Alexandria* (Oxford 1972) 454 f.

[11] We are fortunate in having at last a fresh, scholarly, and witty work on Lucian's vast corpus in J. Hall's detailed study *Lucian's Satire;*, see her ch. 3 on Lucian's religious and philosophic themes. Earlier works tended either to exaggerate the self-contained 'literary' qualities of Lucian's writing or to find contemporary references too readily; for the former tendency see esp. J. Bompaire, *Lucien écrivain* (Paris 1958); G. Anderson, *Lucian: Theme and Variation in the Second Sophistic* (*Mnem.* Suppl. 41, Leiden 1976); id., *Studies in Lucian's Comic Fiction* (*Mnem.* Suppl. 43, Leiden 1976); for the other approach,

Lucian's parody of fantastic travel-tales, the *Verae Historiae*, represents (like his *de Conscribenda Historia*) a reaction against existing tendencies and writings. Elsewhere, particularly in the *Alexander*, the *Peregrinus*, and the *Philopseudes*, his attack is directed more against the hypocrisy of would-be magicians and other such charlatans, and against those who credulously accept and unconsciously exaggerate their fantastic claims. In the *Philopseudes* Tychiades, whose views clearly represent Lucian's own, has just come from the house of Eucrates, where he has heard 'many unbelievable and fairy-tale stories' (5 πολλὰ τὰ ἄπιστα καὶ μυθώδη ἀκούσας). It is all the more shocking, he goes on, when Eucrates is a man of sixty, with a long beard, and a great devotee of philosophy.[12]

Eucrates has been ill and is now recovering; this provides the point of departure for a long discussion of far-fetched cures involving sympathetic magic,[13] incantations,[14] holy names,[15] and Babylonian sorcery.[16] Tychiades, at first politely sceptical, later becomes more forthright in his contempt for such superstitious claptrap. The key word used by Lucian in describing him is ἄπιστος, as in the passage from the *Meditations* quoted at the beginning of the section. Thus Cleodemus, another of the gathering, remarks to him 'I was formerly more sceptical than you about such things' (13 ἀπιστότερος); and still another speaker protests 'you are making fun of it all by refusing to believe in anything' (16 ἀπιστῶν ἅπασιν). This speaker then goes

B. Baldwin, *Studies in Lucian* (Toronto 1973). See now also Jones, *Culture and Society in Lucian*.

[12] The beard is a conventional attribute of the philosopher stereotype in Lucian (e.g. *Hermot.* 18, [*Cynicus*] 14) and elsewhere (Juv. 2. 15, 14. 15), but has some basis in fact: see esp. Muson. fr. 21; Epict. iv. 1. 116; van Geytenbeek, *Musonius Rufus* 119–23. For the social history of beards see Courtney on Juv. 4. 103. For other aspects of Cynic/philosophic dress see Kindstrand on Bion T 19; Apul. *Apol.* 22 (the philosopher's 'uniform').

[13] Lucian, *Philops.* 7 f. Cf. Hor. *Epod.* 17. 76; *Sat.* i. 8. 32 ff.; Virg. *Ecl.* 8. 80; Dodds, *The Greeks and the Irrational* 247, 292 f.

[14] For an early example see the necromantic scenes of Aeschylus' *Persae*: here as often the Oriental colouring reinforces the exotic quality of magic. Later, see e.g. Rohde (n. 7) 320, 326–7; A. Abt, *Die Apologie des Apuleius von Madaura und die antike Zauberei* (Giessen 1908) 189 ff. (I cite by the original pagination from *RGVV* iv. 2, reproduced in the separate reprint).

[15] *Philops.* 10; cf. Nock, *Essays* 188 ff.; *RLAC* vii. 50–2.

[16] *Philops.* 11. Babylonians and Chaldeans were particularly associated with astrology (e.g. Hor. *Odes* i. 11. 1, with Nisbet–Hubbard's note). On 'Chaldeans' see further Abt (n. 14) 330–1.

on to say 'for my part, I'd like to ask you what you have to say about the people who free the possessed from their terrors by exorcising their spirits so plainly. I needn't say anything about this: everyone knows about the Syrian in Palestine . . .'. Oracles,[17] apparitions,[18] holy men,[19] all make their appearance in this debate, and even the Pythagorean Arignotus, who appears at a late stage and who Tychiades thinks will put a stop to these monstrous tales (29 τεράστια), turns out to be as profound a believer in ghosts and apparitions as the rest—or as big a liar, as Lucian's title implies. The satirist regularly conflates philosopher and fraud; Marcus Aurelius shares his contempt for such incredible tales, but sets true philosophic understanding firmly apart from the showmanship and the large claims of the practising magician. Apuleius' *Apology* also shows how readily these two professions, theoretical philosopher and sorcerer, could be associated in popular belief or forensic invective.[20]

In general, Lucian considers all philosophies to be equally implausible humbug. He maintains that only good pragmatic common sense can come to acceptable conclusions about the world and the way a man should live; this is the upshot of several dialogues involving discussion of philosophy, of which the most substantial is the *Hermotimus*.[21] The very diversity of beliefs held by different philosophic schools proves, for Lucian, not only that there is no time or criteria to explore them all, but that *no* true answers can be found. Instead we should be content with the life of the man in the street (*Hermot.* 84). But however hesitant Marcus might be in committing himself to the established Stoic

[17] *Philops.* 38. For a masterly brief account of Greek attitudes to oracles see Nock, *Essays* 534 ff. See also F. Jaeger, *De Oraculis quid Veteres Philosophi Iudicaverint* (diss. Rostock 1910); MacMullen, *Enemies of the Roman Order* 323 n. 24; Courtney on Juv. 6. 555. For increase of popularity of certain oracles in this period see Hall, *Lucian's Satire* 201, 509 f.

[18] *Philops.* 30–1 (closely paralleled by Plin. *Ep.* vii. 27); also 14, 16, 17; cf. Plut. *Cimon* 2; Philos. *VS* 590 on Hadrian of Tyre; Rohde, (n. 7) 533–5 with nn.

[19] *Philops.* 29, 34; cf. Plutarch's mystic dwelling by the Red Sea near the Troglodytes (*Def. Orac.* 420–1; fictional according to Dodds, *Pagan and Christian* 31); Celsus *ap.* Orig. *Cels.* vii. 9. For another fraudulent prophet of doom see SHA *Marcus* 13. 6.

[20] For doctors suspected of sorcery see V. Nutton on Galen, *On Prognosis* 1, p. 70. 8. See MacMullen, *Enemies of the Roman Order* ch. 3–4; 320 n. 16, 322 n. 20; and e.g. Apul. *Apol.* 27. 1. On this work see the comm. by H. E. Butler and A. S. Owen (Cambridge 1914); Abt (n. 14); J. Tatum, *Apuleius and the* Golden Ass (Ithaca and London 1979) 105–19.

[21] Further, see Chadwick, *Early Christian Thought and the Classical Tradition* 132.

position on matters essentially unknowable, this extreme agnosticism was many stages beyond what he was prepared to accept. On the subject of magic and exorcism, on the other hand, he seems to be closer to the negative, destructive attitude of Lucian. Lucian was not the only critic of such practices. His addressee in the *Alexander*, the Epicurean Celsus, composed a work attacking magicians (*Alex.* 21 κατὰ μάγων; cf. Orig. *Cels.* i. 68).[22] Such works were common in this period: Philostratus knows of several (*V. Ap.* vii. 39, a passage which also amply attests to the prevalence of such beliefs). Elsewhere, in the *Lives of the Sophists*, Philostratus declares that in an earlier part of that work he has 'said enough to show that a well-educated man would never be led astray into the practice of magic arts (ἐς γοήτων . . . τέχνας)' (*VS* 590).

The vocabulary which Marcus uses also links him with contemporary accounts of these wonder-workers. γόης in particular is almost universally pejorative. Already in Euripides' *Bacchae* Pentheus refers to the disguised Dionysus as γόης ἐπῳδός (234), and similarly Theseus jeers at the ascetic Hippolytus: 'Isn't this fellow a charm-singer and a sorcerer?' (*Hipp.* 1038). Demosthenes and Aeschines hurl similar insults at one another (Dem. 18. 276; Aesch. 3. 137). In Dio Cassius the philosophic sage Apollonius of Tyana is called γόης καὶ μάγος (67. 18); in Lucian, the prophet Alexander is called γόης ἄνθρωπος καὶ τερατείᾳ φίλος, ἀληθείᾳ δὲ ἔχθιστος ('a magician, friend to wonder-working and foe to truth', *Alex.* 25), and the words γόης, τερατεία, and the like are associated elsewhere (e.g. *Dial. Mort.* 10; *Gallus* 4). It is characteristic that Lucian also speaks of the τερατολογίαι φιλοσόφων ('the fantastic talk of philosophers', *Philopatris* 2); no species of wise man is immune to the satirist's scepticism. In the programmatic dialogue *Piscator* he says of himself: 'I am a hater of buffoons, a hater of magicians, of liars, of pomposity' (20).

As for τέρας, this word was defined by one ancient lexicographer as what is παρὰ φύσιν, contrary to nature (Ammonius, *Voc. Diff.* 135). In origin and through most of its history the word

---

[22] H. Chadwick, *Origen: contra Celsum* (Cambridge 1953) pp. xxiv–xxix, and Hall, *Lucian's Satire* 512–13 convincingly argue that Lucian's addressee is not the same as the Platonist Celsus whose work Origen attacks (though Origen himself seems to be in some doubt about this, at least in the early books: i. 8, iii. 22, 35, 80, iv. 54).

denotes something that is not only strange but frightening and shocking, such as a monstrous freak, a mythical creature, or an ominous sign.[23] In the period we are considering it has, like γόης and μάγος, suspicious and negative overtones. For Marcus and other a τέρας arouses not so much wonder as incredulity, even scorn: the men he condemns here are charlatans, miracle-mongers, even quacks. There are obvious analogies with Lucian's constant attacks on such men (most conspicuous and outrageous in the *Alexander*); but whereas Lucian treats *all* religious believers as fools or hypocrites, Marcus' scepticism has a positive dimension. Here as in the next passage (see section 3 below) we can surmise that his comments rest not only on knowledge of human nature but also on his sense of the dignity of the divine powers and the decorum of human worship.

Evidence in Book I of the *Meditations* in particular shows Marcus' dislike for sophists and suspicion of false philosophers (esp. i. 16. 5, 17. 9). As already indicated, this is a period in which these professions and that of magician or prophet could be combined—if not in fact, at least in popular expectations.[24] The best example is the ghost-figure Apollonius, the subject of Philostratus' largely fictional biography.[25] Whatever the historical truth, Apollonius was described by Philostratus as an associate of Dio Chrysostom (*VS* 488); he is also said to have composed a work on prayer, a subject much discussed by serious thinkers (Philos. *V. Ap.* iii. 41, iv. 19). But in the life by Philostratus (and perhaps also in earlier accounts) he becomes a superhuman being, a philosopher-cum-miracle-worker, a defiant foe of Domitian (the image of the 'philosophic martyr' has been influential here),[26] and almost a reincarnation of Pythagoras. He can foretell the future, avert famine, defy wicked spirits, exorcise demons, and still enjoy the standard sophistic honours, settling local disputes and associating with the dignitaries of the imperial court. Yet even here we may

[23] See *TDNT* viii. 113 ff., a helpful account. On this range of vocabulary see also Nock, *Essays* 308 ff.

[24] See MacMullen, *Enemies of the Roman Order*, loc. cit. (n. 20).

[25] On which see esp. E. Meyer, *Hermes* 52 (1917) 371–424 = *Kleine Schriften* ii (Halle 1924) 131–91; E. L. Bowie, *ANRW* ii. 16. 1 (1978) 1652–99, with massive bibliog. Anderson, *Philostratus* ch. 7–12 is the fullest recent account, ingenious but credulous.

[26] See above, ch. II nn. 42–9, 58; also D. Tiede, *The Charismatic Figure as Miracle-Worker* (Missoula 1972) 56 f.

observe the philosopher's proper disdain for γοητεία; Apollonius
claims to be no wizard, but one who prophesies on the basis of
divine revelation (v. 7, 12, vii. 17, 39, *et al.*).[27] The ostentation,
the grandiose claims to power and spiritual authority, and the
playing upon uncritical mob-enthusiasm are all alike unsympathetic to Marcus and alien to his ethical outlook, which is
focused above all on self-improvement and is limited by
stringent realism.

Finally, it should be noted that there is no reason whatever to
tie Marcus' reference in i. 6 down to Christian exorcisms and
rituals;[28] exorcism was commonly practised by Jews and pagans
(including, as we have seen, Philostratus' Apollonius), and it has
been convincingly shown by Brunt, in an important article,[29]
that during Marcus' reign Christianity had not yet reached any
special prominence among the many freakish or out-of-the-way
cults of the Empire. The names of the movement and its founder
were known at Rome (see e.g. Suet. *Nero* 16. 2; Tac. *Ann.* xv.
44[30]), and during the reign of Marcus apologists such as
Athenagoras protested the merits of their beliefs in eloquent
Greek orations addressed to the emperor.[31] But we do not know

[27] Compare Euphrates' dig at Apollonius in v. 37. Further, MacMullen, *Enemies of the Roman Order* 322; *TDNT* i. 737. The controversy over Apollonius' status was long-lived: cf. Orig. *Cels.* vi. 41; Jerome, *Ep.* 53. 1 'Apollonius—sive ille magus, ut vulgus loquitur, sive philosophus, ut Pythagorici tradunt.' (Similar ambiguity in the case of Apuleius: e.g. August. *Ep.* 102. 36, 136. 1; Lact. *Inst.* v. 3. 7.) Even Marcus Aurelius is seen as having almost supernatural powers in one version of the Rain Miracle (SHA *Marcus* 24. 4, quoted in the end-note to this chapter p. 222).

[28] Farquharson is right here against (e.g.) Haines ad loc., or F. Martinazzoli, *Parataxis* (Florence 1953).

[29] 'Marcus Aurelius and the Christians' (see Bibliography), at pp. 498–520. See p. 497, esp. n. 36, for the point about exorcisms, on which see further K. Thraede, *RLAC* vii. 44 ff.; Dodds, *The Ancient Concept of Progress* 196.

[30] Further: Suet. *Cl.* 25. 4; Plin. *Ep.* x. 96–7; Fronto ii. 282 = Min. Fel. *Oct.* 9. 8; Epict. iv. 7. 1–6, and perhaps ii. 9. 19–22. For full discussion of these and other early *testimonia* on Christianity see W. den Boer, *Scriptorum Paganorum I–IV Saec. de Christianis Testimonia* (Textus Minores II, 2nd edn., Leiden 1965); P. de Labriolle, *La Réaction païenne* (2nd edn., Paris 1948); and on Galen (including references from Arab texts) R. Walzer, *Galen on Jews and Christians* (Oxford 1949) esp. 14 f., 48–56. More recent treatments, such as S. Benko, *ANRW* ii. 23. 2 (1980) 1055 ff., or R. Wilken, *The Christians as the Romans Saw Them* (New Haven, Conn., 1983) add little. For a sensitive general account see Dodds, *Pagan and Christian* ch. 4.

[31] For these authors see J. Otto, *Corpus Apologetarum Saeculi Secundi* (Jena 1847); E. Goodspeed, *Die ältesten Apologeten* (Göttingen 1914); id., *Index Apologeticus* (Leipzig 1912). There are also editions in the Oxford Early Christian Texts series of Melito (ed. and tr. S. G. Hall, 1979), Athenagoras (R. Schoedel, 1972), and Tatian (M. Whittaker, 1982). See further Reardon, *Courants littéraires grecs* 450–1. For discussion see Reardon, op. cit.

whether he read these works or conducted further investiga-
tions. Nor have we any means of knowing how much he knew
about the behaviour and beliefs of those whom his subordinates
suppressed.[32] There is only one passage in the *Meditations* which
actually names the Christians (xi. 3), and even there the
parenthetic ὡς οἱ Χριστιανοί may be an interpolation.[33] At all
events, we should not suppose that they were ever at the centre
of his concerns; nor does it follow, because we can see affinities
and parallels between the *Meditations* and Christian scripture,
that Marcus himself would necessarily have found the teachings
of Christianity sympathetic or its claims to authority persuasive.
Both these assumptions seem to me the product of *interpretatio
Christiana*.

3. Superstitiousness[34]

... καὶ τὸ μήτε περὶ θεοὺς δεισίδαιμον μήτε περὶ ἀνθρώπους δημοκοπικὸν
ἢ ἀρεσκευτικὸν ἢ ὀχλοχαρές ...

... no superstitious fear of the gods, nor with man any courting of the
public or obsequiousness or gratification of the mob ... (i. 16. 3, from
the description of Antoninus Pius)

... καὶ ὡς θεοσεβὴς χωρὶς δεισιδαιμονίας ...

... and how he was reverent, without superstitiousness ... (from the
parallel passage vi. 30)

Superstitiousness was regarded as a moral vice, and was
indeed included by the Stoics among the emotional states (πάθη,

275–89; Chadwick, *Early Christian Thought* ch. i; Millar, *The Emperor in the Roman World*
561–6. For some chronological points, see also Birley 258–9.
    [32] In general on Roman policy see T. D. Barnes, *JRS* 58 (1968) 32–50; G. E. M. de
Ste Croix, *Past and Present* 26 (1963) 1–38, reprinted, with subsequent discussion, in M. I.
Finley (ed.), *Studies in Ancient Society* (London 1974) 210 ff. Also Sherwin-White on Plin.
Ep. x. 96–7.
    [33] As suggested by Haines and others, and argued in great detail by Brunt, 'Marcus
Aurelius and the Christians' 483–98. Birley 264 offers some points in defence.
    [34] P. J. Koets, Deisidaemonia: *A Contribution to the Knowledge of Religious Terminology*
(Purmerend 1929) is standard, but of very limited scope. See also, for Latin usage, Pease
on Cic. *Div.* ii. 148–50, and on *ND* i. 45, 55–6, 117, ii. 71–2; H. Nettleship, *JPh* 6 (1876)
98–9. On Plutarch's *de Superstititione* (*Mor.* 164e–71e) see H. Moellering, *Plutarch on
Superstition* (Boston 1963); H. Braun, *Plutarch's Critique of Superstition in the Light of the New
Testament* (Occasional Papers of the Inst. of Antiquity and Christianity, v, Claremont
1972); Betz *et al.*, *Plutarch's Theological Writings* 1–35. See also G. Lozza's recent edn.
(Milan 1980). For other moralists on this topic see Kindstrand on Bion fr. 31–2, 34.

affectus) which must be eradicated.[35] A similar view is implicit in Horace's lines reproving himself for self-congratulation on the absence of a single vice, *avaritia*: he proceeds to ask himself 'caret tibi pectus inani / ambitione? caret mortis formidine et ira? / somnia, terrores magicos, miracula, sagas, / nocturnos lemures portentaque Thessala rides?' (*Ep.* ii. 2. 205 ff; cf. Plut. *de Sera Num. Vind.* 556b).

But the fullest accounts of educated, philosophically trained Graeco-Roman attitudes come from Cicero and Plutarch. Those who understand the truth, says the Epicurean speaker in Cicero's *de Natura Deorum*, know that the gods deserve reverence because of their eternal and exalted nature; they cannot be the source of anger or favour, and so need not be feared (*ND* i. 45). By contrast, Stoic doctrines of divination 'would so steep us in superstition that we should be the devotees of soothsayers, augurs, oracle-mongers, seers, and dream-interpreters' (i. 55). The Academic Cotta hits back powerfully: Epicureanism is fatal not only to superstition but to religion itself; 'For what reason can you give for the gods to be worshipped by mankind, when the gods not only take no thought for men but concern themselves with nothing, do nothing whatever?' (i. 115). The Stoic speaker in book ii, Balbus, distinguishes religion from superstition and rebukes 'those who spend whole days in prayer and sacrifice to ensure their children will outlive them' (deriving *superstitio* from *superstes*). 'But the best and also the purest, most holy, and most pious way of worshipping the gods is ever to venerate them with purity, sincerity, and innocence both of thought and of speech' (ii. 71). In other words, our worship should not be grasping or selfish; in Marcus' terms, we should not court or flatter the gods any more than we should lower ourselves by gratifying the mob.

Another important theme in Cicero's discussion, probably closer to his own views, appears in the final sections of the *de Divinatione* as well as in the introduction to the *de Natura Deorum*. If the existence of gods is denied, even on sound philosophic grounds, then piety and morality must perish, at least among the masses. Justice among men depends on reverence for divine authority: 'and in all probability, the disappearance of piety

---

[35] See E. Norden, *Fleck. Jahrb.* Suppl. 18 (1892) 340–1 = *Kleine Schriften* (Berlin 1966) 76 f.

towards the gods will entail the disappearance of loyalty and
social union among men as well as of justice itself, the supreme
virtue' (*ND* i. 4). Therefore, having refuted the validity of
divination, Cicero (who himself hoped to become a member of
the college of augurs) insists that the wise politician should
preserve the ancestral rites.[36] Similarly Varro, a Stoic in his
theology (Tert. *Nat.* ii. 2), approved of the continuation of the
old cults for political and social reasons, 'ut potius [deos] magis
colere quam despicere vulgus velit' (*ap.* August. *Civ. Dei* iv. 31).
Seneca held the same view, as we see in the fragments which
survive of his *de Superstitione*: the wise man will perform the
traditional rites 'tamquam legibus iussa non tamquam deis
grata' (*ap.* August. *Civ. Dei* vi. 10). In any case the Stoics, and
Romans generally, attached importance to the observation of
tradition as such. Thus Marcus praises Pius as a man who
performed 'all things in accordance with the ways of our fathers'
(i. 16. 6), and this includes the traditional religion of the Roman
people.[37]

Criticism of the myths, particularly for their anthropomor-
phic pictures of the Olympian gods, was common among the
moralists, and much polemical material was taken over by
Christianity.[38] Scepticism about the value of statues and
sacrifices, while less common, is well attested from Theophrastus
onwards, and Stoic theology, with its vaguer notions of Nature
and the Cosmos largely replacing the Olympian pantheon,
encouraged an ostensibly more spiritual conception of worship.[39] Zeno had already criticised the building of temples: 'one
ought not to build temples or images; for no building is a worthy
place for the gods to dwell in' (*SVF* i. 264). Seneca went further,

[36] Cf. Cic. *de Leg.* ii. 15 f.; Polyb. vi. 56; Posid. fr. 211b Theiler = 265 Edelstein–Kidd;
Plut. *Non Posse* 1101d–e. For discussion see de Ste. Croix (n. 32) 245–8.

[37] See Brunt, *JRS* 64 (1974) 16 nn. 104a, 105.

[38] Rich material on this theme in Pease on Cic. *ND* i. 41–2; also 77 ff. on
anthropomorphism. The Christian apologists take over these polemical arguments, e.g.
Athenag. *Leg.* 18–22 (cf. also August. *Conf.* i. 20–27).

[39] On Theophrastus' *On Piety* and its critique of traditional religious practice see J.
Bernays, *Theophrastos' Schrift über die Frommigkeit* (Berlin 1860); W. Pötscher, *Theophrastos,
Peri Eusebeias* (Leiden 1964); P. A. Meijer, in H. S. Versnel (ed.), *Faith, Hope and
Worship* (Leiden 1981) 250–61. See also R. Parker, *Miasma* (Oxford 1983) 307. On the
'spiritualising' tendency of philosophic religion see Babut, *La Religion des philosophes grecs*;
TDNT iii. 257–65; H. W. Attridge, *ANRW* ii. 16. 1 (1980) 60 ff., esp. 65–9; van der
Horst on ps.-Phocyl. 228. On Plotinus' attitude see J. M. Rist, *Plotinus: The Road to Reality*
(Cambridge 1967) ch. 15.

declaring that it is not formal religiosity but just action which is the true tribute to God: 'vis deos propitiare? bonus esto. satis illos coluit quisquis imitatus est.' (*Ep.* 95. 50; cf. fr. 123). Seneca's formulation moves some way from criticism of actual cult practices, though his remark is regularly quoted in this connection. It points rather towards a more rarified idea, that of moral and spiritual imitation of the gods. The common factor remains that of a more internal and more personal form of religious behaviour and attitude; the Stoics and other thinkers such as Plotinus (Porph. *Vit. Plot.* 10) concentrate not on setting or ritual acts but on the state of mind. The intellectual philosopher is usually far from sympathetic toward popular ideas of religion. Plutarch's piety and belief, above all in the Delphian Apollo who he so devoutly served and praised, are unquestionable. But his is undoubtedly an educated piety, and in condemning the ignorance of the superstitious he is also criticising the tasteless and messy excesses of their consequent actions—the mud, the fumigation, the shouting aloud of confessions. In similar vein the pagan Celsus was to sneer at the ludicrous and irrational beliefs of the Christians, their preposterous prophecies of doom, their Oriental fanaticism, their pandering to the masses.[40]

Apart from Epictetus, the Stoic thinkers also seem remote from the popular cults; and all of them, including Epictetus, ignore or condemn ecstatic or ostentatious 'irrationalism'.[41] An edict in Marcus' name survives in the *Digest*, prescribing banishment to an island for anyone who so acted that 'leves hominum animi superstitione numinis terrerentur' (Modestinus *ap. Dig.* 48. 19. 30).[42] Here as in the *Meditations* we sense strict

[40] See Chadwick, *Early Christian Thought* ch. i, esp. 22–30; Celsus *ap.* Orig. *Cels.* iii. 48 ff., 87, vi. 1 ff. on anti-intellectualism; vii. 3, 9 on Oriental fanaticism; vi. 14 on mass appeal.

[41] On the nature of Epictetus' religiosity see esp. R. P. Lagrange, *Rev. Bibl.* NS 9 (1912) 5–21, 192–212; also ch. vi below. Against ecstatic or 'enthusiastic' cults see Sen. *de Superstit.* fr. 34–5 Haase (with M. Lausberg, *Untersuchungen zu Senecas Fragmenten* (Berlin 1970) 211–25); *de Vita Beata* 26. 8. With Epictetus there is only the argument from silence, but certainly *Ench.* 31. 1, 4–5 (on piety) suggests a more orderly, sedate ideal that suits the more traditional Roman cults. Cf. Bonhöffer, *Die Ethik des Stoikers Epictet* 75–7. In ii. 20. 27 Epictetus expresses a vigorous contempt for oracular lies, including even Delphi.

[42] Again there is no special reason to suppose that this refers to the Christians. There are parallels in rescripts of Constantine, though in a rather different tone: of one such Nock remarks 'This is hysteria' (*Essays* 317, on *Cod. Theod.* ix. 6. 50). Further on Roman

moral concern mingled with a certain aristocratic hauteur. The emperor was capable of admiring the simple beauty of an old Greek prayer (v. 7), but in general his temperament and principles draw him apart from the common man. 'Philosophic religion' for the most part predominates over the formal piety of the traditional cults. We hear nothing of Marcus' experience of festivals, religious rituals, even of his initiation at Eleusis, of which we know from external sources.[43] In the *Meditations* the individual deities, including Zeus, are seldom named.

4. *Communications from the Gods*

τὸ φαντασθῆναι περὶ τοῦ κατὰ φύσιν βίου ἐναργῶς καὶ πολλάκις οἷός τίς ἐστιν, ὥστε, ὅσον ἐπὶ τοῖς θεοῖς καὶ ταῖς ἐκεῖθεν διαδόσεσι καὶ συλλήψεσι καὶ ἐπιπνοίαις [Casaubon; MSS. ἐπινοίαις], μηδὲν κωλύειν ἤδη κατὰ φύσιν ζῆν με, ἀπολείπεσθαι δέ τι ἔτι τούτου παρὰ τὴν ἐμὴν αἰτίαν καὶ παρὰ τὸ μὴ διατηρεῖν τὰς ἐκ τῶν θεῶν ὑπομνήσεις καὶ μονονουχὶ διδασκαλίας...

To have pictured to myself clearly and often what the life according to Nature is like, so that as far as concerns the gods and the communications from the world beyond, and assistance and inspiration, nothing impedes my now living according to Nature, though I still fall short of this by my own fault and through not observing the reminders and almost the instructions of the gods ... (i. 17. 6).

Here we have a passage of obvious importance for our purposes. The author unmistakably speaks of the gods as in some sense the source of his clear (ἐναργῶς) perceptions of the life according to nature, the central conception of man's τέλος in Stoic ethics.[44] One thing that strikes the reader of Book I is that in i. 9. 1 Marcus has attributed the same lesson to one of his teachers, the Stoic Sextus, a human helper and guide. This is, however, explicable by the word πολλάκις here. Clearly the lesson is one which needs repetition, and this suits well the tone of self-reproach at his continuing failures (παρὰ τὴν ἐμὴν αἰτίαν).

legislation against magic see MacMullen, *Enemies* 124 ff.; A. A. Barb, in A. Momigliano (ed.), *The Conflict between Paganism and Christianity in the Fourth Century* (Oxford 1973) esp. 102–11.
    [43] See J. Beaujeu, *Le Religion romaine à l'apogée de l'empire* i (Paris 1955), citing Philos. *VS* ii. 1 and 12 (the latter seems hardly relevant), SHA *Marcus* 27. 1, and *IG* ii² 3. 620, 632, 411 (AD 176).
    [44] See esp. *SVF* iv, p. 160 s.v. κατὰ φύσιν; also ibid. p. 33 s.v. βίος; iii. 4–5, etc. For a modern account see G. H. Watson, in A. A. Long (ed.), *Problems in Stoicism* (London 1971) 216–38.

Further, ὅσον ἐπὶ τοῖς θεοῖς κτλ. does not exclude the parallel contributions of men, Marcus' friends and advisors as well as himself. The agency of man and God is, as often, parallel, with neither superfluous. We may indeed see the *Meditations* as continuing the work of 'reminder and teaching' begun by the gods and by Marcus' mentors.

The other passages in which Marcus speaks of communications from the divine world concern dreams and oracles. Here the reference is rather less clear. How are the words which refer to these communications to be distinguished? It may be worth noting that the three nouns I have picked out from the quotation above each occur only here in the *Meditations*, and that none of them is a technical term of Stoic or religious language.

(*a*) διάδοσις. Normally this means 'distribution', usually in a contractual sense: distributing of land, provisions, etc. Marcus' use here is unusual, and seems to derive from Epictetus i. 12. 6, an argument comparable to some passages in the *Meditations*: if the gods do not exist, how can it be an end to follow the gods? And what if they exist but care for nothing (the Epicurean view)? Or if, indeed, they do exist, and do feel concern and care for mankind, but there is 'no διάδοσις from them to men and, by Zeus, to me'—if this is the case, then how, asks Epictetus, can the conclusion follow that we ought to obey them? In short, the word denotes a channel of communication between gods and men.

(*b*) σύλληψις. The word does not occur at all in Epictetus, but a relevant passage is to hand in Marcus' own work, namely ix. 40 (discussing how the gods help us in response to our prayers). Marcus has observed that the gods do help us in obtaining the ἀδιάφορα, those things which in Stoic doctrine are 'indifferent', having no intrinsic moral value. He adds: 'Besides, who told you that the gods do not also help (συλλαμβάνουσιν) with regard to the things which are in our power?' In ix. 11 he uses συνεργοῦσιν in a parallel way. These passages suggest that σύλληψις in the present passage is used in a comparable way (cf. LSJ συλλαμβάνω VI).[45]

(*c*) ἐπινοίαις or ἐπιπνοίαις. The former is supposed to mean 'intention' (Haines), presumably with the sense of taking thought for, care of, etc., like ἐβουλεύσαντο περὶ ἐμοῦ in vi. 44. 1 or 'consulant' in Cic. *ND* i. 115 (see above, p. 189). This seems to

[45] Cf. e.g. Philos. *Heroicus* 11, p. 13. 6 de Lannoy.

me far-fetched and out of keeping with Marcus' use of ἐπινοεῖν, which usually means to contemplate or look upon (e.g. x. 18, x. 27. 1; cf. LSJ ἐπινοία, which is essentially similar). Epictetus illustrates a more strictly Stoic usage when he speaks of Zeus as self-sufficient, communing with himself: καὶ ἐν ἐπινοίαις γίνεται πρεπούσαις ἑαυτῷ, οὕτως καὶ ἡμᾶς δύνασθαι αὐτοὺς ἑαυτοῖς λαλεῖν, μὴ προσδεῖσθαι ἄλλων . . . ἐφιστάνειν τῇ θείᾳ διοικήσει . . . ('and he occupies himself with ideas appropriate to himself; so we also ought to be able to converse with ourselves, not to be in need of others . . . we should devote ourselves to studying the divine disposition', iii. 13. 7). This may have some relevance to Marcus' own form of self-address and communion with himself, but it sheds no light on the present passage.

ἐπιπνοίαις should probably be read, though the word introduces a range of ideas which may seem foreign to Marcus. It usually refers to divine inspiration, such as is granted to poets, priests, and prophets, or others who seem to possess some special insight.[46] Marcus means nothing so violent or uncontrollable as possession or ecstasy: the last words of the passage quoted imply a more intellectual, admonitory message. The choice of words suggests that the communication was discontinuous. We are not bound to suppose that this happened in dreams but there is obviously a prima-facie case for this given his reference to these later in the same chapter. He could conceivably be referring to the dictates of conscience, associated with the divine element in himself, the δαίμων in his breast (cf. Socrates' δαιμόνιον, much discussed in philosophic literature).[47] If he speaks of what we would call, however loosely and clumsily, 'religious experience', he gives us little enough clue as to its nature. He nowhere describes any such occasions, but these reticent allusions may still give some sense of their significance to him, as a stimulus to

---

[46] For earlier periods see Dodds, *The Greeks and the Irrational* ch. 3; West on Hes. *Th.* 22–34; Fraenkel on Aesch. *Ag.* 106. On the Jewish prophets see Orig. *Cels.* vii. 1 ff., with Chadwick's notes. Further, e.g. Pl. *Lg.* 811c; *Phdr.* 265b; Arist. *EE* 1214ᵃ24; Long. 13. 2; ps.-Plut. *de Vita et Poesi Hom.* 2. 212. In Latin see the phrases collected by Pease on Cic. *ND* ii. 167.

[47] Besides Plato (*Euthyphro.*, *Ap.*, *Phdr.*, [*Theages*], etc.) and Xenophon, see Apuleius, *de Deo Socr.*; and Plut. *de Genio Socr.* (*Mor.* 575–98). On the tradition of scholarly and literary discussion of the Socratic δαιμόνιον see Pease on Cic. *Div.* i. 122; A. Willing, *De Socratis Daemonio quae Antiquis Temporibus fuerint Opiniones*, Comm. Phil. Ien. 8. 2 (1909) 125–83.

moral effort rather than a vision of divine power.[48] The generosity of the gods is confronted with human failings: this is perhaps the keynote of the *Meditations*.

5. *Dreams and Sickness*

τὸ δι᾽ ὀνειράτων βοηθήματα δοθῆναι ἄλλα τε καὶ ὡς μὴ πτύειν αἷμα καὶ μὴ ἰλιγγιᾶν, καὶ τὸ τοῦ ἐν Καιήτῃ, "ὥσπερ χρήσῃ" . . .

τὸ τοῦ Xylander: τούτου AT: τοῦτο Lugd.   χρήστου Theiler, Dalfen: χρήσει Boot: χρήσῃ Lofft: χρήσῃ AT: 'fort. est *quo utaris*, χρήσῃ' Xylander.

That I was granted assistance in dreams, especially how to avoid spitting blood and fits of giddiness; and the answer of the [?] at Caieta, 'even as you shall employ yourself' [?] . . . (i. 17. 9)

There are considerable difficulties in the interpretation of the last phrase of this sentence. Neither the text nor the point of the allusion is altogether clear. Wonderfully diverse renderings have been suggested. Haines and Farquharson both read ὥσπερ χρήσῃ and take this to be part of what was said to Marcus: 'as you shall use it' (what?) or 'even as thou shalt employ thyself', which are cryptic enough. The reading of the Lyons edition (1626), Χρύσῃ, which is supposed to be a reference to the priest of *Iliad* i, is a curiosity deserving mention only because it has survived in at least one translation (Casaubon: 'as that also that happened to thee in Cajeta, as unto Chryses when he prayed by the seashore'!). Theiler suggested χρήστου, which is accepted by Dalfen in his recent Teubner text; they cite the lexicographer Hesychius, who defines χρήστης as μάντις, 'a prophet'. The phrase would then mean 'and that [remark?] which was said in Caieta, like the word of a prophet'. Clearly, certainty here lies afar. What we can say is that the context encourages some further religious reference (καὶ connects the phrase with the clause on dreams, and ⟨τὸ⟩ ὅπως . . . in what follows this extract marks a new start). Marcus is known to have visited Caieta earlier in his life (Fronto i. 192; but SHA *Marc.* 19 is worthless gossip). It was a notable resort,[49] but our sources do not record an oracle there,

---

[48] On visions in dreams see section 5 below; on other, more direct and clearly supernatural visions see Richardson on *Hy. Dem.* 188–90, 275 ff.; Pfister, *RE* Suppl. iv. 277–323; id., *RLAC* v. 832–909; Nock, *Essays* 356–400, esp. 368–74.

[49] E.g. Stat. *Silv.* i. 3. 87 f.; Juv. 14. 87; cf. *RE* iii. 1323 f.; J. H. D'Arms, *Romans on the Bay of Naples* (Cambridge, Mass. 1970) 210 f.

and the inclusion of one in this sentence is unjustifiable over-translation, probably based on Marcus' combination of these two sources of insight elsewhere (ix. 27; *ap.* Fronto i. 50). Accordingly, I shall concentrate henceforth on the reference to dreams, said by Tertullian to be the prime source of knowledge of God for the majority of mankind (*de Anima* 47. 2).[50]

From the earliest times known to us the Greeks and Romans believed in the significance of dreams, and more specifically in their function of communicating warnings, advice, and occasionally deceitful messages from god to man (cf. Hom. *Il.* ii. 1–83; *Od.* xix. 560–9).[51] Most philosophers discussed the topic, but few with more scepticism and rationality than Aristotle in his works *On Dreams* and *On Divination in Sleep*, which strongly influenced the best surviving treatment of these subjects, Cicero's *de Divinatione*. This essay, like his *de Natura Deorum*, offers a conspectus of opposed views and arguments derived from classical and Hellenistic philosophic schools. Aristotle in *On Divination* rejects both the idea that the soul has innate powers of prophecy and the concept of dreams sent by the gods (*Div. per Somn.* 464[a]20; cf. Cic. *Div.* ii. 126, 129).[52]

But most later thinkers were more receptive to supernatural explanations of dream-phenomena; these included the Stoics Zeno, Cleanthes, Chrysippus, Diogenes, Antipater, and Posidonius.[53] A structure of scholarly study was assembled: case histories were collected and handed on, and a pseudo-science of dream-interpretation developed, represented for us by the *Oneirocriticon* or dream-handbook by Artemidorus, a writer of the second century AD.[54] Artemidorus, however, wrote in a long tradition; already in Homer Achilles speaks of calling for the aid of some interpreter of dreams (ὀνειροπόλον), 'for dreams too

---

[50] See Waszink's note. On dream-divination in antiquity the following works deserve mention: A. Bouché-Leclercq, *Histoire de la divination dans l'antiquité* i (Paris 1879); Dodds, *The Greeks and the Irrational* ch. 4 (cf. id., *The Ancient Concept of Progress* ch. 10); C. A. Behr, *Aelius Aristides and the Sacred Tales* (Amsterdam 1968) esp. ch. 8. For a collection of fragmentary ancient treatises see D. del Corno, *Graecorum de Re Oneirocritica Scriptorum Reliquiae* (Milan 1969). See also Kindstrand on Bion fr. 32 τῶν μάντεων; Pease on Cic. *Div.* index s.v. 'dreams'; *TDNT* v. 220 ff., s.v. ὄναρ.

[51] Further, Dodds, *The Greeks and the Irrational* 122.

[52] See Dodds, *The Ancient Concept of Progress* 179–82.

[53] For a long list of philosophers who believed in dream-divination see Clem. Al. *Strom.* i. 21. For modern lists see Bouché-Leclercq (n. 50) i. 29–91. See also the doxography in Cic. *Div.* i. 5–7, with Pease's notes.

come from Zeus' (*Il.* i. 63, cf. v. 148 ff.). The earliest known dream-book is by an Antiphon, in the fifth or fourth century BC (Cic. *Div.* i. 39; Diog. Laert. ii. 46), but the tradition may go back much earlier.[55] The Stoics were the school which most firmly espoused the truth of divination, and the arguments marshalled in its favour by Quintus Cicero in the first book of Cicero's *de Divinatione* are essentially Stoic (e.g. i. 82). It may indeed be guessed that some of the argument comes from Posidonius, who wrote five books on the subject, was well known to Cicero (*Att.* ii. 1. 2; Plut. *Cic.* 4), and is expressly cited as authority for two longish passages (i. 64, i. 125 with 129–30).[56] Basic is the Stoic assumption that deity and divination are related facts. If the gods exist, then they are bound to help us through divination, while if the forms of divination traditionally employed at Rome have validity, then the gods exist (*Div.* i. 9). Cicero replies 'arcem tu quidem Stoicorum . . . defendis' (*ibid.* 10). The argument is indeed well known in various forms (cf. Arist. fr. 10 Rose; Cic. *ND* ii. 12), and a concise parody of it is to be found in Lucian: εἰ γὰρ εἰσὶ βωμοί, εἰσὶ θεοί· ἀλλὰ μὴν εἰσὶ βωμοί, εἰσὶν ἄρα καὶ θεοί ('if there are altars, then there are gods; yes, there are altars, therefore there are gods', *Jup. Trag.* 51).[57] It rests on the assumption that the gods exist, are friendly to mankind, and themselves know what the future will be. This argument and its premises are vigorously attacked by Cicero in the second book of *de Divinatione* (41 f., 101 f., 104–6).

Posidonian theory added hypotheses about the actual mechanism of communication. In his view the soul is itself naturally clairvoyant because of its kinship with God (a fundamental premise for all Stoics); and true divination requires the highest possible degree of dissociation from the body. Consequently it is best achieved in frenzy, in dreams, or in a state close to death (*Div.* i. 64).

[54] Ed. R. Pack (Leipzig 1963); tr. by R. J. White, *The Interpretation of Dreams* (New Jersey 1975). See also R. Pack, *TAPA* 86 (1955) 280–90. For discussion see Behr (n. 50) ch. 8; S. R. F. Price, *Past and Present* 113 (1986) 3–37.

[55] For the identification of the various Antiphons see Dodds, *The Greeks and the Irrational* 132 n. 100; Gomme–Andrewes–Dover on Thuc. viii. 68. 1; R. G. A. van Lieshout, *Greeks on Dreams* (Utrecht 1980) 217 ff. For the tradition of dream-books see del Corno (n. 50); Bouché-Leclercq (n. 50) i. 277; Dodds, op. cit. 134 n. 119.

[56] Fr. 107–8, 110 E.–K. (= 377, 372–3a, 378 Theiler).

[57] See Hall, *Lucian's Satire* 182 ff. for further examples.

Despite Cicero's counterblast, belief in the significance of dreams was certainly not extinguished, and a surprising number of notable figures in the first and second centuries were powerfully influenced by them. Pliny the Elder once had a dream about his old comrade-in-arms Nero Drusus (the father of Claudius), who insisted that he should not allow his deeds in life to be forgotten, an injunction which Pliny took so seriously that he composed twenty books de Bello Germanico (Plin. Ep. iii. 5. 4). Somewhat similar is the case of Dio Cassius, who dedicated to the emperor Severus a work recounting the dreams and portents by which the latter had learned that he would gain the throne (72. 23), and who further asserts that a divine force told him to write on Severus' wars and continued to encourage him in his work through dreams.[58] In Apuleius' novel Lucius receives a number of dreams encouraging him to dedicate himself to the service of the goddess who has saved him (e.g. Met. xi. 19 'nec fuit nox una vel quies aliqua visu deae monituque ieiuna, sed crebris imperiis sacris suis me, iam dudum destinatum, nunc saltem censebat initiari').[59]

Clearly, however, the most directly relevant parallels to Marcus' case are the curative dreams received by the sick. Here again we find several parallels in the literature of the period. Plutarch took such dreams seriously, as shown by a charming passage in the Table-Talk: 'because of a dream, I had for a long time now been avoiding eggs, and I was acting so for this reason, that I might test by an egg . . . the vision which came to me so clearly and frequently' (τῆς ὄψεως ἐναργῶς μοι πολλάκις γενομένης, 635e). Elsewhere he calls dreams 'the most ancient form of prophecy' (Sept. Sap. Conv. 159a). Plutarch is also mentioned by Artemidorus (iv. 72), who describes a dream which presaged his death.[60]

Another familiar figure who appears in Artemidorus is Fronto, described as 'the arthritic' (cf. Gell. ii. 26, xix. 10 for his

---

[58] See Millar, A Study of Cassius Dio 179 f.; cf. 119–20. Arrian also claimed to have embarked on his Anabasis 'not without God's help' (οὐδὲ αὐτὸς ἄνευ θεοῦ, vii. 30. 3). On dream-commands see also Apul. Ap. 54 (p. 41. 1 Helm); Artem. ii. 70; P. Oxy. 1381 (c. 100 AD); Abt (n. 124) 283; F. Kudlien, in V. Nutton (ed.), Galen: Problems and Prospects (London: Wellcome Inst. for the Hist. of Medicine, 1981) 117–30.

[59] See J. Gwyn Griffiths' comm. p. 139.

[60] See R. Pack, TAPA 86 (1955) 285. On the egg passage see also F. W. Brenk. In Mist Apparelled (Leiden 1977) 74–7.

gout). 'After he had prayed for a cure, he dreamed that he was walking around in the suburbs. He obtained sufficient relief by being rubbed with bee-glue' (iv. 22; there is an untranslatable pun on πρόπολις, which means both 'suburb' and 'bee-glue'!).

Finally there is the case of Aristides, about whom we know so much from his dream-records, the so-called *Sacred Tales* ('Ιεροὶ Λόγοι).[61] Peculiar and unpleasant though his personality may seem to us today, the depth of his belief in his elect status, as one specially favoured by the healer god Asclepius, is hardly open to question. But in every way his belief and devotion seem more passionate, his emotions more extravagant, than anything we have any hint of in the work of Marcus. He believed he had had spectacular and glorious visions, and was ready to tell his readers about them in vivid detail. The famous passage in *Sacred Tales* ii (*Or.* 48) 31 f. shows something of the character of the work:

> I dreamed that I stood at the propylaea of the Temple. And many others were also gathered together, as whenever there is a purificatory ceremony. And they wore white garments, and the rest was of an appropriate form. Here I cried out other things to the God [Asclepius] and called him 'arbiter of fate' . . . Countless other things clearly contained the presence of the God. For there was a seeming, as it were, to touch him and to perceive that he himself had come, and to be between sleep and waking, and to wish to look up and to be in anguish that he might depart too soon, and to strain the ears and to hear some things as in a dream, some as in a waking state. Hair stood straight, and there were tears of joy, and the pride of the heart was inoffensive. And what man could describe these things in words? If any man has been initiated, he knows and understands. (Tr. C. A. Behr)

We may note also the interesting passage (too long to quote) in *Or.* 50. 38–70, in which Aristides describes the divine encouragement he has enjoyed in his literary activities. In one dream he is being crowned at the temple of Zeus for his speeches, 'for he is invincible in rhetoric'; in another he is given the name Theodorus, 'and, I think, "Asiarch" was added to the salutation' (50. 48; 53). Asclepius tells him that it is fitting that his

---

[61] See now esp. Behr (n. 50); this work contains a complete translation of the *Sacred Tales*. See also Festugière, *Personal Religion among the Greeks* ch. 7; Dodds, *The Greeks and the Irrational* 109 f., 13–16; id., *Pagan and Christian* 40 ff.; Lane Fox, *Pagans and Christians* 159–63. P. Brown, *The Making of Late Antiquity* (Princeton 1978) 40–5 offers a very different, and to my mind paradoxical, reading of Aristides' character and role.

mind be changed together with his name, and that henceforth he should associate with gods and surpass mankind. Although some of Dodds' psychoanalytical readings of ancient writers are out of favour today, it is hard not to agree with his diagnosis of these passages as megalomaniacal self-compensation, making up for Aristides' insecurity, physical weakness, and thwarted ambition.[62]

Aristides is a figure of Marcus' world and times: Alexander of Cotiaeum tutored them both, and the emperor was once moved to tears by Aristides' (extant) monody on Smyrna (Philos. VS 582). Poles apart though they are in style and character, they both believed in dream-communications. The difference between Marcus and Aristides lies in the former's reticence and humility rather than in matters of belief. Marcus himself refers, without irony or scepticism, to harsh prescriptions of Asclepius, including cold baths such as Aristides underwent so readily (Med. v. 8; cf. e.g. Or. 48. 45 ff.). There is no sign, however, of any special devotion to Asclepius; an apparently effusive reference to the god in a letter to Fronto simply uses him as one deity in a string of rhetorically balanced examples (i. 50). We may conclude from i. 17 that Marcus experienced what he felt certain was divine contact, but without any prior assumptions and expectations which might prompt him, like Aristides or other devotees, to identify it with the voice of any particular god.

6. Prayer[63]

ἤτοι οὐδὲν δύνανται οἱ θεοὶ ἢ δύνανται. εἰ μὲν οὖν μὴ δύνανται, τί εὔχῃ; εἰ δὲ
δύνανται, διὰ τί οὐχὶ μᾶλλον εὔχῃ διδόναι αὐτοὺς τὸ μήτε φοβεῖσθαί τι
τούτων μήτε ἐπιθυμεῖν τινος τούτων μήτε λυπεῖσθαι ἐπί τινι τούτων,
μᾶλλον ἤπερ τὸ μὴ παρεῖναί τι τούτων ἢ τὸ παρεῖναι; . . . τίς δέ σοι εἶπεν ὅτι

---

[62] For criticisms and assessments of Dodds' readings see R. Gordon, Didaskalos 4 (1972) 48–60; Brown, Religion and Society in the Age of St Augustine 74–81; cf. id., Augustine of Hippo (London 1967) 31 n. 4; also H. Lloyd-Jones, in P. Horden (ed.), Freud and the Humanities (London and New York 1985) 152–80. For a balanced view which singles out Dodds' treatment of Aristides for praise see D. A. Russell, PBA 67 (1981) 357–70.

[63] Bibliography on prayer: RLAC viii. 1134 ff., ix. 1 ff.; TDNT ii. 775 ff.; Kindstrand on Bion fr. 29 (pp. 231 f.); Nisbet–Hubbard on Hor. Odes i. 31 (note esp. Ep. i. 18. 104 ff.). Special studies: E. Norden, Agnostos Theos (Berlin 1913) esp. 144 ff.; H. Schmidt, Veteres Philosophi quomodo Iudicaverint de Precibus (RVV iv. 1, Giessen 1907); H. Brune, περὶ εὐχῆς: Veterum de Precibus Sententiae (diss. Marburg 1935); G. Soury, Aperçus de philosophie religieuse chez Maxime de Tyr (Paris 1942) ch. 2. See also above, ch. i n. 14; ch. iii n. 2.

οὐχὶ καὶ εἰς τὰ ἐφ’ ἡμῖν οἱ θεοὶ συλλαμβάνουσιν; ἄρξαι γοῦν περὶ τούτων εὔχεσθαι καὶ ὄψει. οὗτος εὔχεται· πῶς κοιμηθῶ μετ’ ἐκείνης. σύ· πῶς μὴ ἐπιθυμήσω τοῦ κοιμηθῆναι μετ’ ἐκείνης.

The gods are either powerless or powerful. If they are powerless, then why do you pray? But if they are powerful, then why not rather pray that they should grant you not to fear any of these things, not to desire any of them, not to feel grief about any of them, rather than that any of them should be present or absent? . . . Besides, who told you that the gods do not co-operate even with regard to those things which are in our power? Begin at least to pray about these things, and you will see. This man prays: How may I lie with that woman? *You* ought to pray: How may I not desire to lie with her? (ix. 40)

Two other relevant passages in the same book are:

καὶ οἱ θεοὶ δὲ εὐμενεῖς τοῖς τοιούτοις εἰσίν, εἰς ἔνια δὲ καὶ συνεργοῦσιν, εἰς ὑγίειαν, εἰς πλοῦτον, εἰς δόξαν· οὕτως εἰσὶ χρηστοί.

And the gods are kindly to such men, and help them to some objects, such as health, wealth, reputation—so good are they to men. (ix. 11)

. . . φύσει γὰρ φίλοι, καὶ οἱ θεοὶ δὲ παντοίως αὐτοῖς βοηθοῦσι, δι’ ὀνείρων, διὰ μαντειῶν, πρὸς ταῦτα μέντοι, πρὸς ἃ ἐκεῖνοι διαφέρονται.

. . . for by nature these men are akin to you; and also the gods help them in all manner of ways, through dreams, through prophecies—to get, however, the objects with which they are concerned. (ix. 27)

The second is a rather more acid version, implicitly condemning these objects as unworthy of attention.

Prayer has a place in the communicative rituals of man and god as early in Greek literature as we can trace. Already in Homer it represents the channel of requests or pleas in response to which the gods may intervene to give aid or to supplement human weakness with divine strength. It was the work of the philosophers, performed first by Socrates and probably taken further by Plato, to subject prayer to a more stringent set of standards. In Socrates' opinion there were some things for which it was proper to ask, and other things which the gods, however well disposed, would not grant, either because the request was in itself evil or because it would bring evil. Nor should we suppose that human offers of a *quid pro quo* could carry any weight with a just and self-sufficient god (the idea of men swaying the gods thus is criticised by Plato in *Euthyphro* 14e: ἐμπορικὴ ἄρα τις ἂν εἴη . . . τέχνη ἡ ὁσιότης ('Piety, then, would be

---

a kind of art of trading goods'); cf. *Rep.* i. 331b, ii. 364). Each of these arguments is comprehensible as a means of explaining why some prayers seem to succeed, some not. But this does not exclude an actual increase of religious feeling and moral awareness in thinking about prayer. Such a change does seem to be perceptible in the figure of Socrates.[64]

According to Xenophon Socrates prayed to the gods for the gift of 'good things' without qualification (ἁπλῶς), thinking that the gods themselves know best what kind of things are good (*Mem.* i. 3. 2). Somewhat similar is the Pythagorean dictum that wise men ought to pray for good things from the gods on behalf of the foolish, as the foolish do not know what is truly good (Diod. x. 9. 7), or Diogenes' criticism of men who prayed for reputed, not real goods (Diog. Laert. vi. 42). In the *Phaedrus* Socrates' prayer is for his own moral improvement, not for conventional wealth: I would consider the wise man rich, he adds, anticipating one of the Stoic paradoxes (*Phdr.* 279bc).[65] A sustained discussion of prayer and its proper objects is to be found in the pseudo-Platonic *Second Alcibiades*, where such conventional wishes as tyranny, military commands, and so forth are dismissed as valueless. This work is echoed in the most famous ancient treatment of 'the vanity of human wishes', Juvenal's tenth satire.[66] Another, less well known but more explicitly Stoic discussion is the second satire of Persius, in which the poet expresses contempt for the popular notion of deity as ignorant and compliant. The only appropriate offering is spiritual and moral purity; thus Persius concludes his poem:

> quin damus id superis, de magna quod dare lance
> non possit magni Messalae lippa propago?
> compositum ius fasque animo sanctosque recessus
> mentis et incoctum generoso pectus honesto.
> haec cedo ut admoveam templis et farre litabo.

---

[64] On Socrates' prayers see B. D. Jackson, *Phronesis* 16 (1971) 14–37; P. A. Meijer, in Versnel (n. 39) 234–45; D. Clay, in G. W. Bowersock *et al.* (eds.), *Arktouros*, Fest. B. Knox (Berlin 1979) 345–53. On Socrates' religious attitudes in general see Babut (n. 39) ch. 2; W. K. C. Guthrie, *History of Greek Philosophy* iii (Cambridge 1969) 402 ff., 467 ff.

[65] *SVF* iii. 593–600, 603; Cic. *Paradoxa* vi; Hor. *Ep.* i. 1. 106. See further Nisbet–Hubbard on Hor. *Odes* ii. 2 (e.g. on line 4); Griffin, *Seneca* ch. 9, esp. 295 ff. In the *Phaedrus* itself the reference to gold wittily picks up earlier passages (228a4, 235de) in a manner typical of Socratic irony and Platonic word-play.

[66] See the commentaries by Mayor and Courtney.

Let us make the gods an offering which the great platter of great
Messala's bloodshot progeny could never furnish—a heart's blend of
Justice and Right, a mind profoundly pure, a breast pervaded with
heroic virtue! Give me these for offerings, then groats alone are
sacrifice enough. (Pers. 2. 71–5, tr. J. Jenkinson)[67]

As Persius' treatment shows, Stoic views on this subject were
close to those of Socrates. But the Stoics placed much more
emphasis on the supreme importance of 'the things within our
power' (τὰ ἐφ' ἡμῖν), namely one's own moral nature, as opposed
to external possessions or assets popularly believed to be goods
but denied that title by the Stoics. These popular goods included
not only wealth, rank, and power, but even health and long life
(cf. *Med.* ix. 11, quoted above). All of these, the Stoics held, were
technically irrelevant to virtue, for their possession or absence
made no difference to moral choice.[68] If, however, the true
goods are by definition what is in our power, it is hardly
necessary to ask the gods to grant them to us: as Seneca puts it,
'facis rem optimam . . . si, ut scribis, perseveras ire ad bonam
mentem, quam stultum est optare cum possis a te impetrare'
(*Ep.* 41. 1).[69] But it is not surprising that Seneca's position on
this point, as elsewhere, is inconsistent; for the strict logic which
excludes the need for *any* external aid, within or outside the soul,
demands a strength of mind and a self-assurance scarcely
human. It is more common for philosophic writers to see health
of mind and body as analogous, and both dependent upon
divine aid as well as human self-discipline. Thus Horace prays
'frui paratis et valido mihi, / Latoe, dones et[70] precor integra
cum mente' (*Odes* i. 31. 17 f.), or Seneca advises Lucilius 'roga
bonam mentem, bonam valetudinem animi, deinde tunc
corporis' (*Ep.* 10. 4).
    What then was Marcus' position? In ix. 40 he clearly rejects

[67] Note also the related motif of frankness in prayer, speaking your desires out loud,
without shame or secret reservations: S. Sudhaus, *ARW* 9 (1906) 185–200; Schmidt
(n. 63) 55–71; H. Wagenvoort, *Pietas* (Leiden 1980) 206 ff., 210 ff.; H. S. Versenel in id.,
op. cit. (n. 39) 25 ff. See Pythag. *ap.* Clem. Al. *Strom.* iv. 26; Hor. *Ep.* i. 16. 59; Pers. 2.
3 ff.; Sen. *Ep.* 10. 5; Mart. i. 39; Apul. *Ap.* 54.
    [68] Cf. *SVF* iii. 29–48, and the exposition in Cic. *Fin.* iii (32 on this point).
    [69] Further, see Pohlenz, *Die Stoa* ii. 160; K. Schneider, *Juvenal und Seneca* (Wurzburg
1930) ch. 7.
    [70] The text of these lines is a long-standing crux; see Nisbet–Hubbard ad loc. The
structure of Horace's sentence seems to demand 'et'; thus from line 15 we have the
balance 'me . . . me . . . et . . . et . . . nec . . . nec . . .'.

the orthodox Stoic position but advances the hypothesis that the gods may help us also to command our moral intentions and emotional impulses. This chapter is concerned with what is in our power, that is, a proper mental attitude, whereas ix. 11 and 27 refer to the 'indifferents', the popular goods which are irrelevant to virtue. Perhaps these two chapters take a more worldly line with reference to more worldly men, those who do not intellectually grasp philosophic truths. Marcus here suggests that the gods grant 'second-best' goods to such men; he himself, however, should be concerned with what is really and truly good.

A famous passage of Epictetus also deserves mention. Rather than prayer, he is speaking of hymns, songs of praise. Rather than seeking benefits from the deity, he is asserting God's goodness and reciting the benefits which are already with us, in the nature of the world itself.

Ought we not, as we dig and plough and eat, to sing the hymn of praise to God? 'Great is God that he hath furnished us with these instruments wherewith we shall till the earth. Great is God that he hath given us hands, and power . . . to breathe while asleep.' This is what we ought to sing on every occasion, and above all we ought to sing the greatest and most divine hymn because God has given us the capacity to comprehend these things and to follow the right path [i.e. the path of reason]. (Epict. i. 16. 15–21, extracted)[71]

Thus Epictetus regards our own faculties as originally God-given, but entrusted to us to make proper and free moral use thereof. A more precise contrast with *Med.* ix. 40, with which we began, is provided by Epict. iv. 9. 3, a more positive, downright approach to the problem of unlawful desire and temptation: 'Another has a comely wife, you have the ability not to desire a comely wife. Is all this small in your eyes?' For Epictetus the philosopher is immune through God's favour and his own moral authority; for Marcus this goal is in the future, and in the present it is a matter for hope and prayer.

The identification of sources for particular doctrines of prayer is less important than trying to understand the human needs from which the rationalisation springs.[72] The ideal of self-

[71] Cf. Epict. iii. 26. 28 ff., iv. 1. 108 f.
[72] On prayer see the historical survey by F. Heiler, *Das Gebet* (Munich 1919; abbreviated Eng. tr. Oxford 1932); *ERE* x. 154–205; *ODCC* s.v.

sufficiency has its own attraction, and is inspiring enough when developed with the eloquence of Seneca or Epictetus. But it is understandable that at other times a man should find it an irresistible temptation to look to something outside himself, and to seek the aid of greater powers, as Marcus does, to strengthen this self-sufficiency. Furthermore, we have seen that Marcus himself believed that this kind of support had been granted to him: his reference to his dreams, and to the 'generosity' of the gods (εὐποιία) in another passage of Book I (i. 17. 1), make clear that ix. 40 is putting forward as precept something that he at least partially believes has been confirmed by experience. Even the particular temptation can be related to 'confessional' passages in the same chapter of Book I, where Marcus thanks the gods 'that I was not brought up longer with my grandfather's concubine . . . that I did not touch Benedicta or Theodotus' (i. 17. 2 and 7). He ends the same chapter with the words 'for all these things require the gods to help and the aid of fortune' (πάντα γὰρ ταῦτα θεῶν βοηθῶν καὶ τύχης δεῖται). These final words have been thought to be a quotation,[73] but from what has been said it should be obvious that they are no mere metaphor.

7. Heavenly Powers

τρίτον εἰ ἄφνω μετέωρος ἐξαρθεὶς κατασκέψαιο τὰ ἀνθρώπεια καὶ τὴν πολυτροπίαν κατανοήσαις, ὅτι καταφρονήσεις συνιδὼν ἅμα καὶ ὅσον τὸ περιοικοῦν ἐναερίων καὶ ἐναιθερίων· καὶ ὅτι, ὁσάκις ἂν ἐξαρθῇς, ταὐτὰ ὄψῃ· τὸ ὁμοειδές, τὸ ὀλιγοχρόνιον· ἐπὶ τούτοις ὁ τῦφος.

Thirdly, realise that if you could be suddenly caught up into the air and could look down upon human life and see all its variety, you would disdain it, seeing at the same time how great a company of beings in air and ether surrounds you; and that, however often you were caught up, you would see the same things: uniformity, transience, and pomp as well as these.[74] (xii. 24)

In the previous chapter we have considered Marcus' use of

---

[73] A. J. Kronenberg, *CR* 19 (1905) 301, without argument, followed by a number of editors; the rhythm of the phrase gives some support to this suggestion.

[74] The translation here is not entirely satisfactory. Perhaps preferable is '*these* are the object of your/their [i.e. other men's] pride'; that is, despite the transience and uniformity, men (perhaps even including Marcus himself) actually put on a show and exult in these. On τῦφος see D. R. Dudley, *A History of Cynicism* (London 1937) 56 f.; Kindstrand on Bion fr. 7; Brunt, *Athen*, 55 (1977) 42.

this motif, the 'view from above', which symbolically presents the philosopher's austere detachment and superior vision. The special interest of this passage lies in the phrase 'how great a company of beings in air and ether'. Commentators take this to be a reference to some doctrine of daemonology, although the word δαίμων is not actually used. Most thinkers of this period had views about such entities, of varying metaphysical and cosmological complexity: we find detailed accounts in Philo,[75] Albinus,[76] Apuleius,[77] Numenius,[78] and Maximus of Tyre.[79] It is another matter to say which, if any, of the various theories about these beings was in Marcus' mind. The Stoics certainly believed in the existence of superhuman powers in the atmosphere, or in the sublunar sphere (Diog. Laert. vii. 151; SVF ii. 1101–5), but the fullest development of these ideas was by the Platonists, notably Apuleius in his de Deo Socratis and Plutarch in his myths.[80]

One theory which we find in Plutarch and others is that the daemones, or some of them, are in fact the disembodied souls of men. This idea ultimately goes back to Hesiod (whom Plutarch quotes, Def. Orac. 415b). For Plutarch a few souls of heroes may attain supreme purity and, like Hesiod's golden race, become daemones, intermediaries between gods and men. The ideas which Plutarch expresses in a highly Platonic, literary mould are in fact much older and more deeply rooted in ancient beliefs and superstitions about the soul. Many believed that the soul's natural home was in the heavens, to which it would return after death. Such notions find expression in popular epitaphs, as in one fifth-century epigram on the dead at Potidaea: αἰθὴρ μὲν ψυχὰς ὑπεδέξατο, σώματα δὲ χθών (Kaibel, Epigrammata Graeca 21b. 1).[81]

---

[75] See J. Dillon, The Middle Platonists (London 1977) 171 ff.
[76] Dillon 287 on Albinus, Didaskalikos 15.
[77] Dillon 317 ff. on Apul. de Plat. 10.   [78] Dillon 378 on Numen. fr. 37.
[79] Dillon 399–400. Maximus' eighth and ninth Discourses embody similar views to those presented by Apuleius, loc. cit. For other aspects of this subject see Dodds, Pagan and Christian ch. 2; Nock, Essays 653–75; F. Conybeare, 'The Demonology of the New Testament', JQR 8–9 (1896–7).
[80] See G. Soury, La Démonologie de Plutarque (diss. Paris 1942); D. A. Russell, G&R 15 (1968) 33–5. Note esp. Is. Os. 360d–1d with Griffiths' notes; Def. Orac. 415a ff.; de Genio Socr. 590 ff.; de Facie 943a ff. For a detailed and highly interesting study of Plutarch's religious themes see Brenk, In Mist Apparelled, with exhaustive bibliog.
[81] See further R. Lattimore, Themes in Greek and Latin Epitaphs (Illinois 1942) 31 f., 311 ff.; van der Horst on ps.-Phocyl. 107 f.

One reason for supposing these ideas to be relevant to Marcus Aurelius is the unusual passage in *Meditations* iv. 21, in which he seems to show interest in this kind of speculation. The chapter begins with the question: εἰ διαμένουσιν αἱ ψυχαί, πῶς αὐτὰς ἐξ ἀϊδίου χωρεῖ ὁ ἀήρ; ('If souls do remain in existence, how does the air find room for them from time eternal?'), and goes on to discuss the point.

Marcus here states that after death souls move into the atmosphere (εἰς τὸν ἀέρα) before being altered again: 'then they change and are poured out and kindled (χέονται καὶ ἐξάπτονται) into the generative principle[82] of the universal whole, and so provide room for those which succeed to their place'. The passage gives a new slant to Marcus' favourite motif of a succession of deaths, in an apparently orderly sequence.[83] (Also, the striking juxtaposition χέονται καὶ ἐξάπτονται, almost an oxymoron, seems to be a reminiscence of the Stoic notions of the world ending in flood and fire, κατακλυσμός and ἐκπύρωσις.[84] Marcus is doing a little cosmology on his own account.) But the whole description is then qualified, as the author returns to his habitual agnosticism: 'This, then, would be the answer supposing that souls do remain in existence.'

Marcus' language in iv. 21 recalls Stoic discussions of the duration of the soul after separation from the body. Cleanthes seems to have held that all souls survived (ἐπιδιαμένειν) until the end of the world-cycle, Chrysippus that only those of the wise do so (Diog. Laert. vii. 157). Most later Stoics seem to have believed that all souls survived for at least a certain length of time, though Epictetus speaks more in terms of transformation and resolution into elements than of survival.[85] The handbook of Arius Didymus provides one possible parallel to Marcus' thought in xii. 24. Arius says that the world-soul exists in the αἰθήρ and the ἀήρ, and that both living creatures' souls and 'all those which are in the surrounding region' (ἐν τῷ περιέχοντι) have their origin in it, 'for the souls of the dead live on there' (διαμένειν γὰρ ἐκεῖ τὰς τῶν ἀποθανόντων ψυχάς, Arius fr. 39 *ap.* Diels, *Doxographi Graeci* 471. 10 ff.[86]).

---

[83] See ch. IV 5 (ii).
[82] σπερματικὸς λόγος; cf. iv 14, vi 24; SVF iv, p. 93.
[84] See Pease on Cic. *ND* ii. 51; Nisbet–Hubbard on Hor. *Odes* i. 2. 5.
[85] See R. Hoven, *Stoïcisme et stoïciens face au problème de l'au-delà* (Liège 1971).
[86] Quoted in part in *SVF* ii. 809, 821. Cf. Diog. Laert. vii. 157 f.; Tert. *de Anima* 54 f. (attacking Stoic ideas), with Waszink ad loc.

These passages do suggest that in xii. 24 Marcus may be talking of the dead souls of men, now freed from their confinement on the earth below. But this is not a motif that regularly figures in the otherwise similar chapters describing the philosopher's view from above; nor does it seem quite clear why he has brought in the reference here. It is left quite obscure what these beings themselves do or think about the world below. Presumably, however, they also disapprove of it and provide confirmatory authority for Marcus' gloomy criticisms. The absence of reference to their moral superiority may in that case seem surprising; but on the whole it seems that Marcus' belief in this kind of survival was tentative and uncommitted (as the passage from iv. 21 shows; see further below on xii. 5).

An alternative explanation of this passage is to read the words ἐναερίων and ἐναιθερίων as neuter rather than masculine, and to take both words as referring to the heavenly bodies. This idea finds close parallels in Cicero's *Somnium Scipionis*: the wise man, raised above earthly trivialities, can contemplate the planets and stars with wonder and delight.[87] Elsewhere Marcus refers to the purity and detachment of the heavens compared with the filth and scum of earthly life (vii. 47, xi. 27). In this passage the inner atmosphere (ἀήρ) would include the sun, moon, and planets; more remote and still purer is the αἰθήρ, which was thought to contain the stars.[88]

I find it surprising that this interpretation has not been considered in the past; in particular, it explains the absence of response or interest in these heavenly entities. The stars are not given personalities or presented as having any interest in Marcus or his subjects. Whichever explanation of this passage is correct, it shows the author's other-worldliness in the most literal sense. We should also note that there is no word of divine judgement or retribution from these powers. Whether astral spirits or dead men's souls, they are detached from Marcus' concerns, and his imagined sojourn in the heights can bring him no rewards or reassurance, but only morose reflection.

---

[87] On the *Somnium Scipionis* see ch. IV n. 93.
[88] Arist. *de Caelo* iii–iv; Cic. *Somn.* 17; see also M. Nilsson, *Eranos* 44 (1946) 20 ff. = *Opuscula Selecta* (Lund 1960) iii. 31–9; Dodds, *Pagan and Christian* 6.

8. Apprehension of the Gods

πρὸς τοὺς ἐπιζητοῦντας· "ποῦ γὰρ ἰδὼν τοὺς θεοὺς ἢ πόθεν κατειληφὼς ὅτι
εἰσίν, οὕτω σέβεις;" πρῶτον μὲν καὶ ὄψει ὁρατοί εἰσιν· ἔπειτα μέντοι οὐδὲ
τὴν ψυχὴν τὴν ἐμαυτοῦ ἑώρακα καὶ ὅμως τιμῶ· οὕτως οὖν καὶ τοὺς θεούς,
ἐξ ὧν τῆς δυνάμεως αὐτῶν ἑκάστοτε πειρῶμαι, ἐκ τούτων ὅτι τε εἰσὶ
καταλαμβάνω καὶ αἰδοῦμαι.

To those who ask the question 'Where have you seen the gods or
whence have you apprehended that they exist, that you thus worship
them?', first, they are visible even to the eyes [?]; second, I have not
seen my own soul, and yet I honour it. And so too with the gods; from
my repeated experiences of their power, from these I apprehend that
they exist, and I do them reverence. (xii. 28)

Here as in the discussion of prayer and its efficacy Marcus is
influenced by the stock arguments in textbooks. The question
posed here is almost a θέσις of the philosophical and rhetorical
schools; it is certainly related to a known thesis, 'Is the world
governed by Providence?' (Quintilian iii. 5. 6, xii. 2. 21; Theon
ii. 126 Spengel).[89] Marcus' answer here is somewhat perfunctory, particularly when we remember that the whole of the
second book of Cicero's de Natura Deorum (the longest of the
three) is devoted to this subject.

Another common question was how one apprehended the
gods: are they 'known' or perceived through the senses, or the
intellect, or how? Stoics recognised that this was a difficult
problem, and it was one of their stock puzzles under the heading
of the criterion of truth. Diogenes Laertius puts it simply and
clearly: 'It is by sense perception, they hold, that we get
cognition of white and black, rough and smooth, but it is by
reason that we get cognition of conclusions reached through
demonstration, such as the gods' existence or providence' (vii.
52).[90] Chrysippus argued that the Epicurean denial of divine
providence could not be reconciled with our common conception that the gods are kind and good to mankind (SVF ii. 1126).
The problem of course arises that not everyone would assent to
this allegedly universal conception. There remains a gap
between the will to believe and the ability to demonstrate.

[89] Further, see S. F. Bonner, Roman Declamation (Liverpool 1949) 3.
[90] Cf. A. A. Long and D. N. Sedley, The Hellenistic Philosophers i (Cambridge 1987)
241–53.

In arguing for the existence of the gods and their concern for men,[91] Epictetus and others appeal to the evidence provided by the beauty and order of the universe (Epict. ii. 14. 25–7). Many writers refer to the stately movement of the stars and planets as a decisive proof of providential design (Pl. *Lg.* x. 897c, 898c, xii. 966e; cf. Ps. 19: 1, and especially the noble fragment of Aristotle's *de Philosophia* preserved by Cicero, *ND* ii. 95).

It is usually assumed that Marcus' first reply to the imaginary opponent, ὄψει ὁρατοί εἰσιν, makes the same point. This is very probably correct, but should perhaps not be assumed as certain. Of course Stoics and other thinkers regarded the heavenly bodies as divine, as they did the universe as a whole;[92] Marcus speaks of the sun as one of the gods (viii. 19), and, as we have seen, he may refer to the stars and planets as divine observers in xii. 24. But he may be thinking here of another common 'proof' of the gods' existence, their manifestation in epiphanies. This is another reason given by Cicero's Stoic for belief in the gods, though he does not develop the point at any length (*ND* ii. 6). On the Epicurean side, Lucretius refers to men's visions of the gods, both waking and sleeping, as the origin of religious belief (v. 1161 ff.). The word ὄψις need not exclude apparitions in dreams, so that we might connect this passage with Marcus' references to divine aid and admonition in i. 17. This is, however, only an alternative suggestion, made in the belief that we should leave open the question what exactly Marcus refers to in this cryptic phrase.

The second argument he gives is more explicit and more eristic. It is another commonplace of the schools, found already in Xenophon (*Mem.* iv. 3. 14) and used several times by Cicero; thus *Mil.* 84: 'proinde quasi nostram ipsam mentem ... qua haec ipsa agimus et dicimus, videre aut plane qualis sit aut ubi sit sentire possimus', or *Tusc.* i. 70: 'sic mentem hominis, quamvis eam non videas, ut deum non vides, tamen, ut deum agnoscis ex operibus eius, sic ex memoria rerum et inventione et celeritate motus omnique pulchritudine virtutis vim divinam mentis agnoscito.' In the lines that follow Marcus presents an

---

[91] Cf. the division of his subject by the Stoic Balbus in Cic. *ND* ii. 3, with 35 and iii. 6; other doxographic treatments follow a similar order of discussion; see Pease on ii. 3.

[92] See e.g. Pease on Cic. *ND* ii. 39 (note esp. ii. 30 'deum esse mundum'; cf. i. 37 on Zeno); Posid. fr. 127 E.–K.; Diog. Laert. vii. 139.

analogy ('so too it is with the gods . . .'); his apprehension of
their power, at all times (ἑκάστοτε), is the proof for him. But here
again there is a slight elusiveness, in ἐξ ὧν . . . ἐξ τούτων . . .; what
exactly are the experiences which constitute this proof? Perhaps
the world around Marcus, with all the goodness within it which
the gods have brought about; perhaps the inner sensations of
encouragement and advice to which we have already referred
(but would these be frequent enough to justify ἑκάστοτε?).
One more general point may be made here. It is common in
other writers and in popular response to religious teaching for
the worshipper to expect evidence of divine power and interven-
tion, spectacular or miraculous proofs.[93] Thus in Apuleius the
irreligiosi will be convinced of their error, now that they behold
Lucius saved and restored to human shape through the favour of
Isis (*Met.* xi. 15). Similarly the followers of Iamblichus see 'the
manifest proofs' of his power and believe accordingly (Eunapius
VS 458–9, where Iamblichus makes the spirits of two streams
visible to them). So too in the New Testament both the disciples
and the Scribes and Pharisees expect 'a sign (from heaven)',
supernatural proof of Christ's power and status (see esp. Mark 8:
11–13; Matt. 12: 38; 16: 1–4, where Christ comments that it is 'a
wicked and adulterous generation' that seeks a sign; 24: 3; Luke
23: 8).[94] Marcus Aurelius' expectations seem more modest; he is
less inclined to point to any specific events as decisive proof. It is
rather contemplation of the workings of the whole universe that
convinces the Stoic that it is the reasoned design of greater
powers. In fact the reasons Marcus gives here are perfunctory
and undeveloped, and his final words in xii. 28 neatly express
the convergence of reason and reverence: καταλαμβάνω is a word
of reasoned argument and intellectual apprehension (cf. κατάλ-
ηψις), while the last word of the chapter, αἰδοῦμαι, carries more
religious emotion, reverence, and awe. καταλαμβάνω picks up

[93] See MacMullen, *Paganism* 94–7, from whom I draw some of these examples. For
belief in divine epiphanies in this period see also Nock, *Essays* 934 n. 17, citing Celsus *ap.*
Orig. *Cels.* iii. 24, vii. 35, viii. 45; Max. Tyr. *Or.* ix. 7. 1; Alex. Aphrod. *Fat.* 32; add
Philos. *VS* ii. 4. 568; *V. Ap.* iv. 10, viii. 7; Lane Fox, *Pagans and Christians* ch. 4, a
magnificently wide-ranging account.
[94] It may seem strange that the miracles which Jesus does perform do not qualify as
'signs', but rather give rise to the demand that he produce authentic proof of deity. This
is presumably because for his contemporaries the deeds of Jesus could be seen as merely
sorcery, manipulation of demons, and the like. They did not prove him the son of God
(so *TDNT* vii. 235).

κατειληφώς, and ὄψει ὁρατοί and ἑώρακα pick up ἰδών; so too
αἰδοῦμαι picks up σέβεις and τιμῶ, but the author intensifies the
rhetorical effect of his words by giving αἰδοῦμαι the emphatic
final place. Theory and abstraction are a thin mask for genuine
hope and intense personal involvement.

9. Survival of the Good[95]

πῶς ποτε πάντα καλῶς καὶ φιλανθρώπως διατάξαντες οἱ θεοὶ τοῦτο μόνον
παρεῖδον, τὸ ἐνίους τῶν ἀνθρώπων καὶ πάνυ χρηστοὺς καὶ πλεῖστα πρὸς τὸ
θεῖον ὥσπερ συμβόλαια θεμένους καὶ ἐπὶ πλεῖστον δι' ἔργων ὁσίων καὶ
ἱερουργιῶν συνήθεις τῷ θείῳ γενομένους, ἐπειδὰν ἅπαξ ἀποθάνωσι, μηκέτι
αὖθις γίνεσθαι, ἀλλ' εἰς τὸ παντελὲς ἀπεσβηκέναι;

How was it that the gods, who ordered all things aright and out of love
for mankind, overlooked this one thing only, that some men altogether
good, those who had, so to speak, most commerce with the divine, and
who by holy acts and solemn rites had grown most intimate with
divinity, should, once dead, never come into being again, but be
wholly extinguished? (xii. 5)

Apart from iv. 21 (discussed in section 7 above), this is the
principal passage in the *Meditations* to give extended consideration to the thought of an afterlife in the sense of continued (or
renewed) consciousness for the individual. Indeed, Marcus goes
still further than even the gentler Stoic views allowed, and
speaks, although hypothetically, of a rebirth, a renewed life
(αὖθις γίνεσθαι). It should be noted that he nowhere envisages
this for *himself*. His concern is broader, and is expressed
speculatively, as a question (πῶς ποτε). The rest of the chapter,
not quoted here, responds to the initial question. If this is so, it is
as it should be; for if it should be otherwise, the gods would have
made it so. Moreover, our very argument and disputation about
questions of justice with the gods presuppose that we believe
them ready to respond to such appeals. We hold that they are
ἄριστοι καὶ δικαιότατοι (xii. 5 *ad fin.*). And if this is so, they would
not have overlooked or neglected anything in their ordering of
the world out of injustice or unreason. Thus the end of the
chapter echoes its beginning, οὐκ ἄν τι περιεῖδον answering
παρεῖδον, and ἀδίκως καὶ ἀλόγως contrasting with καλῶς καὶ
φιλανθρώπως. Yet the very neatness of the argument emphasises

[95] See Hoven (n. 85) on this whole subject, and his pp. 147-8 on *Med.* xii. 5.

its circularity: the Stoics hold that 'whatever is, is right', and consequently, once we grant their premises of an ordered world and just gods, we have no alternative but to suppose that our human judgement is in error where it sees injustice in divine dispensation.[96] But the inadequacy of Marcus' logic is perhaps less important than the self-denial which his position involves. Even professed Stoics such as Seneca might waver over the possiblity of conscious posthumous survival,[97] and Marcus' reflections here seem particularly austere when contrasted with the high-flown imaginative myths in Plutarch or the bizarre speculations of the neo-Platonists. Although elsewhere he allows himself some more ingenious theorising as to the future destination of the disembodied soul (iv. 21), this is considered only 'on the hypothesis that souls do continue to exist' (see above, p. 207). He maintains a firm agnosticism, though this does not exclude a note of hope and longing, if not for himself, then for those better than himself.

The argument is couched in such a way as to avoid any direct criticism of the divine disposition; we may profitably contrast the chorus of Euripides' *Heracles*, who also speak of the gods' failure to make proper recompense to the virtuous with a second life, and ascribe this to a deficiency in divine ξύνεσις and σοφία which the play will make horrifyingly apparent (*HF* 655–72). Marcus has no such fault to find with divine providence, but the length of the question he asks here, with its straggling clauses piled up to describe these good and holy men, does suggest that he sees this as a real problem, one which needs an answer. At the same time we must not exaggerate: the form of xii. 5 is that of an intellectual problem. The posing and the hypothetical resolution of this problem do not constitute a *crise religieuse*. Marcus ponders and redeploys his beliefs rather than repudiating them. Contrast the words of Fronto, writing to Marcus and voicing his own grief at the loss of a grandson: 'saepe enim expostulo cum deis immortalibus et fata iurgio compello' (ii. 222 ff.; cf. Marcus'

---

[96] On the idea of reproaching the gods and pleading to them for justice see (for early Greece) J. Griffin, *CQ* 28(1978) 1–6 (add Theogn. 373–80, 733 ff.); Collard on Eur. *Supp.* 734–6. Later, see Epict. i. 6. 38 f., iii. 22. 13 (with Billerbeck's note), 58 f.; M. Aur. vi. 16, 41, xi. 13, xii. 12. Cf. the language of litigation in Job (10: 2, 23: 3–6, 31: 35, etc.; see G. B. Caird, *The Language and Imagery of the Bible* (London 1980) 157–8).

[97] See Hoven (n. 85) 109–26; Pohlenz, *Die Stoa* i. 322 and notes; A. L. Motto, *Guide to the Thought of L. Annaeus Seneca* (Amsterdam 1970) 61–2.

reference in xii. 5. 3 to those who 'dispute' with God (δικαιο-
λογῇ); also xii. 24 οὔτε δὲ τῇ ἐπιτυχίᾳ μεμπτέον οὔτε τῇ προνοίᾳ
ἐγκλητέον, 'one should neither find fault with what befalls nor
cry out against Providence'). Fronto goes on to criticise the very
ideas of Providence, destiny, or the gods which it is so often
Marcus' concern to defend to himself.[98] Marcus never
denounces Providence, but his advocacy is not always whole-
heartedly persuasive.

The reference in xii. 5 to pre-eminently good men recalls a
number of the passages in which Stoics maintained that only the
sapientes would survive after death (see p. 207 above, with n. 85).
This declaration is less arrogant than it sounds, since Stoics
commonly held that no certain example of a *sapiens* had ever
existed![99] Marcus certainly did not claim to be one (x. 1, x. 36,
etc.[100]), and his description is less intellectual, more religious in
tone. What kind of men did he mean and what kind of
'commerce' or 'communion' with the divine did these fortunate
few enjoy? The closest parallel is probably iii. 4. 3, describing in
eloquent terms the man who is open, straightforward, and
unmalicious:

ὁ γάρ τοι ἀνὴρ ὁ τοιοῦτος, οὐκ ἔτι ὑπερτιθέμενος τὸ ὡς ἐν ἀρίστοις ἤδη εἶναι
[cf. xii. 5 πάνυ χρηστούς], ἱερεύς τίς ἐστι καὶ ὑπουργὸς θεῶν [cf. xii. 5
ἱερουργιῶν], χρώμενος καὶ τῷ ἔνδον ἱδρυμένῳ αὐτοῦ . . .

Such a man, putting off no longer to be one of the elect, is surely a priest
and minister of gods, employing aright that which is seated within him
also . . .

Similarly, iii. 7 refers to 'the man who puts first of all his own
mind and divinity, and the holy rites (τὰ ὄργια) of its excellence'.
These parallels confirm the view[101] that Marcus need not be
speaking in xii. 5 of literal acts of worship; rather, it is the moral
qualities of the good man that qualify him for such titles. We are
moving again in the area of *spiritual* service to the gods, both to
the powers that govern the cosmos and to their image, the
daemon that dwells within each rational being, his conscience or

---

[98] The whole of Fronto's epistle is moving and convincing. Cf. ch. III n. 6 above. For
arguments defending Providence in the *Meditations* see ii. 11, vi. 44, x. 6–7.
[99] See above, ch. III nn. 72–3.
[100] See Brunt, *JRS* 64 (1974) 6 n. 32.
[101] Ibid. 17.

better self.[102] In the same vein, the image of the 'priest' is used for the ministry of the true Cynic philosopher by Epictetus (iii. 22. 82 τοῦ κοινοῦ πατρὸς ὑπηρέτης τοῦ Διός).[103] Both authors doubtless recall, but do not phrase so exclusively, the old Stoic principle that only the *sapiens* is the true ἱερός or μαντικός (*SVF* iii. 608; cf. 605, 611–24).[104]

We might perhaps go further, and recall that ἱερός is one of the titles given by many authors (including Plutarch and Lucian) to the kind of figure usually known as the θεῖος ἀνήρ, and well exemplified in Philostratus' Apollonius.[105] Celsus, quoted by

[102] The use of the word δαίμων by thinkers of this period is, as will already be clear, frequently ambiguous. Besides the works cited in nn. 75–80 above, see Theiler on *Med.* ii. 13; Bonhöffer, *Epictet und die Stoa* 81–6, who attempts to distinguish the different senses in Epictetus and Marcus. Here I offer only a very summary set of distinctions, with a few references. (1) δαίμων as intermediary (spirit) between gods and men, as in (e.g.) Pl. *Symp.* 202d–4a; Epict. iii. 13. 15; Diog. Laert. ix. 7. (2) δαίμων as individual 'genius' in the Roman sense, a tutelary deity: for this concept see Hor. *Ep.* ii. 2. 187, with Brink's comm. appendix 19; cf. Pl. *Tim.* 90. (3) Stoic use: a localised god within oneself, one's rational self, the portion of divine fire which exists in all rational beings. This sense in particular makes for ambiguity, as this spark or deity can be regarded either as a part of oneself (the soul? the higher part of the soul?) or as an independent deity which has its temporary residence within one's body. See e.g. Sen. *Ep.* 41. 2; Epict. i. 14. 12 ἐπίτροπος; M. Aur. v. 27 ὃν ἑκάστῳ προστάτην καὶ ἡγεμόνα ὁ Ζεὺς ἔδωκεν ἀπόσπασμα ἑαυτοῦ. (4) δαίμων in the modern sense of 'demon', that is, an evil and dangerous spirit. Pagans as well as Christians believed in such beings; see Dodds, *Pagan and Christian* 37 f. (though they lacked the concept of the Devil). But in Marcus this sense is found only in i. 6 (the reference to exorcism already discussed: see p. 181 above). Socrates' famous divine sign, his δαιμονίον (see above, n. 47) could be regarded as either (2) or (3). Most of Marcus' uses of the word (see Dalfen, index s.v.) fall into category (3), though v. 27, quoted above, comes closer to (1); vii. 17 is more akin to everyday usage, with δαίμων ἀγαθὸς meaning little more than 'good luck' (cf. x. 13); iii. 6, iii. 7, and iii. 12 particularly suggest the independent and conscious existence of the δαίμων. Note also xii. 9. I do not think as relevant the area of religious belief discussed by Nock, 'The Emperor's Divine *Comes*', *Essays* 653–75, however rich and stimulating his account. Marcus, like Epictetus, clearly thinks of such a δαίμων as dwelling in every man: the emperor is not specially privileged. Nock's treatment, however, does suggest another contrast between Marcus and his fellow emperors, who often thought of themselves as under the protection of a particular god (thus Octavian and Apollo, Domitian and Minerva, Julian and Mithras). We find no such evidence in the case of Marcus.

[103] See Billerbeck's note, and for the priest image see also Apul. *Ap.* 41 (p. 48. 2 Helm); 1 Pet. 2: 9; Porph. *de Abstin.* 2. 49.

[104] For a parody see Lucian, *Vit. Auct.* 20. Further, *TDNT* iii. 257–65.

[105] For this range of vocabulary and concepts see H. D. Betz, *Lukian von Samosata und das Neue Testament* (Berlin 1961) 102–3. On the whole subject see the very helpful survey by M. Smith, *JBL* 90 (1971) 174 ff., which includes much recent bibliography. See also L. Bieler, Θεῖος ἀνήρ (Vienna 1935–6); M. Hadas and M. Smith, *Heroes and Gods* (London 1965); D. Tiede, *The Charismatic Figure as Miracle Worker* (SBL Dissertation Series i, Missoula 1972). Some aspects of their presentation in literature are also treated by P. Cox, *Biography in Late Antiquity* (Berkeley and Los Angeles 1983). See also n. 113 below.

Origen, gives the title ἱερός to inspired poets, sages, and pagan philosophers (*Cels.* vii. 41). Marcus himself seems to allude to the conception in vii. 67: 'to live the blessed life rests on very few conditions; and do not, just because you have given up hope of being expert in dialectics and physics, therefore despair of being a free man, reverent, sociable and readily obedient to God. For it is possible to be a holy man (θεῖον ἄνδρα) and yet not be recognised by anyone.'[106]

I would read this as a sour reflection on two common beliefs: first, that intellectual activities such as dialectic or physics have value *per se*, without their ethical consequences; and second, that a θεῖος ἀνήρ is bound to be very much a 'showman', a grandiose, immensely impressive individual, a 'charismatic figure' and 'miracle-worker' to use the terms adopted by one student of the phenomenon.[107] This latter view Marcus clearly rejects. We should relate his comment here to his disapproval of ostentation, grand gestures,[108] and showmanship, visible in many passages of his work, including i. 6 (his distrust of 'what is said' (not 'done') by the miracle-workers, the γόητες). A revealing phrase in the chapter on Antoninus Pius sums up his own ideal: 'acting always according to the traditions of our forefathers, but not endeavouring that his regard for these traditions should be noticed' (i. 16. 6).[109]

Meditations vii. 66 also offers an instance of this disapproval, and on comparable grounds: 'how do we know that Telauges was not superior in character to Socrates? It is not enough that

[106] More relevant than Democritus and others quoted by Farquharson on this passage is Epict. iii. 24. 118, or Sen. *Ep.* 79 (esp. 13–18). But note that Seneca characteristically paints a rosier picture: fame and recognition will come to the philosopher after death. It is commonly maintained in ancient literature that, despite their protestations, philosophers too want fame: see above, ch. IV n. 107.

[107] Tiede (n. 105).

[108] See i. 16. 4. χρηστικὸν ἀτύφως, ibid. 5 οὔτε πρὸς καλλωπισμὸν, v. 18, ix. 29, xi. 3. As has often been noted, the ostentatious self-immolations of Peregrinus and others (including many of the Christian martyrs) carry to a further extreme the self-consciously heroic ends of the Stoic opposition (Tac. *Agr.* 42. 3–4; *Ann.* iv. 20. 3, etc.; cf. above, ch. II n. 44).

On death-wishes see Sen. *Ep.* 24. 25; Nock, *Conversion* 194–201; W. Rutz, 'Amor Mortis', *Hermes* 88 (1960) 462 ff.

[109] Cf. Pl. *Rep.* ii. 361b κατ' Αἰσχύλον οὐ δοκεῖν ἀλλ' εἶναι ἀγαθὸν ἐθέλοντα (alluding to Aesch. *Sept.* 574); also e.g. Sen. *Ep.* 80. 10, with Summers' note; Epict. iii. 24. 50. Epictetus also criticises a 'philosopher' who has always wanted those who meet him to admire and cry out ὦ μεγάλου φιλοσόφου (i. 21. 3). See further Epict. iii. 12. 16–17, iii. 24. 118, iv. 1. 155, iv. 6. 24, iv. 8. 15–20, 35 ff.; M. Aur. vii. 73, xi. 13.

Socrates perished more gloriously.[110] It is not enough . . . that Socrates argued more fluently with the sophists, spent the night in the open more enduringly . . . we have to consider what sort of soul Socrates had'. These remarks are striking, not least because Marcus is certainly not the man to deride Socrates, whom he quotes so often. But Socrates is a man who is above all others celebrated, in this period and much earlier, in hagiographic literature, including works which come close to treating him as a θεῖος ἀνήρ (Plutarch's *de Genio Socratis* provides much illustrative material).[111] Part of what Marcus surely objects to is the automatic idolisation of Socrates, not because he dissents from the general view that Socrates is a figure who deserves admiration, but because Socrates like everyone else—like Marcus himself—should be judged according to proper, philosophic standards, not accorded unquestioned special status.[112]

These passages are sufficient to show how out of sympathy Marcus Aurelius would be with the kind of hero-worship received in this period and later by a still more famous kind of 'holy man', the type of magician-cum-sage which has been described in detail by Peter Brown and his followers.[113] The

[110] The resolution of Socrates to die, so memorably captured in Plato's *Apology* (contrast the feeble justification offered in Xen. *Ap.* 5–8) always had something paradoxical about it, given that the options of exile or escape were available. His later imitators often followed his example with greater theatricality: cf. the case of Seneca, and Petronius' mockery of such ostentation (Tac. *Ann.* xvi. 18). Note also Tacitus' language at *Agr.* 42. 4, esp. 'ambitosa morte'.

[111] See D. A. Stoike, in Betz *et al.*, *Plutarch's Theological Writings*, esp. 239 ff.; see also M. Riley, *GRBS* 18 (1977) 257 ff.

[112] The oddity of vii. 66 (as Professor Russell observes) is that it is hard to see how we can consider the ψυχή of Socrates, or anyone else, except by observing such actions as his standing up to the Thirty in the case of Leon. Epict. iv. 1. 160 and iv. 7. 30 f., passages which single out this episode for praise, show the incongruity. It may be, then, that Marcus is making a somewhat unreal distinction here, between moral action and inner moral attitude, to be explained, as I suggest, by his impatience with eccentricity and showmanship. (Professor I. G. Kidd offers a different account: there is, he suggests, a contrast between isolated instances or actions, not in themselves evidence for the reasons for doing them, and consistent διαθέσεις ψύχης.)

The presence of Telauges, a ghostly figure absent from Plato and Xenophon but known to have been the subject of a lost Socratic dialogue by Aeschines, makes the passage all the more baffling. On Telauges see Farquharson's helpful note; K. Krauss, *Aeschinis Socratici Reliquiae* (Leipzig 1911) 102–13; H. Dittmar, *Aeschines von Sphettos* (Berlin 1912) 213 ff.; J. Humbert, *Socrate et les petits socratiques* (Paris 1967) 229–31. I would say only that the question with which Marcus begins the chapter is surely rhetorical; whatever Aeschines may have said, Marcus need not be preferring Telauges to Socrates, and the lack of further attention paid to him counts against any such view.

[113] Esp. Brown's seminal article in *JRS* 61 (1971) 80–101 = *Society and the Holy in Late*

kind of men Marcus most admires are delineated, in their humanity and their earthly, social activities, in the first book of the *Meditations*. As for the relationship between men and the gods, while Marcus did believe, as has been shown, in divine aid through dreams and prophecies, there is no sign that he believed that even the most gifted of men could exert power, magical or theurgical, to control or command heaven—the claim that was essential to the authority and function of the holy man in late antiquity. The gods *grant* aid, they cannot be forced to yield it.[114] Here, as in his literary tastes or indeed his choice of philosophy, Marcus stands apart from the trends and interests of his age. *Meditations* xii. 5 shows both the affinities of language and the fundamental difference of attitude: religious devotion expressed in ethical conduct may bring one nearer to God, but that is an inner, private, unostentatious affair; it has nothing to do with magic; and it does not necessarily hold out any hope of reward to Marcus or to any man.

10. *Conclusion*

From the disparate material surveyed in this chapter so far I now attempt to draw some broad and summary conclusions, and add a few supplementary points.

(1) Marcus acknowledges, in the Fronto correspondence (esp. i. 50; cf. 246 *ad fin.*) and in the *Meditations*, his belief in divine communication and aid to human beings through dreams, oracles, and other means. He believes that he himself has experienced such aid, in particular through dreams, that the gods have helped him in the specific case of his health, and more broadly that it is their εὐποιία (i. 17. 1) that has protected him in certain moral crises.

(2) Although he says and implies that the gods sometimes appear to men, he does not describe any such experience or identify the protection or patronage of any individual god in his own case. The reference in v. 8 to the cures prescribed by

---

Antiquity (London 1982) 103–52, and several of the other papers reprinted in that volume. See also id., *The Making of Late Antiquity* (Cambridge, Mass. 1978) esp. 24–5; G. Fowden, *JHS* 102 (1982) 33–59. Anderson, *Philostratus* 146–8 draws parallels between the holy men and the 2nd-cent. sophists, but somewhat overstates the resemblances.

[114] See K. Thomas, *Religion and the Decline of Magic* (London 1971) 69 ff. on the crucial distinction between prayer and spell.

Asclepius could be purely general (as v. 8. 1 τὸ λεγόμενον in fact suggests).[115] Otherwise in the *Meditations* he refers once to Clotho (iv. 34), once to the Muses (xi. 18), and several times to Zeus (iv. 23, v. 7 (a quotation), 8, 27, xi. 8). Far more common are the vaguer θεός or θεοί,[116] or references to the cosmos, its motions, and its processes (in iv. 23 κόσμος and φύσις are invoked as if gods). Nor is there any trace of his having had recourse to astrology, theurgy, or the like. We do not even find references to his initiation in mysteries such as those of Eleusis, about which we have external testimony (see n. 43 above).

(3) In contexts that suggest more of Marcus' religious attitudes we often find obscurities and ambiguities. The author is frequently elliptical, his language memorable but imprecise or allusive. The parallel with his reserve about sexual experiences (i. 17. 2 and 7) is striking; it seems plausible that the emperor was uneasy about expressing himself with complete frankness, and in the sphere of religious experience he may have found it hard to know exactly what he had to recount. It seems unlikely that his guarded references mask anything like the relationship of Aristides with Asclepius or Lucius-Apuleius with Isis. We are dealing rather with a spirituality without a clear personal object. Stoicism preserved the names of the traditional gods, but only through the purifying medium of allegory.[117] Hence Marcus' relatively impersonal, inscrutable gods are in accord with orthodox Stoicism; what is alien to the Stoa is the melancholy reflectiveness with which he contemplates the working-out of Nature's laws.

(4) The *Meditations* are Stoic in their ethics and cosmology, but hints of other teachings and other, perhaps richer, religious language permeate the religious thought of the work. It is difficult to isolate any single passage which a doctrinaire Stoic could not or should not have written, but certain aspects set Marcus apart from the main trend of the school. Among these we may note two in particular: his negative attitude to the material, physical world, and his recurrent reflections on change, transience, and death. In both areas Marcus' indivi-

[115] For the fame and popularity of the cult in general, see Beaujeu (n. 43) 60 ff.; E. and L. Edelstein, *Asclepius* (Baltimore 1945); Behr (n. 50) ch. 2; Hall, *Lucian's Satire* 507; Lane Fox, *Pagans and Christians* 151–3, etc.
[116] See Brunt, *JRS* 64 (1974) 15.
[117] See e.g. Diog. Laert. vii. 147; P. de Lacy, *AJP* 69 (1948) esp. 256–71.

duality may be demonstrated by sustained comparisons between his work and the teachings of Epictetus, his literary and ethical mentor, as the next chapter is intended to show.

I confine to the inferior status of an appendix some material from other sources which has often been cited in discussions of Marcus' religious beliefs, but which in my view has little evidential value or significance. In the narratives of Marcus' campaigns in Dio Cassius' *Roman History* (epitomised with additions by Xiphilinus)[118] and in the *Historia Augusta* we find recounted two 'miracles' involving rain and lightning (combined in most accounts), which are also commemorated on the Column of Marcus Aurelius and on coins of AD 172-3.[119] In 172 a bolt of lightning is said to have answered Marcus' prayers and destroyed an enemy war-engine (SHA *Marcus* 24. 4; *BMC* IV, ΜΛ, 566-7). In 173 a more spectacular rain storm relieved the thirst of the Roman army and in the end brought a halt to some desperate fighting (Dio: see below). The events, originally separate (they are depicted in different scenes on the Column[120]), were easily conflated at an early date. The sources[121] differ as to whether Marcus was present or not on the second occasion; moreover, the agency, human or divine, which brought about the storm was a matter of dispute. Even the dating of the events in the course of Marcus' German campaigns is hard to determine; but it is usually held that the Column illustrates events from the wars of AD 172-5 only.[122]

The epitome of Dio is probably the most reliable account, but is marred by the Christianising 'corrections' of Xiphilinus. According to Dio (72. 14) Marcus won an unexpected victory against the Quadi, 'or rather it was vouchsafed to him by heaven'. The Romans were hemmed in and deprived of water, which seemed to spell victory for their enemies;

---

[118] See Millar, *A Study of Cassius Dio* 1-4.

[119] For a detailed presentation and discussion of the Column see C. Caprini, A. M. Colini, M. Pallotino, and P. Romanelli, *La colonna di Marco Aurelio* (Rome 1955); select illustrations also in Birley, *Marcus Aurelius* (revised edn.) plates 24-38. For the coinage of Marcus' reign see H. Mattingly, *Coins of the Roman Empire in the British Museum* iv (London 1940).

[120] See Caprini *et al.* (n. 119) figs. 18 (lightning) and 23-4 (rain); Birley, plates 25 (lightning) and 26 (rain).

[121] For full literary sources and discussion see J. Lightfoot, *The Apostolic Fathers II*, *Ignatius* i (London 1885) 469 ff.; Mayor on Tert. *Ap.* 5. 6; A. B. Cook, *Zeus* iii (Cambridge 1940) 324 ff.; J. Guey, *RPh* 22 (1948) 16-62. See also Beaujeu (n. 43) 342 ff.; Birley 171-4; Liebeschuetz, *Continuity and Change in Roman Religion* 210-13. For Christians in the Roman army see J. Helgeland, *ANRW* ii. 23. 1 (1979) 725 ff. (766-73 on this episode).

[122] But see J. Morris, *Journ. of Courtauld and Warburg Inst.* 15 (1952) 32 ff. (reprinted in German in Klein (ed.), *Marc Aurel*).

suddenly many clouds gathered and a mighty rain, not without divine interposition, burst upon them. Indeed there is a story (λόγος ἔχει) that Arnouphis, an Egyptian *magus*, who was a companion of Marcus, had invoked by enchantments various *daimones*, among them Hermes lord of the air, and by this means attracted the rain . . .

At this point Xiphilinus steps in to correct Dio: it was not Arnouphis, he claims, 'for Marcus, it is recorded, never took any pleasure in acquaintance with magicians or in sorcery (γοητείαις)'; rather, a legion of Christian soldiers offered their services and at Marcus' request prayed for aid;

and their God immediately gave ear and smote the enemy with a thunderbolt and comforted the Romans with a shower of rain. Marcus was greatly astonished by this and not only honoured the Christians by an official decree but also named the legion κεραυνοβόλον ['Thundering']. It is also reported that there is a letter of Marcus' extant about these matters. But the Greeks, although they know that the division was named the Thundering legion and themselves bear witness to this fact, make no statement whatever about the reason for its name.

By contrast, the account in the *Historia Augusta* is unusually moderate, though no doubt resting on slender foundations: 'fulmen de caelo precibus suis contra hostium machinamentum extorsit suis pluvia impetrata, cum siti laborarent' (24. 4). This appears to refer to the lightning miracle, not mentioned by Dio; but the detail about the soldiers' desperate thirst should belong rather to the rain miracle.

The following discrepancies or errors in these accounts, in addition to the points already mentioned, should arouse misgivings. (1) On the Aurelian Column it is generally accepted that the emperor himself is not present on the occasion of the rain miracle; the general involved may be Pertinax.[123] Dio does not assert that Marcus was present (συνόντα τῷ Μάρκῳ, said of Arnouphis, need not imply this); Xiphilinus has him asking the Christians to pray, witnessing their success, and honouring them; the *Historia Augusta*, apparently combining the two incidents, might be taken as attributing the prayers (or spells) to Marcus himself. (2) Xiphilinus is mistaken about the name of the legion he cites, the XII Legio Fulminata, which had possessed this title for over a century.[124] (3) Both Dio and Xiphilinus rely to some degree on hearsay and doubtful evidence (λόγος ἔχει . . . λέγεται), though the existence of Arnouphis is adequately confirmed by an inscription.[125] (4) The episode of the rain miracle was clearly

---

[123] See Birley 173; Caprini in Caprini *et al.* (n. 119) 89, citing Eusebius. ('Forse Pertinace' is a common phrase in his survey of the Column: pp. 91, 92, 105, 108, 115.)
[124] See Birley 173, with n. 27, citing e.g. Dio 55. 23; *CIL* iii. 30.
[125] See *L'Année Épigraphique* 1934, 245.

sensational; another who claimed responsibility for the Roman success was Julianus the theurgist, composer of the so-called Chaldaean oracles (*Suda* s.v. *Ιουλιανός*).[126] The Christians already laid claim to the achievement in Marcus' lifetime, as we see from a fragment of an *Apology* addressed to him by the bishop Apollinaris (*ap*. Euseb. *Hist. Eccl*. v. 5. 4; later, Tert. *Ap*. 5; *ad Scap*. 4). A letter from Marcus reporting the Christians' success to the senate is referred to by Tertullian and survives in the manuscripts of Justin's *Apology*, but it is certainly, like others of its kind, a Christian forgery.[127] Xiphilinus' account is in the same tradition. (5) The presentation on the Column of a very Roman god, probably Jupiter, sending the rain,[128] must show the official version, whatever truth lies behind the story of Arnouphis. Coinage attributed the victory to Mercury or to Jupiter himself. If, then, a foreign deity was involved at all, he was rapidly naturalised: perhaps Hermes Trismegistus or Thoth became the Roman Mercury of the coins.[129] At all events, there seems no place for the Christians here, though of course there may have been some serving in the army.

In view of the epigraphic evidence for his presence at Marcus' headquarters a year or so before, the case for Arnouphis' involvement is strong; but as we have seen, there is no good reason to suppose that Marcus himself was present at the rain miracle, or that either of these events bear significantly upon his religious outlook. Their prominence in our sources owe much to status-seeking by others, perhaps little to his own initiative. Supernatural aid in a military crisis is a common mythical-historical motif (as at Marathon or the Milvian Bridge).[130] The evidence reviewed here does not warrant any conclusions about Marcus' interest in Egyptian or other foreign cults, nor need we deplore a lapse into primitive superstition.[131]

Still more tenuous is the anecdote preserved only in Lucian, *Alexander* 48, again referring to the period of wars against the

[126] On this man see further Dodds, *The Greeks and the Irrational* 283–5; MacMullen, *Enemies of the Roman Order* 104, 107; H. Lewy, *Chaldean Oracles and Theurgy* (Cairo 1956) 3 ff., who quotes the evidence.

[127] See Lightfoot (n. 121) for other such instances; also T. D. Barnes, *JTS* 19 (1968) 209–31, an attempt to distinguish genuine and elaborated documents among the martyr-acts.

[128] *Pace* Birley 173.

[129] So Brunt, *JRS* 64 (1974) 17 n. 108.

[130] See further Cic. *ND* iii. 11 ff.; W. K. Pritchett, *The Greek State at War* iii (Berkeley and Los Angeles 1979) ch. 2; F. Pfister, *RE* Suppl. iv. 293 ff.; Brenk, *In Mist Apparelled* 105 n. 20.

[131] See also SHA *Marcus* 13. 1 f. on ceremonies of *lustratio* (Beaujeu (n. 43) 340–1). This too wins harsh words from condescending moderns, e.g. W. Warde Fowler, *The Religious Experience of the Roman People* (London 1911) 429; F. M. Altheim, *History of Roman Religion* (Eng. tr. London 1938) 453.

Marcomanni and the Quadi.[132] (This passage refers to Marcus as deified, θεός; it may therefore be assumed that the work is later than 180.) According to Lucian, the oracle of the prophet Alexander urged the emperor (as Lucian tells the story, without first being consulted) to cast two live lions into the Ister (the lower Danube) along with many prayers and rich sacrifices. Since this rite was followed by a crashing defeat for the Romans, the oracle had to excuse its failure with a plea of ambiguity in the tradition of Delphi and Croesus: 'for the god, Alexander claimed, foretold victory, but did not make clear whether it was the victory of the Romans or their opponents'. Some have identified the unfortunate lions in another scene on the Aurelian column, but the counter-arguments are strong.[133] Not the least of these is the question whether the Romans would have preserved the memory of such a ceremony, however bizarrely picturesque, when it had preceded a defeat. The episode, with its Herodotean model and its obvious aptness for Lucian's satirical exposé, may be pure fiction (geography also raises some doubts: does a Roman emperor naturally consult a new oracle in Asia about pressing campaigns in Germany?). At all events, it tells us nothing reliable about Marcus' attitudes. Even if it is true that he was prepared to resort to such desperate and spectacular measures, it may have been under pressure from his legions rather than from any personal belief in Alexander's remedy.[134]

---

[132] On Alexander and Glycon see Jones, *Culture and Society in Lucian* ch. 12; Lane Fox, *Pagans and Christians* 241–50, a splendid rehabilitation. Both authors draw on the landmark study by L. Robert, *À travers l'Asie Mineure* (Paris 1980) 393–421. This new approach undoubtedly makes Alexander's oracle look less of a freak and a fraud than Lucian would have us believe, but I continue to feel very sceptical about this particular episode.

[133] The scene in question is fig. 13; counter-arguments, Caprini in Caprini *et al*. (n. 119) 87.

[134] Thus, for instance, the account of this episode by F. H. Hayward, *Marcus Aurelius: A Saviour of Men* (London 1935) seems to me over-credulous. K. Hopkins, *Conquerors and Slaves* (Cambridge 1978) 233, in the course of a demonstration of the wide prevalence of superstitious beliefs at Rome, also places excessive trust in Lucian ('. . . induced even the emperor Marcus Aurelius . . .'); similarly J. Ferguson, *The Religions of the Roman Empire* (London 1970) 189 ('most astonishing of all, Marcus Aurelius listened to one of his oracles . . .'); Beaujeu (n. 43) 347–9; Jones (n. 132) 144.

VI

Life and Death in the Religion of Epictetus and Marcus Aurelius

Man that is born of woman hath but a short time to live, and is full of misery.

(Book of Common Prayer, *Burial of the Dead*, First Anthem)

You are a philosopher, Dr Johnson. I have tried too in my time to be a philosopher; but, I don't know how, cheerfulness was always breaking in.

(Oliver Edwards (d. 1791), in Boswell, *Life of Johnson*, 17 April 1778)

1. *Two Stoics Compared*

The freed slave Epictetus is widely regarded as the thinker closest to and most influential upon the emperor Marcus Aurelius. They can never have met,[1] but in the first book of the *Meditations* Marcus expresses his gratitude to Rusticus for acquainting him with the ὑπομνήματα (discourses) of Epictetus, 'of which he lent me his own copy' (i. 7). He quotes him often, and still more frequently echoes his language, his patterns of thought, and the types of imagery he favours. It is evident that he knew the *diatribai* of Epictetus very well indeed, and he probably took over some of his older quotations from the earlier Stoic. Both authors, for instance, quote the saying of Antisthenes, βασιλικὸν μὲν εὖ πράττειν, κακῶς δὲ ἀκούειν ('A king's part is to act well and be spoken ill of in return': Epict. iv. 6. 20 and M. Aur. vii. 36), and Marcus' version is closer to Epictetus' citation than to another version of the dictum which we find in Plutarch (*Alex.* 41. 2).

---

[1] This is plain even if Epictetus did survive until the reign of Hadrian, as SHA *Hadr.* 16. 10 implausibly suggests: cf. *PIR*[2] E 74. Marcus would surely have mentioned such an encounter in Book I.

In general, it seems most likely that he read Epictetus in the collection which has come down to us, compiled by Arrian by the time (probably) of Hadrian's reign and known, for instance, to the sophist Favorinus (Gell. xvii. 19, xix. 1. 14 ff.).[2] We are told that Arrian composed eight books (T vi Schenkl), of which only four have survived;[3] and Marcus occasionally quotes sayings of Epictetus which are not preserved elsewhere (e.g. iv. 41 = Epict. fr. 26 Schenkl, ψυχάριον εἶ βαστάζον νεκρόν, ὡς Ἐπίκτητος ἔλεγεν: 'you are a poor soul carrying a corpse, as Epictetus put it'; see also xi. 36–8). It therefore seems probable that Marcus at least consulted the whole of Epictetus' œuvre.

It is unnecessary to spend further labour in assembling obvious parallels between Epictetus and Marcus in their language and thought. Much material bearing on this will be found in the earlier chapters of this study.[4] My present object is to focus on a central topic in both authors, their religious outlook—that is, their conception of man in the divinely governed universe. It could reasonably be said that this is the most important of all subjects for both these authors. Logically, their further doctrines of the needs, powers, and duties of the individual man all depend on the conception of man as the offspring and servant of God, pursuing the ideal of self-improvement by submission of his will to God, by so disciplining his mind as to approximate, so far as possible, to a divine state of serenity and purity (ὁμοίωσις θεῷ).[5] With this self-discipline and reverence for the soul as the most important part of oneself goes a proper evaluation of the external things conventionally regarded as good and evil but in reality, according to the Stoics, 'indifferent'. This category included not only wealth, health, power, and status but their opposites. Poverty, oppression, the

---

[2] The exact date of Arrian's attendance at Epictetus' lectures and compilation of his record (probably not at the same time) is uncertain. On the chronology of Arrian see A. B. Bosworth, CQ 22 (1972) 164 ff.; id., From Arrian to Alexander (Oxford 1988) 16 n. 1, with earlier bibliog. It seems plausible that he heard Epictetus in the first decade of the second century (Bosworth, art. cit. 184 n. 1; Millar, JRS 55 (1965) 142). The compilation was known to Herodes Atticus (T viii Schenkl = Gell. i. 2) and probably to Lucian (T xiii–xvi). See further Schenkl's ed. maior of Epictetus, praefatio; RLAC v. 616 ff.

[3] Arrian was also responsible for compiling the Encheiridion; see Simplicius' preface to the Ench. (= T iii Schenkl), in which he cites a letter of Arrian. There seem to have been still further works by Arrian on Epictetus, if we believe Photius and others who speak of twelve books of Ὁμιλίαι (T vi). See Schenkl, praef. xi–xii.

[4] See further RLAC v. 619; Breithaupt 45–64.

[5] On this conception see above, ch. v n. 5.

disapproval of others, even death, were all numbered among the indifferents.[6]

All this is standard doctrine in Marcus as well as in Epictetus; but I shall argue that there are signs, even in small details of language, that his attitude to it is significantly more sceptical and pessimistic; that he diverges from his creed in ways that reveal his own ambiguity of attitude and also expose Stoicism's weaknesses. In some respects this is an argument from silence: points which Epictetus stresses strongly do not always appear in Marcus, from which we may infer that they did not impress him so much. Other themes and arguments do appear, but are given a more depressing or pessimistic twist. Finally, there are some basic differences in their approach to these questions, for all their similarity on doctrine: among these differences I would number the greater emphasis on the closeness of man and God in Epictetus, conveyed especially in his passages of or about prayer, where he is warm and devout (Epict. i. 16. 15 ff.; iii. 26. 28 ff.; iv. 1. 108 f.). For Marcus deity seems much more remote and impersonal, shrouded in mystery. Another important difference, on which I have touched elsewhere, is the strongly ascetic strain in Marcus,[7] which has very great influence upon his religious attitudes: he will extend the Stoic belittling of the body's needs and sensual pleasures to condemnation and hatred of bodily experience, and an insistence that only the soul's life is valuable or indeed truly *real*.[8] In general this asceticism is accompanied in the *Meditations* by a strange other-worldliness; both seem scarcely Stoic. The former tendency is in fact castigated in general terms by Epictetus in an interesting essay (iv. 11) which strikingly portrays extreme self-punishment, of a kind that seems to foreshadow the Desert Fathers (note especially § 16 εἰς ἐρημίαν).[9] It is true that Epictetus is attacking more the neglect of cleanliness and appearance in the name of holiness; but contempt for the body itself, as an unworthy and

[6] Diog. Laert. vii. 102–7; *SVF* iii. 117–23, iv. p. 5; see I. G. Kidd, in Long (ed.), *Problems in Stoicism* 150 ff.

[7] See further pp. 241–3; also the general discussion in ch. III 5 above. Marcus seems to have cultivated ascetic habits in his youth (i. 5–6), as Seneca dabbled in Pythagoreanism and vegetarianism (*Ep.* 108. 17 f.; see Griffin, *Seneca* 38–41).

[8] This has been finely discussed by Dodds, *Pagan and Christian* 8–12, 27 ff.

[9] See Dodds, *Pagan and Christian* 29 f.; J. Leipoldt, 'Griech. Philosophie und frühchristliche Askese', *Verh. Sachs. Akad.*, Phil.-hist. Kl. 106, iv. (1961); Meredith, *JTS* 27 (1976) 313–32. Note also *RLAC* i. 749 ff.; van der Horst on ps.-Phocyl. 76.

unclean receptacle for the soul, is nevertheless a feature of the *Meditations* not apparent in the earlier thinker.

Further, much of the material from Marcus collected in the last chapter shows his attitudes to be of a less orthodox, more speculative and unusual kind than the undeveloped Stoic religiosity which we find in Epictetus. The latter has nothing, for instance, of that recurrent theme in Marcus, the 'view from above', the *contemptus mundi*, which has its origin in philosophies and creeds, above all Platonism, which put less stress than the Stoics on the importance of one's behaviour and choices in this life. Even the most distinguished Latin example of this topos, Cicero's *Somnium Scipionis*, which naturally does place much importance upon Scipio's distinguished career, is still tinged with a remoteness from everyday life and politics quite uncharacteristic of its author. Conversely, we may observe that the perennial Stoic argument from the beauty and order of the natural world to the existence of a providential divine plan and artificer, which does appear in Epictetus (ii. 14. 25–6), is absent from Marcus.[10]

We should make every allowance for differences in circumstance and genre in distinguishing Epictetus' ideas from Marcus'. The implications of these differences are far-reaching. Epictetus is a sermoniser, haranguing a potentially unreceptive audience. He is concerned to move and excite that audience; his works are exhortations to philosophy as much as an exposition thereof. It is natural that he should dwell on its potential, its power and attractions. This is not to say that he does not emphasise the difficulty of the road (see e.g. iii. 21 and 22), but he has his eyes upon an ideal potentially attainable or approachable by others even if not by himself. Diogenes and Socrates are for him *exempla* to inspire his hearers, not to humble himself.

Contrast with this the role, and the mode of composition, of Marcus Aurelius. Writing for himself alone, he cannot take refuge in topics or discussions which are not ultimately relevant to his own case. He can discern the weak points or the deceptive arguments in his own exposition. His own status and the calls upon his time, of which he sometimes complains and of which he must always have been conscious, forbid his prolonging his

[10] On the theme in general see A. S. Pease, *HTR* 34 (1941) 163 ff.

studies in order to grapple seriously with the problems that perplex him. Above all, there is the difference in philosophic authority between the two Stoics: Epictetus' professionalism, combining eloquence and wisdom,[11] should be contrasted with Marcus' unconfident, tentative approach, characteristic of a man now without teachers, feeling his way towards an always unsatisfactory resolution of disorganised and even contradictory views. Furthermore, whereas Epictetus can sublimate his philosophic principles in the heroic vision of the sage defying the tyrant[12]—the supreme translation of those principles into action—that refuge is denied to Marcus by virtue of his unique position. He himself, in potential, *is* the tyrant. Greek authors stressed the unaccountability of the ruler as his greatest source of power and the greatest danger to himself and his people.[13] Yet in a sense the *Meditations* show us Marcus' accounts, his self-examination and also his self-defence before the higher authority of conscience and of his δαίμων.[14] In a word, Epictetus is a freed slave and therefore intensely conscious of the meaning and limits of human freedom (cf. esp. iv. 1);[15] Marcus, supreme and independent, possessor of the power which in popular thought bestowed the greatest freedom and the greatest happiness, is none the less bound both by his strong sense of duty and by his consciousness of his own limitations.

In Epictetus iii. 13. 9 ff. we read:

Behold now, Caesar seems to provide us with profound peace, there are no wars any longer, no battles, no violent brigandage, no piracy, but at any hour we can travel by land, or sail from the rising of the sun to the setting. Can he, then, provide us in any way with peace from fever,

[11] A traditional ideal: cf. e.g. Cic. *Inv.* i. 1; *de Or.* iii. 142–3; Fronto ii. 50, perhaps 68 (Pericles); August. *de Doctrina Christiana* iv. 7. Cf. Hubbell, op. cit. (ch III n. 43).
[12] See C. G. Starr, 'Epictetus and the Tyrant', *CPh* 44 (1949) 20–9; MacMullen, *Enemies of the Roman Order* 70–94, 310, etc.; and my ch. II. 3 above, with examples in n. 58.
[13] See e.g. Hdt. iii. 80. 3; Aesch. *PV* 324; Ar. *Vesp.* 587; Eur. *Supp.* 430 ff., with Collard's notes.
[14] On conscience see esp. H. Chadwick, *RLAC* x. 1025–1107 (1047–52, 1058–60 on Stoics, including Marcus). See also J. de Decker, *Juvenalis Declamans* (Gand 1913) 62–3; *TDNT* vii. 898 ff., s.v. σύνοιδα; R. Parker, *Miasma* (Oxford 1983) 252 ff.; A. Dihle, *The Theory of Will in Classical Antiquity* (Berkeley and Los Angeles 1982) 129, 209 n. 149, 236 n. 46.
[15] See Brunt, *JRS* 64 (1974) 7 n. 36.; Pohlenz, *Die Stoa* i. 330, ii. 162; id., *Freedom in Greek Life and Thought* (Dordrecht 1966) ch. 4, esp. 151–9. For a cooler view see G. E. M. de Ste Croix, *The Class Struggle in the Ancient Greek World* (London 1981) 142, 423.

from shipwreck, from fire, from earthquake, from lightning? Can he give us peace from love? He cannot. From grief? From envy? He cannot, not from a single one of these things. But the doctrine (λόγος) of the philosophers promises to give peace from these troubles also. What says it? 'Mankind, if you heed me, wherever you may be, whatever you may be doing, you will feel no pain, no anger, no compulsion, no hindrance, but you will pass your lives in tranquillity, and be free from every disturbance.' When a man has had this kind of peace decreed to him—not by Caesar, for how could *he* possibly decree it?—but by God, through the λόγος, is he not satisfied?

This brilliant passage not only exemplifies perfectly the inner-ness of first-century Stoic morality, but also points the way to a fuller understanding of the attraction which philosophy must have had for Marcus. The one thing a monarch cannot command is his own peace of mind; yet, strikingly, that is exactly what Stoicism defines as the *only* thing in any man's power. That theme is prominent in Epictetus above all Stoics. We should note also the religious element, introduced casually here in a way which shows how readily Epictetus slides from philosophy to religion and vice versa. 'By God, through reason', ὑπὸ τοῦ θεοῦ . . . διὰ τοῦ λόγου, emphasises that reason, like philosophy itself, can be regarded as God's gift (e.g. Sen. *Ep.* 90. 1), and that in Stoicism the place of man is intimately related to religious presuppositions. At the same time, however, Epictetus' attention is not primarily directed to the divine, although it is basic to his whole doctrine. Speculation about God, his nature and his powers, is not common in Epictetus, and this is a significant difference from Marcus.

This much in broad summary of the importance of religion in the philosophy of Epictetus and Marcus, and as illustration of the distinctions which may need to be drawn. I turn now to detail, and propose to discuss two main topics which offer an opportunity to compare and contrast the two authors: first, the imagery employed to describe the place of man in the cosmos, his role in the divine creation—images such as θεατής, ἀθλητής, ὑποκριτής (the spectator, the contender, the actor); and second, death and dissolution, the mortality of man and his return to the elements from which he came. The different uses of the metaphors for life and human activity indicate different atti-tudes in the authors; the theme of death and mortality is conspicuously more prominent and more depressingly put in Marcus than in Epictetus.

2. Metaphors for the Life of Man

A number of metaphors commonly applied to the life of man by Epictetus are rare or non-existent in Marcus. Two of these are often found together, that of the θεατής, the spectator at a splendid festival or procession (πανήγυρις, πομπή, etc.), and that of the ἀθλητής, the champion performing and triumphing in the demanding game of life, suffering trials (ἆθλα) which he willingly endures in the service of God. These two images neatly represent the complementary ideals of contemplation and action, a pair which can be traced far back in Greek thought,[16] and which might indeed both be seen in the figure of Odysseus, especially as interpreted by Stoics and other moralists.[17]

A revealing example of the spectator image[18] occurs at Epict. iv. 1. 103–10, where the philosopher reproaches another man who complains at having to leave the festivities:

Did not God also bring you to it? Did he not show you the sun? Did he not give you fellow workers, senses, reason? As what kind of being did he bring you here? Was it not as a mortal? Was it not as one who was to live on earth with a little portion of flesh and gaze upon his dispositions, and share in the ceremonies with him and join in the celebrations, for a little time? Are you not willing to admire the proceedings while you are allowed to, and then, when he leads you off, to depart paying obeisance and offering thanks[19] for what you have heard and seen? . . . 'Why then did he bring me here?' Well, if it doesn't suit you, depart. He has no need of a fault-finding spectator. What he

[16] For the earlier history of these motifs see (on πομπή and similar terms) Kindstrand on Bion fr. 68 (p. 282), and (for life as an athletic contest) Billerbeck on Epict. iii. 22. 56. See also V. Pöschl, *Bibliographie der antiken Bildersprache* (Heidelberg 1964) s.v. 'Athlet', p. 452. For the contrast between the active and contemplative lives see esp. Griffin, *Seneca* 339–43; ch. II n. 81 above; Winterbottom on ps.-Quint. *Decl. Min.* 268.

[17] See F. Boll, *Kleine Schriften* (Leipzig 1950) 307. On *Odysseus philosophicus* see also R. B. Rutherford, *JHS* 106 (1986) 145–62.

[18] For the image see Bion fr. 68 with Kindstrand's note; Lucr. iii. 938 ff.; Hor. *Ep.* ii. 2. 213–16, with Brink's note and appendix 20 (contrast my comments in *CQ* 31 (1981) 379–80).

[19] Cf. J. H. Quincey, *JHS* 86 (1966) 133–58; H. S. Versnel, in id. (ed.), *Faith, Hope and Worship* (Leiden 1981) 42–55, on εὐχαριστεῖν and related terms. For singing of thanks to God in Stoicism see Cleanthes, *SVF* i. 537, 36 ff. (the hymn to Zeus).

needs are those who join in the feast, . . . join in the dance, so that they may applaud, admire, sing the praises of the festival.

Similarly, i. 6. 19: 'he brought man into the world as a spectator, to behold him and his deeds, and not only as a spectator, but as an interpreter of them . . .'.

We can see immediately how much stress Epictetus lays upon the pleasure and satisfaction of this communal life, conveyed through the metaphors of dancing and festivity. Marcus' imagery usually conveys a more isolated picture. The uplifting quality of Epictetus' words is reinforced by the vivid way in which God is brought into the picture, as the immediate and obvious source of all man's blessings, and a very personalised source.[20] Man should be giving thanks and offering hymns of joy and praise throughout his earthly life. He should depart from life too in the same spirit of thanksgiving. The word Epictetus uses is εὐχαριστήσας (cf. M. Aur. ii. 3 only; much rarer than in Epictetus). There are resemblances between this comparison and another which Marcus does use, that of man's life as a part to play upon the world-stage (e.g. Epict. *Ench.* 17; M. Aur. xii. 36);[21] but in Marcus' usage the image is less joyous, more impersonal, as in xii. 36:

Mortal man, you have been a citizen in this great city . . . Why is it hard, then, if Nature who brought you in sends you out of the city?— she who is no tyrant or unjust judge. It is as though the master of the show, having engaged an actor, were to dismiss him from the stage. 'But I have not spoken my five acts, only three.' What you say is true, but in life three acts are the whole play. For he determines the perfect whole, the cause yesterday of your composition, today of your dissolution; you are the cause of neither.[22]

Consider next the frequency with which Epictetus employs the comparison of man on earth with an athlete competing in the Olympic games: for instance, *Ench.* 51. 2: '. . . and if you meet anything that is laborious, or sweet, or held in high repute or no repute, remember that *now* is the contest, and here before you are the Olympic games, and that it is impossible to delay

---

[20] Cf. M. Spanneut, *RLAC* v. 616.

[21] On this range of imagery see above, ch. iv n. 13.

[22] Note the detached use of ἡ φύσις instead of a deity; and the more clinical vocabulary characteristic of Marcus (συγκρίσεως . . . διαλύσεως: both these abstract nouns are frequent in Marcus, whereas Epictetus has only their cognate verbs).

longer; that it depends on a single day and a single action whether you are to lose or save your progress.' Similar is ii. 18. 27: 'The man who exercises himself against such external impressions is the true athlete in training. Hold hard, unhappy man: do not be swept along. Great is the struggle (ὁ ἀγών), divine the task; the prize is a kingdom, freedom, serenity, peace.' Or again, iii. 22. 50 ff., where moral strength is compared with the athlete's shoulders, sinews, etc. Here we recognise the Cynic-Stoic idea of endurance (*labor*, πόνος), often associated with the mythical models of Heracles and Odysseus. A classic instance is Juvenal's strident finale to *Satire* 10: 'fortem posce animum, mortis terrore carentem ... qui ferre queat quoscumque labores/ ... et potiores/Herculis aerumnas credat saevosque labores/et Venere et cenis et pluma Sardanapalli' (10. 357 ff.). More broadly, Stoics often regard hardships as a test for mankind. Seneca goes so far as to use this as an explanation for the existence of evil and misfortune in the world (especially in his *de Providentia* and *de Constantia Sapientis*),[23] an idea also found in Epictetus, e.g. i. 24, which begins: 'It is hardships that show what men are. Consequently, when a difficulty befalls you, remember that God, like a physical trainer, has matched you against a rugged young man. What for?, someone asks. So that you can become an Olympic victor; but that cannot be done without sweat.'[24]

In Marcus this lame and inhumane account of human suffering is not used. While there is a very strong sense that life is a constant struggle, there is also much less confidence that anything can be made of it in the long run, that anyone can actually be the 'victor'. The existence of evil and of wicked men, instead of being explained by this rather sophistical rationale, is treated more as an inevitable by-product of universal processes which we cannot control (e.g. iv. 6).[25] The comparison with the

---

[23] See E. Norden, *Kleine Schriften* (Berlin 1966) 33–40, who also deals with Christian developments of the theme (e.g. 1 Cor. 9: 24–7). (One possible instance in the *Meditations* may require qualification of the argument in the text: x. 31 τί γάρ ἔστι πάντα ταῦτα ἄλλο πλὴν γυμνάσματα λόγου ἑωρακότος ἀκριβῶς καὶ φυσιολόγως τὰ ἐν τῷ βίῳ;—but here there is no reference to the gods imposing such a test; it is a description from the human side. This is how one ought to face such challenges.)

[24] See further Epict. i. 29. 33 ff., iii. 22. 57 (where Heracles is mentioned, as in Juvenal).

[25] For attempted explanations of the existence of evil see also Cleanthes *SVF* i. 537. 15 ff.; Cic. *ND* ii. 167, iii. 65–93; A. D. Nock's comm. on Sallustius, *Concerning the Gods and*

athlete occurs only once in the *Meditations*, in an unusually high-flown passage in which Marcus imagines a man of complete purity and simplicity:

... ἱερεύς τίς ἐστι καὶ ὑπουργὸς θεῶν, χρώμενος καὶ τῷ ἔνδον ἱδρυμένῳ αὑτοῦ, ὃ παρέχεται τὸν ἄνθρωπον ἄχραντον ἡδονῶν, ἄτρωτον ὑπὸ παντὸς πόνου, πάσης ὕβρεως ἀνέπαφον, πάσης ἀναίσθητον πονηρίας, ἀθλητὴν ἄθλου τοῦ μεγίστου, τοῦ ὑπὸ μηδενὸς πάθους καταβληθῆναι ...

... [such a man] is surely a priest and minister of the gods, employing that which is seated within him, which makes it possible for the man to be unstained by pleasures, unscathed by any pain, untouched by any wrongdoing, unconscious of any wickedness, a wrestler in the greatest contest of all, not to be overthrown by any passion ... (iii. 4. 3)

But this description is not of himself or of any individual, but of an ideal; nor is the image ever attached by Marcus even to mythological heroes or great men of the past such as Cato.

Marcus' conviction that he is not one who deserves the title of philosopher, but only a *proficiens*, makes him very reluctant to see himself as an example or instructor to mankind, on behalf of God or philosophy—another concept prominent in Epictetus, for instance in his account of the ideal 'Cynic' (iii. 22).[26] There Epictetus speaks of the Cynic as the common educator of men, their *paedagogus* (§ 17); he will be the overseer of all mankind (§ 18);

he must know that he has been sent by Zeus to men, partly as a messenger (ἄγγελος),[27] in order to show them that in questions of good and evil they have gone astray ... he must accordingly be able to lift up his voice, and, mounting the tragic stage, to speak like Socrates: 'Alas, mankind, where are you rushing? What are you doing, poor wretches? Like blind men you go tottering around ...' (iii. 22. 23 and 26).

the Universe (Cambridge 1926) lxxviii f.; E. Schröder, *Plotins Abhandlung πόθεν τὰ κακά, Enn. i. 8* (diss. Borna–Leipzig 1916) part i, esp. 38–47 on Stoics; Arnold, *Roman Stoicism* 206–10; A. A. Long and D. N. Sedley, *The Hellenistic Philosophers* i (Cambridge 1987) 311, 328–33, 386. Some of the explanations are in fact contradictory; within the *Meditations*, the last sentence of xii. 5 might be thought to rule out some arguments that Marcus seems to accept elsewhere: contrast iv. 6, v. 17, ix. 42.

[26] On which see the detailed comm. by M. Billerbeck. Some of the images discussed in this section are further illustrated by J. L. Moles, *JHS* 103 (1983) 112 n. 73, in a discussion of Cynicism as a 'missionary philosophy'. I doubt if he is justified in seeing all of these as specifically Cynic vocabulary, but the point is not of great importance for the period of Marcus Aurelius (and Marcus was familiar with Cynicism; see i. 6).

[27] ἄγγελος: *TDNT* i. 74 ff., with special reference to the function of divine messengers to men. Cf. Hermes, Iris, holy men (see above, ch. v nn. 105, 113), and of course Judaeo-Christian angels.

Similarly in Epict. iii. 24. 111 ff. the ideal philosopher is to see
that he is a witness, a μάρτυς²⁸ on behalf of Zeus. Compare
further iii. 26. 27: 'Does God so neglect his own creations, his
servants, his witnesses, whom alone he uses as examples to the
uninstructed, to prove that he both exists and governs the
universe well . . .'; also iv. 8. 30–1.

Marcus, despite his position of supremacy, does not see
himself in his private writings as an instructor or preacher to his
people, still less as communicating the will of God to man. (We
may contrast the dubious report in Aurelius Victor, who
portrays him as lecturing amid a crowd of philosophic enthu-
siasts before departing on campaign: de Caesaribus 16. 9–10. Yet
this improbable picture is regularly retailed in biographies.)
Indeed, the one use of the word paedagogus in the Meditations
provides a marked contrast to Epictetus' use in iii. 22; for
Marcus is reflecting on how a wise king's associates would use
the term disparagingly, in their relief after the king's death: 'We
shall breathe more freely with that schoolmaster gone . . . I
could feel all along that he was tacitly condemning us.' (x. 36).
Nor is there any suggestion in the Meditations that Marcus, or
any of his predecessors, had by virtue of his status any privileged
access to the divine power (as Epictetus comes near to suggesting
of his Cynic). We have seen in the last chapter how rare are his
references to possible divine communication (esp. i. 17 ad fin.),
and such dreams and oracles were accessible to all mankind.
Again the unimaginative idealisation of his subjects and his
biographers may be contrasted: the Historia Augusta tells us that
'there were not lacking men who supposed that he foretold
many things in dreams, prophesied future events, and did so
truthfully' (SHA Marcus 18. 7).²⁹

For the rest of our examples it will be necessary to begin from
Marcus himself. One passage is particularly rich in metaphors
for life; its density of imagery and its sense of the unreality of
human existence are alike alien to Epictetus.

τοῦ ἀνθρωπίνου βίου ὁ μὲν χρόνος στιγμή, ἡ δὲ οὐσία ῥέουσα, ἡ δὲ αἴσθησις

²⁸ μάρτυς: TDNT iv. 474 ff., esp. 480–1 on Epictetus' usage. Here again the
connection with the theme of the free man versus the tyrant is evident: though Epictetus
does not use the word in the Christian sense of 'martyr', the philosopher is the witness for
God against those who accuse or mock him: i. 22. 44–9.
²⁹ On the SHA's picture of Marcus see above, ch. IV n. 130.

ἀμυδρά, ἡ δὲ ὅλου τοῦ σώματος σύγκρισις εὔσηπτος, ἡ δὲ ψυχὴ ῥόμβος [better, ῥεμβός?], ἡ δὲ τύχη δυστέκμαρτον, ἡ δὲ φήμη ἄκριτον. συνελόντι δὲ εἰπεῖν, πάντα τὰ μὲν τοῦ σώματος ποταμός, τὰ δὲ τῆς ψυχῆς ὄνειρος καὶ τῦφος, ὁ δὲ βίος πόλεμος καὶ ξένου ἐπιδημία, ἡ δὲ ὑστεροφημία λήθη. τί οὖν τὸ παραπέμψαι δυνάμενον; ἓν καὶ μόνον φιλοσοφία.

Of man's life, his time is a tiny point, his existence a flux, his sensation is clouded, his whole body's composition swiftly corruptible, his vital spirit an eddy, his fortune hard to predict, his fame uncertain. To put it briefly: all the things of the body, a river; all the things of the spirit, dream and delirium; life a warfare and a sojourn in a strange land; and as for renown hereafter, it is oblivion. What then can be man's escort through life? One thing only, philosophy. (ii. 17)[30]

Although Marcus goes on to describe the philosophic life as one which keeps the spirit immune to external things and makes it content with all experience, including even death, the remainder of the chapter does not seem to cancel out the overwhelmingly bleak picture of human life offered in this passage. We may note especially the emphasis on the fluidity and obscurity of life: ῥέουσα, ῥεμβός, and the river image[31] emphasise the former, ἀμυδρά and δυστέκμαρτον the latter. The minuteness of the human life-span in eternity, a theme frequent in Marcus' work, is emphasised at the start of the whole sequence and again at the end, in the equation of ὑστεροφημία λήθη. Epictetus nowhere shows such consciousness of the vastness of infinity and eternity. Nor does he focus so often on death and the extinction of his existence. Marcus' praise of philosophy in this chapter (a common rhetorical theme,[32] but surprisingly rare in the Meditations themselves) turns swiftly to its capacity to reconcile us to the expectation of death. Epictetus too alludes to the Platonic idea of philosophy as a meditatio mortis (see Ench. 21, with Schenkl's parallels; also ch. 1 n. 52 above), but his eyes and words are always turned much more towards the duties and possiblities of life. Nor, when he does speak of death, is

---

[30] ῥόμβος = a whirling eddy or motion; ῥεμβός (the reading of most of the MSS, revived by Dalfen) = roaming, wandering, movement at random: this reading is supported by Marcus' use of ἀπορρέμβεσθαι (iii. 4 init., iv. 22); ῥέμβεσθαι (ii. 7); κρεμάμενος ἐκ τοῦδε καὶ τοῦδε (xii. 1); ῥιπτάζεσθαι (v. 5). See also G. Zuntz, JTS 47 (1946) 85–8.
[31] Cf. Pohlenz, Die Stoa ii. 170; ch. IV p. 147–8 above, with nn. 55–6.
[32] Laudes philosophiae: e.g. Arist. Protr.; Cic. Tusc. v. 1 ff.; or the proems to Lucretius, books v and vi, and Manilius, book i; also Sen. Ep. 88 and 90. For more formal rhetorical exercises see Max. Tyr. Or. i; Themist. Or. xxiv (protreptic to philosophy).

there the same striking mixture as in Marcus of gruesome detail
(εὔσηπτος) and clinical vocabulary (σύγκρισις, picked up later
in Marcus' chapter by λύσιν τῶν στοιχείων ἐξ ὧν ἕκαστον ζῷον
συγκρίνεται, 'the release of the elements from which each living
creature is constituted').[33]
A number of points in ii. 17 deserve special comment. It is
surprising that Marcus dismisses with equal force and distaste τὰ
μὲν τοῦ σώματος and τὰ δὲ τῆς ψυχῆς, 'all the things of the body'
and 'all the things of the soul'. It may be answered that
elsewhere he uses a tripartite division, σῶμα, ψυχή, νοῦς, 'body,
vital spirit, mind' (iii. 16 init.; similarly ii. 2, xii. 3). In each of
these divisions the νοῦς or ἡγεμονικόν, the intellectual element, is
the only one which should be valued.[34] But there is no third
element here, unless the δαίμων within, the guiding spirit, is to be
so regarded. It is not, however, introduced at the same point in
the chapter; and μὲν . . . δὲ seems to suggest a dualistic picture.
The difficulties of the concept of δαίμων as used by the later
Stoics are notorious:[35] does this 'guiding spirit' come from
outside, from God, or is it innate, the best part of ourselves? Or is
this an academic distinction to which the writers are in fact
indifferent? Is it identifiable with the divine 'cohabitant'
(σύνοικος) described in Plato's Timaeus (90c), or has it more in
common with the Roman genius (Hor. Ep. ii. 2. 188)? In
Meditations ii. 17 all that is apparent is that the δαίμων came from
another world and will return there, but in the meantime its
purity must be preserved with truly religious devotion. It must
be protected from outside influence, even from every disturbing
thought. Epictetus seems to speak of the daemon in language
like that of Marcus only in one passage, i. 14. 12:

Yet none the less he [Zeus] has stationed by each man's side as
guardian his own particular spirit, and has committed the man to his
care: and this is a guardian who never sleeps and is not to be beguiled.
To what other guardian, better or more careful, could he have
committed each one of us? Therefore, when you close your doors and
make darkness within, remember never to say you are alone, for you
are not. God is within, and your own guardian spirit . . .

---

[33] On medical vocabulary in Marcus see Schekira 236; J. E. G. Whitehorne, Latomus
36 (1977) 419 n. 32. Also ch. IV p. 145 above.
[34] So e.g. Dodds, Pagan and Christian 9 n. 4.
[35] See above ch. V n. 102.

Marcus, as often, is less impassioned, less specific, perhaps less certain.[36]

If the state of one's νοῦς or δαίμων (they seem to be equated at *Med.* iii. 16) is supremely important, then it is a possible but not an inevitable step to make it all-important, to feel and therefore to argue that the rest of one's life and thoughts are actually unreal, or of a lower, inferior order of reality compared with the pure life of one's intellectual being. This is a step which Epictetus does not take, but which Marcus does, not only in ii. 17 but also elsewhere. Comparable are v. 10. 2, v. 23 (the latter chapter is close to ii. 17 in its imagery, but lacks the positive section to counterbalance it), vii. 3, ix. 24, and x. 9: the last passage opens with the words 'Play-acting, warfare, excitement, lethargy, slavery!'. All these passages refer to the chaos and formlessness of everyday life, the general absence of order or sense. In ii. 17 the phrase τὰ δὲ τῆς ψυχῆς ὄνειρος καὶ τῦφος is particularly vivid: life is a dream and an illusion (or delusion?). The dream image for life has a distinguished pedigree in ancient literature:[37] it tends to be used of the insignificance and transience of human achievements, although an interesting exception to this rule may be seen in the *Prometheus Bound*, where the image describes the hopelessness of man's natural state until Prometheus, the proto-philosopher, gave him the gifts of reason and invention (Aesch. *PV* 448–9). This might seem analogous to the saving and protecting power of philosophy in *Med.* ii. 17, but the other passages cited suggest that Marcus' faith in this power varied, and that he did not believe that reason invariably or always helps man to find meaning or certainty (notice ii. 17. 1 'his fortune hard to predict'; also v. 10). In the passage from ii. 17 quoted above philosophy's task is not ambitious or osten-

[36] For uncertainty and questioning in the *Meditations* see v. 10 (where Marcus perhaps dissociates himself from 'the Stoics'; cf. Rist, art. cit. (ch. I n. 2)); ibid. § 2 ἐν τοιούτῳ οὖν ζόφῳ καὶ ῥύπῳ καὶ τοσαύτῃ ῥύσει τῆς τε οὐσίας καὶ τοῦ χρόνου καὶ τῆς κινήσεως καὶ τῶν κινουμένων τί ποτέ ἐστι τὸ ἐκτιμηθῆναι ἢ τὸ ὅλως σπουδασθῆναι δυνάμενον οὐδ' ἐπινοῶ; also vi. 15. Note how regularly imagery of change and aimless fluctuation counters the ideal of stablity, uprightness, and direction towards a goal (σκοπός). Cf. ch. IV nn. 86, 138 above.

[37] Dream imagery: Headlam–Thomson on Aesch. *Ag.* 1327 ff.; Stanford on Soph. *Aj.* 125 ff.; Pöschl (n. 16) 573; Dodds, *Pagan and Christian* 9. Cf. ch. IV n. 41 above; and compare the similar notion that life is really a form of death (ch IV n. 12). In ix. 24 Marcus seems to be saying that the world of the dead in Homer has more reality than the fussing and triviality of daily life on earth.

tatious, but inwardly directed: he does not extol her civilising power or the benefits she bestows upon enraptured humanity, but only her protection, shielding the soul from the world outside (cf. viii. 48). As for τῦφος, a condemnatory word favoured by the Cynics, the meaning 'delirium' need not exclude the more common meaning in Marcus, pomposity and empty show. Both senses reinforce the idea in ὄνειρος, that of the shallowness and insubstantiality of life.[38]

In the same passage of ii. 17 ξένου ἐπιδημία ('the sojourn of a stranger in a foreign land') also deserves comment. This is an image which Marcus has inherited directly from Epictetus, who says of a man who is concerned about popular acclaim: 'I call him first of all a stranger [or "foreigner"], and I say, this man does not know where in the world he is; although he has been residing here (ἐπιδημῶν) all this time, he is ignorant of the laws of the city and its customs, what is and is not possible there.' (Epict. ii. 13. 6). Here we recognise the more straightforward and expansive style characteristic of Epictetus' diatribes.[39] Marcus elsewhere uses the same idea as Epictetus, for instance in iv. 29, another passage in which the imagery is richer, more varied, and more significant than is customary in the earlier author. Another use occurs in xii. 13: 'How ridiculous and how like a stranger in the world is the man who is surprised at any one of life's events.' Imagery of this kind has earlier background, but seems particularly apt to Stoic cosmopolitanism: 'the universe is a kind of commonwealth' (iv. 4).[40] But it is noteworthy that

[38] For τῦφος see above, ch. v n. 74.

[39] Expansiveness: note the much greater average length of one of Epictetus' discourses compared with a chapter of the *Meditations*; also the greater frequency of examples enumerated and discussed, imagined arguments or conversations, and simple exposition. Epictetus does not stress brevity, as Marcus does, in his discussions of style. 'Straightforwardness' of style is hard to document, but it seems relevant to observe that there are fewer cruces of interpretation in Epictetus; that he has fewer rare, unique, or obscure words than Marcus; and that he does not cultivate the compressed, epigrammatic style that makes many of Marcus' reflections so cryptic. Even the *Encheiridion* is more discursive than (e.g.) Epicurus' *Kuriai Doxai*, and some portions are clearly derived from longer discourses (e.g. *Ench.* 29 = *Diss.* iii. 15). Some of this stylistic lucidity may be the result of Arrian's classicising editorial work (cf. nn. 2–3 above); but since Marcus appears to have read Epictetus in Arrian's version (if indeed there was any alternative), the comparison remains valid.

[40] Cicero in *Fin.* iv. 7 regards this as a rich rhetorical theme treated unworthily by the Stoics. On the theme, see the full treatment of instances in Epictetus and Marcus by G. R. Stanton, *Phronesis* 13 (1968) 183 ff. Further examples: Billerbeck on Epict. iii. 22. 4, 22, 47, 83. See also E. Elorduy, *Die Sozialphilosophie der Stoa* (*Philol.* Suppl. 28. 3, 1936);

Marcus in ii. 17 alters the use of the metaphor, applying it to man's residence in life *tout court*: rather than criticising an attitude which makes one act like a stranger in one's homeland, he speaks as if his time here were a forced visit to an alien place. The word for 'visit', ἐπιδημία, may have additional point. As seen above, it appears in a similar context in Epictetus; it has remoter ancestry in Greek popular philosphy. Thus, in the pseudo-Platonic *Axiochus* the saying παρεπιδημία τίς ἐστιν ὁ βίος ('life is a kind of temporary visit') is described as a commonplace (365b). But in Roman times the term is sometimes used of an emperor's official visits (*OGI* 517. 7; Herodian iii. 14. 11), and so might here be used sardonically by Marcus of his whole life as emperor. So here again we find something which appears to be a topos in earlier authors, including Epictetus, but which is given more personal bite by Marcus.

There is a strongly Platonic note in this range of ideas: the body as an imperfect fleshly vessel for something far superior, something which is akin to the divine and should not be polluted by earthly substance. Indeed, the *Phaedo*, the dialogue in which Plato most fervently maintains the antithesis of body and soul, offers a close parallel to Marcus' usage. This occurs at 67b, and forms part of a very influential passage, frequently anthologised and quoted.[41]

ὥστε ἥ γε ἀποδημία ἡ νῦν μοι προστεταγμένη μετὰ ἀγαθῆς ἐλπίδος γίγνεται καὶ ἄλλῳ ἀνδρὶ ὃς ἡγεῖταί οἱ παρεσκευάσθαι τὴν διάνοιαν ὥσπερ κεκαθαρμένην.

And it follows that the journey now appointed for me may also be made with good hope by any other man who regards his intellect as prepared by its having been, as it were, purified.

Here ἀποδημία is akin to the usage of ἐπιδημία discussed above, while προστεταγμένη alludes to the metaphor of *militia dei*, life as a period of service under God, the divine general, which is prominent in the *Phaedo* and is taken over by all the Roman Stoics (as later by the early Christians).[42] Seneca comments

Long and Sedley (n. 25) 330, 332, 348, 429–37. It seems not to involve social consequences or political reform: see Brunt, *Athen.* 55 (1977) 47, citing H. C. Baldry, *The Unity of Mankind in Greek Thought* (Cambridge 1965) 151–66, and Epict. iii. 13. 9 ff., quoted above on p. 229–30.

[41] See Chadwick, *RLAC* vii. 1142.

[42] Cf. Pl. *Ap.* 28d; *Phaedo* 61e; D. Steyns, *Étude sur les métaphores et comparaisons de Sénèque*

'vivere, Lucili, militare est' (*Ep.* 96. 5); Epictetus frequently uses the image (e.g. iii. 22. 69, iii. 24. 31 ff., 95 ff.); and we find it in Marcus in the chapter we have been discussing: ὁ δὲ βίος πόλεμος (ii. 17. 1). Yet the image in Marcus conveys weariness rather than confident assertion. Contrast the spirit of Epict. iii. 24. 99, 'whatever station and post you assign me, I shall die ten thousand times over, as Socrates says, before I abandon it' (Socrates' actual words were rather less grandiose; see Pl. *Ap.* 30c1); or the solidarity of the Christian 'fight the good fight'.

In Marcus such imagery conveys a more bitter attitude toward life's duties and expectations than we find in Epictetus, who indeed seems almost untinged by the Platonic dualism of body and soul.[43] We find Marcus describing death as repose (ἀνάπαυλα),[44] 'from sense-perception, impulse, intellectual effort, and all one's duty done in service to the flesh (καὶ τῆς πρὸς τὴν σάρκα λειτουργίας)' (vi. 28). Or again, in v. 31, reviewing his conduct in social obligations, he reminds himself 'that the story of your life is written and your service accomplished' (ὅτι πλήρης ἤδη σοι ἡ ἱστορία τοῦ βίου καὶ τελεία[45] ἡ λειτουργία). Here also the metaphors are both characteristic of Marcus and appropriate to his situation: his service to God is to fulfil his public role; and historiography, with its absorption in the lives of rulers (cf. Suetonius and the *Historia Augusta*), was destined, as he knew well, to focus on his life in due course.

Another such passage is iii. 3, in which the likelihood that death brings oblivion is welcomed, as this will mean release from the body: 'if death leads to unconsciousness, you will cease to suffer pains and pleasures and to be the servant of an earthly

(Ghent 1907) 22–34; R. Reitzenstein, *Die Hellenistischen Mysterienreligionen* (Leipzig and Berlin 1910) 66 ff. The image is taken over by Christianity, though not necessarily from Stoicism, as the usage is widespread: see e.g. Teles p. 42. 10 H. ἀβίωτος ὁ βίος, στρατεία, λειτουργία, πολιτικὰ πράγματα, σχολάσαι αὐτῷ οὐκ ἔστιν, a passage very much in Marcus' manner. See also Hense on Teles 54. 2, and for Christian developments Gataker on *Med.* ii. 17 (e.g. Eph. 6: 12; 1 Pet. 2: 11, 4: 1); H. Emunds *ap.* A. von Harnack, *Militia Christi* (revised edn., Darmstadt 1963) 131 ff.

[43] On all this see Arnold, *Roman Stoicism* 257–9; Lagrange, art. cit. (ch. v n. 41).

[44] Used only here, but cf. v. 1 (ἀναπαύεσθαι, *bis*); for Marcus' lack of sleep see ii. 1, vi. 2, viii. 12; Fronto i. 188 (but contrast i. 54; ii. 18 and that whole exchange are more frivolous). On insomnia in later life see Dio 71. 24. 4; p. 120 above (in general, Nisbet–Hubbard on Hor. *Odes* ii. 11. 8). For metaphorical/symbolic use of sleep and wakening see above, ch. iv n. 41; below, Envoi n. 8.

[45] τελευταία, resurrected in Dalfen's text, seems to me to have nothing to recommend it.

vessel as far inferior as that which does it service is superior: for
the one is mind and deity, the other matter and gore.' Ths vivid
antithesis concludes the chapter. Here the words for 'do service',
λατρεύειν and ὑπηρετεῖν, again recall Plato, but are used in a
rather different sense. Socrates speaks of his *service* to God in the
pursuit of his enquiries, testing and seeking wisdom among his
fellow men (*Ap.* 23c; 30a), and Epictetus echoes this (iii. 22. 56,
his only use of λατρεύειν). But Marcus is bemoaning his
enslavement to the body, the container of the soul, in the spirit of
the ascetic motto σῶμα σῆμα ('the body is a tomb').[46] Epictetus
certainly also ranks the body as inferior to the governing mind or
spirit, but it is rare for him to pour scorn or contempt upon it *per
se*: he usually condemns only those who are too attached to it,
too indulgent with its appetites. One exception might be seen in
Epict. fr. 23 (quoted by Stobaeus), which is indeed quite close to
Marcus, even to the use of the λειτουργία image, employed by
Epictetus only here. The fragment runs, in part:

> At all events, we love and tend our body, the most unpleasant and
> dirtiest thing there is. Why, if we had to tend our neighbour's body for
> a mere five days, we would not be able to endure it. Just think what a
> nuisance it is to get up in the morning and brush some other person's
> teeth, and then after attending to the call of nature, having to wash
> those parts. Truly it is a wonderful thing to love something to which we
> devote our services (λειτουργοῦμεν) in so many respects every single
> day. I stuff this bag here, then I empty it—which is the more
> wearisome? Still, one has to serve God . . .

But even here, there is more jocularity and agreeable vulgarity
than actual *hatred* of the body.[47]

This seems a common contrast between Epictetus and
Marcus, the one employing the familiar coarseness and cheerful
argumentative style of diatribe,[48] the other more compressed,
employing a more unusual style and syntax, a wider and more

---

[46] On which see Dodds, *The Greeks and the Irrational* 169–71; C. J. de Vogel, in H. J.
Blumenthal and R. A. Markus (eds.), *Neoplatonism and Early Christian Thought* (Fest. A. H.
Armstrong) (London 1981) 79–95.

[47] For other possible examples see Pohlenz, *Die Stoa* ii. 165 (note to i. 336).

[48] For vulgarity as a characteristic of 'diatribe' see above, ch. 1 n. 62. In Epictetus see
e.g. *Ench.* 7 (comic touches, esp. 'packed in like sheep', added to the image of the voyage
of life, on which see above, ch. IV n. 54), 11, 12; *Diss.* ii. 20. 10, ii. 23, iii. 7, iii. 24. 38 ff.
(largely polemic against Epicureanism; contrast the more sympathetic and dignified
attitude of Marcus in e.g. ix. 41, xi. 26, xii. 34), iii. 22. 77, 80, 90 (abuse of unworthy
Cynics).

recondite vocabulary, and often reaching greater depths of gruesomeness, a tendency which seems to spring from a deeper dissatisfaction and distaste. Their respective treatments of death (see section 3 below) will provide further contrasts. But before taking up that topic two further quotations from the *Meditations* should be cited, both of which are particularly violent and unconventional passages pungently characterising human life as a whole.

ὁποῖόν σοι φαίνεται τὸ λούεσθαι, ἔλαιον, ἱδρώς, ῥύπος, ὕδωρ γλοιῶδες, πάντα σικχαντά—τοιοῦτον πᾶν μέρος τοῦ βίου καὶ πᾶν ὑποκείμενον.

As your bath appears to your senses—oil, sweat, dirt, greasy water, all disgusting—such is every piece of life and every object. (viii. 24)

τὸ σαπρὸν τῆς ἑκάστῳ ὑποκειμένης ὕλης· ὕδωρ, κόνις, ὀστάρια, γράσος, ἢ πάλιν· πῶροι γῆς τὰ μάρμαρα καὶ ὑποστάθμαι ὁ χρυσός, ὁ ἄργυρος, καὶ τριχία ἡ ἐσθὴς καὶ αἷμα ἡ πορφύρα, καὶ τὰ ἄλλα πάντα τοιαῦτα, καὶ τὸ πνευματικὸν δὲ ἄλλο τοιοῦτον καὶ ἐκ τούτων εἰς ταῦτα μεταβάλλον

The rottenness of the matter that underlies all things. Water, dust, bones, stench. Or again: marble, an incrustation of earth; gold and silver, sediments; your dress, the hair of animals; the purple dye, blood; and so on with all the rest. What is of the nature of breath too is similar and changes from this to that. (ix. 36)

This is more than 'diatribal vulgarity'. In the first of these passages it is hard to exaggerate the tone of revulsion from the physical, which is intensified by the precision of the picture and the bizarre choice of example. We should contrast the argument of Chrysippus, who deduced from the beauty and excellence of the universe[49] 'omnia hominum causa facta esse et parata' (Cic. *ND* ii. 154; cf. ii. 133, i. 23)—'that all things are made and prepared for man's use'.[50] In the second passage we see again the reductive, brutally physical analysis of matter and earthly objects, the self-imposed insistence on the 'reality' of things. There is no room given to positive values that might counter this depressingly negative picture; no sense that God, or λόγος, is immanent in and working on the material world, giving it shape and purpose.

This revulsion from the physical and condemnation of

---

[49] See F. Solmsen, *AJP* 72 (1951) 4 = *Kleine Schriften* i (Hildesheim 1968) 464.

[50] This optimistic view was attacked especially by the Epicureans: see Lucr. ii. 167–83, iv. 822–59, v. 156–234; Cic. *ND* i. 21 ff.

worldly objects suggests how strongly Marcus inclines toward a more transcendent view of deity as existing apart from the physical world, on another plane, and to a more elevated conception (at least in the eyes of Platonists, Christians, and others) of the soul.[51] But he does not take the final step towards postulating the existence of such a transcendent divinity (this would have been a quite unorthodox step for a Stoic), or affirming the continued, conscious existence of the disembodied soul.[52] He speaks constantly of 'the gods'—rarely personified or individualised as they are by Epictetus. He speaks of himself after death as undergoing change, transformation, or resolution into separate elements—rarely and hesitantly of what could reasonably be termed an afterlife.

3. Death and Dissolution[53]

'Death is nothing to us' (e.g. Epict. Ench. 5 'it is nothing terrible').[54] This precept was as fundamental to Stoicism as to the Epicurean Principal Doctrines (Kuriai Doxai 2 = Sent. Vat. 2).[55] Yet to Marcus Aurelius death seems to have been a great deal more. He constantly returns to the subject of his own and others' demise. It has been estimated that 62 chapters of the Meditations deal prominently with this theme: this amounts to about one in eight chapters of the work.[56] More significant than such undigested statistics is the way in which he treats the theme. Here he is very different from Epictetus, although he can be seen to be imitating him in several passages.

Firstly, Epictetus does not refer to the subject nearly as often, and he also deals with it much more casually. Death is often referred to as one of a string of obstacles or 'indifferents' which are to be overcome by the aspiring philosopher: thus death and exile are paired at Epict. iii. 22. 19–22, or grouped with disease and poverty in Ench. 2. Death does not figure even once in the

---

[51] For another striking instance see vii. 68 τὰ μελύδρια τοῦ περιτεθραμμένου τούτου φυράματος. See further viii. 50 τὰ σαπρότερα; ix. 14; xii. 7 τὴν ἀσθένειαν πάσης ὕλης.

[52] Cf. Waszink on Tert. de Anima 5.

[53] On this topic the indexes to Haines' Loeb edn. of Marcus remain a useful guide, s.v. 'Death', 'Destruction, 'Dissolution', 'Soul', etc. See also Hoven, Stoïcisme et stoïciens.

[54] Further, SVF i. 196 = Sen. Ep. 82. 7. Cf. SVF i. 190, iii. 70, 118, 256, etc.

[55] Further, e.g. Diog. Laert. x. 124; Lucr. iii. 830.

[56] Brunt, JRS 64 (1974) 20.

titles (admittedly sometimes unsatisfactory) which are given to the individual diatribes in our texts of Epictetus. Although he does give it more extended treatment upon occasion (ii. 1. 17 f., ii. 6. 12 ff., iii. 24. 84–94, iii. 26. 3 ff., iv. 1. 103–10), there is not the same fascination with the topic which we can discern in Marcus. Epictetus' eyes are more on life. Death will come when God wills, there is nothing we can do about it, but let it find us doing our work well and yet ready to depart (iii. 5. 7 f.; cf. iv. 10. 14 ff.).

This is in harmony with two of Epictetus' favourite quotations: 'as God wills, so let it come to pass' (Socrates in Pl. *Crito* 43d), and 'lead me, O Zeus, and thou, O Destiny' (Cleanthes, *SVF* ii. 537 = fr. 2. 1 Powell).[57] Neither appears in the *Meditations*. These quotations bring out the personal quality of Epictetus' devotion. Epictetus has no questions or uncertainty about the nature of God: his existence and his goodness are basic presuppositions, not subjects for discussion (ii. 14. 11 ff.). In speaking of these qualities of divinity he moves directly to human action, to deducing the consequences of his simple theism.[58] This attitude is apparent also in the imagined speeches Epictetus makes to God, giving an account of himself and his life (ii. 5. 9 ff.; iv. 10. 14 ff., from which I quote).

If death finds me occupied with these matters, it is enough for me if I can lift up my hands to God and say 'The faculties which I received from you to enable me to understand your governance and follow it, these I have not neglected. I have not dishonoured you as far as in me lay.... Have I ever blamed you?[59] Have I been discontented with any of those things which happen, or wished that it might have been otherwise? ... The length of time for which I had the use of your gifts is enough for me. Take them back again and assign them to what place you will, for they were all yours, and you gave them to me.' Is it not enough for a man to take his departure from the world in this state of mind?

In his protreptic zeal here Epictetus borders on bravado (Demetrius the Cynic, quoted in Seneca's *de Providentia* 5. 5–6, decidedly oversteps the borderline). We can perhaps best

---

[57] For the former see Epict. i. 4. 24, i. 29. 18, iv. 4. 21; *Ench.* 53. For the latter see ii. 23. 42, iii. 22. 95, iv. 1. 131; *Ench.* 53.
[58] See also Bonhöffer, *Die Ethik des Stoikers Epictet* 40–2.
[59] On blaming and reproaching the gods see also ch. v n. 96 above.

understand his attitude to death if we think of it as another
ethical *labor*, a Herculean obstacle to be conquered.[60]

A second difference between the two Stoics is that Epictetus is
relatively unconcerned with the mechanism of death, that is,
how it affects one's body, where the soul goes, and by what
process. In one passage he gives an orthodox definition which
bears close resemblances to Marcus' language. ' "But now it is
time to die." Well, why say "die"? Don't give the business a
spurious tragic grandeur, but say it as it is, "Now is the moment
for the matter to be transformed back into the elements from
which it came together before." What is terrible about that?
What novel or unreasonable thing will have taken place?' (iv. 7.
15-16). Or again, Epictetus argues as follows:

What is death? A bugbear [μορμολύκειον, a Platonic word: cf. *Med.* xi.
23]. Turn it about and see what it is. See, it doesn't bite! The paltry
body has got to be separated from the tiny portion of spirit, either now
or later, just as it existed separately before. . . . Why? So that the
revolution of the universe may be accomplished; for it has need of the
things that are coming now into being, of the things that will be, of the
things that are ended. What is hardship? A bugbear . . . (ii. 1. 17-19)

We notice again how death has no special authority, no unique
horror, for Epictetus: it is only one in a series of false bogies.

Here the ideas are very close to Marcus', and the diminutives
(esp. 'the paltry body') are precisely in his manner.[61] We find
references to the Stoic concept of the cycle of the universe, the so-
called *magnus annus*, in the *Meditations* also.[62] But the overall
effect of Epictetus' lively dismissal of human fears, with his
humorous touches and question-and-answer technique, is very
different. Moreover, the details of the soul's separation, the
process by which it is reabsorbed into the cosmic whole, the
theoretical foundation of the cyclical renewal, are not subjects
which interest him. They are thrown in merely for argumenta-

---

[60] On Heracles as a Stoic hero, overcoming obstacles and resisting pleasure, see
F. Buffière, *Les Mythes d'Homère et la pensée grecque* (Paris 1956) 376-7; G. K. Galinsky, *The
Heracles Theme* (Oxford 1972) ch. 5 and 9. On ethical *labores*, n. 23 above.

[61] Cf. ψυχάριον in v. 33, vii. 16, etc.; ἀνθρωπάριον in iii. 10, vii. 23; Farquharson on iv.
20. See further D. Szumska, 'De Diminutivis apud M. Aurelium Obviis', *Eos* 44 (1964)
230-8 (Polish, with Latin summary). For Epictetus see Halbauer, *De Diatribis Epicteti* 34
(list); Billerbeck on iii. 22. 21.

[62] On the *magnus annus* see *Med.* xi. 1 (παλιγγενεσία); Pease on Cic. *ND* ii. 51 ff.; Long
and Sedley (n. 25) 274-9, 308-13.

tive impact, as an unanswerable response to the repeated question 'Why?'. Marcus by contrast has the freedom and the compulsion to ponder traditional difficulties, even if he does not hope to resolve them. He is also fascinated by the idea of the transmutation of the body and the soul into their elements: he repeatedly makes of this subject a strange kind of poetry.[63] A parallel example is Epict. iv. 1. 106 (in the festival passage quoted above, p. 231). Here again a humorous, casual tone is adopted by Epictetus when he is dealing with a subject which falls under physics or cosmology rather than within his own immediate didactic province. To the man who objects 'I wanted to go on with the holiday', he retorts:

Leave, depart as a grateful, reverent spectator should. Make room for others; others must be born, just as you were, and once born they must have land and houses and provisions. But if the first comers do not move along, what is left for those who follow after? Why are you insatiable? Why are you not satisfied? Why do you keep crowding the universe? (τί στενοχωρεῖς τὸν κόσμον;)

This down-to-earth diagnosis of population problems may be contrasted with Marcus Aurelius' comments in *Med.* iv. 21, echoing Stoic discussions of the survival of body and soul within the world:

... as on earth change and dissolution after a continuance for so long make room for more dead bodies, so also in the atmosphere souls pass on and continue for a certain length of time, and then change and are poured out and are kindled into the generative principle of universal nature, and so provide room for those which succeed in their place. At least, that is what one would answer on the hypothesis that souls do continue.[64]

In Epictetus, a jocular debating point; in Marcus, a serious source of uncertainty, a starting-point for speculation.

Marcus' eye is regularly on the workings of time and infinite space. He doubtless wishes to look beyond the everyday world of chaotic human activity (iv. 32. 1, etc.), to something more

---

[63] Death is a φύσεως πυστήριον (*Med.* iv. 5). See further ch. IV n. 25 above; Pohlenz, *Die Stoa* ii. 170.

[64] See also viii. 18 'What is dead does not fall outside the universe', etc. On σπερματικὸς λόγος see above, ch. V n. 82. Note also the contrast between this cosmic speculation and a blunter, more practical sense of στενοχωρία ('cramped housing') satirically exploited in diatribal writing; see Nock's comm. on Sallustius p. xxxi n. 85.

impersonal and lasting. In this spirit he contemplates the stars: 'Watch and see the courses of the stars as if you ran with them; and continually dwell in mind upon the changes of the elements into one another, for such imaginations wash away the foulness of life upon the ground.' (vii. 47; cf. xi. 27, esp. on 'purity').[65] There is nothing of this sour asceticism in Epictetus, who indeed seems to consider earth and heavenly bodies as equally worthy of contemplation: 'A man who has this to think upon, and who beholds the sun and moon and stars, and enjoys land and sea, is no more forlorn than he is without help.' (Epict. iii. 13. 16). In this respect Marcus' attitude is again reminiscent of Platonism, with its condemnation of the sublunar world (Pl. *Tht.* 176a, etc.).[66] Epictetus, concentrating on the life of this world, is content; the disillusionment of Marcus seeks a purer and higher existence beyond this mortal sphere.

The third and final point on which Epictetus and Marcus are at variance is the question of the individual soul's survival after death. This is a subject which Epictetus, apparently close here to the views of the early Stoics, seems to consider less significant than it has been thought to be by most religious writers. Orthodox Stoicism reserved judgement on the subject.[67] Tacitus, like Marcus himself, could refer to the afterlife as a standard topic of philosophic discourse (*Ann.* xvi. 19 'de immortalitate animae et sapientium placitis'; *Med.* iv. 48. 1). But his contemporary Epictetus is indifferent; he never commits himself to any view on the topic. The stated opinions of the early Stoics had been varied. They all declared that the soul was corporeal and therefore perishable (*SVF* ii. 809 ff.); but most held that it survived for some time after its separation from the body, and then perished, an opinion ridiculed by Cicero as having the worst of both worlds (*Tusc.* i. 77–8). Some held that all souls survived until the conflagration that was to end the world-cycle (so Cleanthes *ap.* Diog. Laert. vii. 157 = *SVF* ii. 811). Chrysippus, however, thought that only the souls of the wise survived that long (ibid.; cf. Arius, *Doxogr.* 471. 18 = *SVF* ii. 809). Panaetius suspended judgement entirely (Cic. *Tusc.* i. 79).

[65] Star-gods and purity of the stars: see above, ch. IV n. 91.
[66] See Dodds, *Pagan and Christian* 12 ff.
[67] See Hoven (n. 52) esp. ch. 2; also my ch. V. 7 above. Hoven remarks (p. 133) that Musonius seems to show no interest in the question of posthumous survival; I agree.

Such 'survival' presumably means survival of *consciousness*, for the Stoics believed that no matter fell outside the universe;[68] rather, it was reabsorbed, resolved into its original elements, and eventually reshaped, 'so making boundless eternity ever young', as Marcus himself put it (vi. 15; cf. vii. 25, viii. 50, xii. 23). Marcus regularly comments on the speed with which this is happening: e.g. ii. 12 πῶς πάντα ταχέως ἐναφανίζεται ('how swiftly all things are vanishing away'), vi. 15 σπεύδει (*bis*), διηνεκῶς, ἀεί, παραθέοντων, παραπετομένων, etc.[69] It is clear that he does not envisage continuous survival until the end of the *magnus annus*. Rather, the changes in matter are incessant (v. 23) and affect even living bodies (ii. 3). This obsession with perpetual change, and how one should regard it in and outside oneself, is very typical of Marcus, though not of Epictetus. Marcus' allusions to Heraclitus' notion of life as a river or flux are a symptom of this—again, an author and a range of ideas almost wholly ignored by Epictetus.[70]

For the most part Marcus' emphasis suggests that he assumes immediate extinction of consciousness. This is most concisely put at vii. 32: 'On death: either dispersal, if [we are] atoms; or, if [we are] a living unity, either extinction or a change of place.' Only the last option gives any hint of a prolonged life elsewhere, and this does not necessarily imply continuity of consciousness, for the word that Marcus uses (μετάστασις) could as well denote reincarnation as a completely different person. In v. 13 Marcus speaks of every separate μέρος, every portion of himself, being assigned by change to some part of the cosmos, and so on again into infinity or until the end of the cycle. This conception is put most vividly in vii. 23: 'Universal Nature out of its whole material, as from wax, models now the figure of a horse, then melting this down uses the material for a tree, next for a man, next for something else. Each of these exists for a very brief time

---

[68] Besides *Med.* viii. 18 already quoted, and viii. 50, see Sen. *Ep.* 36. 10 f.; *NQ* iii. 9; *Ben.* v. 8. 5; Plut. *Sto. Rep.* 39. 1052d (attacking Chrysippus).

[69] Of 25 examples in Dalfen's index of ταχύς and cognates all but 9 occur in contexts of death and dissolution, of which the passage cited in the text is typical. ἐναφανίζεσθαι is also a favoured word in such contexts: iv. 14, v. 23, vi. 36, vii. 10, xii. 32.

[70] On Heraclitus and the Stoa see A. A. Long, *Philosophia* 5–6 (1975–6) 133–56; on Marcus in particular, Rist, art. cit. (ch. I n. 2) 36 ff. In Epictetus Heraclitus is mentioned only once, though with high praise (*Ench.* 15), and never quoted. Contrast the string of quotations at *Med.* iv. 46 and numerous other allusions (see Haines, index s.v.; Pohlenz, *Die Stoa* ii. 170, note to i. 349). For Seneca see Pohlenz i. 322, ii. 160.

. . .' (cf. vii. 25, iv. 36).[71] In this frame of reference there is plainly no room for an afterlife. Elsewhere Marcus wavers (esp. viii. 58; cf. xii. 5, discussed on ch. v above). His assertions of faith in divine providence, even his most lyrical submission to what is decided by powers outside himself (iv. 23), are more than balanced by these endless doubts and ponderings on the ways of the Universal Nature. It is these doubts and qualms which above all differentiate his religious utterances from the confident relationship of Epictetus to a God who, as he believed, knows him and cares for him. A striking instance is Epictetus' declaration 'I am a free man and a friend of God,[72] and so I willingly obey him' (iv. 3. 9). It is difficult to imagine Marcus saying these words.[73] Again, Epictetus says that 'Wherever I go, there are sun, moon, stars, dreams, signs, my converse with the gods (ἡ πρὸς θεοὺς ὁμιλία)' (iii. 22. 22).[74] The optimism of this passage, with its grateful confidence in the rightness of the world and the possibility of continuous contact with divine powers, stands in sharp contrast with the remote uncertainty of supernatural communication in Marcus Aurelius (i. 17. 6 and 9).

But if the transformation of the soul after death finds no place in Epictetus' works, the subject is prominent in the writings of two other Roman Stoics, who also merit a brief comparison with Marcus as a concluding pendant to this chapter. I refer to Seneca, especially in his *Consolatio ad Marciam* (25–6), in which he envisages the posthumous ascent of Marcia's lost son,[75] and to Lucan, who presents in the prologue to Book IX of his epic the apotheosis of the murdered Pompey. I consider first the poet.

---

[71] Haines interestingly compares Romans 9: 20–1 (the image of the potter (κεραμεύς) and the pot). For yet another contrast see the much more sceptical and bantering use of the same image by R. Fitzgerald, *Rubáiyát of Omar Khayyám* (1859) stanzas lix–lxiv.

[72] Cf. ii. 17. 29. Contrast Aristotle's famous remark that it would be curious for anyone to claim that he 'loved' Zeus (*NE* 1159ᵃ4; [*Magna Mor.*] 1208ᵇ30). On friendship with God see *TDNT* ix. 115, 168; P. Brown, *The Making of Late Antiquity* (Cambridge, Mass. 1978) ch. 3.

[73] On Marcus' use of φιλία and cognates see ch. III. 5, p. 123 above.

[74] On communion and association between men and gods see Nock, *Essays* 582 ff. Again the eleventh book of Apuleius' *Metamorphoses*, with its picture of the intimate and loving relationship between the narrator and the goddess, provides a vivid contrast with the starkness of Marcus' religion. See J. Gwyn Griffiths' comm. on *Met.* xi, pp. 53–4.

[75] See commentaries by C. G. Grollios (*Seneca ad Marciam: Tradition and Originality* (Athens 1956)) and C. E. Manning (*Mnem.* Suppl. 69, Leiden 1971). For other relevant passages see Pohlenz, *Die Stoa* ii. 160, note to i. 322.

at non in Pharia manes iacuere favilla,
nec cinis exiguus tantam conpescuit umbram:
prosiluit busto semustaque membra relinquens
degeneremque rogum sequitur convexa Tonantis.
qua niger astriferis conectitur axibus aer
quodque patet terras inter lunaeque meatus,
semidei manes habitant, quos ignea virtus
innocuos vita patientes aetheris imi
fecit, et aeternos animam collegit in orbes:
non illuc auro positi nec ture sepulti
perveniunt. illic postquam se lumine vero
inplevit, stellasque vagas miratus et astra
fixa polis, vidit quanta sub nocte iaceret
nostra dies, risitque sui ludibria trunci.
hinc super Emathiae campos et signa cruenti
Caesaris ac sparsas volitavit in aequore classes,
et scelerum vindex in sancto pectore Bruti
sedit et invicti posuit se mente Catonis.

But the spirit of Pompey did not linger down in Egypt among the embers, nor did that handful of ashes imprison his mighty ghost. Soaring up from the burning-place, it left the charred limbs and the unworthy pyre behind and sought the dome of the Thunderer. Where our dark atmosphere—the intervening space between earth and the moon's orbit—joins on to the starry spheres, there after death dwell heroes, whose fiery quality has fitted them, after guiltless lives, to endure the lower limit of ether, and has brought their souls from all parts to the eternal spheres: to those who are coffined in gold and buried with incense that realm is barred. When he had steeped himself in the true light of that region, and gazed at the planets and the fixed stars of heaven, he saw the thick darkness that veils our day, and smiled at the mockery done to his headless body. Then his spirit flew above the field of Pharsalia, the standards of bloodthirsty Caesar, and the ships scattered over the sea, till it settled, as the avenger of guilt, in the righteous heart of Brutus, and took up its abode in the heart of unconquerable Cato. (Lucan ix. 1–18, tr. J. D. Duff).

In this passage we can immediately recognise Stoic elements: in the conception of *virtus* as the qualification for divinity (cf. Hor. *Odes* iii. 3. 9 ff.), and in the idea of the soul's return to its heavenly home. 'Ignea' in line 7 refers to the fiery nature of the soul. We are shown Pompey rising majestically above this worthless earthly sphere, admiring the heavenly beauties (l. 12

'miratus'), and looking back with a sense of superiority and contempt (ll. 13–14; as Pompey smiles at the sight of his own corpse, the 'view from above' theme is given a bizarre new twist!). In what follows, Pompey's spirit settles in the hearts of Brutus and Cato; this seems remotely comparable with the idea of a guardian spirit or δαίμων, not always kept theoretically distinct from that of a disembodied soul.[76] But it would be hard to parallel, in Stoicism or Platonism, the notion of a particular guardian, a former contemporary, inhabiting *two* separate souls.

Lucan, in fact, here as often, outstrips straightforward Stoicism and general consistency for an immediately striking effect which is, on reflection, overdrawn and unconvincing. The detail of his cosmology is abruptly introduced and grandiloquently expressed (esp. 'astriferis axibus', 'ignea virtus', 'patientes aetheris imi'). The topos of simple virtue, in any case inappropriate to Pompey in his lifetime, is twisted to fit the circumstances by the statement that nobody *buried* in gold or with incense can reach the astral realm, a regulation which hardly satisfies either heavenly justice or common sense (ll. 10–11). Finally, the portrait of Pompey given elsewhere in the epic does not justify Lucan's description of him as one of the 'innocui' (l. 8); nor do we feel that he merits such posthumous honour as is here described. The inconsistency is made still more glaring by the passage which follows: we are promptly told that Cato had hated Pompey as much as Caesar (confirmed by Lucan's earlier narrative, especially ii. 319 ff.). Hence, even within the historical fantasy of the epic, it is hard to accept that Cato reckoned Pompey after his death as a worthy cause or a source of inspiration. Lucan is merely drawing on high-sounding ideas, Stoic in the main but going outside strict orthodoxy, to create a superficially impressive but in fact ill-conceived episode. Contrast the enthronement of Pompey's spirit in Cato with the more realistic emulation of Pius by Marcus; and contrast the virtual apotheosis of Pompey with the absence of any divinised human benefactors, or euhemerist ideas of this kind, from Marcus' world-picture. None of his predecessors is referred to by him as

---

[76] See above, ch. v n. 102. A partial parallel to Lucan's conception is the curious passage in Plut. *de Genio Socr.* 585d–6a, where the spirit of the dead man has moved into a different body, coexisting with its owner; the story is told by a Pythagorean. (I owe this reference to Professor Russell.)

divine: Augustus, Hadrian, and the rest all died at the appointed time, and so will he.[77] The Senecan passage is both more extended and more self-consciously literary, rich in allusion to Cicero's celebrated *Somnium Scipionis* (note esp. the appearance of Scipio in *Marc.* 25. 2).[78] The highly Platonist vision of the cosmos presented in Cicero's work also tempers the Stoic rigour of Seneca. This softening effect is enhanced by the very un-Stoic picture of great men communing with one another after death. It is this assemblage ('coetus sacer', *Marc.* 25. 2) that Marcia's son Metilius has now joined. There, Seneca assures the grieving mother, the dead boy will be reunited with his illustrious grandfather, the historian Cremutius Cordus,[79] who will reveal to him the secrets of the universe and the course of future events.

Here too we have, in extended form, the soul's view of earth from above, and also, with strongly emotive colouring, the release from the body: 'vincula animorum tenebraeque sunt; obruitur his, offocatur inficitur, arcetur a veris et suis in falsa coiectus' (24. 5). But whereas in the *Meditations* this sombre antipathy to the flesh is countered by no hope or at least no certainty of a freer, more fulfilled state after death, Seneca's eschatology is, at least for the purpose of this consolation, clearly defined and optimistic. There will be only a brief period of purgation ('paulumque supra nos commoratus, dum expurgatur et inhaerentia vitia . . . excutit'—very Platonic, and indeed Virgilian,[80] but scarcely Stoic). Thereafter the fortunate boy will ascend to the heights of the universe and join the blessed: 'ad

[77] For Marcus and his predecessors see ch. IV n. 102. Nowhere does he speak of any of them as divine; nor did he himself encourage or attract imperial honours in his own lifetime: see Beaujeu, *La Religion romaine* 363; J. H. Oliver, *Marcus Aurelius: Aspects of Civic and Cultural Policy in the East, Hesp.* Suppl. 13 (1970) 87; Brunt, *JRS* 64 (1974) 17. In general on emperors' and intellectuals' attitude to the cult see G. W. Bowersock, in W. den Boer (ed.), *Le Culte des souverains,* Fond. Hardt Entretiens xix (Geneva 1972) 177 ff.; S. R. F. Price, *Rituals and Power* (Cambridge 1983) 66–9, 72–5, 114–16 (though as for p. 116, the *Meditations* are hardly 'in public'!), 227–31, and *passim.*

[78] On the *Somnium* see above, ch. IV n. 93. But Marcus' sense of alienation from the world around him brings him closer to the detached superiority of Africanus than to the gloating *Schadenfreude* of Cremutius (see the passages quoted in the text).

[79] For littérateurs in the afterlife see Nisbet–Hubbard on Hor. *Odes* ii. 13 (p. 204). On Cremutius Cordus see esp. Tac. *Ann.* iv. 34 f.; MacMullen, *Enemies of the Roman Order* 299.

[80] Cf. Virg. *Geo.* iv. 219 ff.; *Aen.* vi. 724 ff. On the mythological and philosophic background to these passages see F. Solmsen, *Proc. of the Amer. Philos. Soc.* 112 (1968) 8–14; id., *CPh* 67 (1972) 31–41, both reprinted in his *Kleine Schriften* iii (Hildesheim 1983).

excelsa sublatus inter felices currit animas' (25. 1; the verb is in the prophetic present tense). Again a contrast with Marcus is clearly discernible, and made sharper by unmistakable similarities of language. In vii. 47, quoted earlier, he urges himself to watch the courses of the stars ὥσπερ συμπεριθέοντα, 'as if you were running with them' (cf. 'currit' in Seneca).[81] Thus Marcus' eyes are on the heavens, but his feet are grounded in mortality and pessimism.

The imagined address to Marcia by her father Cremutius also includes some themes which recall Marcus without any deeper resemblance. The paternal authority forbids further mourning and assures her of Metilius' well-being; he also expatiates on his improved historical insight, being now apprised of all past and future events (26. 4).[82] Not only does Cremutius contemplate the cosmos, he even deigns to look back at earth. As Seneca pointedly phrases it, 'iuvat enim ex alto relicta despicere' ('It is delightful to look down on what one has left behind', 25. 2). Indeed, the shade shows a somewhat morbid delight in the future changes and devastation which time will bring to pass in the world he has left (25. 6, especially 'alibi hiatibus vastis subducet urbes, tremoribus quatiet, et ex infimo pestilentiae halitus mittet', etc.). He also anticipates the culmination, at the end of the world-cycle, when the souls themselves 'will be transformed into our former elements' (26. 7). This theme, central to Marcus' thought, receives only a passing allusion in Seneca, as his consolatory purpose makes natural. Almost inevitably, Seneca concentrates on the *survival* of Metilius. None the less, Marcus is closer to Seneca than to Lucan. There are affinities between Cremutius' delight in the vastness of his historical panorama and Marcus' retrospectives across time: 'ruitura regna et magnarum urbium lapsus' (26.5) are philosophic themes as well as historical set pieces.[83] But Marcus' view

---

[81] See parallels in Gataker, and in R. M. Jones, *CPh* 21 (1926) 97 ff. It seems plausible that Marcus here echoes the myth of Plato's *Phaedrus*, with its celestial panorama (esp. 247–8); for his knowledge of that work see esp. Fronto's *Erotikos* (i. 20 ff., esp. 32 and 42).

[82] See my remarks in ch. IV 5 (i) above on the use of this topos in *Med.* xi. 1.

[83] See above, ch. III n. 82 on the death of cities. See also Aesch. *Sept.* 287–368; Virg. *Geo.* ii. 498; in historiography, Polyb. ii. 56. 10–13 (on Phylarchus), xxiii. 10–11 (Livy xl. 3. 3 ff.), xxxix. 2; F. W. Walbank, *JHS* 48 (1938) 55–68; id., *Polybius* (Berkeley and Los Angeles 1972) 39; Ogilvie on Livy i. 29, ii. 33. 8; Tac. *Ann.* iv. 32 'ingentia illi bella, expugnationes urbium, fusos captosque reges'. In other genres, Sen. *Ep.* 91; Lucian,

of human society is considerably more jaundiced (iv. 48; vii. 48, etc.), and his treatment of the theme of change in this world, while less cataclysmic, is more poignant.

It would be unjust to the variety and vivacity of Seneca's works to suppose the climax of the *ad Marciam* to embody his settled views on death and survival. Elsewhere his confidence in the afterlife is more temperate and in many ways more moving.[84] Yet his general attitude, while not dogmatic, seems to incline toward greater confidence and more imaginative optimism about posthumous survival than we find anywhere in the *Meditations*. It could also be shown that this optimism is accompanied by more ambitious claims for the powers of human reason, as aided by and conversant with God (*Ep.* 31. 9 ff.; 41. 4 ff., *et al.*).[85] Here too he may be used to illuminate by contrast the pessimism of Marcus Aurelius.

Charon 23. For cataclysms in Senecan tragedy see *Thy.* 830–5, with Tarrant's note; *Tro.* 386–92; D. and E. Henry, *The Mask of Power* (Warminster 1985) ch. 2. For Lucan's use of the theme see M. Lapidge, *Hermes* 107 (1979) 344–70.

[84] See further Pohlenz, loc. cit. (n. 75); also H. MacL. Currie, in D. R. Dudley (ed.), *Neronians and Flavians* (London 1972) 34 ff.

[85] See e.g. Sen. *Ep.* 73. 16 'deus ad homines venit, immo quod est propius, in homines venit: nulla sine deo mens bona est' (though what follows raises some doubt as to whether Seneca really means more than the divine spark which is in all men; for such ambiguity see ch. v n. 102). See also *Ep.* 41. 1–2 (daemon language). In general, see J. N. Sevenster, *Paul and Seneca* (Leiden 1961) 89, 128–9; Dihle, *The Theory of Will in Classical Antiquity* ch. 6.

Envoi

uno itinere non potest pervenire ad tam grande
secretum.

(Symmachus, *Relationes* iii. 10)

Justin Martyr in the opening chapters of his *Dialogue*
recounts to the Jew Trypho the narrative of his spiritual
progress, in an episode which, as has often been recognised,[1]
offers a paradigm of the status and the limitations of philosophy
in the second century AD. Trypho greets him as a philosopher
and expects to learn something of profit from him, 'for do not the
philosophers turn every discourse on God? Do not questions
continually arise to them about his unity and providence? Is this
not truly the task of philosophy, to investigate the deity?' (ch. 1.
3). Justin answers that this is indeed so, but many philosophers
(he means the Stoics) pay no attention to the question whether
God cares for us individually, and even deny it, with woeful
consequences to morality and happiness. Others assert that the
soul is immortal and immaterial and consequently needs
nothing from God.

Justin goes on to describe his quest for philosophic truth in
terms which significantly echo the 'search' of Socrates for one
wiser than himself (Pl. *Ap.* 20e–23b). Whereas Socrates questioned the practitioners of various professions about their
subjects and concluded that their expertise was limited and no
true wisdom, Justin has tried the teachings of various philosophic schools in turn,[2] finding Platonism the most satisfying,
but was finally persuaded by a conversation with a mysterious
old man in a secluded spot by the sea that his faith in Plato's
philosophy was ill-founded, and that long before the Greek
thinkers, there were men

who spoke by the Divine Spirit, and foretold events which would take

---

[1] See esp. N. Hyldahl, *Philosophie und Christentum: Eine Interpretation der Einleitung zum Dialog Justins* (Copenhagen 1966).

[2] For such circuits see Galen v 41–2 Kühn; ps.-Clement, *Recogn.* 1. 1; Nock, *Essays* 475 n. 41 (cf. ibid. n. 37). Cf. and contrast the attitude of Lucian, *Menippus* 3 ff., etc.; see Chadwick, *Early Christian Thought* 132 n. 56.

place and which are now taking place. They are called prophets. These
alone both saw and announced the truth to men, neither reverencing
nor fearing any man, nor influenced by any desire for glory . . .

. . . Their
writings are still extant, and he who has read them is very much helped
to know about the beginnings and the end and those things which the
philosopher ought to know, if he only trusts in them. For they did not
use demonstration in their treatises, since they were witnesses worthy
of belief, of truth beyond all demonstration. [There follows a reference
to the evidence of prophecies and miracles, topics of which the
apologists make much.[3]] But pray [the old man tells Justin] that above
all things the gates of light shall be opened to you. For these things (i.e.
the nature of the soul and God) cannot be perceived or understood by
all, but only by the man to whom God and his Christ have imparted
understanding.[4] When he had spoken these and many other things
which there is no time for mentioning at present, he went away bidding
me attend to them, and I have not seen him since. But immediately a
flame was kindled in my heart (πῦρ ἐν τῇ ψυχῇ ἀνήφθη[5]), and a love of
the prophets and of those men who are friends of Christ possessed me.
And as I spoke his words over again to myself, I found this philosophy
to be a source of safety and profit.[6] So it was that for these reasons I
became a lover of wisdom. Moreover, I would wish that all, making a
resolution similar to my own, would not keep themselves away from
the words of the Saviour. For they possess a terrible power in
themselves, and are sufficient to inspire[7] those who turn aside from the
path of rectitude with awe, while the sweetest rest (ἀναπαύσις[8]) is
afforded those who practise them (ἐκμελετῶσιν αὐτούς[9]). (Dial. 7. 1–8.
2)

---

[3] Cf. esp. Orig. Cels. i. 2 and vii. 1–26 with Chadwick's notes.
[4] Compare Dial. 92. 1 (grace needed to understand Scripture).
[5] Surely another Platonic echo: cf. Pl. (?) Ep. vii. 341cd (cf. ch. 1 n. 110).
[6] For the description of Christianity as a 'philosophy' cf. Melito fr. 1 Hall (= Euseb.
Hist. Eccl. iv. 26. 7); Miltiades, author of a work 'in defence of the Christian philosophy'
referred to by Euseb. ibid. v. 17. 5; Tatian, Or. ad Gr. 35; Tert. Ap. 46 with Mayor's notes;
Min. Fel. Oct. 4. 4. Galen, by contrast, called the Christians 'people who . . . draw their
faith from parables, and yet in discipline and self-control, in their keen pursuit of justice,
have attained a pitch not inferior to that of genuine philosophers' (Arabic text tr. by R.
Walzer, Galen on Jews and Christians (Oxford 1949) 15; S. Benko, ANRW ii. 23. 2 (1980)
1098–1100). See also Proclus, in Rem Publ. ii. 255. 21 Kroll, describing Christianity as
'the barbarian theosophy'.
[7] Cf. the material on philosphic conversion quoted or cited above in ch. III 3 (esp. n.
35; also ch. II n. 33).
[8] On this ideal see further Med. v. 1, v. 4 (cf. iv. 31 προσαναπαύεσθαι), v. 10. 2, vi. 12
(the close parallel in Sen. Ep. 103. 4 does not have the same note of exhaustion that we
find in Marcus' words). See also Betz's preface to Plut. Tranq. in id. (ed.), Plutarch's
Ethical Writings 198–208, esp. 206–7.
[9] On the meanings of μελετάω and the like, see LSJ s.v.; D. A. Russell, Greek

Justin's exhortation is greeted with some scepticism by the traditionalist Jews, and Trypho declares that, while he admires Justin's zeal in the study of the divine,

it would be better for you still to abide in the philosophy of Plato, or of some other man, cultivating endurance, self-control, or moderation, than to be deceived by false words and follow the opinions of men of no reputation. For if you remain in that mode of philosophy and live blamelessly, a hope of a better destiny might remain for you, but when you have forsaken God and set your confidence in man, what salvation still remains? (8. 3)[10]

The remainder of the dialogue moves more in the realm of Old Testament typological interpretation than in that of Greek philosophy, as Justin attempts to show that Christians are the chosen race and that the worship of God needs more than orthodox obedience to the Mosaic Law.

In this episode, the whole of which is regrettably too long to quote, we find much that is relevant to our main themes. The centrally religious orientation of philosphy is clear from Trypho's expectations when he meets the author, from the old man's opening exchange with Justin (not quoted), and from Justin's own description of his new convictions. The teachings of Stoicism are concisely sketched, and Justin focuses on two areas which had traditionally received violent criticism: the equivocation over the extent and detailed workings of divine Providence,[11] and the doctrine of cycles which repeat themselves eternally in every respect.[12] The status of philosophers as 'truly holy men' (2. 1 ὅσιοι ὡς ἀληθῶς οὗτοί εἰσιν) is conceded, but qualified by far-reaching criticisms of their acceptance of doctrines inherited from their teachers (one thinks of the notorious Pythagorean *ipse dixit* and of the veneration of Epicureans for the master),[13] their eagerness for payment,

---

Declamation (Cambridge 1983) 10 f. The basic sense is to exercise oneself in, to rehearse or practise something, and hence to recite (e.g. a declamation). Here again the rhetorical technique serves a higher philosophic or religious end. Cf. the use of the word in the passages quoted in ch. 1, pp. 17, 19 above; Rabbow, *Seelenführung* 338.

[10] Philosophy gives (or promises) σωτηρία; see Nock, *Essays* 78 n. 115, 121 ff. See further *TDNT* vii. 965 ff., esp. 968–9 on Epictetus and others.

[11] Cf. Pease on Cic. *ND* ii. 164, iii. 86; Plut. *Sto. Rep.* 31–7, 1048c–51d.

[12] Cf. Pease on Cic. *ND* ii. 51; Orig. *Cels.* v. 21, etc.

[13] Pease on Cic. *ND* i. 10 (Pythagoreans and *ipse dixit*); i. 43 (Epicureans). Note also the commemoration of Epicurus' birthday (Cic. *Fin.* ii. 101).

hypocritically concealed,[14] and their unnecessary involvement with subsidiary propaedeutic studies such as music, astronomy, geometry, and the like.[15] Above all Justin is a man of his time in his concentration upon the limits and incapacity of human reason, even when it is the reasoning genius of Plato. The final, crucial, galvanising factor must be something outside, God-given: for the Jews, the Law revealed to Moses; for the Christians, the revelation through Christ. Yet in the face of his audience's incredulity Justin also seeks to give a rational, argumentative account, 'if you are prepared to accept a λόγον about this' (9. 1).[16] Most of the Dialogue is devoted to this attempt to prove the ineffable and incommunicable. Here, as in the work of Marcus Aurelius, the combination of philosophic exposition and persuasive eloquence can take one only so far: there must be a final imaginative leap in the dark. Belief is not something the honest mind can buy or inherit or obtain. Yet it is characteristic of most ancient philosophy of religion, and perhaps especially of Stoicism, that it elevates the reasoning man as its ideal, and tries to establish and communicate evidence of deity, to prove the rational order of the world. Hence the vehemence with which Graeco-Roman thinkers abuse Christianity for its exaltation of faith, its denigration of reason.[17] By contrast, Christian writers could mock the philosophers for their lack of *divina auctoritas* (Lact. *Inst.* iii. 15. 2–5; August. *Civ. Dei* xviii. 41). The exaggerated claims made in this polemic for the philosophic integrity of pagan religion, for its

[14] The criticism is rooted in Plato's attacks on the sophists: cf. Dodds and Irwin on Pl. *Grg.* 519cd; G. B. Kerferd, *The Sophistic Movement* (Cambridge 1981) 24 ff. It frequently recurs: see e.g. Caesar in Plut. *Cat. Min.* 52. 6 ff.; Lucian, *Piscator* 34–6. Similar is the sardonic pronouncement of the Emperor Pius, *Dig.* 27. 1. 6. 7: 'I feel sure that those who are wealthy will voluntarily provide financial assistance to their cities. And if they quibble about the size of their estate, they will thereby make it quite clear that they are not philosophers' (for similar pronouncements see Millar, *The Emperor in the Roman World* 501).

[15] See esp. Stuckelberger on Sen. *Ep.* 88 *passim*; Kindstrand on Bion (?) fr. 3. For later transformations of the theme see Philo, *de Congressu*, ed. M. Alexandre (Paris 1967) editor's introd., 27 ff.; Clem. Al. *Strom.* i. 28 ff., vi. 93; August. *Conf.* iv. 28 ff.; *Ep.* 101; Fuchs, *RLAC* iii. 368 ff.; A. Dihle, Fond. Hardt Entret. xxxii (Geneva 1986) 185 ff.

[16] For the multiple complexities of λόγος in earlier literature and thought see LSJ and W. K. C. Guthrie, *History of Greek Philosophy* i (Cambridge 1962) 419 ff. For this period and the sense here see Arndt–Gingrich s.v., esp. 1 β–γ.

[17] Cf. Walzer (n. 6) 48–56; Dodds, *Pagan and Christian* 120 ff.; Chadwick, *Early Christian Thought* ch. 1, esp. 24–5. For modern studies see R. Swinburne, *Faith and Reason* (Oxford 1981); J. Hick (ed.) *Faith and the Philosophers* (London 1964); *ODCC* s.v. 'Faith'.

sheer rationality, tend to obscure a more fundamental similarity in the questions both sides sought to answer.

In his brilliant survey of the state of pagan religious beliefs in the first and second centuries, A.D. Nock concentrated on the change, no doubt partly social and political in origin, in intellectual attitudes to religion, on the shift in religious needs and expectations which, as he saw it, led men to welcome 'the inspired teacher and the divine revelation', the Chaldean and Clarian oracles, the influence of Oriental cults, and the rise of magic and of neo-Platonic theurgy.[18]

Philosophy became more and more linked to piety and revelations, and less averse from magic . . . Hard thinking and dialectics had a place in this philosophy, but much of its appeal was to the heart and to the soul rather than to the head. In influential circles an inturned piety which offered to the supreme being 'the sacrifice of reason', and an ascetic salvationism overshadowed Greek self-sufficiency.[19]

This picture has been profoundly influential,[20] but the antithesis is too forced. We may continue to rate the world of astrological magic[21] and curses as inferior intellectually to the system of a Plotinus, while recognising that the presuppositions of Plotinus, as of Plato, are not immune to questioning and criticism. We may concede that Seneca or indeed Paul appeals to heart as well as to head; but so did Plato. In the *Gorgias* Socrates concludes the statement of his profoundest beliefs with a myth of the soul's fate in the afterlife: he accepts that his audience may scoff at this as an old wives' tale (527a5), but passionately asserts: 'You may think this is a μῦθον, but I take it as a λόγον. For I shall tell you what I am about to tell you as what

---

[18] *Cambridge Ancient History* xii. 409–49, esp. 438–49. Cf. *CAH* x. 465–511.

[19] *CAH* xii. 441. Here Nock cites his own essays in *Gnomon* 12 (1936) 605 ff. = *Essays* 444 ff., and *JRS* 27 (1937) 112 = *Essays* 456.

[20] Especially on Dodds in *Pagan and Christian*; for a sustained critique on a number of fronts see the works of Peter Brown, esp. *Religion and Society in the Age of St Augustine* (London 1972) 74–81 (cf. 17, 119 ff.), and *The Making of Late Antiquity* (Cambridge, Mass. 1978) 4–11, 15, 21, 27–8, etc. See also ch. v nn. 9 and 61–2 above.

[21] The absence from the *Meditations* of any reference to astrology or the power of the stars is noteworthy (and note the disparaging reference to Chaldeans in iii. 3). Almost all of the emperors, and many others, believed in or showed interest in astrology (though there were occasional purges): see MacMullen, *Enemies of the Roman Order* 128–33 and *Anc. Soc.* 2 (1971) 105–16; Mayor's *Juvenal*, index s.v. 'Astrology'; Liebeschuetz, *Continuity and Change* 123; Wallace-Hadrill, *Suetonius* 194–7.

is *true*' (*Grg.* 523a).[22] There are some things which even Socrates must take on faith. The *Gorgias*, like Justin's *Dialogue*, ends with the listeners moved (cf. *Grg.* 513c4–6)[23] but unconvinced. We may appositely recall Marcus' words: δόγμα γὰρ αὐτῶν τίς μεταβαλεῖ; ('Who can change man's convictions?', ix. 29). Each of us is trapped within his own selfhood.

In another paper Nock wrote 'The historian of religion cannot, however, solve the riddles of the universe'.[24] What can and does legitimately fall within his scope is to study the way in which men of the past have tried to approach a solution of those riddles, and the ways in which they have commented on or criticised each other's attempts, and so to strive for a better understanding of those individual men and also of himself. It is to make a historical and biographical observation, not an evaluation, to comment that Marcus Aurelius seems on the evidence of his work to have set his face deliberately against tendencies known to him in the philosophy and religion of his own day,[25] even though these movements included elements which might well have satisfied or consoled him more effectively than the Stoicism to which his upbringing and his own earlier choices committed him. The Platonism of his time, with its strong sense of dualism and its exaltation of the intellectual quest for religious truth, left its traces on his thought; the eschatological promises of the mysteries and the salvationist cults affected his language and metaphors without being accepted by his intellect; the pursuit of dreams, visions, and oracles which both dominated and gave spiritual strength to an Aristides is attenuated in the religion of Marcus to hesitant expression of questions unsupported by hope. He recapitulated the arguments of his school while often flinching at their rigour. His principles rejected the palliatives which his temperament might have welcomed.

These comments are not intended as denigration of Marcus. He has suffered much in the past from casual or ill-informed

---

[22] See Dodds' notes, and add *Meno* 81a, perhaps *Alc.* 1 130d; *Tim.* 28c, 29b–d, 72d; *Epinomis* 980a.

[23] I follow Irwin's interpretation of this passage, against Dodds. Callicles *is* strangely moved, but remains too angry and set in his own beliefs to respond fully (or, by the end, at all) to Socrates' appeal. His silence at the end of the dialogue signifies not consent but a breakdown of all communication, the failure of dialectic. Socrates is talking in a void.

[24] *Essays* 445.

[25] See above, n. 21, and pp. 158, 180, 211, 217–18, 219, 229.

praise and blame, which sometimes fails to take full account of the complexity of his work. The description 'the last of the Stoics' has occasionally carried with it the implication that he is also the least worth considering. If this study is to serve any useful purpose, I hope that it will encourage others to take Marcus' *Meditations* more seriously as a literary and highly articulate expression of philosophy, and as a statement, however strange or fragmented its form, of a view of human life which may seem unfamiliar or unsympathetic, but which has its own coherence and, like many such systems, its own tragic and undermining limitations.

This is not the place to resume the long-standing debate over the relative merits of Stoicism and Christianity, a traditional comparison which must now appear somewhat restricted in its range.[26] Under the Roman empire of the second century, and within the reign of Marcus Aurelius himself, the apologists[27] who addressed the emperor defended their creed in terms adopted from Greek philosophy; the spirit of the Second Sophistic, its language, its rhetoric, and its polemic, runs strong in the orations of Athenagoras, Justin, and Tatian. Tertullian is an example of a Stoic converted to Christianity; the apology of Melito, Bishop of Sardis, finds its closest stylistic parallels in the Platonist Maximus of Tyre; Tatian's initiation into many mysteries (29. 1) recalls the experiences of Apuleius (*Ap.* 55, *Flor.* 18).[28] It should be obvious that these religious and philosophic movements are influenced by one another, and respond each in their different ways to general human longings and instincts. At the same time there are significant differences which may be insuperable in many cases (including Marcus' own) as a

[26] For worthy comparative studies of this kind see e.g. E. Hatch, *The Influence of Greek Ideas and Usages upon the Christian Church* (London 1907); W. R. Halliday, *The Pagan Background to Early Christianity* (Liverpool 1925). Outstanding for range and detail, but highly indigestible, is J. Stelzenberger, *Die Beziehungen der frühchristlichen Sittenlehre zur Ethik der Stoa* (Munich 1933). See also M. Spanneut, *Le Stoïcisme des Pères de l'Église* (Paris 1957); Nock, 'Early Gentile Christianity and its Hellenistic Background', in *Essays* 49–133 (also published separately, New York 1964); Dodds, *Pagan and Christian* ch. 4. On a more popular level H. Chadwick, in J. Boardman *et al.* (eds.), *The Oxford History of the Classical World* (Oxford 1986) 821–3 says a good deal in short compass.

[27] In general see esp. Chadwick, *Early Christian Thought* ch. 1; Reardon, *Courants littéraires grecs* 275–308. For further bibliography see above, ch. v nn. 30–2.

[28] On Tertullian the final chapters of Barnes, *Tertullian*, entitled 'A Pagan Education' and 'The Christian Sophist', make the point amply and stimulatingly. For possible links between Tertullian and Apuleius see ibid. 256–8.

consequence of education, upbringing, temperament, and all that these entail. Prejudice, inhibitions, snobbery social and intellectual, may all also play their part. No one's judgement is ultimately fair and free. Many Christians might be repelled by the harshness and insensitive dismissal of the softer emotions and virtues which is undeniably present in orthodox Stoicism, and not only in parodies thereof.[29] They also rejected the materialist and impersonal, mechanistic idea of God as inherent in the *mundus*, and the Stoics' anti-individualist conception of the world which saw each man's body and soul as material in a cosmic workshop; and they were shocked by the Stoics' uncompromising determinism. The Stoics on the other hand might criticise the Christian reliance on faith over reason,[30] the dependence of their system on sacred books the interpretation of which was known to be hotly disputed,[31] their insistence on divine revelation as the only key to humanity's prison. Again, they found the incarnation degrading to the concept of God, the resurrection of the flesh both preposterous and disgusting (cf. Acts 17. 32);[32] and they would in all probability have viewed with doubt and unease the Christian emphasis on human imperfectibility and sin.[33] The historian and critic can chart the points of contact and divergence in the two schools, can discern the routes by which the one may have influenced the other, and can point to the prominence of particular doctrines in the authors whom they study; but they should not suppose that the satisfactions and the difficulties of one who lives by and in these beliefs are thus to be finally calculated, or the validity of either world-view disproved. Here only the individual can choose.

[29] Such as Cic. *Mur.* 61 ff. (contrast *Fin.* iv. 74), or Hor. *Sat.* i. 3. 124–42, iii. 3 throughout; Lucian, *saepissime*: see Hall, *Lucian's Satire* 168 ff., 187. See also Addison, *Cato* i. iv. ' 'Tis pride, rank pride, and haughtiness of soul;/I think the Romans call it Stoicism.'

[30] Galen *ap.* Walzer (n. 6) 11, 48–56; Lucian, *Peregr.* 13 (see K. Praechter, 'Skeptische bei Lukian', *Philol.* 51 (1892) 285 ff.); Celsus *ap.* Orig. *Cels.* i. 9; Porphyry, *contra Christianos* fr. 1 and 73 Harnack; Dodds, *Pagan and Christian* 120 f.

[31] See Brunt, 'Marcus Aurelius and the Christians' 516 n. 111.

[32] E.g. Porphyry, *contra Christianos* fr. 92–4 Harnack (whether these passages genuinely come from Porphyry need not be pursued here: see A. Meredith, *ANRW* ii. 23. 2 (1980) 1125 ff.). Cf. Brunt, loc. cit. (n. 31); W. Nestle, *Griechische Studien* (Stuttgart 1948) 597 ff.; H. Chadwick, *HTR* 41 (1948) 83–102. See also van der Horst on ps.-Phocyl. 103–4; and the wide-ranging comparisons between Judaeo-Christian and Hellenic thought in Dihle, *The Theory of Will in Classical Antiquity* (Berkeley and Los Angeles 1982) esp. ch. 1, and e.g. pp. 71–7.

[33] Cf. *ODCC* s.v. 'Sin', and works cited there. On pagan concepts of sin see above all K. Latte, *Kleine Schriften* (Munich 1968) 3–35.

Select Bibliography

A. EDITIONS AND TRANSLATIONS OF THE *MEDITATIONS*

M. Antonini Imperatoris de Rebus Suis . . . Libri xii commentario perpetuo explicati atque illustrati studio . . . Thomae Gatakeri (Cambridge 1652). Irreplaceable treasure-house of learning, but hard to use.

The Fourth Book of the Meditations of M. Aurelius, ed. Hastings Crossley (London 1882).

M. Antonini Imperatoris in Semet Ipsum Libri xii, rec. H. Schenkl (Leipzig 1913).

The Communings with Himself of M. Aurelius Antoninus, ed. and tr. by C. R. Haines (Loeb Classical Library, Harvard 1916). Good literal translation with valuable if unsystematic notes and good indexes.

The Meditations of the Emperor M. Antoninus, ed. with trans. and comm. by A. S. L. Farquharson (Oxford 1944). Standard and sympathetic commentary, though dated in approach and rather inconveniently arranged.

Kaiser Marc Aurel, Wege zu sich selbst . . ., ed. W. Theiler (Zurich 1951). Compressed and interesting introduction; text and German translation; laconic but often original notes. No indexes.

M. Aureli Antonini ad Se Ipsum Libri xii, ed. J. Dalfen (Leipzig 1979; 2nd edn. 1987). Replaces Schenkl's edition in the Teubner series, and like his is most valuable for the complete index verborum. Text sound but not substantially improved (too many passages bracketed as interpolations); useful illustrative passages. (See F. H. Sandbach, *CR* 31 (1981) 188–9.)

For fuller lists see esp. Dalfen's edition, pp. xxvii–xxxi, xl; also Klein (ed.), *Marc Aurel* (cited below) 503–5. I have tried to inspect all those which they mention, though some were inaccessible to me. Few offer more than brief or derivative notes. For serious study of the *Meditations* the essential texts are those cited here.

The *Meditations* have often been translated: the earliest English translation was by Meric Casaubon (London 1634, dedicated to Archbishop Laud; reprinted in Everyman's Library, London 1906). The editions by Haines, Farquharson, and Theiler include translations. Also noteworthy are those by J. Jackson (Oxford 1906) and George Long (London 1862, often reprinted), which Matthew Arnold singled out for praise in his essay. Farquharson's translation is shortly to be reissued (without text) in the World's Classics series (Oxford University Press), with a new introduction and notes by myself.

In the text and notes I have sometimes adapted or directly quoted from the translations by Haines and Farquharson.

B. COMMENTARIES ON OTHER RELEVANT AUTHORS

I omit from this list most standard commentaries on well-known works, to which I refer in the conventional manner (e.g. 'see Nisbet–Hubbard on Hor. *Odes* i. 1. 1'). I include here more obscure or specialised commentaries which deal with works contemporary with the *Meditations* or relevant for other reasons.

Billerbeck, M., *Epiktet vom Kynismus* (iii. 22) (Philosophia Antiqua Monograph Series, Leiden 1978).
Düring, I., *Aristotle's* Protrepticus (Stud. Graec. et Latina Gothoburgensia 12, Göteborg 1961).
Hillyard, B. P., *Plutarch*, de Audiendo (New York 1981).
Horst, P. W. van der, *The* Sentences *of Pseudo-Phocylides* (Leiden 1978).
Kindstrand, J. F., *Bion of Borysthenes* (Uppsala 1976).
Mayor, J. E. B., *Tertullian's* Apology (Cambridge 1917).
Nock, A. D., *Sallustius:* Concerning the Gods and the Universe (Cambridge 1926, repr. Hildesheim 1966).
Slings, S. R., *A Commentary on the Platonic* Clitophon (Amsterdam 1981).
Stuckelberger, A., *Senecas 88. Brief über Wert und Unwert der freien Künste* (Heidelberg 1965).
Valgiglio, E., *Plutarch*, de Audiendis Poetis (Turin 1973).
Waszink, J. H., *Tertullian*, de Anima (Amsterdam 1947).

I wish also to record here the help I have gained from consulting a number of unpublished Oxford D.Phil. theses which are occasionally cited in my notes:

Abbot, N. J. S., 'Commentary on Ps.-Plutarch *de Liberis Educandis*' (1980).
Geiger, T., 'Commentary on Plutarch, *Cato Minor*' (1971).
Moles, J. L., 'Commentary on Plutarch, *Brutus*' (1979).

C. SECONDARY AND SCHOLARLY STUDIES

I include here only works which have proved regularly useful. For fuller lists on various subjects relating to Marcus Aurelius and his reign see esp. Klein (ed.), *Marc Aurel* 503–29; Stanton's *ANRW* survey, cited below; A. Garzetti, *From Tiberius to the Antonines* (Eng. tr. London 1974) 708–25, 768–73; and, on the text, Dalfen's Teubner edition, pp. xxxv–xl. More detailed bibliography on many topics is given in the footnotes.

Works listed here and regularly cited in the notes are often referred to by author's name alone (where unambiguous) or by a shortened title.

Anderson, G., *Philostratus: Biography and Belles-Lettres in the Third Century AD* (London, Sydney, and New Hampshire 1986).
Arnold, E. V., *Roman Stoicism* (London 1911).
Arnold, M., 'Marcus Aurelius', in *Essays in Criticism: First Series* (London 1865).
Babut, D., *La Religion des philosophes grecs* (Paris 1974).
Barnes, T. D., 'Legislation against the Christians', *JRS* 58 (1968) 32–50.
—— *Tertullian: A Literary and Historical Study* (Oxford 1971).
—— *The Sources of the* Historia Augusta (Collection Latomus vol. 155, Brussels 1978).
Beaujeu, J., *La Religion romaine à l'apogée de l'empire* i (Paris 1955).
Behr, C. A., *Aelius Aristides and the* Sacred Tales (Amsterdam 1968).
Beranger, J., *Recherches sur l'aspect idéologique du principat* (Basle 1953).
Betz, H. D. (ed.), *Plutarch's Ethical Writings and Early Christian Literature* (Studia ad Corpus Hellenisticum Novi Testamenti iv, Leiden 1978).
—— (ed.), *Plutarch's Theological Writings and Early Christian Literature*, (Studia ad Corpus Hellenisticum Novi Testamenti iii, Leiden 1975).
Birley, A. R., *Marcus Aurelius* (London 1966; revised and repaginated edn., London 1987).
Bonhöffer, A., *Epictet und die Stoa* (Stuttgart 1890).
—— *Die Ethik des Stoikers Epictet* (Stuttgart 1894).
—— *Epiktet und das Neue Testament* (RVV 10, Giessen 1911).
Boulanger, A., *Aelius Aristide et la sophistique* (Paris 1923).
Bowersock, G. W., *Greek Sophists in the Roman Empire* (Oxford 1969).
—— (ed.), *Approaches to the Second Sophistic* (Pennsylvania 1974).
Bowie, E. L., 'The Greeks and their Past in the Second Sophistic', *Past and Present* 46 (1970) 3–41; also in M. I. Finley (ed.), *Studies in Ancient Society* (London 1974) 166–209.
—— 'The Importance of Sophists', in J. J. Winkler and G. Williams (eds.), *Later Greek Literature* (= *YCS* 27 (1982)) 29–59.
Bramble, J. C., *Persius and the Programmatic Satire* (Cambridge 1974).
Brenk, F. W., *In Mist Apparelled: Religious Themes in Plutarch's* Moralia and Lives (Mnemos. Suppl. 48, Leiden 1977).
Breithaupt, G., *De M. Aurelii Antonini commentariis quaestiones selectae* (diss. Göttingen 1913).
Brock, M. D., *Studies in Fronto and his Age* (Cambridge 1911).
Brown, P., *Religion and Society in the Age of St Augustine* (London 1972).

Brunt, P. A., 'Marcus Aurelius in his *Meditations*', *JRS* 64 (1974) 1–20.
—— 'Stoicism and the Principate' *PBSR* 43 (1975) 7–39.
—— 'From Epictetus to Arrian', *Athen.* NS 55 (1977) 19–48.
—— 'Marcus Aurelius and the Christians', in C. Deroux (ed.), *Studies in Latin Literature and Roman History* i (Brussels 1979) 483–520.
Bushnell, C. C., 'Comparisons and Illustrations in the τὰ πρὸς ἑαυτόν', *TAPA* 36 (1905) xxix–xxx.
—— 'A Classification . . . of the Comparisons and Illustrations in the *Meditations* of Marcus Aurelius Antoninus', *TAPA* 39 (1908) xxix–xxxi.
Chadwick, H. (tr. with notes), *Origen: contra Celsum* (Cambridge 1953; 2nd edn. 1965).
—— *Early Christian Thought and the Classical Tradition* (Oxford 1966).
Champlin, E. H., 'The Chronology of Fronto', *JRS* 64 (1974) 136–59.
—— *Fronto and Antonine Rome* (Cambridge, Mass. 1980).
Cherniss, H., 'Ancient Forms of Philosophic Discourse', in id., *Selected Papers*, ed. L. Taran (Leiden 1977) 14–35.
Colardeau, T., *Études sur Épictète* (diss. Paris 1903).
Dalfen, J. *Formgeschichtliche Untersuchungen zu den Selbstbetrachtungen Marc Aurels* (diss. Munich 1967).
D'Alton, J. F., *Roman Literary Theory and Criticism* (London 1931).
Dihle, A., 'Ethik', in *RLAC* vi (1966) 646–796.
—— *The Theory of Will in Classical Antiquity* (Berkeley and Los Angeles 1982).
Dill, S., *Roman Society from Nero to Marcus Aurelius* (London 1904).
Dillon J., *The Middle Platonists* (London 1977).
Dodds, E. R., *The Greeks and the Irrational* (Berkeley and Los Angeles 1951).
—— *Pagan and Christian in an Age of Anxiety* (Cambridge 1965).
—— *The Ancient Concept of Progress and Other Essays . . .* (Oxford 1973).
Farquharson, A. S. L., *Marcus Aurelius: His Life and his World* (Oxford 1951).
Festugière, A. J., *La Révélation d'Hermès Trismégiste* i–iv (Paris 1944–54).
—— *Personal Religion among the Greeks* (Berkeley and Los Angeles 1954).
Geytenbeek, A. C. van, *Musonius Rufus and Greek Diatribe* (Assen 1963).
Gibbon, E., *The Decline and Fall of the Roman Empire*, ed. J. B. Bury (London 1896) vol. ii.
Griffin, M. T., *Seneca: A Philosopher in Politics* (Oxford 1976).
—— *Nero: The End of a Dynasty* (London 1984).
—— 'Philosophy, Cato and Roman Suicide', *G&R* 33 (1986) 64–77, 192–202.
Hadot, I., *Seneca und die griechisch-römische Tradition der Seelenleitung* (Berlin 1969).

Hadot, P., *Exercises spirituels et philosophie antique* (Paris 1981).

Halbauer, O., *De Diatribis Epicteti* (diss. Leipzig 1911).

Hall, J., *Lucian's Satire* (New York 1981).

Hoven, R., *Stoïcisme et stoïciens face au problème de l'au-delà* (Liège 1971).

Ingenkamp, H. G., *Plutarchs Schriften über die Heilung der Seele* (*Hypomnemata* Bd. 34, Göttingen 1971).

Jones, C. P., *Plutarch and Rome* (Oxford 1971).

—— *The Roman World of Dio Chrysostom* (Cambridge, Mass. 1978).

—— *Culture and Society in Lucian* (Cambridge, Mass. 1986).

Kassel, R., *Untersuchungen zur griechischen und römischen Konsolationsliteratur* (*Zetemata* 18, Munich 1958).

Kennedy, G., *The Art of Persuasion in Greece* (Princeton, NJ, 1963).

—— *The Art of Rhetoric in the Roman World* (Princeton, NJ, 1972).

Klein, R. (ed.), *Marc Aurel* (Wege der Forschung 550, Darmstadt 1979).

Labriolle, P. de, *La Réaction païenne* (Paris 1934; 2nd edn. 1948).

Lagrange, R. P., 'La Philosophie religieuse d'Épictète et le christianisme', *Revue Biblique* NS 9 (1912) 5–21, 192–212.

Lameere, W., 'L'Empereur Marc Aurèle', in J. Preaux (ed.), *Problèmes d'histoire du christianisme* v (Brussels 1974–5), 5–54.

Lane Fox, R., *Pagans and Christians in the Mediterranean World from the Second Century AD to the Conversion of Constantine* (Harmondsworth 1986).

Leibeschuetz, J. H. W. G., *Continuity and Change in Roman Religion* (Oxford 1979).

Long, A. A., *Hellenistic Philosophy* (London 1974).

—— 'Epictetus and Marcus Aurelius', in T. J. Luce (ed.), *Ancient Writers: Greece and Rome* ii (New York 1982) 985–1002.

—— (ed.), *Problems in Stoicism* (London 1971).

Lutz, C. E., 'Musonius Rufus: the Roman Socrates', *YCS* 10 (1947) 3–147.

McGann, M. J., *Studies in Horace's First Book of Epistles* (Brussels 1969).

Macleod, C. W., *Collected Essays* (Oxford 1983).

MacMullen, R., *Enemies of the Roman Order* (Cambridge, Mass. 1966).

—— *Paganism in the Roman Empire* (New Haven, Conn. 1981).

Malingrey, A. M., '*Philosophia*': *Étude d'un groupe de mots dans la littérature grecque* (Études et Commentaries 40, Paris 1961).

Meredith, A., 'Asceticism—Christian and Greek', *JTS* NS 27 (1976) 313–32.

Millar, F., *A Study of Cassius Dio* (Oxford 1965).

—— 'Epictetus and the Imperial Court', *JRS* 55 (1965) 141–8.

—— *The Emperor in the Roman World* (London 1977).

Misch, G., *A History of Autobiography in Antiquity* (Eng. tr. by Misch and E. W. Dickes, London 1950).

Moles, J. L., 'The Career and Conversion of Dio Chrysostom', *JHS* 98 (1978) 79–100.

Momigliano, A., *The Development of Greek Biography* (Cambridge, Mass. 1971).

—— *Alien Wisdom: The Limits of Hellenization* (Cambridge 1975).

Murray, O., Review-discussion of MacMullen, *Enemies of the Roman Order*, in *JRS* 59 (1969) 261–5.

Nock, A. D., *Conversion* (Oxford 1933).

—— *Essays on Religion and The Ancient World*, ed. Z. Stewart (Oxford 1972).

Norden, E., *Die Antike Kunstprosa* (Leipzig and Berlin 1909).

Oliver, J. H., *The Civic Tradition and Roman Athens* (Baltimore 1983).

Pohlenz, M., *Die Stoa* (3rd edn., Göttingen 1964).

—— *Kleine Schriften*, ed. H. Dörrie (Hildesheim 1965).

Rabbow, P., *Seelenführung* (Munich 1954).

Reardon, B. P., *Courants littéraires grecs des IIe et IIIe siècles après J.-C.* (Paris 1971).

Renan, E., *Marc Aurèle et la fin du monde antique* (= *Hist. des origines du Christianisme* vii) (Paris 1882; Eng. tr. London, n.d.).

Rendall, G. H., article on 'Marcus Aurelius' in *ERE* viii. 409–15.

Rist, J. M. *Stoic Philosophy* (Cambridge 1969).

—— 'Are you a Stoic? The Case of Marcus Aurelius', in B. F. Meyer and E. P. Saunders (eds.), *Jewish and Christian Self-Definition*, iii. *Self-Definition in the Graeco-Roman World* (London 1982).

Russell, D. A., *Plutarch* (London 1973).

Schadewaldt, W., *Monolog und Selbstgespräch* (Berlin 1926).

Schekira, R., *De Imperatoris M. Aurelii Antonini Librorum Sermone Quaestiones Philosophicae et Grammaticae* (diss. Greifswald 1919).

Sedgwick, H. D., *Marcus Aurelius: A Biography* (Oxford 1921).

Stanton, G. R., 'The Cosmopolitan Ideas of Epictetus and Marcus Aurelius', *Phronesis* 13 (1968) 183–95.

—— 'Marcus Aurelius, Emperor and Philosopher', *Historia* 18 (1969) 570–87, reprinted (in German) in Klein (ed.), *Marc Aurel* 359–88.

—— 'Marcus Aurelius, Lucius Verus and Commodus', in *ANRW* ii. 5 (Berlin and New York 1975) 478–549.

Stertz, S. A., 'Marcus Aurelius as Ideal Emperor in Late Antique Greek Thought', *CW* 70 (1977) 433–9.

Striller, F., 'De Stoicorum Studiis Rhetoricis', *Breslauer philol. Abhandlungen* I (1886).

Syme, R., *Tacitus* (Oxford 1958).

Wallace-Hadrill, A., 'The Emperor and his Virtues', *Historia* 30 (1981) 298–323.

—— '*Civilis Princeps*: Between Citizen and King', *JRS* 72 (1982) 32–48.

—— *Suetonius: The Scholar and his Caesars* (London 1983).
Whitehorne, J. E. G., 'Was Marcus Aurelius a Hypochondriac?',
  Latomus 36 (1977) 413–21.
Williams, W., 'Individuality in the Imperial Constitutions: Hadrian
  and the Antonines', *JRS* 66 (1976) 67–83.
Wirszubski, C., *Libertas as a Political Idea at Rome* (Cambridge 1950).
Zilliacus, H., *De Elocutione M. Aurelii Imperatoris Quaestiones Syntacticae*
  (Helsingfors and Leipzig 1936).

NOTE: I regret that I have been unable to take account of two
important publications which appeared while my own book was in
proof: M. P. J. van den Hout's expanded revision of his text of Fronto
(Leipzig 1988), and L. Holford-Strevens, *Aulus Gellius* (London 1988)
which includes much of relevance to my second chapter in particular.

Index of Passages of the *Meditations* Discussed

This index covers all substantial discussions of passages, and a selection of more casual references; on the whole it excludes pages or footnotes in which a passage is merely cited as one in a list of examples, without particular comment.

Index of Subject-matter

This index covers the text of the book but includes only more substantial or significant items treated in the footnotes. Proper names are included only when the entry seems likely to be of use to the reader. The names of modern scholars are deliberately excluded.

278   INDEX OF SUBJECT-MATTER

Dreams 195-200
Drusus (the elder) 71

Egnatius Celer, P. 74
elogia 51, 112
Emperor, expectations of 78-9, 111-12
Encomium 55
see also Kings and Rulers, praise of
End of World 254-5
Epictetus 7, 8, 25, 30, 33, 34, 36, 38,
    43 n., 57, 58, 65, 76, 86, 95, 97, 98,
    104, 105, 119, 165, 167, 204, 210,
    Ch. VI *passim*
contrasted with Marcus Aurelius
    Ch. VI *passim*, esp. 225-31, 239
on reading 26
on self-discipline 17
Epicurean writers in Latin 4
Epicurus, Epicureanism 24-5, 57, 59,
    159-61, 179 n., 189, 209, 210,
    243 n., 244
Epigrams 128-31, 206
see also Aphorisms
Epitaphs 128
Euphrates 58, 73, 80
Euripides 15, 185, 213
Evil, existence of 233-4
Exclamations 134-5
Exempla 25, 55-9, 140
Exorcism 181, 184-6

Fabianus 41, 58, 72
Fadius Gallus, M. 60
Fannia 62
Fannius, C. 63
Faustina xv, xvi, 45, 117
Favorinus 87, 108
Flattery 99, 122
Food 117-19
Freedom as philosophic ideal 76, 166,
    174-5, 229-30
Freedom of speech 100
Friendship 99, 121-3, 179 n.
Friendship with God 250
Fronto, M. Cornelius xvii, 5, 29, 81, 84,
    85, 94, 98, 105-6, 107, 113-14,
    116-23 *passim*, 127, 195-6, 198-9,
    213, 254 n.
Funeral speeches 51-3, 112

Galen 23, 86, 87, 120, 257 n.
Games, gladiatorial 98, 117
Gellius, Aulus 41, 88
Glycon (epigrammatist) 129

God, assimilation to (ὁμοίωσις θεῷ) 180,
    226
Gods, arguments about 23, 136, 197,
    200-5, 208, 209-14, 218-19
see also Prayer
Gracchus, C. and Ti. 49, 67
Greek
as language of philosophy 7
Romans proficient in 7-8, 72
Greek Anthology (*Anthologia Palatina*)
    128-31
Greeks in Roman government 74, 76

Hadrian, Roman emperor xv, 50, 75,
    108-9, 116, 118, 164
Headings (κεφάλαια) 33, 131
Heirs 136, 164
Heliodorus (sophist) 108
Helvidius Priscus 59, 61, 64, 70, 76
Heraclitus 15, 27, 31, 128, 146, 148,
    173, 249
Hercules/Heracles 233, 246 n.
Herennius Senecio 61
Herodes Atticus 81-9 *passim*, 91 n.
Herodian 174 n.
Herodotus 224
Hesiod 31, 54, 155, 206
Historia Augusta xv, xvii, 66, 85, 91 n.,
    174, 221-2, 235, 241
History, historiography 29
Holy men 184, 217-18
Homer 14, 26, 43, 54, 163, 196, 201
Horace 16, 21, 26, 30, 31, 38, 54, 58, 60,
    95, 104, 117, 130, 189, 203
Hunting 116

Iamblichus 211
Imagery 22, 28, 34-5, 115, 122, 133,
    135-6, 138-9
Images, specific
animals 148-50
awakening 142, 143
body politic 150-1
death as falling of a fruit 151-2
life as athletic contest 232-4
life as a battlefield 148, 240-1
life as a dream 129, 238
life as a play 130, 166-7, 232
man as spectator of life 231-2, 247
material world as filth, etc. 118, 154
men as marionettes 149
nature as moral analogy 122, 134,
    148-55

Images (*cont.*)
   philosopher as priest 170, 214–15
   river 129, 147–8, 236
   spring of goodness 154
   storm 148
Imperial cult 253 n.
Inspiration 194
Intellectual achievement, thrill of 120,
   156
Isaeus (rhetorician) 80
Isocrates 23, 54, 55, 106, 113

Julian the Apostate 10, 109
Julianus (theurgist) 223
Julius Caesar 5–6, 50, 60, 69, 252
Julius Genitor 73
Julius Kanus 71
Junius Rusticus (*cos* II 162) *see* Rusticus
Junius Rusticus, Stoic martyr 61–2
Justin Martyr xvii, 179, 256–8, 262
Juvenal 3, 75, 98, 146, 202, 233

Kings and rulers, praise or exhortation
   of 54, 96, 111–15, 123 n., 165

Laelius 59
Lectures, how to behave at 103–4
Letters, gnomic 12 n.
Liberality 97–8
Licinius Murena 71
Lists of virtues and vices 132 n., 153
Livia, wife of Augustus 71
Livy 56, 68
Lucan 250–2
Lucian 21, 58, 80, 81, 129, 155, 160,
   182–6, 197, 215, 223–4, 256 n.
   Scholia to 9
Lucilius (friend of Seneca) 73
Lucius (disciple of Musonius) 58, 89
Lucius Verus (co-emperor with Marcus)
   xv–vi, 45, 98 n., 114
Lucretius 7, 16 n., 21, 30, 159, 210
Lucullus 67

magic 87, 181–8
magnus annus 246
Marcellus (nephew of Augustus) 71
Marcia (addressee of Seneca's
   Consolation) 250, 253–5
Marcus Aurelius
   asceticism 116–21, 227, 241–3
   attends lectures in old age 89
   attitude to his predecessors 108–10,
      164, 165 n., 252–3

campaigns xvi, 2–3
career and offices held xv
'conversion' to philosophy 92, 103–7
cosmology, speculations on 205–8
disapproves of the Christians? 188
dislikes gladiatorial games 98, 117
dislikes sophists 40, 85
edict on superstition 191
education 52–3, 91–107 *passim*
endows chairs in philosophy 77, 81–2
ill-health 118, 120, 241 n.
indifference to imperial cult 253 n.
initiated at Eleusis 192, 219
limited philosophic interests 88,
   119–20
modesty on his own achievements
   93–4
not a hypochondriac 120 n.
not an opium addict 118 n.
pessimism 122–4, 172–5
philhellenism 8, 81
preoccupation with death 161–7,
   244–50
puritanical tendencies 117–19, 144–7
quotes from memory 34 n.
rarely names individual gods 218–19
reading 28–9, 64 n., 65, 225–6
religious beliefs Ch. v *passim*, esp. 181,
   192, 194–5, 209–11, 212–14,
   218–20; 235, 249–50, 261
sense of isolation 122–4
sexual experiences 118–19, cf. 201
simple style of life 117
Stoic 3, 47, 238 n., 244
style 39
teachers 52–3, 91 n., ch. III *passim*
tolerance of free speech 89
youth contrasted with later years
   28–9, 115–25
Martyr-literature 62–4
Mausoleum 164
Maximus of Tyre 80, 87, 127, 206, 262
***Meditations*, The**
ancient references to 9
attempts to describe the work's style
   5, 10–11
compositional methods 126–53 *passim*
contradictions, dilemmas in 168–72
date of composition 45–7
described by the author 34–5
diminutives in 246 n.
generic status 7, 8–14
not a didactic work 9, 23

Index of Greek Words